Lecture Notes in Computer Science 11833

More information about this series at http://www.springer.com/series/7410

Sonia Belaïd · Tim Güneysu (Eds.)

Smart Card Research and Advanced Applications

18th International Conference, CARDIS 2019
Prague, Czech Republic, November 11–13, 2019
Revised Selected Papers

Editors
Sonia Belaïd
CryptoExperts
Paris, France

Tim Güneysu
Ruhr-Universität Bochum
Bochum, Germany

ISSN 0302-9743 ISSN 1611-3349 (electronic)
Lecture Notes in Computer Science
ISBN 978-3-030-42067-3 ISBN 978-3-030-42068-0 (eBook)
https://doi.org/10.1007/978-3-030-42068-0

LNCS Sublibrary: SL4 – Security and Cryptology

This Springer imprint is published by the registered company Springer Nature Switzerland AG
The registered company address is: Gewerbestrasse 11, 6330 Cham, Switzerland

Preface

These proceedings contain the papers selected for presentation at the 18th International Conference on Smart Card Research and Advanced Applications (CARDIS 2019), held in Prague, Czech Republic, during November 11–13, 2019. The conference was organized by the Faculty of Information Technology of the Czech Technical University in Prague, Czech Republic.

CARDIS provides a space for security experts from industry and academia to exchange ideas on security of smart cards and related applications. Those objects have been part of our daily life for years: banking and SIM cards, electronic passports, etc. But the world is constantly changing; a secure element, such as smart cards, is now being implemented in many cases, for example as a hardware root of trust for larger systems. As such, smartcard security and core ingredients such as applied cryptography is a key enabler for the security of the entire system. At the same time, and with the growing use of smartcard technology, the attack surface is increasing, from physical attacks to logical attacks, from local attacks to remote attacks, and more recently combined attacks. It is more important than ever that we understand how smart cards and related systems, can be secured.

This year, CARDIS received 31 papers from a large number of international countries. Each paper was reviewed by three independent reviewers. The selection of 15 papers to fill the technical program was accomplished based on 142 written reviews. This task was performed by the 31 members of the Program Committee with the help of 28 external reviewers. The technical program also featured two invited talks. The first invited speaker, Peter Schwabe (Radboud University in Nijmegen, The Netherlands), presented "Post-quantum crypto on ARM Cortex-M" and the second speaker, Gilles Barthe (Max-Planck Institute in Bochum, Germany, and IMDEA Software Institute, Spain), presented "Formal Verification of Side-Channel Resistance." We would like to thank the general chair, Martin Novotný, for the great venue and smooth operation of the conference.

We would also like to thank the Program Committee and the external reviewers for their thorough work, which enabled the technical program to be of high quality, as well as the Steering Committee for giving us the opportunity to serve as program chairs at such a prestigious conference. The financial support of all the sponsors was highly appreciated and greatly facilitated the organization of the conference. We would like to thank the sponsors Thales, Infineon, Rambus, PQSHIELD, NewAE, Riscure NAGRA and FortifyIQ, CryptoExperts, ima, and KAOS for their support and collaboration. Furthermore, we would like to thank the authors who submitted their work to CARDIS 2019, without whom the conference would not have been possible.

January 2020

Sonia Belaïd
Tim Güneysu

Organization

Program Committee

Josep Balasch	Katholieke Universiteit Leuven, Belgium
Alessandro Barenghi	Politecnico di Milano, Italy
Sonia Belaïd	CryptoExperts, France
Begül Bilgin	Cryptography Research, USA
Thomas De Cnudde	Katholieke Universiteit Leuven, Belgium
Elke De Mulder	Cryptography Research, USA
Thomas Eisenbarth	WPI, USA
Junfeng Fan	Open Security Research, The Netherlands
Jean-Bernard Fischer	NagraVision, Switzerland
Domenic Forte	University of Florida, USA
Dahmun Goudarzi	PQShield, UK
Daniel Gruss	Institute for Applied Information Processing and Communications, Graz University of Technology, Austria
Tim Güneysu	Ruhr-Universität Bochum and DFKI, Germany
Annelie Heuser	CNRS, IRISA, France
Kerstin Lemke-Rust	Bonn-Rhein-Sieg University of Applied Sciences, Germany
Roel Maes	Intrinsic ID, USA
Amir Moradi	Ruhr-Universität Bochum, Germany
Debdeep Mukhopadhyay	IIT Kharagpur, India
Colin O'Flynn	NewAE Technology Inc., Canada
Axel Poschmann	xen1thLabs, UAE
Emmanuel Prouff	ANSSI, France
Thomas Pöppelmann	Infineon Technologies AG, Germany
Francesco Regazzoni	ALaRI – USI, Switzerland
Thomas Roche	NinjaLab, France
Kazuo Sakiyama	The University of Electro-Communications, Japan
Erkay Savas	Sabanci University, Turkey
Tobias Schneider	NXP Semiconductors, The Netherlands
Peter Schwabe	Radboud University, The Netherlands
Carolyn Whitnall	University of Bristol, UK
Yuval Yarom	The University of Adelaide and Data61/CSIRO, Australia
Rina Zeitoun	IDEMIA, France

Additional Reviewers

Andreeva, Elena
Barbu, Guillaume
Bermudo Mera, Jose Maria
Bouffard, Guillaume
Bronchain, Olivier
Cao, Yang
Costa Massolino, Pedro Maat
Cuong, Bien
De Meyer, Lauren
Fritzmann, Tim
Fritzsch, Clemens
Giner, Lukas
Gonzalez, Ruben
Hara-Azumi, Yuko
Kannwischer, Matthias
Kavun, Elif Bilge
Li, Yang
Maniatakos, Mihalis
Pelletier, Hervé
Rebeiro, Chester
Richter, Bastian
Saha, Sayandeep
Seker, Okan
Tunstall, Mike
Villegas, Karine
Wood, Tim
Yao, Yuan

Contents

System-on-a-Chip Security

In-situ Extraction of Randomness from Computer Architecture Through Hardware Performance Counters . . . 3
Manaar Alam, Astikey Singh, Sarani Bhattacharya, Kuheli Pratihar, and Debdeep Mukhopadhyay

Optimized Threshold Implementations: Minimizing the Latency of Secure Cryptographic Accelerators . . . 20
Dušan Božilov, Miroslav Knežević, and Ventzislav Nikov

Breaking the Lightweight Secure PUF: Understanding the Relation of Input Transformations and Machine Learning Resistance . . . 40
Nils Wisiol, Georg T. Becker, Marian Margraf, Tudor A. A. Soroceanu, Johannes Tobisch, and Benjamin Zengin

Post-Quantum Cryptography

Improving Speed of Dilithium's Signing Procedure . . . 57
Prasanna Ravi, Sourav Sen Gupta, Anupam Chattopadhyay, and Shivam Bhasin

An Efficient and Provable Masked Implementation of qTESLA . . . 74
François Gérard and Mélissa Rossi

Side-Channel Analysis

Side-Channel Attacks on Blinded Scalar Multiplications Revisited. . . . 95
Thomas Roche, Laurent Imbert, and Victor Lomné

Remote Side-Channel Attacks on Heterogeneous SoC . . . 109
Joseph Gravellier, Jean-Max Dutertre, Yannick Teglia, Philippe Loubet Moundi, and Francis Olivier

Optimal Collision Side-Channel Attacks. . . . 126
Cezary Glowacz and Vincent Grosso

Microarchitectural Attacks

A Bit-Level Approach to Side Channel Based Disassembling . . . 143
Valence Cristiani, Maxime Lecomte, and Thomas Hiscock

CCCiCC: A Cross-Core Cache-Independent Covert Channel on AMD Family 15h CPUs 159
Carl-Daniel Hailfinger, Kerstin Lemke-Rust, and Christof Paar

Design Considerations for EM Pulse Fault Injection 176
Arthur Beckers, Masahiro Kinugawa, Yuichi Hayashi, Daisuke Fujimoto, Josep Balasch, Benedikt Gierlichs, and Ingrid Verbauwhede

Cryptographic Primitives

Lightweight MACs from Universal Hash Functions. 195
Sébastien Duval and Gaëtan Leurent

FELICS-AEAD: Benchmarking of Lightweight Authenticated Encryption Algorithms. 216
Luan Cardoso dos Santos, Johann Großschädl, and Alex Biryukov

Advances in Side-Channel Analysis

A Comparison of χ^2-Test and Mutual Information as Distinguisher for Side-Channel Analysis 237
Bastian Richter, David Knichel, and Amir Moradi

Key Enumeration from the Adversarial Viewpoint: When to Stop Measuring and Start Enumerating? 252
Melissa Azouaoui, Romain Poussier, François-Xavier Standaert, and Vincent Verneuil

Author Index 269

System-on-a-Chip Security

In-situ Extraction of Randomness from Computer Architecture Through Hardware Performance Counters

Manaar Alam(✉), Astikey Singh, Sarani Bhattacharya, Kuheli Pratihar, and Debdeep Mukhopadhyay

Indian Institute of Technology Kharagpur, Kharagpur, India
alam.manaar@gmail.com, astikey070@gmail.com, tinni1989@gmail.com, its.kuheli96@gmail.com, debdeep.mukhopadhyay@gmail.com

Abstract. True Random Number Generators (TRNGs) are one of the most crucial components in the design and use of cryptographic protocols and communication. Predictability of such random numbers are catastrophic and can lead to the complete collapse of security, as all the mathematical proofs are based on the entropy of the source which generates these bit patterns. The randomness in the TRNGs is hugely attributed to the inherent noise of the system, which is often derived from hardware subsystems operating in an ambiguous manner. However, most of these solutions need an add-on device to provide these randomness sources, which can lead to not only latency issues but also can be a potential target of adversaries by probing such an interface. In this paper, we address to alleviate these issues by proposing an *in-situ* TRNG construction, which depends on the functioning of the underlying hardware architecture. These functions are observed via the Hardware Performance Counters (HPCs) and are shown to exhibit high-quality randomness in the least significant bit positions. We provide extensive experiments to research on the choice of the HPCs, and their ability to pass the standard NIST and AIS 20/31 Tests. We also analyze a possible scenario where an adversary tries to interfere with the HPC values and show its effect on the TRNG output with respect to the NIST and AIS 20/31 Tests. Additionally, to alleviate the delay caused for accessing the HPC events and increase the throughput of the random-source, we also propose a methodology to cascade the random numbers from the HPC values with a secured hash function.

Keywords: True Random Number Generator · Hardware Performance Counters · Cryptographic post-processing

1 Introduction

Random Numbers Generators (RNGs) form the backbone in the development of almost all of the devices requiring secure communication, device authentication, or data encryption. Applications of such devices include Smart Cards, RFID

S. Belaïd and T. Güneysu (Eds.): CARDIS 2019, LNCS 11833, pp. 3–19, 2020.
https://doi.org/10.1007/978-3-030-42068-0_1

tags, and IoT devices. The unpredictability of random numbers is a crucial component in parameter and key generation for both symmetric and asymmetric cryptography, generation of random masks for padding data, generating session keys between communicating parties and several other secured applications. The RNGs rely on inherent chaos and unpredictability of various physical factors from the environment or hardware components to provide the much-needed randomness, which signifies that infinitely long history of previous random numbers provides no advantage over deciding or predicting the future random occurrences.

True Random Number Generators (TRNGs) derive its randomness from physical factors in the environment, and thus when implemented in hardware, the randomness is extracted from the physical parameters such as gate delay. Fault in design and fabrication procedure of TRNG results in insufficient entropy (randomness) or improper functioning of the TRNG. Depending on the type of randomness source and the post-processing involved, there have been quite a large number of TRNG designs in the literature. A popular TRNG based on Thermal Noise was first introduced by Intel [14] and recently can be found in [10,19]. The most commonly used entropy source for both FPGA and ASIC TRNG's is metastability, which can be found in [12,20]. Timing jitter in electronic systems was also considered as TRNG source in [11,26]. However, along with the design challenges involved in designing these TRNGs, an equally complex task is to develop test strategies for TRNGs. Owing to the fact that most tests are statistical and can only evaluate the statistical quality of the generated numbers and not their entropy, modern methods for certification of TRNGs involve a carefully chosen bag of tests. These tests mainly include: **(1)** *NIST* standard tests [22], which aims at estimating the min-entropy, i.e., evaluating the information content of the most likely outcome, and **(2)** *AIS 20/31* Tests [15] proposed by the German Federal Office for Information Security, which estimates Shannon entropy, targeted at evaluating the average information content of the random variable associated with the random source.

Furthermore, the TRNGs which are often implemented using external hardware are susceptible to physical attacks. In [16] attackers inject periodic signals to the power supply in order to destroy the randomness of the Ring Oscillators (ROs) by reducing the entropy of the generated keystream. In [7], the adversaries used strong magnetic fields to tamper the randomness generated by 50 ROs. In other instances, usage of power, clock glitches, and other techniques of physical attacks have threatened the deployment of TRNGs. Though there exist methods of on-the-fly testing of TRNGs which can be effective during such attacks [21,27], it would be desirable to develop TRNG sources which are available to a program without resorting to an external component. The TRNG should derive its randomness from the underlying hardware artifacts which are available in the computer architecture and which exhibit its randomness owing to the various processes which execute on them. Such an *in-situ* TRNG design would also make physical attacks more challenging, as compared to when the TRNG is an add-on hardware device which the adversary can target more effectively.

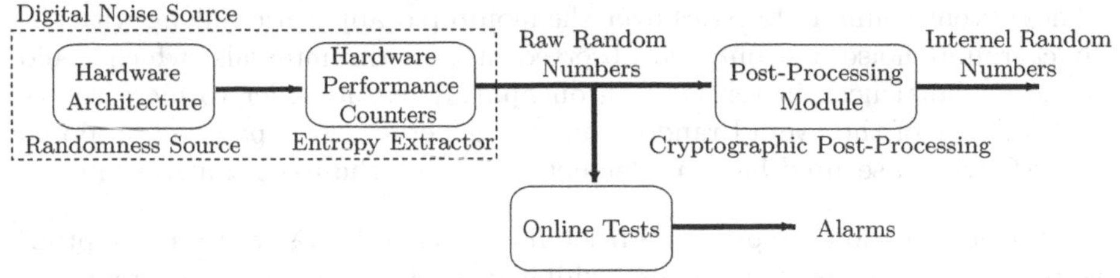

Fig. 1. Generic structure of the proposed True Random Number Generator (TRNG) circuit

In this paper, we analyze and propose an *in-situ* design for TRNG based on the randomness derived from various hardware activities as observed in the underlying computer architecture. These hardware activities (like instruction-counts, CPU-cycles, etc.) are observed through Hardware Performance Counters (HPCs) allowing detailed, low-level measurement of different process behavior executed in CPUs. HPCs provide valuable information about program execution, which were extensively used in the literature to attack strong cryptographic algorithms [3,9] and also used to detect the execution of malicious programs [1,2,5]. The information provided by HPCs are also used to identify vulnerabilities which aid reverse engineering of proprietary software [4]. However, modern processor vendors do not make any guarantee about determinism of these hardware activities (or HPC events) [25]. We analyze the source of non-determinism exhibited by these HPC events and aim to utilize this non-determinism in designing our TRNG module. We observe that the least significant bits of these HPC events display high-quality randomness and high entropy. We also propose a hybrid model coupled with a secure hash implementation in order to cope up with the latency in accessing the HPC events and thus to increase the throughput of the TRNG design where required.

Contribution

The major highlights of the paper in context to the general structure of a TRNG (as illustrated in Fig. 1) are explained in details as follows:

- We propose a TRNG derived from computer architecture, which thrives on the randomness observed through the architectural events from the underlying hardware. The HPC counters, which monitors these architectural events, exhibits inherent non-determinism in their implementation [25] and are also affected due to a vast number of processes running on a processor core in a fixed quantum of time. HPC event counters provide a cumulative count to these architectural events and thus proposed to be a high source of entropy.
- It was also observed that the randomness was highest in the Least Significant bits (LSBs) for the observed values from these counters. The entropy reduces as we consider the bits more towards the Most Significant Bit (MSBs).

– These event counter statistics over the monitored application along with the background noise can only be observed at periodic intervals, which could create a bottleneck in terms of throughput. Thus, in order to increase the throughput of the overall random number generation, we pair the proposed TRNG with a secured hash implementation using the Keccak algorithm.

In the next section, we present a brief discussion on HPCs, which is the primitive tool to extract the randomness exhibited by the architectural component.

2 Preliminaries on Hardware Performance Counters

Hardware Performance Counters (HPCs) are special purpose registers present in most of the modern-day microprocessors which store the hardware related activities during the execution of a program. The HPCs provide detailed, low-level hardware utilization statistics to advance user modules and are thus very useful in code optimization and process tuning operations. The HPCs typically count the number of occurrences of various hardware events such as number of instructions executed, number of bus-cycles consumed, number of CPU-cycles consumed, different operations related to the cache memory, branch misprediction operations and many more events related to the architectural activities of a system. There are a wide variety of events that can be measured with HPCs, and the event availability varies considerably among CPUs and vendors. A full list of available events can be found in various vendor's architectural manuals. As these events are immensely useful in computer architectural design and optimizations, these were available to users having user-level privileges. However, various researchers developed security implications of such user-level accesses to these counter values for the cryptographic implementations, which led the security engineers to push the HPCs to higher privilege scale and thus the counters can only be accessed in modern systems with administrative privileges. It has already been shown in [25] that the HPC values obtained by monitoring a process are not deterministic in nature. In the next section, we analyze the reason behind the inherent non-determinism exhibited by the HPC events, which is the primary motivation behind the proposed TRNG design.

3 Non-determinism of HPCs and Motivation

All Linux based systems with kernel version 2.6.31 and above have a utility named `perf`, which can be used to access and read the HPC registers through the `perf_event` system call. The `perf` utility provides a simple command line interface to observe the detailed, low-level hardware based event counter values during the execution of a process. A user can monitor desired events for the entire duration of the execution or can observe them periodically with a fixed interval of time. The command to observe the values of a monitored event (`<event_name>`) with a fixed interval (`<interval_duration>`) of time during the execution of an executable (`<executable_name>`) is given as follows:

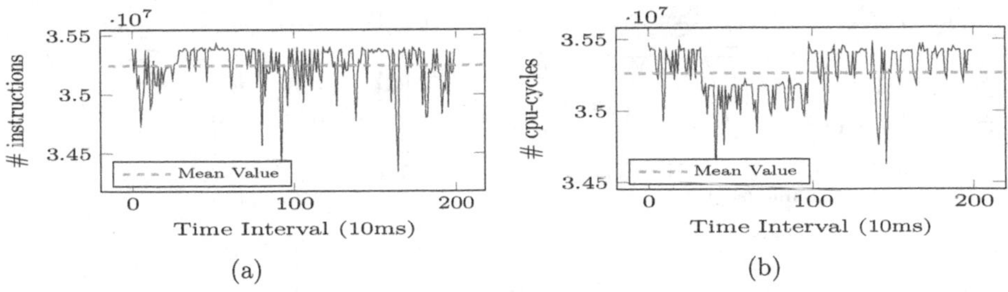

Fig. 2. Variation of the HPC events (a) `instructions` and (b) `cpu-cycles` monitored over an infinite loop on different time intervals

```
perf stat -e <event_name> -I <interval_duration> <executable_name>
```

In all of our experiments, we took a `C` code snippet which does nothing but loops infinitely, over which we observed various event counts such as `instructions`, `bus-cycles`, `cpu-cycles`, `cache-misses`, `branch-misses` and many more. As an example, we observed two performance counter events `instruction` and `cpu-cycles` over the executable of infinite loop with 10 ms[1] interval of time and the corresponding observations are shown in Fig. 2. In an ideal case, the HPC events `instruction` and `cpu-cycles` should report constant values over the duration of time, as the executable is doing nothing except looping infinitely. But, it can be observed from Fig. 2 that the number of instructions and the number of CPU cycles is not constant over time, which shows the significant amount of non-determinism exhibited by these performance counters.

Measuring exact event counts using HPCs can be difficult because of several external sources of variation such as program layout [18,24], multiprocessor variation [6], operating system interaction [17], measurement overhead [29], and hardware implementation details [23,24]. As discussed in [25], after carefully avoiding these sources of variation as much as possible, it was found that internal hardware interrupt is the potential source that leads to non-deterministic behaviour. Most of the HPC events get incremented an extra time for every hardware interrupt that occurs in the system. Hence, if an event is affected by hardware interrupts, then it cannot be a deterministic event, as it is impossible to predict in advance when these interrupts will happen. There are several types of interrupts affecting these HPC events such as Local Timer Interrupts (LOC), IRQ Work Interrupts (IWI), Rescheduling Interrupts (RES), Function Call Interrupts (CAL), and TLB Shootdowns (TLB). The effect of these interrupts can be monitored efficiently using `/proc/interrupts`, which also includes additional interrupt counts that happen outside of process context, adding extra assistance to the non-determinism of HPC events.

In order to validate this, we again monitored the events `instructions` and `cpu-cycles` as before and along with that we also measured the total number

[1] We selected 10 ms as it is the lowest interval of time that the `perf` tool supports, and thus corresponds to the highest supported frequency.

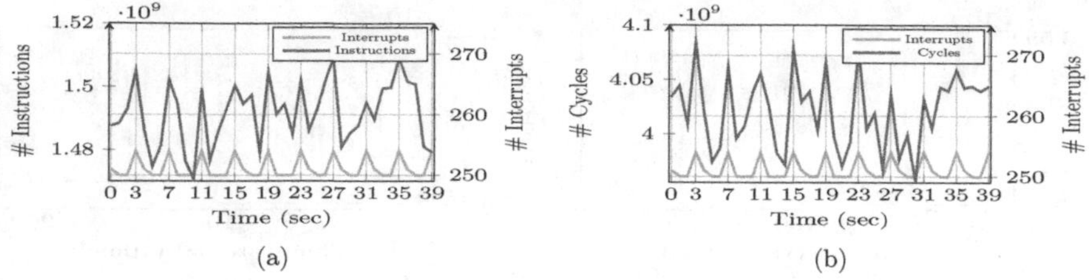

Fig. 3. Effect of hardware interrupts on the HPC events (a) `instructions` and (b) `cpu-cycles` monitored over an infinite loop on different time instances

of interrupts received per second using the Linux `mpstat` command which uses `/proc/interrupts` as a subroutine. We performed the experimentation on a per-core approach using the Linux `taskset` command. We present the effect of these hardware interrupts on both the HPC events in Fig. 3. We can easily observe from both the figures that whenever there is a surge in the number of interrupts, the counts of the events also increases validating the association between hardware interrupts and HPC events.

HPCs are registers dedicated to each core of a processor. Apart from being affected by the hardware interrupts, these event counts are also affected by the execution of various processes which are running in the background. The Operating System entirely administrates the execution of all the processes on the actual hardware of the architectural components, which are extremely complex to model as it is mostly dominated by the effect of speculative executions, out-of-order execution, interrupts, instruction prefetching and many more optimization techniques. Most of the modern processors are multicore, and an innumerable number of processes can get executed concurrently on each of these processor cores. The HPCs measure the event counts for all the events for all those processes which are concurrently running on the same processor core along with their fine-grained context switches. Thus if these HPCs are monitored for a per-core based approach, the counters are not only affected by the event counts from the operations in the monitored process but also from the all other processes which are running concurrently to the monitored application. Hence the background processes also have a significant impact on the event count of the target process, which is being monitored. In the next section, we propose an efficient construction of TRNG using the statistics obtained from these HPCs.

4 Randomness Extraction Using HPCs

In this section, we briefly discuss about the selection of appropriate architectural events to design the TRNG and the methodology to extract the randomness from such events. In the previous section, we have seen that the performance counter values range between a particular interval with low deviation from the mean, which makes the most significant bits of the observed values to be highly predictable. On the other hand, the noise component in these performance counter

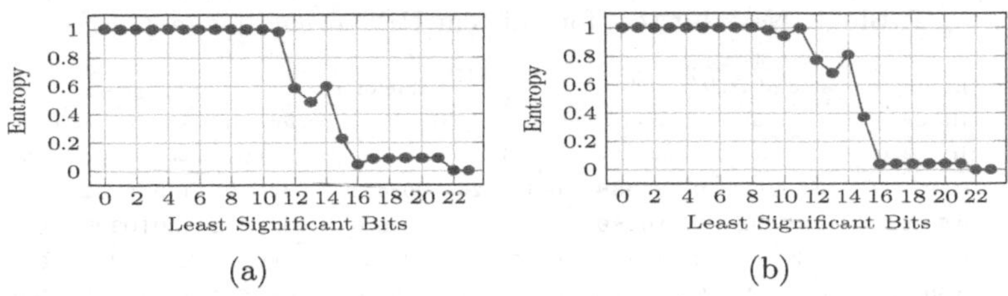

Fig. 4. Entropy of each LSBs for HPC event (a) `instructions`, and (b) `cpu-cycles`

values is very high if we consider only the least significant bits. The analysis of selecting the LSBs is elaborated next.

4.1 Selection of the Least Significant Bits

In the previous section, we claimed that the performance counter events which are observed over a straightforward executable exhibit a high source of entropy as they inherently possess a considerable amount of noise which is entirely contributed by the unpredictable hardware interrupts in the system and various processes running in the background. It should be further noted that the entropy of each bit position would not be the same for the binary sequences converted directly from the monitored values. The entropy is highest with the LSB, which can be considered as the most random bit output while the MSB is highly predictable. In support of our claim, we observed 500,000 instances of the performance counter events `instructions` and `cpu-cycles`, and calculated the entropy for each bit position. Figure 4 shows entropy values of all the bit positions for both the events. We can observe from the figures that the LSBs have the highest entropy, and as we move towards the MSBs, the entropy gets reduced. Hence, instead of considering the observed HPC value, we transform the data into binary sequences and consider the last 9[2] bits for our further analysis.

4.2 Selection of HPC Events Using Yao's Next-Bit Test

In all of our experiments, we considered the sampling interval time as 10 ms. Hence, the `perf` tool will generate data points for any HPC event after each 10 ms time interval. Let us consider last n LSB bits of a single instance of data as the source of randomness. At any time instant t, we considered the sequence of bits $S(n,t) = \left(b_0^t, b_1^t, \cdots, b_{n-2}^t, b_{n-1}^t\right)$ derived directly from the value obtained by `perf` tool for each HPC events. Our conjecture to consider an HPC event as a source of TRNG is based on the idea that there will be no bias in predicting a bit, even if we know the previous values. In order to determine the bias in observation, we provide Yao's next-bit test [28], which we discuss as follows.

[2] We empirically selected last 9 least significant bits for our experimental setup as for most of the events the last 9 bits provide highest entropy values.

Table 1. Next-bit test for different HPC events for $m = 4$

Known bits	Estimated value of $\hat{\mathbf{Pr}}[b_4^t = 0]$				Value of δ			
	Hardware performance counter events				Hardware performance counter events			
	`instructions`	`cpu-cycles`	`cache-misses`	`branches`	`instructions`	`cpu-cycles`	`cache-misses`	`branches`
0000	0.499362	0.499119	**0.483038**	**0.511926**	0.000638	0.000881	**0.016962**	**0.011926**
0001	0.500616	0.498508	**0.510286**	0.5	0.000616	0.001492	**0.010286**	0
0010	0.50388	0.499933	**0.61523**	**0.473591**	0.00388	0.000067	**0.11523**	**0.026409**
0011	0.503006	0.501612	**0.538575**	**0.472271**	0.003006	0.001612	**0.038575**	**0.027729**
0100	0.497589	0.500212	**0.465892**	0.494755	0.002411	0.000212	**0.034108**	0.005245
0101	0.501385	0.503288	0.499264	**0.489194**	0.001385	0.003288	0.000736	**0.010806**
0110	0.497944	0.499307	0.49388	**0.480069**	0.002056	0.000693	0.00612	**0.019931**
0111	0.497515	0.498644	**0.545499**	**0.529411**	0.002485	0.001356	**0.045499**	**0.029411**
1000	0.501878	0.497065	**0.532874**	**0.480286**	0.001878	0.002935	**0.032874**	**0.019714**
1001	0.509205	0.500564	**0.325212**	**0.473333**	0.009205	0.000564	**0.174788**	**0.026667**
1010	0.503668	0.498804	**0.588985**	0.507633	0.003668	0.001196	**0.088985**	0.007633
1011	0.500938	0.500415	**0.345577**	**0.476785**	0.000938	0.000415	**0.154423**	**0.023215**
1100	0.49932	0.504391	**0.681509**	**0.483871**	0.00068	0.004391	**0.181509**	**0.016129**
1101	0.499705	0.499179	**0.578446**	**0.470919**	0.000295	0.000821	**0.078446**	**0.029081**
1110	0.502052	0.501125	**0.357142**	**0.477891**	0.002052	0.001125	**0.142858**	**0.022109**
1111	0.500587	0.497146	**0.437479**	**0.481415**	0.000587	0.002854	**0.062521**	**0.018585**
Average δ					0.002236	0.001493	**0.073995**	**0.018411**

Table 2. Experimental setups for validation of the proposed claim

Processor	Linux version
AMD A10-8700P Radeon R6	Ubuntu with Kernel 4.13.0-36
Intel Core i7-7567U	Ubuntu with Kernel 4.15.0-33

Suppose we know first m-bits of the n possible bits for any sequence $S(n,t)$, i.e., the sequence $S(m,t)$ is already given (where $m < n$). Now, according to Yao's Next-bit test, we say that the sequence $S(n,t)$ has no bias if probability of the $(m+1)^{th}$ bit being zero is $0.5 \pm \delta$ (i.e., $\mathbf{Pr}[b_m^t = 0] = 0.5 \pm \delta$), given the knowledge of $S(m,t)$, when δ is negligible (with respect to the security parameter). There are 2^m possibilities for $S(m,t)$, and we perform the test for all such possibilities. In order to estimate the $\mathbf{Pr}[b_m^t = 0]$, we consider N such sequences by observing an HPC event at N successive interval of time. Let the sequence $S(m,t)$ occurs at $\mathcal{T}$ times out of N possibilities. We now count the occurrences of $b_m^i = 0$ and $b_m^i = 1$ as $\mathcal{C}_0$ and $\mathcal{C}_1$ respectively, where $i = 1, 2, \cdots, \mathcal{T}$. We define the estimated probabilities as $\hat{\mathbf{Pr}}[b_m^t = 0] = \frac{\mathcal{C}_0}{\mathcal{T}}$ and $\hat{\mathbf{Pr}}[b_m^t = 1] = 1 - \hat{\mathbf{Pr}}[b_m^t = 0]$. Without loss of generality we first consider the case of $m = 4$, i.e., first 4 bits of the binary sequence is known. There are 2^4 possibilities of $S(m,t)$, which are shown in **Known Bits** column of Table 1. We observed $N = 500,000$ values for the events `instructions`, `cpu-cycles`, `cache-misses`, and `branches` and estimated the probability $\hat{\mathbf{Pr}}[b_4^t = 0]$ as discussed previously. The estimated probability values for all the events and for all the combination of **Known Bits** and the corresponding values of δ (as mentioned previously) are shown in Table 1. The first cell in Table 1 contains the value 0.499362, which signifies that for the event instructions if we known that the first 4 bits are 0000, then the estimated probability that the next bit will be 0 is 0.499362. We can also observe from the table that the corresponding value of δ is 0.000638. It is clear from the table that all the combinations have probabilities close to 0.5 for the events instructions and cpu-cycles. The corresponding values of δ are also negligible. In case of events cache-misses and branches the probability values are highly biased for some combinations with high value of δ and are shown with **bold** faces. The average values of δ for all the sequences corresponding to each of the performance counter events are also shown in Table 1 and justifiably these values are higher for the events cache-misses and branches. Similar results are observed for other values of m. Hence, we conclude after this analysis that the events instructions and cpu-cycles can act as better candidate for source of randomness while we discard the other two events cache-misses and branches in our further analysis. In the next section, we validate our conclusion through an extensive set of results with the help of NIST and AIS 20/31 Test suite.

5 Experimental Validation

In this section, we first provide results on TRNG output obtained from the raw HPC events followed by the results on the TRNG output in the presence of a strong adversarial perturbation.

5.1 Results on TRNG Output Obtained from HPC Events

All the experiments are conducted on two different processors as listed in Table 2, where the access to HPC events is available to users with administrative privilege. There exists a diverse set of HPC events which can be accessed via the perf utility. We considered some of the primitive events such as instructions, cpu-cycles, bus-cycles, cache-misses, branches etc., as the obtained values for each of these events are high compared to the other events. The perf statistics are recorded after every time interval of 10 ms for an executable which runs infinitely over time. The idea behind the selection of events which showed high values compared to the lower ones is because the ones reporting very high values can be expected to produce decent randomness in the Least Significant Bits. On the contrary, events which show low values as output are intuitively more predictable compared to the earlier case.

The NIST Test suite is observed to work the best for the events instructions and cpu-cycles in all the setups as mentioned in Table 2. The perf statistic is recorded for more than 15 hours of execution time, which resulted in altogether 10 sets, each set having more than 5.5×10^7 performance counter values. For each set, we selected the last 9 bits from the LSB of each observation and appended one after another to generate a consolidated binary string. We applied the NIST Test suite on this consolidated binary sequence. We furnish our results from the NIST suite for both Intel and AMD processors in Table 3. We can observe from the table that both the events instructions and cpu-cycles pass all the 15

Table 3. NIST test results on TRNG output for different HPC events on two different processors

NIST test	Intel			AMD		
	instructions	cpu-cycles	cache-misses	instructions	cpu-cycles	cache-misses
Frequency	PASS	PASS	FAIL	PASS	PASS	FAIL
BlockFrequency	PASS	PASS	FAIL	PASS	PASS	FAIL
CumulativeSums	PASS	PASS	FAIL	PASS	PASS	FAIL
Runs	PASS	PASS	FAIL	PASS	PASS	FAIL
LongestRun	PASS	PASS	FAIL	PASS	PASS	FAIL
Rank	PASS	PASS	PASS	PASS	PASS	FAIL
FFT	PASS	PASS	PASS	PASS	PASS	FAIL
NonOverlappingTemplate	PASS	PASS	FAIL	PASS	PASS	FAIL
OverlappingTemplate	PASS	PASS	PASS	PASS	PASS	FAIL
Universal	PASS	PASS	FAIL	PASS	PASS	FAIL
ApproximateEntropy	PASS	PASS	FAIL	PASS	PASS	FAIL
RandomExcursions	PASS	PASS	FAIL	PASS	PASS	FAIL
RandomExcursionsVariant	PASS	PASS	FAIL	PASS	PASS	FAIL
Serial	PASS	PASS	PASS	PASS	PASS	FAIL
LinearComplexity	PASS	PASS	PASS	PASS	PASS	FAIL

tests under the NIST Test suite. We perform the same experimentation on each of the 10 sets and obtain similar results for all the sets. Table 3 also shows the NIST Test results for the HPC event `cache-misses` on both the processors. We can observe that most of the tests under the NIST Test suite fails for this event, which aligns with the results shown in Table 1.

In order to further analyze the TRNG property of the events `instructions` and `cpu-cycles`, we applied the AIS 20/31 Test procedures on the consolidated binary output string as obtained before. The results of the tests for both Intel and AMD processors are shown in Table 4. We can observe from the table that all the tests under Procedure A and Procedure B of AIS 20/31 Test suite pass for both the events `instructions` and `cpu-cycles`. The details of the parameters mentioned under Procedure B can be found in the AIS 20/31 Test Manual. Hence, with the outcomes of these two test suites, we conclude that the HPC events which are affected by various hardware interrupt and the background noises can be effectively used to design a TRNG module.

5.2 Perturbation in TRNG Output in Presence of an Adversary

In the previous subsections, we tested the sources of entropy through normal process execution framework in a multi-core processor setup, where we show that the inherent chaos of the various process execution and the unpredictability of hardware interrupts have an extensive impact on the HPC values. We claim with suitable results that the values obtained from HPCs qualify for a pure computer architecture based TRNG. But we are also interested in understanding the effect on the HPCs in the presence of a powerful adversary.

Let us consider a server setup, where there are multiple users logged into the same server, and all of the users are having administrative privileges. Thus all of

Table 4. AIS 20/31 test results on TRNG output for different HPC events on two different processors

AIS 20/31 test	Intel		AMD	
	`instructions`	`cpu-cycles`	`instructions`	`cpu-cycles`
Procedure A				
T0	PASS	PASS	PASS	PASS
T1	PASS	PASS	PASS	PASS
T2	PASS	PASS	PASS	PASS
T3	PASS	PASS	PASS	PASS
T4	PASS	PASS	PASS	PASS
T5	PASS	PASS	PASS	PASS
Procedure B				
T6	PASS $d = 0.001990 < 0.025$ $s = 0.001080 < 0.02$	PASS $d = 0.001760 < 0.025$ $s = 0.000970 < 0.02$	PASS $d = 0.001640 < 0.025$ $s = 0.001120 < 0.02$	PASS $d = 0.001790 < 0.025$ $s = 0.000560 < 0.02$
T7	PASS $s_1 = 0.008000 < 15.13$ $s_2 = 0.050002 < 15.13$	PASS $s_1 = 0.079000 < 15.13$ $s_2 = 0.047869 < 15.13$	PASS $s_1 = 0.010000 < 15.13$ $s_2 = 0.049847 < 15.13$	PASS $s_1 = 0.047000 < 15.13$ $s_2 = 0.069748 < 15.13$
T8	PASS $s = 8.109696 > 7.976$	PASS $s = 10.479683 > 7.976$	PASS $s = 8.214734 > 7.976$	PASS $s = 9.975684 > 7.976$

these users can observe perf statistics over executables which run on processor cores shared across various user processes. Hence it is feasible for an adversary running on the same processor core as the TRNG module to modify these HPC values in regular time intervals. We performed several experiments where the adversary process runs on the same processor core as the target core and uses `asynchronous perf ioctl system` calls to set the value of the HPC event `instructions` to zero periodically. This manipulation by the adversary hampers the instruction counts observed over a synchronous measurement procedure to a great extent. The range of the instruction counts varied widely when a concurrent adversary module refreshed the instruction counts, which is also expected if the adversary wishes to modify the counter values instead of resetting it. Any modification to the counter values by a powerful adversary does have an impact in changing the overall values of the instruction counts but does not have any impact on the entropy of the least significant bits of the counter values. The reason behind it is that of the inherent chaos of a large number of concurrent process executions and optimization constructs of the Operating System and their effect on the underlying computer architecture modules. Hence, a powerful adversary needs to not only model the chaos exhibited by the background concurrent processes but also needs to have complete control of hardware interrupts appearing in the system, both of which is assumed to be a challenging task to execute. Without loss of generality, we tested the TRNG sequences generated by the HPC event `instructions` on the Intel processor in the presence of this adversary with both NIST and AIS 20/31 Test suites. The results are furnished in Table 5, which shows that all the tests under both of these test suites pass with the modified TRNG sequence. In the next section, we discuss a hybrid TRNG

Table 5. NIST and AIS 20/31 test results on TRNG output for the HPC event `instructions` on Intel processor after adversarial modification

NIST test		AIS 20/31 tests	
Frequency	PASS	Procedure A	
BlockFrequency	PASS	T0	PASS
CumulativeSums	PASS	T1	PASS
Runs	PASS	T2	PASS
LongestRun	PASS	T3	PASS
Rank	PASS	T4	PASS
FFT	PASS	T5	PASS
NonOverlappingTemplate	PASS	Procedure B	
OverlappingTemplate	PASS	T6	PASS
Universal	PASS		$d = 0.003479 < 0.025$
ApproximateEntropy	PASS		$s = 0.002547 < 0.02$
RandomExcursions	PASS	T7	PASS
RandomExcursionsVariant	PASS		$s_1 = 0.008429 < 15.13$
Serial	PASS		$s_2 = 0.094531 < 15.13$
LinearComplexity	PASS	T8	PASS
			$s = 8.047369 > 7.976$

construction using a secure hash implementation for enhancing the throughput of the design to cope up with the latency in accessing HPC events.

6 Hybrid Construction to Enhance Throughput

In this section, we describe an efficient generation of random bit string through a secured hash implementation using Keccak algorithm [8] followed by its validation as TRNG using NIST and AIS 20/31 Test suites. The design is simple yet effective in context to generating a high-speed sequence of random numbers. In the previous section, we elaborate on how True Random Numbers were obtained from the Hardware Performance Counter values. The proposed design only considers last 9 bits from the LSB of each cumulative sample of event count for a periodic interval of 10 ms. This latency of 10 ms of the generation of 9 random bits is inappropriate when compared to real-life random number generation requirements. Thus we bridge the gap with a hybrid model which uses a shift register, the Keccak algorithm, and a control block by considering the random bits obtained from HPCs as input. If an application asks for a random number within the interval of 10 ms, the hybrid model uses its deterministic algorithm to generate a more extensive number of random bits using the previous inputs.

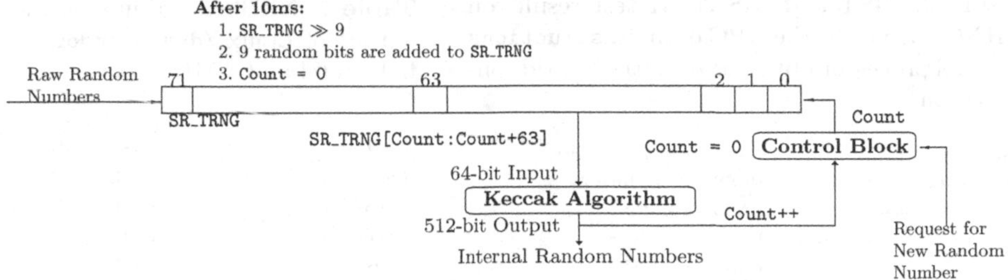

Fig. 5. Hybrid Construction for generating internal random numbers

6.1 Cryptographic Post-processing of the TRNG Output

The hybrid TRNG construction as shown in Fig. 5, takes the output of the true random number sequence obtained from the HPC events as its input and generates a sequence of more number of bits using a shift register (`SR_TRNG`), a Control Block, and Keccak (or SHA-3) Algorithm. The hybrid construction works with two operational modes as follows:

1. **Initialization:** The HPC based TRNG construction generates 9 random bits in every 10 ms interval. The hybrid construction waits for the first 80 ms after the start of the system. The shift register `SR_TRNG`, which is of length 72 bits, is filled from the LSB to MSB after each 10 ms in such a way that after first 80 ms the register `SR_TRNG` is filled with 72 bits of a random string. In this mode a register `Count` is also set to 0.
2. **Generation:** If a user needs a true random number from the system, it requests the Control Block to generate it. The Control Block then takes the 64-bit string `SR_TRNG[Count:Count+63]` and produces a 512-bit string using SHA-3 algorithm and provides these bits as an output to the request. The Control Block then increments the value of `Count` register by 1. After 10 ms the register `SR_TRNG` is right shifted by 9 bits, 9 random bits obtained from the new HPC value after the 10 ms are added to the shift register, and the register `Count` is again reset to 0.

Any user can obtain a maximum of $9 * 512 = 4608$ bits of a random string within the latency of 10 ms. Hence the maximum throughput of the hybrid design is $46,080$ bits per second (or 45 Kbps). It is evident that the throughput of the hybrid design is directly proportional to the length of the shift register `SR_TRNG`, which can be tuned to support different kinds of applications with varying requirements of throughput.

6.2 Results on TRNG Output Obtained from Hybrid Construction

The TRNG output obtained from the HPC event values are used as input to the hybrid construction. As discussed previously, after every 10 ms the shift register

Table 6. NIST and AIS 20/31 test results on TRNG output for the HPC event `instructions` on Intel processor obtained from the hybrid construction

NIST test		AIS 20/31 tests	
Frequency	PASS	Procedure A	
BlockFrequency	PASS	T0	PASS
CumulativeSums	PASS	T1	PASS
Runs	PASS	T2	PASS
LongestRun	PASS	T3	PASS
Rank	PASS	T4	PASS
FFT	PASS	T5	PASS
NonOverlappingTemplate	PASS	Procedure B	
OverlappingTemplate	PASS	T6	PASS
Universal	PASS		$d = 0.004060 < 0.025$
ApproximateEntropy	PASS		$s = 0.005410 < 0.02$
RandomExcursions	PASS	T7	PASS
RandomExcursionsVariant	PASS		$s_1 = 0.499285 < 15.13$
Serial	PASS		$s_2 = 0.612501 < 15.13$
LinearComplexity	PASS	T8	PASS
			$s = 8.107012 > 7.976$

Table 7. NIST test results on the output of Linux `/dev/urandom` on both Intel and AMD Processors

NIST test	Intel	AMD
Frequency	FAIL	FAIL
BlockFrequency	FAIL	FAIL
CumulativeSums	FAIL	FAIL
Runs	FAIL	FAIL
LongestRun	FAIL	FAIL
Rank	FAIL	FAIL
FFT	FAIL	FAIL
NonOverlappingTemplate	FAIL	FAIL
OverlappingTemplate	FAIL	FAIL
Universal	FAIL	FAIL
ApproximateEntropy	FAIL	FAIL
RandomExcursions	FAIL	FAIL
RandomExcursionsVariant	FAIL	FAIL
Serial	FAIL	FAIL
LinearComplexity	PASS	PASS

`SR_TRNG` holding the recent history of random bits from the TRNG is right shifted by 9 bits to accommodate fresh random bits. In an interval of 10 ms, we obtain the upper bound of 4608 bits of random binary string which requires only 72 bits of extra storage. The storage will be marginally higher for higher throughput design. We also take the output from the hybrid construction and run both the NIST and AIS 20/31 Tests on the sequences. Without loss of generality, results for the event `instructions` on the Intel processor are furnished in Table 6, which shows that the sequences pass all the tests under both the test suites.

7 Discussion

In this paper, we proposed a TRNG construction using the values obtained from the HPC events through the Linux based tool perf. However, all the Linux based systems have special character files `/dev/urandom` providing an interface to the kernel's random number generator, which gathers environmental noise from device drivers and other sources into an entropy pool. However, several weaknesses of such random number generation with a detailed cryptographic analysis is shown in [13]. In order to stress the weakness, we collected "random" data using `/dev/urandom` and applied NIST Test suite on the output. The result of the tests on both Intel and ARM processors are shown in Table 7. We can easily observe that apart from the *LinearComplexity* test under the NIST Test suite the dataset fails to qualify for all other tests. Since the dataset did not qualify the NIST Test suite, we did not provide any results on AIS 20/31 Test to show its weakness further. The objective of this discussion is to stress on the fact that the proposed approach can be used as a TRNG source in modern Linux based systems as an alternative to apparently weaker random number generator using `/dev/urandom`.

8 Conclusion

In this paper, we showed that components of architecture infuse a huge level of randomness because of the Operating System optimization constructs and unpredictability of different hardware interrupts, which gets manifested through the Hardware Performance Counters. These counters digitize the randomness of the architectural constructs and various experimental results using standard NIST, and AIS 20/31 Test suites show that these counters can indeed be considered as a TRNG source. We have also shown that the proposed TRNG construction is robust and fault tolerant in the presence of a powerful adversary. The proposed TRNG module has a latency of 10 ms because of the time to access HPC events. Thus to enhance the throughput of the design, we combine the TRNG module with a simple yet effective Keccak hash implementation and a shift register to design a hybrid module which also qualifies NIST and AIS 20/31 Tests.

Acknowledgement. The authors thankfully acknowledge the Defence Research & Development Organisation (DRDO) for funding the project through JCBCAT, Kolkata, India.

References

1. Alam, M., Bhattacharya, S., Dutta, S., Sinha, S., Mukhopadhyay, D., Chattopadhyay, A.: RATAFIA: ransomware analysis using time and frequency informed autoencoders. In: 2019 IEEE International Symposium on Hardware Oriented Security and Trust (HOST), pp. 218–227 (2019)
2. Alam, M., Bhattacharya, S., Mukhopadhyay, D., Bhattacharya, S.: Performance counters to rescue: a machine learning based safeguard against micro-architectural side-channel-attacks. IACR Cryptology ePrint Archive 2017, 564 (2017)
3. Alam, M., Bhattacharya, S., Sinha, S., Rebeiro, C., Mukhopadhyay, D.: IPA: an instruction profiling-based micro-architectural side-channel attack on block ciphers. J. Hardw. Syst. Secur. **3**(1), 26–44 (2019)
4. Alam, M., Mukhopadhyay, D.: How secure are deep learning algorithms from side-channel based reverse engineering? In: Proceedings of the 56th Annual Design Automation Conference 2019, p. 226. ACM (2019)
5. Alam, M., Mukhopadhyay, D., Kadiyala, S.P., Lam, S.K., Srikanthan, T.: Side-channel assisted malware classifier with gradient descent correction for embedded platforms. In: PROOFS@ CHES, pp. 1–15 (2018)
6. Alameldeen, A.R., Wood, D.A.: Variability in architectural simulations of multi-threaded workloads. In: 2003 Proceedings of the Ninth International Symposium on High-Performance Computer Architecture, HPCA-9 2003, pp. 7–18. IEEE (2003)
7. Bayon, P., et al.: Contactless electromagnetic active attack on ring oscillator based true random number generator. In: Schindler, W., Huss, S.A. (eds.) COSADE 2012. LNCS, vol. 7275, pp. 151–166. Springer, Heidelberg (2012). https://doi.org/10.1007/978-3-642-29912-4_12

8. Bertoni, G., Daemen, J., Peeters, M., Van Assche, G.: Keccak. In: Johansson, T., Nguyen, P.Q. (eds.) EUROCRYPT 2013. LNCS, vol. 7881, pp. 313–314. Springer, Heidelberg (2013). https://doi.org/10.1007/978-3-642-38348-9_19
9. Bhattacharya, S., Mukhopadhyay, D.: Who watches the watchmen?: utilizing performance monitors for compromising keys of RSA on Intel platforms. In: Güneysu, T., Handschuh, H. (eds.) CHES 2015. LNCS, vol. 9293, pp. 248–266. Springer, Heidelberg (2015). https://doi.org/10.1007/978-3-662-48324-4_13
10. Chen, W., et al.: A 1.04 μW truly random number generator for Gen2 RFID tag. In: 2009 IEEE Asian Solid-State Circuits Conference, pp. 117–120. IEEE (2009)
11. Cherkaoui, A., Fischer, V., Fesquet, L., Aubert, A.: A very high speed true random number generator with entropy assessment. In: Bertoni, G., Coron, J.S. (eds.) CHES 2013. LNCS, vol. 8086, pp. 179–196. Springer, Heidelberg (2013). https://doi.org/10.1007/978-3-642-40349-1_11
12. Güneysu, T.: True random number generation in block memories of reconfigurable devices. In: 2010 International Conference on Field-Programmable Technology, pp. 200–207. IEEE (2010)
13. Gutterman, Z., Pinkas, B., Reinman, T.: Analysis of the Linux random number generator. In: 2006 IEEE Symposium on Security and Privacy (S&P 2006), pp. 15–pp. IEEE (2006)
14. Jun, B., Kocher, P.: The Intel random number generator. White Paper, vol. 27, pp. 1–8. Cryptography Research Inc. (1999)
15. Killmann, W., Schindler, W.: A proposal for: functionality classes for random number generators. Ser. BDI, Bonn (2011)
16. Markettos, A.T., Moore, S.W.: The frequency injection attack on ring-oscillator-based true random number generators. In: Clavier, C., Gaj, K. (eds.) CHES 2009. LNCS, vol. 5747, pp. 317–331. Springer, Heidelberg (2009). https://doi.org/10.1007/978-3-642-04138-9_23
17. Mc Guire, N., Okech, P., Schiesser, G.: Analysis of inherent randomness of the Linux kernel. In: Proceedings of the 11th Real-Time Linux Workshop. Citeseer (2009)
18. Mytkowicz, T., Diwan, A., Hauswirth, M., Sweeney, P.F.: Producing wrong data without doing anything obviously wrong!. ACM SIGARCH Comput. Archit. News **37**(1), 265–276 (2009)
19. Petrie, C.S., Connelly, J.A.: A noise-based IC random number generator for applications in cryptography. IEEE Trans. Circuits Syst. I: Fundam. Theory Appl. **47**(5), 615–621 (2000)
20. Robson, S., Leung, B., Gong, G.: Truly random number generator based on a ring oscillator utilizing last passage time. IEEE Trans. Circuits Syst. II Express Briefs **61**(12), 937–941 (2014)
21. Rožić, V., Yang, B., Mentens, N., Verbauwhede, I.: Canary numbers: design for light-weight online testability of true random number generators. In: NIST RBG Workshop, Gaithersburg, MD, USA, vol. 386, p. 2016 (2016). Cryptology ePrint Archive, Technical report
22. Rukhin, A., Soto, J., Nechvatal, J., Smid, M., Barker, E.: A statistical test suite for random and pseudorandom number generators for cryptographic applications. Technical report, Booz-Allen and Hamilton Inc., Mclean, VA (2001)
23. Weaver, V.M.: Using dynamic binary instrumentation to create faster, validated, multi-core simulations. Ph.D. thesis, Cornell University (2010)
24. Weaver, V.M., McKee, S.A.: Can hardware performance counters be trusted? In: 2008 IEEE International Symposium on Workload Characterization, pp. 141–150. IEEE (2008)

25. Weaver, V.M., Terpstra, D., Moore, S.: Non-determinism and overcount on modern hardware performance counter implementations. In: 2013 IEEE International Symposium on Performance Analysis of Systems and Software (ISPASS), pp. 215–224. IEEE (2013)
26. Yang, B., Rožic, V., Grujic, M., Mentens, N., Verbauwhede, I.: ES-TRNG: a high-throughput, low-area true random number generator based on edge sampling. IACR Trans. Cryptogr. Hardw. Embed. Syst. **2018**, 267–292 (2018)
27. Yang, B., Rožić, V., Mentens, N., Dehaene, W., Verbauwhede, I.: TOTAL: TRNG on-the-fly testing for attack detection using lightweight hardware. In: Proceedings of the 2016 Conference on Design, Automation & Test in Europe, pp. 127–132. EDA Consortium (2016)
28. Yao, A.C.: Theory and application of trapdoor functions. In: 23rd Annual Symposium on Foundations of Computer Science (SFCS 1982), pp. 80–91. IEEE (1982)
29. Zaparanuks, D., Jovic, M., Hauswirth, M.: Accuracy of performance counter measurements. In: 2009 IEEE International Symposium on Performance Analysis of Systems and Software, pp. 23–32. IEEE (2009)

Optimized Threshold Implementations: Minimizing the Latency of Secure Cryptographic Accelerators

Dušan Božilov[1,2](✉), Miroslav Knežević[1], and Ventzislav Nikov[1]

[1] NXP Semiconductors, Leuven, Belgium
[2] COSIC KU Leuven and imec, Leuven, Belgium
dusan.bozilov@esat.kuleuven.be

Abstract. Threshold implementations have emerged as one of the most popular masking countermeasures for hardware implementations of cryptographic primitives. In this work, we first provide a generic construction for $d+1$ TI sharing which achieves the minimal number of output shares for any n-input Boolean function of degree $t = n - 1$ and for any d. Secondly, we demonstrate the applicability of our results on a first-order and second-order $d+1$ low-latency PRINCE implementation.

Keywords: Threshold implementations · PRINCE · SCA · Masking

1 Introduction

Historically, the field of lightweight cryptography focused on algorithm designs occupying smallest possible silicon area. Small area results in low power consumption, another equally important optimization target. However, hitting these two targets degrades performance of lightweight cryptographic primitives, and for most online applications, they frequently do not meet the requirements. Only a handful of designs consider latency among their main design goals. PRINCE [6] and Midori [1] are two prominent examples.

Vulnerability to physical attacks, e.g. side-channel analysis (SCA) is a threat faced by the field of (lightweight) cryptography since its creation, with significant effort being invested in SCA resistant implementation design. To resist an adversary that has access up to d wires in a circuit [11] the secret value has to be shared into at least $d+1$ random shares using a masking technique, such as Boolean masking.

Circumventing a masked implementation requires attackers to recover the secret information from several shares, i.e. they need to employ a d-th order higher-order attack at least. These attacks are harder to mount due to their susceptibility to measurement noise. Higher-order SCA protection incurs penalties in silicon area, execution time, power consumption and the amount of random bits required for secure execution. Additional cost comes from the increasing number of shares required. The number of output shares grows exponentially

S. Belaïd and T. Güneysu (Eds.): CARDIS 2019, LNCS 11833, pp. 20–39, 2020.
https://doi.org/10.1007/978-3-030-42068-0_2

with the algebraic degree of the function, the number of nonlinear terms the function has, and the security order that needs to be achieved.

Secure cryptographic circuit design becomes significantly harder once the requirements have to be met for latency, energy consumption, silicon area or power. In the context of this paper, and as stated in [12], we consider latency as the total time needed to execute a single cryptographic operation. Minimizing latency can be achieved by increasing the frequency the circuit can operate on or by reducing clock cycle count of the operation. Hence, one design outperforms another with regards to latency if the product of the number of clock cycles and the minimal clock period is smaller in that design.

In [14], the authors provide the first example in the literature where latency and SCA protection are considered as the main design goal. Their results indicate that this is a significantly more difficult problem than designing a countermeasure by optimizing area or the amount of randomness, which are the typical design criteria addressed by the scientific community. Therefore, designing side-channel countermeasures for low-latency or low-energy implementations is considered to be an important open problem. The authors of [8] introduced a generalized concept for low-latency masking that is supposed to be applicable to any implementation and protection order, however they have applied their concept to designs which are not low-latency and therefore it is difficult to compare their approach. We have to stress that the goal to achieve minimal latency is not equivalent to get only execution within less cycles, since at the same time the complexity of the circuit grows resulting in longer critical path. In other words one gets a design which can be executed in less cycles but also with lower max frequency. It has been pointed out in [13] that the generalized concept has to use another re-sharing technique, since the original one has a flaw for $d > 2$.

Threshold Implementations (TI) [15] is a provably secure masking scheme specifically designed to counter side-channel leakage caused by the presence of glitches in hardware. Later the approach of TI was extended to counter higher-order (uni-variate) attacks [3]. The theory suggests the usage of at least $td + 1$ number of input shares in order to make a Boolean function with algebraic degree t secure against a d-th order side-channel attack. That is the reason why these TI schemes are often referred to as a $td + 1$ TI. Consolidated Masking Scheme (CMS) [17] reduced the required number of input shares needed to resist a d-th order attack to $d + 1$, regardless of the algebraic degree of the shared function. Recall that this is theoretically the lowest bound on the number of input shares with respect to the order of security d. After that, many schemes using $d + 1$ shares such as Domain Oriented Masking (DOM) and Unified Masking Approach (UMA) emerged [9,10], where the essential differences among them is in the way the refreshing of the output shares is performed. Since the security against glitches of all these schemes (CMS, DOM, UMA, etc.) relies on the TI principles, these are also referred as $d + 1$ TI.

While the established theory of TI guarantees that the number of input shares linearly grows with the order of protection d, it does not provide efficient means to keep the exponential explosion of the number of output shares under control.

The state-of-the-art is a lower bound of $(d+1)^t$ given in [17], while in [3] the authors described a method to obtain a TI-sharing with $\binom{td+1}{t}$ output shares. The latter work also notes that the number of output shares can sometimes be reduced by using more than $td+1$ input shares. Aside from a formula for the lower bound in [17], there was not much other work of applying $d+1$ TI to functions with higher degree than 2. The only exception is the AES implementations by [19, 20] where $d+1$ TI is applied to the inversion of $GF(2^4)$, which is a function of algebraic degree 3. However, even for this particular case, the first attempt [20] resulted in sharing with minimal number of output shares but it did not satisfy the non-completeness property of TI. Only in the follow-up publication [19] the sharing was correct and minimal. It has to be noted that for the particular case of cubic function, it is fairly easy to find the minimal first-order sharing of 8 output shares by exhaustive trial and error approach.

Our Contribution: In this paper we first introduce a method for optimizing Threshold Implementations. In particular, we provide a constructive solution for $d+1$ TI that achieves the optimal number of output shares for any n-input Boolean function of degree $t = n - 1$ for any security order d. Using this construction we demonstrate how to reduce the latency to achieve faster TI-protected implementation of PRINCE. Third, we also show the most energy efficient round-based first-order secure implementation of PRINCE using $d+1$ TI sharing.

Finally, we would like to point out that the method of minimizing the number of output shares is of general interest since it can equally well be applied to any cryptographic implementation and any design optimisation criteria.

2 Preliminaries

The elements of the finite field $\mathcal{F}_2^n$ are represented with small letters. Subscripts are used to specify each bit of an element or each coordinate function of a vectorial Boolean function, for example $x = (x_1, \cdots, x_n)$, where $x_i \in \mathcal{F}_2$. Subscripts are used to represent shares of one-bit variables. The reader should be able to distinguish from the context if the text is referring to specific bits of unshared variable or specific shares of a variable. Next we denote Hamming weight, concatenation, cyclic right shift, right shift, composition, multiplication and addition with $wt(.)$, $||$, $\ggg$, $\gg$, $\circ$, $.$ and $+$ respectively. We will use Algebraic Normal Form representations of Boolean functions and will refer to the algebraic degree of such Boolean function.

Two permutations S and S' are affine equivalent if and only if there exists two affine permutations C and D satisfying $S' = C \circ S \circ D$. We refer to C as the output and D as the input transformation. Last the TI sharing which is designed to protect against the d-th order attack we will simply refer to as the d-th order TI.

2.1 Threshold Implementations

The most important property that ensures security of TI even in the presence of glitches is *non-completeness*. The d-th order non-completeness property requires any combination of up to d component functions to be independent of at least one input share. When cascading multiple nonlinear functions, the 1-st order sharing must also satisfy the *uniformity*: namely a sharing is uniform if and only if the sharing of the output preserves the distribution of the unshared output. In other words, for a given unmasked value, all possible combinations of output shares representing that value are equally likely to happen. For higher-order sharing and to achieve uniformity one can always apply refreshing of the output shares.

Given the shares $x_1, \ldots, x_n$ a (first- and second-order) refreshing can be realized by mapping $(x_1, \ldots, x_n)$ to $(y_1, \ldots, y_n)$ using n random values $r_1, \ldots, r_n$ as follows:

$$y_1 = x_1 + r_1 + r_n \qquad y_i = x_i + r_{i-1} + r_i, \qquad i \in \{2, \ldots, n\} \tag{1}$$

This refreshing scheme is called *ring re-masking.* An improvement regarding the number of random bits used when multiplication gate is shared has been achieved in [10] where the amount of randomness required is halved compared to CMS. In [9], the authors have shown that the amount of randomness for sharing a multiplication gate can be further reduced to one third, although this comes at the significant performance cost. Since our goal is to build low-latency side-channel secure implementations, we do not take the approach of UMA. Instead, we choose CMS/DOM for d + 1 TI designs In this paper we will interchangeably use terms mask refreshing and re-masking.

In order to prevent glitch propagation when cascading nonlinear functions, TI requires register(s) to be placed between the nonlinear operations. Otherwise, the non-completeness property may be violated and the leakage of the secret internal state is likely to be manifested.

When sharing a nonlinear function the number of output shares is typically larger than the number of input shares. This is likely to occur when applying $td + 1$ TI and it always occurs when applying $d + 1$ TI. In order to minimize the number of output shares we need to refresh and recombine (compress) some shares by adding several of them together. To prevent glitches from revealing unmasked values, decreasing the number of shares can only be done after storing these output shares into a register. The output shares that are going to be recombined together still need to be carefully chosen such that they do not reveal any unmasked value.

While using $d + 1$ TI the relation between the input shares needs to obey a stronger requirement, namely shared input variables need to be *independent* [17]. This can be achieved in various ways - for example by refreshing some of the inputs or by using a technique proposed in [10].

2.2 Minimizing Implementation Overheads Using S-box Decomposition

Similar to other side channel countermeasures, the area overhead of applying TI increases polynomially with respect to the security order and exponentially with respect to the algebraic degree of the function we are trying to protect. To keep the large overheads caused by exponential dependency under control, designers often use decomposition of the higher degree functions into several lower degree functions. This approach has originally been demonstrated in [16] where the authors implemented a TI-protected PRESENT block cipher [5] by decomposing its cubic S-box into two simpler quadratic S-boxes. Finally, decomposition of all cubic 4-bit S-boxes into chains of smaller quadratic S-boxes was given in [4], which eventually enables compact, side-channel secure implementations.

Although a decomposition of nonlinear functions into several simpler functions of smaller algebraic degree is the proper approach to use for area reduction of the TI-protected implementations, its side-effect is the increased latency of the S-box evaluation and hence the entire implementation. Recall that the TI requires registers to be placed between the nonlinear operations in order to prevent the glitch propagation, which in turn increases the latency. We will not use this approach since our goal is to achieve low-latency.

2.3 A Note on Latency and Energy Efficiency

As already mentioned, most of the effort the scientific community has spent on designing secure implementations has been focused on reducing area overheads. Another important metric that had been given lots of attention is the amount of randomness used in protected implementations. While both of these metrics are important, performance and energy consumption of secure implementations have been unjustly treated as less significant. It has been widely accepted that performance is the metric to sacrifice in order to achieve the lowest possible gate count. Contrary to this view, most of the practical applications nowadays require (very) fast execution and it is often latency of the actual implementation that matters rather than the throughput. Energy consumption is another equally important metric and, unlike power consumption, it cannot be well controlled by keeping the area low while sacrificing performance. Optimizing for energy consumption is in fact one of the most difficult optimization problems in (secure) circuit design since the perfect balance between the circuit power consumption and its execution speed needs to be hit.

The absolute latency is directly proportional to the number of clock cycles a certain operation takes to execute. At the same time, the absolute latency is inversely proportional to the clock frequency the system is running at. While the clock frequency is determined by taking into account multiple factors from the whole system, most important of which is the overall power/energy consumption, the number of clock cycles a certain algorithm takes to execute is under full control of the designer. Especially when considering embedded devices, the tendency is to keep the clock frequency as low as we can while still meeting the performance requirements. That is the reason why minimizing the number of clock cycles of a certain algorithm is the most important strategy when it comes to minimizing the overall latency of that algorithm.

Although the majority of results available in public literature deal with area-efficient hardware architectures, there are still a few notable examples where the latency reduction has been the main target. In [14], the authors particularly explore the extreme case of a single clock cycle side-channel secure implementations of PRINCE and Midori. Moreover, they conclude that designing a low-latency side-channel secure implementation of cryptographic primitives remains an open problem.

3 Finding an Efficient Sharing

To find a $d+1$ sharing for a quadratic vectorial Boolean function is straightforward and especially easy for the functions that have a simple ANF e. g., a quadratic function with a single second degree term. However, finding an efficient sharing for a vectorial Boolean function of higher algebraic degree with several high degree terms may not be evident, requiring increasingly more effort to find the minimal number of the output shares.

Minimizing the number of output shares becomes even harder the higher the security order d is. In this section we propose methods to deal with this complexity and we describe an optimal solution for the $d+1$ sharing for any security order d.

To achieve d-th order security using $d+1$ sharing for a single term of degree t, i.e. a product of t variables, one gets exactly $(d+1)^t$ shares for the product [17].

For *non-completeness*, in the $d+1$ TI sharing each output share should contain only one share per input variable. In other words if in an output share there are two shares of an input variable then the d-th order non-completeness will be violated. We can see this in the $d+1$ sharing of Eq. (3), the first output share only has one input share of x, y and z: x_0, y_0 and z_0, respectively. All other output shares in Eq. (3) adhere to this rule as well.

Therefore, to ensure *non-completeness* it is enough to have only one share of each input variable present in any given output share. We will assume that the independence of input shares is always satisfied.

Correctness is achieved by verifying that each monomial of a shared term (product) in the unshared function f must be present in one of the output shares.

Consider again the function $xy+z$. One possible first-order $d+1$ sharing of it is given in Eq. (2).

$$
\begin{array}{ll}
(x, y, z) & \\
(0,0,0) & o_1 = x_0 y_0 + z_0 \\
(0,1,*) & o_2 = x_0 y_1 \\
(1,0,*) & o_3 = x_1 y_0 \\
(1,1,1) & o_4 = x_1 y_1 + z_1
\end{array} \tag{2}
$$

Shorter representation of the sharing is shown within the brackets in Eq. (2). Each output share is a row of a table, and each column represents the shares of different input variable. Entry in row i and column j is the allowed input share of j-th input variable for i-th output share.

Columns are representing the variables x, y and z respectively. The asterisk values indicate that we do not care about what input share of z is there, since the sharing of linear term z is ensured by combining rows 1 and 4 of the table. This also shows that the table representation of the sharing does not uniquely determine the exact formula for each output share, and there is certain freedom in determining where we can insert the input shares.

For example, we can use the table of Eq. (2) to share function $x+y+xy+z$. There are two options for terms x_0 and x_1, rows 1 and 2, and rows 3 and 4, respectively. Similarly, y_0 can be in either shares 1 or 3, y_1 can be in share 2 or 4.

Non-completeness and *correctness* can be easily argued from the table representation. Since for every table row, each column entry in the table can represent only one input share of that column's variable, *non-completeness* is automatically satisfied. For row 3 of the table in Eq. (2) by fixing the entries representing x to 1 and y to 0 we ensure that only x_1 and y_0 can occur in that output sharing. Hence, there is no way that x_0 or y_1 can be a part of that particular output share, which is the only way to violate *non-completeness* in $d+1$ sharing. *Correctness* of the table can be verified by checking correctness for every monomial in unshared function f individually. If the combined columns representing variables of the monomial contain all possible combinations of share indexes, sharing is correct, since all terms of shared product for each monomial can be present in the output sharing. Following example from Eq. (2), for monomial xy we see that all four combinations $\{(0,0),(0,1),(1,0),(1,1)\}$ are present in two columns representing variables x and y, allowing all the terms of shared product $xy = (x_0+x_1)(y_0+y_1) = x_0y_0+x_0y_1+x_1y_0+x_1y_1$ to be present in at least one output share. The same holds for $z = z_0 + z_1$ as both combination $\{(0),(1)\}$ are present in output table of Eq. (2). Also, the number of rows in correct sharing table is lower-bounded by the $(d+1)^t$, when the degree of the function is t.

Now, consider a function $xy+xz+yz$. One possible first-order $d+1$ sharing and its table is given in Eq. (3). Columns represent x, y, and z, respectively.

$$\begin{array}{ll} (0,0,0) & o_1 = x_0y_0 + x_0z_0 + y_0z_0 \\ (0,1,1) & o_2 = x_0y_1 + x_0z_1 + y_1z_1 \\ (1,0,0) & o_3 = x_1y_0 + x_1z_0 \\ (1,1,1) & o_4 = x_1y_1 + x_1z_1 \\ (*,0,1) & o_5 = \qquad\qquad\quad y_0z_1 \\ (*,1,0) & o_6 = \qquad\qquad\quad y_1z_0 \end{array} \tag{3}$$

The table has 6 rows representing different output shares, which is larger than theoretically minimal 4 shares. Sharing given by Eq. (3) is also very easily obtained when we try to derive it by hand. Naive approach is to start by sharing xy into four shares. Next, we try to incorporate xz into these four shares by setting all indexes of z to be equal to y. The problem arises when we try to add sharing of yz. In the existing four output shares we have z and y have same indexes, thus we are required to add two more shares for terms y_0z_1 and y_1z_0.

Further on, we will show that for any function with n input variables of degree $t = n - 1$ it is possible to have a $d + 1$ sharing with minimal $(d + 1)^t$ shares.

Definition 1. *Table with n columns representing output sharing of a function of degree t with n input variables is referred to as a D^n-table. The number of rows of the table is the number of output shares for a given sharing. If the output sharing is correct then D^n-table is t-degree correct D^n-table. t-degree correct D^n-table with minimal numbers of rows is called an* optimal *D^n-table. Optimal D^n-table that has $(d + 1)^t$ rows is called* ideal *D^n-table, denoted D^n_t-table.*

For $t = n$ ideal D^n_n-table is just a table that contain all different $(d + 1)^t$ indexes of input variables in the terms of shared product that occur when sharing a function of degree t. We can also consider each row of a D^n-table as an ordered tuple of size n. i-th value in a such tuple represents the i-th input variable, and it's value is the allowed input share of that variable in the output share represented by the tuple. All tuple entries have values from the set $\{0, \ldots, d\}$.

Definition 2. *D^t-table D_1 is t-subtable of D^n-table D_2 for given t columns if D_2 reduced to these t columns is equal to D_1.*

We have shown with the sharing in Eq. (2) how one can check the correctness of the table. Now we generalize this by showing how to check if a given D^n-table can be used for sharing of any function of degree t. It is sufficient to check correctness only for the terms of degree t, since if a product of t variables can be shared with a number of output shares, any product of a subset of these t variables can also be shared using the same output shares.

It is easy to see that a D^n-table D can be used to share any function of degree t if and only if for any combination of t columns, D^t-table formed by chosen t columns contains all possible $(d+1)^t$ ordered tuples of size t. In, other words, t-subtable of D for any t columns is t-degree correct D^t-table. This comes from the fact that D^t-table that contains all possible $(d + 1)^t$ ordered t-tuples represents

Table 1. D^3-table and its 3 2-subtables.

xyz	xy	xz	yz
000	00	00	00
011	01	01	11
100	10	10	00
111	11	11	11
001	00	01	01
110	11	10	10

a correct sharing for functions of degree t. If this is true for any combination of t columns of D we can correctly share any combination of products of size t from n input variables.

An example is given in Table 1 where D^3-table on the left can be used for first-order sharing of any function of degree 2 since all 3 D^2-tables obtained from it have all 4 possible ordered 2-tuples $(0,0)$, $(0,1)$, $(1,0)$ and $(1,1)$ as at least one of its rows. Next we show how one can construct ideal D^n-table for any function for given n, d and $t = n-1$. To recap, we first build a $(d+1)^t \times n$ table D, where every row is a tuple of indexes (in a single row no variable index is allowed to be missing and, naturally, no variable index is duplicated) and t-subtable of D for any t columns is a t-degree correct D^t-table. Since $t = n-1$ we can consider t-subtable generation as one column removal from D. Such a D^n-table D is then equivalent to a sharing which fulfills the *correctness* and the *non-completeness* properties of TI. Constructing an ideal D^n_n-table is trivial by enumerating all ordered index n-tuples. The number of rows in it is $(d+1)^n$.

Showing that a particular D^n-table with $(d+1)^{n-1}$ rows is a D^n_{n-1}-table becomes equivalent to proving that removal of any single column (restriction to $n-1$ columns or, equivalently, variables) from the D^n-table yields a D^{n-1}_{n-1}-table. Alternatively, any $(n-1)$-subtable of D^n_{n-1}-table is a D^{n-1}_{n-1}-table.

Here we will show how to build the D^n_t-table for the case when $t = n-1$. For any given D^n_{n-1}-table and security order d we will prove the existence of other d D^n_{n-1}-tables such that no n-tuple exists in more than one table. In other words, no two tables contain rows that are equal. We call such $d+1$ D^n_{n-1}-tables *conjugate tables*, and the sharings produced from them *conjugate sharings.* Having all rows different implies that these $d+1$ D^n_{n-1}-tables cover $(d+1)(d+1)^{n-1} = (d+1)^n$ index n-tuples, i.e. all possible index n-tuples. Therefore, these $d+1$ D^n_{n-1}-tables together form a D^n_n-table.

We build the $d+1$ conjugate D^n_{n-1}-tables inductively. For a given d we build $d+1$ conjugate D^2_1-tables, then assuming $d+1$ conjugate D^n_{n-1}-tables exist we construct $d+1$ conjugate D^{n+1}_n-tables.

The *initial step* is simple: D^2_1 has two columns (for the variables x and y) and in each row i (enumerated from 0 to d) of each conjugate table j (enumerated from 0 to d) we set the value in the first column to be i, and the value of the second column to be $(i+j) \mod (d+1)$, hence obtaining the $(d+1)$ conjugate

For $0 \leq i \leq d$ we construct the i-th D_n^{n+1}-table as follows:

1. Start with empty D-table P of $n+1$ variables.
2. For $0 \leq j \leq d$:
   (a) Take the j-th D_{n-1}^n-table and append one more column as last column.
   (b) Fill up the last column with the value $(i+j) \mod (d+1)$.
   (c) The obtained extended table is added to the D-table P.

Fig. 1. Algorithm for optimal $d+1$ sharing

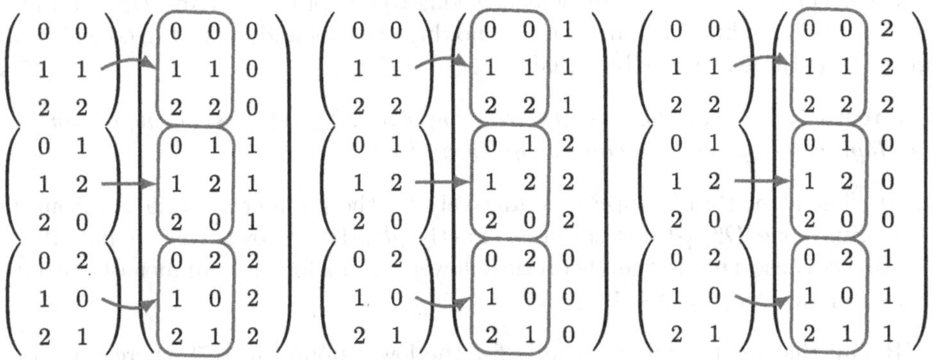

Fig. 2. Generating conjugate D_2^3-tables from D_1^2-tables.

D-tables with $d+1$ rows. Indeed, both columns of any of the constructed D_1^2-tables contain all values between 0 and d, so by removing either column we always obtain a correct D_1^1-table. Also, this construction ensures that second column never has the same index value in one row for different tables, therefore no two rows for different tables are the same, ensuring that formed tables are indeed conjugate.

Induction step - assume we have $d+1$ conjugate D_{n-1}^n-tables. Using them we are now going to build $d+1$ conjugate D_n^{n+1}-tables as described in Fig. 1.

The example of the iterative step from Algorithm 1 is given in Fig. 2.

Lemma 1. *Given $d+1$ conjugate D_{n-1}^n-tables the algorithm described in Fig. 1 constructs $d+1$ conjugate D_n^{n+1}-tables.*

Proof. First, let us show that the constructed $d+1$ D_n^{n+1}-tables are conjugate, i.e. there is no $(n+1)$-tuple which belongs to more than one of them. Let us assume there exists an $(n+1)$-tuple which belongs to two D_n^{n+1}-tables. This implies the existence of an n-tuple which belongs to two of the initial $d+1$ D_{n-1}^n-tables, contradicting the fact that these initial tables are conjugate.

Finally, any restriction to a particular set of columns has to have all the combinations of index n-tuples, i.e. the *correctness* property. In fact, it is sufficient to prove that any set of n columns in any of the new conjugate tables contains all possible n-tuples. Indeed, if we remove the last column in any of the so constructed tables we get the union of the original $d+1$ D^n_{n-1}-tables forming one D^n_n-table. By definition D^n_n-table satisfies this property. Lastly, we are left with the other case of removing one of the first n columns, which results in a table of dimensions $(d+1)^n \times n$. If we prove there are no duplicates among the $(d+1)^n$ tuples within this table, all combinations will be the table, making it again a D^n_n-table. Consider two n-tuples. If they are equal their last indexes are also equal. By Algorithm 1 design, equality of the last indexes (these are in the $(n+1)$-st column) implies that the two $(n-1)$-tuples belong to one of the starting conjugate D^n_{n-1}-tables, i.e. they can't be in different conjugate D^n_{n-1}-tables. However, for the $(n-1)$-tuples which belong to one of the starting D^n_{n-1}-tables by assumption is known that there are no duplications and hence the considered two $(n-1)$-tuples cannot be equal. □

Theorem 1. *Any of the constructed conjugate D^n_{n-1}-tables by algorithm in Fig. 1 provides optimal sharing for given n, d and $t = n-1$.*

Proof. The algorithm is applied inductively for the number of variables from 2 till n. Since one D^n_{n-1}-table contains exactly $(d+1)^{n-1}$ rows, we conclude it is optimal because this is the theoretical lower bound for the number of output shares for the case $t = n-1$. □

Recall that aside from a formula for the lower bound in [17], there was not much other work of applying $d+1$ TI to functions with higher degree than 2 with the only exception: the AES implementations by [19,20] where $d+1$ TI was applied to the inversion of $GF(2^4)$, which function has algebraic degree 3. When we tried to obtain by hand $d+1$ TI for PRINCE S-box of algebraic degree 3 we only managed to find output sharing for the most significant bit of the S-box with 12 and 44 output shares, for the first-order and the second-order $d+1$ TI prior to the discovery of the Algorithm 1. Optimal solution is 8 and 27 output shares for these two cases, respectively, which is easily found using approach described here.

Another benefit of using algorithmic solution is it can easily be automated using a computer, removing the possibility of human error that is likely to occur, the more complex the ANF becomes.

It is well known that a balanced Boolean function of n variables has a degree at most $n-1$. Therefore all $n \times n$ S-boxes which are permutations have a degree of at most $n-1$. Indeed nearly all bijective S-boxes used in symmetric ciphers are chosen to have a maximum degree of $n-1$. In particular, inversion in the field is always has maximum degree of $n-1$, most notable example of its usage being AES S-box. In the particular case of AES inversion, applying the algorithm shown here will produce the minimal number of shares, which is 128. This is however too large for any practical application.

Most notable exception where low-degree function is used is Keccak's [2] χ-function which is a 5×5 S-box of degree 2. A sharing with 8 shares can be easily found for χ by hand while a conjugate D^5-table will have 16 entries which corresponds to the optimal sharing for degree 4. Hence, the method presented in this section is not optimal when the degree of the function is lower than $n-1$.

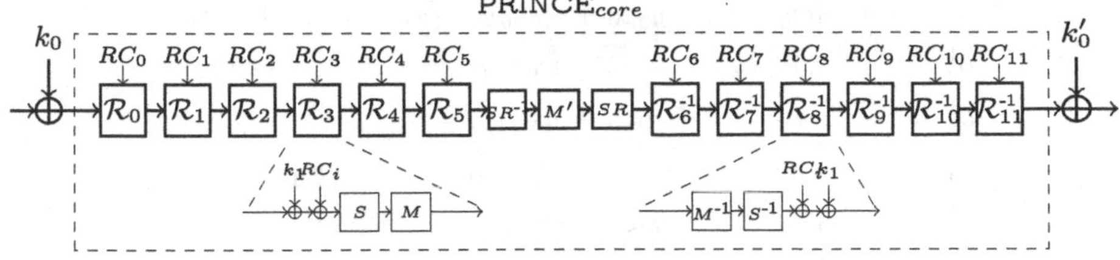

Fig. 3. *PRINCE cipher.*

Therefore, finding the optimal sharing for functions with a degree lower than $n-1$ remains an *open problem.*

4 Hardware Implementation

As a proof of concept we apply the optimal $d+1$ TI to PRINCE [6], a block cipher designed for low-latency hardware implementations. PRINCE block size is 64 bits, with a 128-bit key, used to derived 3 64-bit internally used keys k_0, k_0' and k_1. Figure 3 shows the internal structure of the cipher consisting of 12 rounds.

PRINCE round consists of 4-bit S-box operation, linear layer realized as matrix multiplication, and round constant addition. The S-box look-up table is $S(x) = [B, F, 3, 2, A, C, 9, 1, 6, 7, 8, 0, E, 5, D, 4]$. The algebraic degree of the S-box is 3, and S-box is affine equivalent to its inverse $S^{-1} = A_{io} \circ S \circ A_{io}$. The A_{io} look-up table is $A_{io}(x) = [5, 7, 6, 4, F, D, C, E, 1, 3, 2, 0, B, 9, 8, A]$.

To implement the first-order secure masking of PRINCE S-box, with $d = 1$, we use the algorithm described in Sect. 3 to obtain a conjugate D_3^4-table. This table represents an optimal solution for 2 input shares with 8 output shares for each input/output bit of the S-box. Recall that the PRINCE S-box is a 4×4-bit S-box and that it has a degree 3.

The optimal sharing is given below in Eq. (4) as conjugate D_3^4-table. The exact sharing for four bits of PRINCE S-box is given with Eqs. (5), (6), (7) and (8), respectively.

$$\begin{array}{ccc} (x,y,z,w) & (1,0,1,0) & (0,1,0,1) \\ (1,1,0,0) & (0,0,1,1) & (1,0,0,1) \\ (0,1,1,0) & (1,1,1,1) & (0,0,0,0) \end{array} \tag{4}$$

As an example consider the first coordinate functions of PRINCE. For the first bit we have $o^1 = 1 + zw + y + yz + wzy + x + xw + xy$ with optimal sharing:

$$
\begin{aligned}
o_1^1 &= 1 + z_0w_0 + y_0 + y_0z_0 + w_0z_0y_0 + x_0 + x_0w_0 + x_0y_0 \\
o_2^1 &= w_0z_0y_1 + x_1y_1 \\
o_3^1 &= z_1w_0 + y_1z_1 + w_0z_1y_1 \\
o_4^1 &= w_0z_1y_0 + x_1w_0 \\
o_5^1 &= z_1w_1 + y_0z_1 + w_1z_1y_0 + x_0w_1 \\
o_6^1 &= w_1z_1y_1 \\
o_7^1 &= z_0w_1 + y_1 + y_1z_0 + w_1z_0y_1 + x_0y_1 \\
o_8^1 &= w_1z_0y_0 + x_1 + x_1w_1 + x_1y_0
\end{aligned} \tag{5}
$$

Continuing for the second bit's algebraic function $o^2 = 1+yw+yz+xz+yzw+xyz$ optimal sharing is:

$$
\begin{aligned}
o_1^2 &= 1 + y_0w_0 + y_0z_0 + x_0z_0 + y_0z_0w_0 + x_0y_0z_0 \\
o_2^2 &= y_1z_0w_0 + x_1y_1z_0 \\
o_3^2 &= y_1w_0 + y_1z_1 + y_1z_1w_0 + x_0y_1z_1 \\
o_4^2 &= x_1z_1 + y_0z_1w_0 + x_1y_0z_1 \\
o_5^2 &= y_0w_1 + y_0z_1 + x_0z_1 + y_0z_1w_1 + x_0y_0z_1 \\
o_6^2 &= y_1z_1w_1 + x_1y_1z_1 \\
o_7^2 &= y_1w_1 + y_1z_0 + y_1z_0w_1 + x_0y_1z_0 \\
o_8^2 &= x_1z_0 + y_0z_0w_1 + x_1y_0z_0
\end{aligned} \tag{6}
$$

Optimal sharing for the third bit with algebraic function $o^3 = w + x + zw + xw + xz + xzw + xyz$ is:

$$
\begin{aligned}
o_1^3 &= w_0 + x_0 + z_0w_0 + x_0w_0 + x_0z_0 + x_0z_0w_0 + x_0y_0z_0 \\
o_2^3 &= x_1z_0w_0 + x_1y_1z_0 \\
o_3^3 &= z_1w_0 + x_0z_1w_0 + x_0y_1z_1 \\
o_4^3 &= x_1w_0 + x_1z_1 + x_1z_1w_0 + x_1y_0z_1 \\
o_5^3 &= w_1 + z_1w_1 + x_0w_1 + x_0z_1 + x_0z_1w_1 + x_0y_0z_1 \\
o_6^3 &= x_1z_1w_1 + x_1y_1z_1 \\
o_7^3 &= z_0w_1 + x_0z_0w_1 + x_0y_1z_0 \\
o_8^3 &= x_1 + x_1w_1 + x_1z_1 + x_1z_0w_1 + x_1y_0z_0
\end{aligned} \tag{7}
$$

Finally, for the fourth bit of PRINCE S-box and its function $o^4 = 1 + z + x + yz + xy + yzw + xzw + xyw$ optimal sharing is given with:

$$
\begin{aligned}
o_1^4 &= 1 + z_0 + x_0 + y_0 z_0 + x_0 y_0 + y_0 z_0 w_0 + x_0 z_0 w_0 + x_0 y_0 w_0 \\
o_2^4 &= x_1 y_1 + y_1 z_0 w_0 + x_1 z_0 w_0 + x_1 y_1 w_0 \\
o_3^4 &= y_1 z_1 + y_1 z_1 w_0 + x_0 z_1 w_0 + x_0 y_1 w_0 \\
o_4^4 &= y_0 z_1 w_0 + x_1 z_1 w_0 + x_1 y_0 w_0 \\
o_5^4 &= z_1 + y_0 z_1 + y_0 z_1 w_1 + x_0 z_1 w_1 + x_0 y_0 w_1 \\
o_6^4 &= y_1 z_1 w_1 + x_1 z_1 w_1 + x_1 y_1 w_1 \\
o_7^4 &= y_1 z_0 + x_0 y_1 + y_1 z_0 w_1 + x_0 z_0 w_1 + x_0 y_1 w_1 \\
o_8^4 &= x_1 + x_1 y_0 + y_0 z_0 w_1 + x_1 z_0 w_1 + x_1 y_0 w_1
\end{aligned} \tag{8}
$$

The sharing of the cubic terms is unique while multiple options exist for the sharings of the lower degree terms and that is why one needs to avoid repetitions.

The resharing of the first-order secure implementation is performed according to the DOM [10] rules, in which complementary domains are remasked using the same randomness, with no remasking for output shares containing only one domain. It can be noticed from Eq. 4 that output shares o_1, o_2, o_3, o_4 have complementary domains of shares o_6, o_5, o_8, o_7, respectively. If we consider 8 output shares of 4-bit length, remasking is given with Eq. 9, where o_i, ro_i are S-box outputs output before and after remasking, and r_i are random 4-bit values, requiring 12 random bits. Recombination is achieved by adding shares ro_1, ro_2, ro_3, ro_4 into one, and ro_5, ro_6, ro_7, ro_8 into another recombined share.

$$
\begin{aligned}
&ro_1 = o_1 \quad && ro_2 = o_2 + r_1 \quad && ro_3 = o_3 + r_2 \quad && ro_4 = o_4 + r_3 \\
&ro_5 = o_5 + r_1 \quad && ro_6 = o_6 \quad && ro_7 = o_7 + r_3 \quad && ro_8 = o_8 + r_2
\end{aligned} \tag{9}
$$

If we inspect the PRINCE round structure we can further reduce the first-order randomness requirement. The mixing layer consists of matrices M, M' or M^{-1}, while M can be derived from M' using nibble shuffling SR, i.e. $M = SR \circ M'$. The 64×64 involution matrix M' independently affects 16-bit parts of its input, and can be viewed as 4 independent 16×16 matrices (M_0, M_1, M_1, M_0). PRINCE state composed of 16 nibbles enumerated from 0 to 15 can be separated into 4 groups: $(0, 1, 2, 3)$, $(4, 5, 6, 7)$, $(8, 9, 10, 11)$ and $(12, 13, 14, 15)$. Randomness for the S-boxes can be reused between groups, as the nibble shuffling

$$
\begin{aligned}
SR &: (0,1,2,3,4,5,6,7,8,9,10,11,12,13,14,15) \rightarrow (0,5,10,15,4,9,14,3,8,13,2,7,12,1,6,11) \\
SR^{-1} &: (0,1,2,3,4,5,6,7,8,9,10,11,12,13,14,15) \rightarrow (0,13,10,7,4,1,14,11,8,5,2,15,12,9,6,3)
\end{aligned}
$$

together with M' operation does not cause mixing of the S-box outputs obtained using the same randomness. Additionally, assuming probing model case, the first-order attacker can observe one share out of two at a given cycle, disallowing him to exploit the reuse of randomness. Hence, this structure in round-based implementation reduces the amount of randomness by a factor of four.

The second-order implementation of the PRINCE S-box is again obtained using algorithm explained in Sect. 3. It provides a sharing with 3 input shares

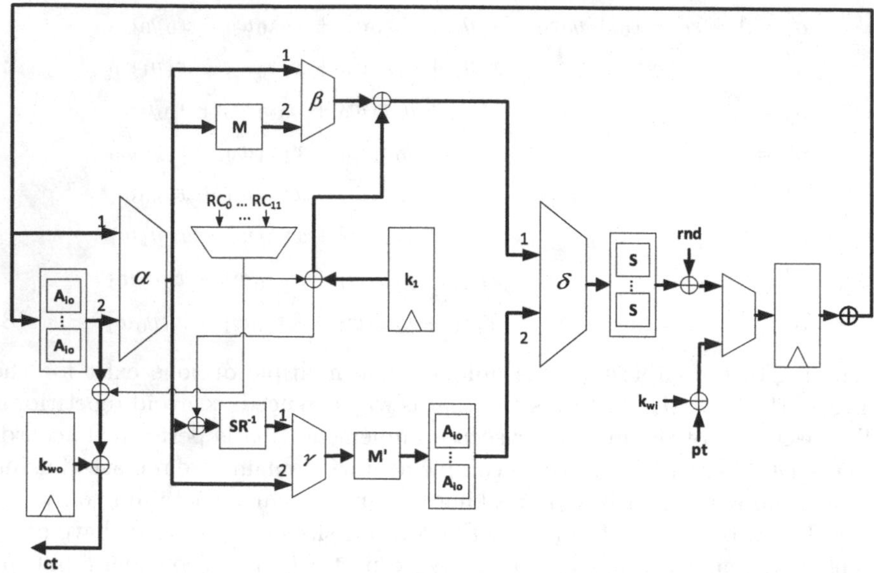

Fig. 4. Protected PRINCE round based architecture with one cycle per round execution.

and 27 output shares. The second order D_3^4-table is given in Eq. 10. Due to space requirements we omit the exact sharing, but a correct sharing can be derived from Eq. 10. For the second-order implementation ring-resharing technique is used, requiring 27 random bits per S-box output bit, or 108 random bits per S-box.

$$\begin{array}{lllll} (x,y,z,w) & (0,0,1,1) & (0,0,2,2) & (2,0,2,1) & (2,0,0,2) \\ (1,1,0,0) & (1,1,1,1) & (1,1,2,2) & (0,2,0,1) & (0,2,1,2) \\ (2,2,0,0) & (2,2,1,1) & (2,2,2,2) & (1,0,0,1) & (1,0,1,2) \\ (0,1,1,0) & (0,1,2,1) & (0,1,0,2) & (2,1,0,1) & (2,1,1,2) \\ (1,2,1,0) & (1,2,2,1) & (1,2,0,2) & (2,0,1,0) & (0,2,2,0) \\ (1,0,2,0) & (2,1,2,0) & (0,0,0,0) & & \end{array} \tag{10}$$

Hardware architecture of two $d+1$ TI PRINCE implementations without S-box decomposition is shown in Fig. 4. Control for the two implementations is exactly the same, while datapath only differs in the numbers of shares that are used. First-order implementation has 2 shares throughout, except for the S-box output, that has 8 shares, recombined back to two after the register stage. Second-order implementation has 3 shares, with S-box output having 27 shares.

Table 2. Area/power/energy/randomness/latency/max frequency comparison

PRINCE	Area @10 MHz (GE)	Power @10 MHz (uW)	Energy @10 MHz (pJ)	Rand/Cycle (bits)	Clock # (cycle)	f_{max} (MHz)	Latency @ f_{max} (ns)
Unprotected	3589	59	71	0	12	393	30.5
[14] 1st $(td+1)$ with S-box decomp.	9484	66	264	0	40	432	92.6
1st $(d+1)$ w/o S-box decomp.	11596	100	241	48	24	376	63.8
2nd $(d+1)$ w/o S-box decomp.	32444	374	898	1728	24	385	62.4

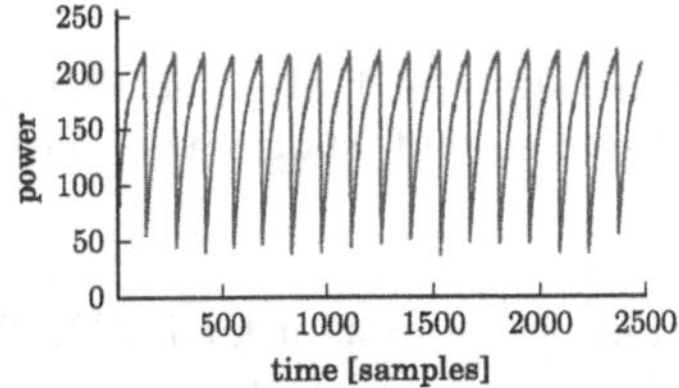

Fig. 5. Example power trace waveform used to perform the t-test on first-order PRINCE.

4.1 Synthesis Results and Side-Channel Evaluation

We have synthesized our designs as well as the previously existing TI PRINCE implementation [14] using TSMC 90 nm library using the typical case of +25 °C. Synthesis tool is Cadence Encounter RTL Compiler version 14.20-s034. Producing the smallest possible implementation was achieved by setting the frequency well below the critical path, at 10 MHz. The power consumption at 10 MHz is averaged from 100 random inputs simulations of a back-annotated post-synthesis netlist, obtained using Cadence Incisive Enterprise Simulator version 15.10.006. Energy is given for one encryption operation, assuming average power consumption. Table 2 shows area, power and energy consumption, the number of random bits required per clock cycle and maximum frequency for 3 hardware implementations, one given by Moradi [14], and two that newly proposed ones. The authors of [14] provided us with their implementations, allowing for a fair comparison of three designs using the same compiler and library, as the synthesis results for design presented in [14] differ from the original paper.

At the maximum frequency, our first-order design surpasses previous state of the art by reducing latency by almost a third. The energy consumption of our first-order at the frequency of 10 MHz is lower by almost 10%. On the other hand, the implementation from [14] beats our version with respect to area, power consumption, maximal running frequency and randomness required. Potentially, it also can achieve higher throughput, with small modifications to the finite state machine, so it processes three messages at once. Given that our goal was to minimize implementation latency and energy, these results are not surprising.

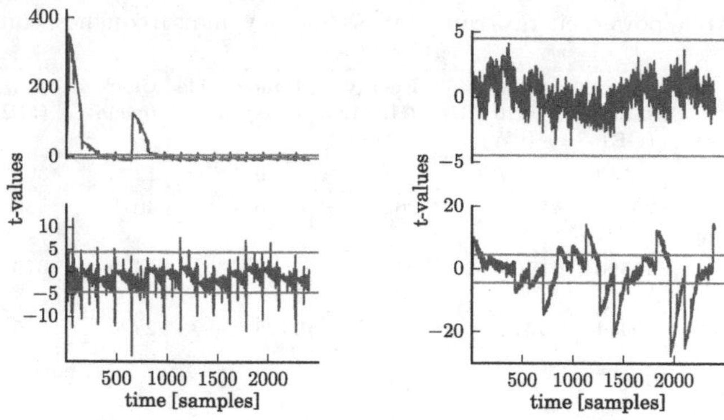

Fig. 6. Leakage detection test results on first-order PRINCE. PRNG off (left) and PRNG on (right). First- (top) and second- (bottom) order t-test results.

We first provide evaluation of the first-order PRINCE without S-box decomposition using optimal $d + 1$ sharing which design was programmed onto a Xilinx Spartan-6 FPGA. The platform used is a Sakura-G board. The design is separated into two FPGAs to minimize the noise: one performs the PRINCE encryption and second FPGA handles the I/O and the start signal. Our core runs at 3.072 MHz while the sampling rate is 500 million samples per second. The power waveform is given in Fig. 5.

We apply a non-specific leakage detection test [7] on the input plaintext following the standard methodology [18], and resulting t-test graphs are shown in the Fig. 6. First, we turn PRNG off to verify validity of the setup and leakage is detected with 1 million traces. The left hand side in Fig. 6 demonstrates a strong first-order leakage during the loading of the plaintext and the key. This can be attributed to one share of both the key and the plaintext being equal to the unshared value, while the other share is zero. Another strong peak is during the first S-box execution as there is still high correlation to the input. Leakage is present in later rounds as well due to lack of additional randomness, although it becomes smaller. Second-order leakage can also be observed when the masks are off. When PRNG is on no first-order leakage is detected after 100 million traces, while second-order leakage is observed as expected.

Due to size and randomness needed, the second-order design did not fit onto the same FPGA board. Instead, the design is tested against simulated power traces. We measured the estimated power consumption by running a post-synthesis simulation with back-annotated netlist. Input-to-output timing delays and current consumption of every gate in the netlist were taken into account and modeled as specified by the technology liberty timing file. In our simulations, one clock cycle is represented with 50 sample points and we cover first seven rounds of the execution. One million traces have been obtained with PRNG switched on, and two thousand traces with PRNG off. Simulated traces are perfectly aligned, they do not contain any measurement noise, and numerical

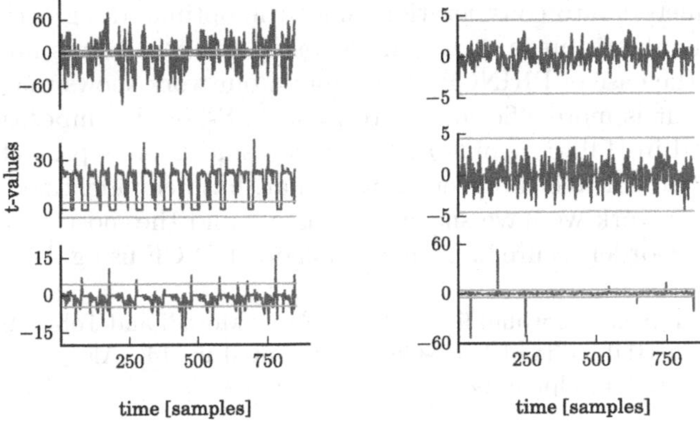

Fig. 7. Leakage detection test results on second-order PRINCE. PRNG off (left) and PRNG on (right). First, second and third-order (top - middle - down) t-test results.

noise of the samples is minimized by having a precision of 32-bit floating point representation compared to 8-bit obtained from the FPGA setup.

The second-order implementation t-test results are shown in Fig. 7. We notice that with PRNG off, leakage occurs in all orders with only two thousand traces. With PRNG on, the design is leakage free in first and second-order, while several points leak in the third order. More precisely, third order leakage occurs during writing of the S-Box output to the register every other cycles.

5 Conclusion and Outlook

In this paper we provided an algorithm which produces a $d + 1$ TI sharing with the optimal (minimum) number of output shares for any n-input Boolean function of degree $t = n - 1$ and for any security order d. We highlight that this contribution is of general interest since the method of minimizing the number of output shares can be applied to any cryptographic design.

Second, we reported, evaluated and compared hardware figures for our proposed TI-protected round-based version of PRINCE cipher, with the previous state of the art. The comparison showed that our designs have more than 30 % lower latency compared to the architecture presented in [14] while the energy consumption is lower by about 10 %. It should, however, be noted that the design presented in [14] still has the highest power efficiency reported in the literature.

We would like to summarize that the generic algorithm for achieving minimal number of output shares is necessary, but not sufficient condition when designing for low-latency and low-energy applications. Applying TI on higher degree functions reduces the total clock count, in effect reducing latency and energy consumed during one operation. However, due to increased circuit complexity it increases the area and the critical path of the design, which have negative impact on energy consumption and latency, respectively. A circuit designer should take all these parameters into consideration, since the optimal design choice heavily depends on the algorithm in question, alongside the constraints imposed upon the design. In the case of PRINCE block cipher, our work shows that for achieving low-latency it is more efficient not to perform S-box decomposition.

As discussed in [14], designing a low-latency side-channel protection in general, and for PRINCE block cipher in particular, has been identified as an open problem. In this work we have shown the fastest and the most energy efficient round based first-order secure implementation of PRINCE using $d+1$ TI sharing.

Acknowledgements. We would like to thank Amir Moradi and Tobias Schneider for providing us with HDL code of PRINCE TI presented in [14]. Also we would like to thank the reviewers for helping us to improve the paper.

References

1. Banik, S., et al.: Midori: a block cipher for low energy. In: Iwata, T., Cheon, J.H. (eds.) ASIACRYPT 2015. LNCS, vol. 9453, pp. 411–436. Springer, Heidelberg (2015). https://doi.org/10.1007/978-3-662-48800-3_17
2. Bertoni, G., Daemen, J., Peeters, M., Assche, G.V.: The Keccak reference, January 2011. http://keccak.noekeon.org/
3. Bilgin, B., Gierlichs, B., Nikova, S., Nikov, V., Rijmen, V.: Higher-order threshold implementations. In: Sarkar, P., Iwata, T. (eds.) ASIACRYPT 2014. LNCS, vol. 8874, pp. 326–343. Springer, Heidelberg (2014). https://doi.org/10.1007/978-3-662-45608-8_18
4. Bilgin, B., Nikova, S., Nikov, V., Rijmen, V., Stütz, G.: Threshold implementations of all 3 × 3 and 4 × 4 S-boxes. In: Prouff, E., Schaumont, P. (eds.) CHES 2012. LNCS, vol. 7428, pp. 76–91. Springer, Heidelberg (2012). https://doi.org/10.1007/978-3-642-33027-8_5
5. Bogdanov, A., et al.: PRESENT: an ultra-lightweight block cipher. In: Paillier, P., Verbauwhede, I. (eds.) CHES 2007. LNCS, vol. 4727, pp. 450–466. Springer, Heidelberg (2007). https://doi.org/10.1007/978-3-540-74735-2_31
6. Borghoff, J., et al.: PRINCE – a low-latency block cipher for pervasive computing applications. In: Wang, X., Sako, K. (eds.) ASIACRYPT 2012. LNCS, vol. 7658, pp. 208–225. Springer, Heidelberg (2012). https://doi.org/10.1007/978-3-642-34961-4_14
7. Cooper, J., DeMulder, E., Goodwill, G., Jaffe, J., Kenworthy, G., Rohatgi, P.: Test Vector Leakage Assessment (TVLA) methodology in practice. In: International Cryptographic Module Conference (2013)
8. Groß, H., Iusupov, R., Bloem, R.: Generic low-latency masking in hardware. IACR Trans. Cryptogr. Hardw. Embed. Syst.-TCHES **2**, 1–21 (2018)
9. Gross, H., Mangard, S.: Reconciling $d + 1$ masking in hardware and software. In: Fischer, W., Homma, N. (eds.) CHES 2017. LNCS, vol. 10529, pp. 115–136. Springer, Cham (2017). https://doi.org/10.1007/978-3-319-66787-4_6
10. Groß, H., Mangard, S., Korak, T.: Domain-oriented masking: compact masked hardware implementations with arbitrary protection order. In: Proceedings of the ACM Workshop on Theory of Implementation Security, TIS@CCS 2016, Vienna, Austria, p. 3, October 2016

11. Ishai, Y., Sahai, A., Wagner, D.: Private circuits: securing hardware against probing attacks. In: Boneh, D. (ed.) CRYPTO 2003. LNCS, vol. 2729, pp. 463–481. Springer, Heidelberg (2003). https://doi.org/10.1007/978-3-540-45146-4_27
12. Knežević, M., Nikov, V., Rombouts, P.: Low-latency encryption – is "Lightweight = Light + Wait"? In: Prouff, E., Schaumont, P. (eds.) CHES 2012. LNCS, vol. 7428, pp. 426–446. Springer, Heidelberg (2012). https://doi.org/10.1007/978-3-642-33027-8_25
13. Moos, T., Moradi, A., Schneider, T., Standaert, F.X.: Glitch-resistant masking revisited - or why proofs in the robust probing model are needed. IACR Trans. Cryptogr. Hardw. Embed. Syst.-TCHES **2**, 256–292 (2019)
14. Moradi, A., Schneider, T.: Side-channel analysis protection and low-latency in action. In: Cheon, J.H., Takagi, T. (eds.) ASIACRYPT 2016. LNCS, vol. 10031, pp. 517–547. Springer, Heidelberg (2016). https://doi.org/10.1007/978-3-662-53887-6_19
15. Nikova, S., Rechberger, C., Rijmen, V.: Threshold Implementations against side-channel attacks and glitches. In: Ning, P., Qing, S., Li, N. (eds.) ICICS 2006. LNCS, vol. 4307, pp. 529–545. Springer, Heidelberg (2006). https://doi.org/10.1007/11935308_38
16. Poschmann, A., Moradi, A., Khoo, K., Lim, C.W., Wang, H., Ling, S.: Side-channel resistant crypto for less than 2,300 GE. J. Cryptol. **24**(2), 322–345 (2011). https://doi.org/10.1007/s00145-010-9086-6
17. Reparaz, O., Bilgin, B., Nikova, S., Gierlichs, B., Verbauwhede, I.: Consolidating masking schemes. In: Gennaro, R., Robshaw, M. (eds.) CRYPTO 2015. LNCS, vol. 9215, pp. 764–783. Springer, Heidelberg (2015). https://doi.org/10.1007/978-3-662-47989-6_37
18. Reparaz, O., Gierlichs, B., Verbauwhede, I.: Fast leakage assessment. In: Fischer, W., Homma, N. (eds.) CHES 2017. LNCS, vol. 10529, pp. 387–399. Springer, Cham (2017). https://doi.org/10.1007/978-3-319-66787-4_19
19. Ueno, R., Homma, N., Aoki, T.: A systematic design of tamper-resistant Galois-field arithmetic circuits based on threshold implementation with (d + 1) input shares. In: 2017 IEEE 47th International Symposium on Multiple-Valued Logic (ISMVL), pp. 136–141 (2017)
20. Ueno, R., Homma, N., Aoki, T.: Toward more efficient DPA-resistant AES hardware architecture based on threshold implementation. In: Guilley, S. (ed.) COSADE 2017. LNCS, vol. 10348, pp. 50–64. Springer, Cham (2017). https://doi.org/10.1007/978-3-319-64647-3_4

Breaking the Lightweight Secure PUF: Understanding the Relation of Input Transformations and Machine Learning Resistance

Nils Wisiol[1,3](✉), Georg T. Becker[2], Marian Margraf[3], Tudor A. A. Soroceanu[3], Johannes Tobisch[4], and Benjamin Zengin[5]

[1] Chair for Security in Telecommunications of Technische Universität Berlin, Berlin, Germany
nils.wisiol@tu-berlin.de
[2] Digital Society Institute at the ESMT Berlin, Berlin, Germany
georg.becker@esmt.org
[3] Institute of Computer Science of Freie Universität Berlin, Berlin, Germany
{nils.wisiol,marian.margraf,tudor.soroceanu}@fu-berlin.de
[4] Horst Görtz Institute for IT-Security at Ruhr-Universität Bochum, Bochum, Germany
johannes.tobisch@ruhr-uni-bochum.de
[5] Fraunhofer Institute for Applied and Integrated Security at Berlin, Berlin, Germany
benjamin.zengin@aisec.fraunhofer.de

Abstract. Physical Unclonable Functions (PUFs) and, in particular, strong PUFs such as the XOR Arbiter PUF have gained much research interest as an authentication mechanism for embedded systems. One of the biggest problems of strong PUFs is their vulnerability to so called machine learning attacks. In this paper, we take a closer look at one aspect of machine learning attacks that has not yet gained the needed attention: the generation of the sub-challenges in XOR Arbiter PUFs fed to the individual Arbiter PUFs. Specifically, we look at one of the most popular ways to generate sub-challenges based on a combination of permutations and XORs as it has been described for the "Lightweight Secure PUF". Previous research suggested that using such a sub-challenge generation increases the machine learning resistance significantly.

Our contribution in the field of sub-challenge generation is threefold: First, drastically improving attack results by Rührmair *et al.*, we describe a novel attack that can break the Lightweight Secure PUF in time roughly equivalent to an XOR Arbiter PUF without transformation of the challenge input. Second, we give a mathematical model that gives insight into the weakness of the Lightweight Secure PUF and provides a way to study generation of sub-challenges in general. Third, we propose a new, efficient, and cost-effective way for sub-challenge generation that mitigates the attack strategy we used and outperforms the Lightweight Secure PUF in both machine learning resistance and resource overhead.

Georg T. Becker is being supported by Rheinmetall.

S. Belaïd and T. Güneysu (Eds.): CARDIS 2019, LNCS 11833, pp. 40–54, 2020.
https://doi.org/10.1007/978-3-030-42068-0_3

1 Introduction

Physical Unclonable Functions (PUFs) have gained much research attention since their invention in 2002. PUFs use the intrinsic process variations of each chip to build an unclonable function that is device specific. PUFs with an exponential challenge space, often denoted as *Strong PUFs*, are particularly well suited for lightweight authentication scenarios. The most prominent PUF with an exponential challenge space is the XOR Arbiter PUF [5,16]. Using strong PUFs in a challenge-and-response protocol remains challenging due to machine learning attacks [10]. In these attacks, challenge-and-response pairs are collected and machine learning algorithms are used to approximate the PUF using a software model. While these attacks are very efficient small XOR Arbiter PUFs, the machine learning complexity increases exponentially with the number of XORs [10,11,18]. However, Becker [1] showed how reliability information can be used for a machine learning attack with only a linear increase complexity.

To determine the number of allowed authentications before a design is known to be insecure, it is crucial to fully understand the machine learning resistance of the underlying PUF construction. In this paper, we will take a closer look at an aspect that has not yet gained the required attention: the input transformation generating the sub-challenges. Rührmair *et al.* [10] have shown that attacking an XOR Arbiter PUF in which each arbiter chain has the same challenge is easier than attacking one in which each arbiter chain gets a different challenge. This was later verified by other researchers [18]. The results of [10] are based on the input transformation by Majzoobi *et al.* [7] for their Lightweight PUF of 2008, which has gained some research attention [8,9,23]. Yet, in how far such transformations are actually optimal to counter current state-of-the-art machine learning attacks has not been studied.

1.1 Main Contribution

In this paper we perform a thorough analysis of the impact of input transformations on state-of-the-art machine learning attacks. Our analysis shows that one has to carefully choose the input transformation to achieve the desired machine learning resistance. In particular, on first sight the often cited Lightweight input transformation from Majzoobi *et al.* [7] seems to be close to the case of random sub-challenges. (In Sect. 3.1, we argue random sub-challenges are hardest to learn.) However, we show that by using this input transformation the logistic regression (LR) learner has a significant probability to converge to a local minimum, providing only a partially accurate model of the XOR Arbiter PUF. We show in a novel attack how these local minima can be exploited to efficiently model PUFs based on the Lightweight input transformation. We furthermore discuss the reasons for these local minima and subsequently present an easy-to-implement input transformation that achieves a modeling resistance comparable to the optimal solution based on random sub-challenges.

2 Background

2.1 Machine Learning Attacks on PUFs

It was already shown in 2004 by Lim [6] that Arbiter PUFs can be modeled using the linear delay model. Subsequently, the XOR Arbiter PUF and Lightweight Secure Arbiter PUF were proposed to increase the machine learning resistance by increasing the non-linearity of the PUF model. In 2010, Rührmair *et al.* [10] provided an extensive study of the machine learning resistance of the XOR Arbiter PUFs. On the one hand, their result showed that these constructions can be modeled quite efficiently for reasonably sized PUFs. On the other hand, they showed that the modeling complexity grows exponentially with the number of XORs. Their results also indicated that Lightweight Secure PUFs require more time and information to be modeled, compared to XOR Arbiter PUFs of the same size.

Side-channel attacks on XOR Arbiter PUFs and variants have also been extensively studied, ranging from power consumption [2,12] to reliability [4] and optical emissions [17]. It is worth noting that the reliability side-channel attack does not require the attacker to have physical access to the device or tamper with it. At the same time, it has been shown to scale linearly in the number of XORs of the given XOR Arbiter PUF [1]. To counter reliability-based machine learning attacks, protocols can be used in which part of the challenge is generated by the PUF device so that the attacker cannot collect responses for the same challenge multiple times to determine the reliability [22], or by removing unreliability of responses [20].

There have also been proposals of novel strong PUFs designs to avoid the modeling by the linear delay model, such as the Bistable Ring PUF [3] which can be implemented on FPGAs. However, it is still vulnerable to machine learning attacks [14].

2.2 Notation

Throughout this paper, we will use natural numbers n, k. Unless specified otherwise, lowercase Latin variables represent vectors, with their elements referenced by a subscript index; lowercase Greek letters and f will represent functions. Note that we also use subscript indices to refer to elements of vectors that are function values, e.g. $\sigma(c)_i$ for the i-th entry of $\sigma(c) \in V^n$ for a function σ and vector space V^n. For two vectors $v, w \in V^n$, we define $\langle v, w \rangle = \sum_{i=1}^n v_i w_i$ to be the inner product of v and w. Lists of vectors $v^{(i)}$ will often be denoted as $(v^{(1)}, ..., v^{(k)})$, i.e., vectors of that list are referred to by the superscript index. We denote bits as $-1, 1$ rather than $0, 1$, where -1 is True. Note that the XOR operation is hence represented by the product of two bits. We define $\operatorname{sgn} x$ to be the sign of any real number x, and define $\operatorname{sgn}(0) = 1$ arbitrarily. Unless otherwise specified, probabilities are taken uniformly random for independent bits.

2.3 Modeling XOR Arbiter PUFs

Figure 1a depicts a 2-XOR Arbiter PUF that consists of two individual Arbiter PUFs with their response XORed. Each Arbiter PUF consists of n delay stages consisting of 2-input multiplexers through which two signals are propagated. The multiplexers interchange the two signals depending on the applied challenge and an arbiter at the end measures if a signal arrives first at the top or bottom line to determine the response bit. The delays of the individual Arbiter PUFs are additive, i.e., the final delay difference between the two signals is the sum of the delay difference of the individual stages. A challenge bit $c_i = -1$ swaps the two signals and can be modeled by multiplying the delay difference $\delta(i)$ at stage i with minus one. This way a recursive formula can be constructed to model the delay difference $\delta(i)$ at the i-th stage, $\delta(i) = \delta(i-1, c) \cdot c_i + s_i(c_i)$ where $s_i(c_i)$ is the delay difference introduced at stage i for challenge c_i. The sign of the final delay difference $\delta(n)$ at stage n then defines the response bit. The above recursive formula can be simplified into a linear threshold function [6]. We follow the same approach as other researchers (e.g., [10]) and model an n-bit k-XOR Arbiter PUFs based on a product of *linear threshold functions (LTF)* given by

$$f(c) = \prod_{l=1}^{k} \operatorname{sgn} \left\langle w^{(l)}, x^{(l)} \right\rangle = \operatorname{sgn} \prod_{l=1}^{k} \left\langle w^{(l)}, x^{(l)} \right\rangle, \tag{1}$$

where the *weight vectors* $w^{(1)}, ..., w^{(k)} \in \mathbb{R}^{n+1}$ model the physical properties of the k arbiter chains (derived from s), and $x^{(1)}, ..., x^{(k)} \in \{-1, 1\}^{n+1}$ are the *feature vectors* for the given master-challenge $c \in \{-1, 1\}^n$. The feature vectors $x^{(l)}$ can be computed from the k *sub-challenges* $c^{(l)}$ given to the individual arbiter chains using the function $\mathrm{ATT} : \{-1, 1\}^n \to \{-1, 1\}^{n+1}$, $x^{(l)} = \mathrm{ATT}(c^{(l)})$

$$x_i^{(l)} = \prod_{j=i}^{n} c_j^{(l)} \text{ for } 1 \leq i \leq n \tag{2}$$

and $x_{n+1}^{(l)} = 1$. In analogy to LTF, we call ATT the *arbiter threshold transform.*

3 Input Transformations: Classic vs. Random

When XOR Arbiter PUFs were proposed by Suh and Devadas [16], the first step was to provide all arbiter chains with the same challenge (here called *classic* design). Subsequently, Majzoobi et al. [7] proposed to modify the challenge before feeding it into the individual arbiter chains, to let the PUF fulfill the strict avalanche criterion. Although initially designed to harden XOR Arbiter PUFs against chosen-challenge attacks, it became clear that the design twist also has an impact on the passive (that is, non-adaptive) regression attack introduced by Sölter [15] and Rührmair et al. [10]. In this work, we generalize the idea of transforming challenges for each arbiter chain and call it *input transformation.* To shed some light on how machine learning hardness can be increased using

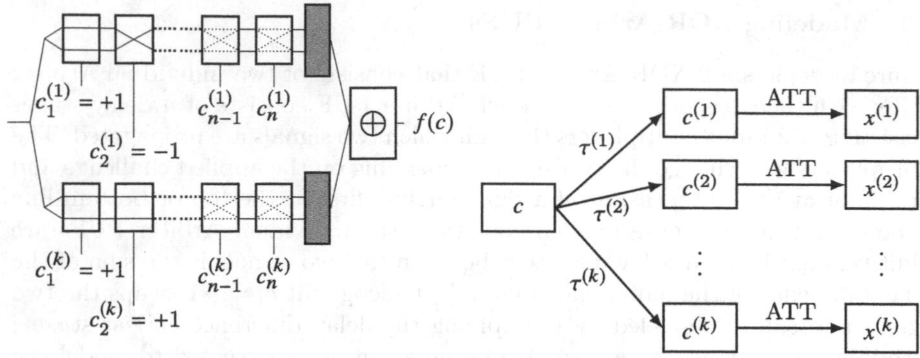

Fig. 1. (a) Schematic representation of an XOR Arbiter PUF with $k = 2$. After the challenge is set up, a rising edge is applied on the left-hand side, with the arbiters at the end of each chain (gray rectangles) measuring if the top line or bottom line shows the signal first, the result is xored. Duing this process, the $n{\cdot}k$ challenge bits $c^{(l)} \in \{-1, 1\}^n$, $1 \leq l \leq k$ decide at each stage (white rectangles), if the signal paths are crossed or not. The parity of result bits output as $f(c)$. (b) Generation of sub-challenges $c^{(l)} \in \{-1, 1\}^n$ and feature-vectors $x^{(l)} \in \{-1, 1\}^{n+1}$ from the master-challenge $c \in \{-1, 1\}^n$ using functions $\tau^{(l)} : \{-1, 1\}^n \to \{-1, 1\}^n$ and $\mathrm{ATT} : \{-1, 1\}^n \to \{-1, 1\}^{n+1}$. Note that we abbreviate $\mathrm{ATT}(\tau^{(l)}(c)) = \sigma^{(l)}(c)$ for all master-challenges c, where $\sigma : \{-1, 1\}^n \to \{-1, 1\}^{n+1}$.

an input transformation, we studied the impact of input transformations on the success rate of logistic regression attacks.[1]

We use the linear model introduced in the background section for modeling the XOR Arbiter PUFs and assume that the sub-challenges $c^{(l)}$ can be computed from a single master-challenge $c \in \{-1, 1\}^n$. We call a list of functions $(\tau^{(1)}, ..., \tau^{(k)})$ with $\tau^{(l)} : \{-1, 1\}^n \to \{-1, 1\}^n$ that transform the master-challenge c into sub-challenges $\tau^{(l)}(c) = c^{(l)}$ the *sub-challenge generators.*

We take the classic design as an example for our notation. As all arbiter chains are fed the master-challenge, we have $\tau^{(1)} = \cdots = \tau^{(k)} = \mathrm{id}$. Hence, we can compute any feature vectors $x^{(l)}$ directly from the master-challenge given,

$$x^{(l)} = \mathrm{ATT}(\tau^{(l)}(c)) = \mathrm{ATT}(c) = (c_1 c_2 \cdots c_n, c_2 \cdots c_n, ..., c_n, 1).$$

It is crucial to distinguish sub-challenges $c^{(i)}$ from feature vectors $x^{(i)}$. Sub-challenges represent the bits that are physically fed into the arbiter chains, whereas features vectors are used to enable a modeling of arbiter chains as linear threshold function (LTF) as given in (1).

For our analysis, the feature vector structure for a given input transformation is crucial. We hence abbreviate the value $\mathrm{ATT}(\tau^{(l)}(c))$ to $\sigma^{(l)}(c)$ and formally define *input transformation* to be the list of functions $(\sigma^{(1)}, ..., \sigma^{(k)})$ that

[1] Attack and analysis implementation can be found at https://github.com/nils-wisiol/pypuf/.

transforms the master-challenge into the feature vectors. Figure 1b summarizes our notation.

Applying our notation to the model given in (1), the model for an XOR Arbiter PUF with input transformation $(\sigma^{(1)}, ..., \sigma^{(k)})$ is given by

$$f(c) = \operatorname{sgn} \prod_{l=1}^{k} \left\langle w^{(l)}, \sigma^{(l)}(c) \right\rangle \tag{3}$$

where $\sigma^{(1)} = \cdots = \sigma^{(k)}$. We have for all master-challenges c that $\mathrm{ATT}(\tau^{(i)}(c)) = x^{(i)} = \sigma^{(i)}(c)$.

3.1 Pseudorandom Input Transformation

We demonstrate the influence of input transformations on the learning hardness of logistic regression attacks in Fig. 2. To contrast the classic design, where all arbiter chains receive the same challenge, we implemented a simulation of XOR Arbiter PUFs with pseudorandom sub-challenge generators, where all arbiter chains receive an individual pseudorandom challenge chosen by seeding the generator with the master-challenge and the index of the sub-challenge. For our implementation, we used the standard Python pseudorandom generator based on the Mersenne Twister. Assuming security of the pseudorandom generator, we can guarantee that the sub-challenges are chosen indistinguishable from truely random sub-challenges and feature vectors (for all polynomially time-bounded observers, i.e. including the machine learning attacker).

By the absence of any observable correlation, the pseudorandom input transformation is, while not being a reasonable real-world design choice, an extremal

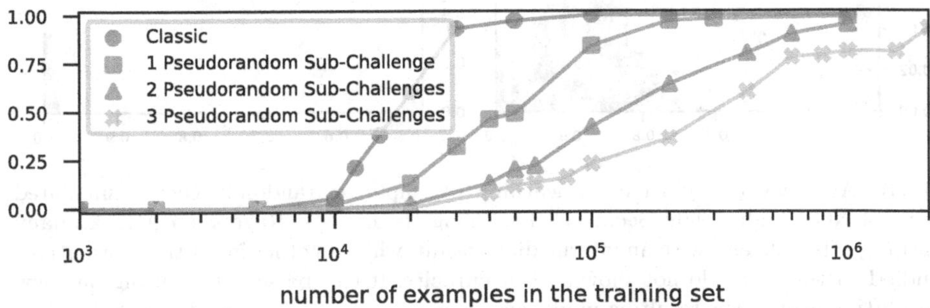

Fig. 2. Success rate of logistic regression attacks on simulated XOR Arbiter PUFs with 64-bit arbiter chains and four arbiter chains each, based on at least 250 samples per data point shown. Accuracies better than 70% are considered success, but we only observe accuracies around 50% and 99%. Four different designs are shown: of the four arbiter chains in each instance, an input transform is used that transforms zero, one, two, and three challenges pseudorandomly, keeping the remaining challenges unmodified.

example among all input transformations. As elaborated in Sect. 4, the absence of correlation results in a decrease of the number of minima in the logistic regression attack.

The empirical results match this rationale: Fig. 2 shows that, compared to the classic design, the required size of the training set to achieve a high success rate increases substantially. Figure 2 also shows designs in which only a subset of arbiter chains receive pseudorandom challenges, whereas the others receive the same unmodified challenge. For those designs, the required size of the training set is, as could be expected, in between the pure classic and the pure pseudorandom case.

3.2 Local Minima

Logistic regression uses gradient descent over a function f defined by the provided training set to conduct the modeling attack. The algorithm's ability to find a "good" minimum depends, among other parameters, on the algorithm's random initialization. Empirical results obtained by repeatedly attacking the same XOR Arbiter PUF show that the probability to guess successful initializations significantly changes with the input transformation in use (Fig. 4).

Whenever an input transformation of an XOR Arbiter PUF sends the same challenge to several arbiter chains, this will be reflected in function f as symmetry. Using the classic input transformation, the attacker has at least $k!$ equally good minima[2] to choose from. This idea of f's symmetry can be generalized to the case where properties of the input transformation allow permutations of the original weights to approximate the XOR Arbiter PUF with mediocre accuracy,

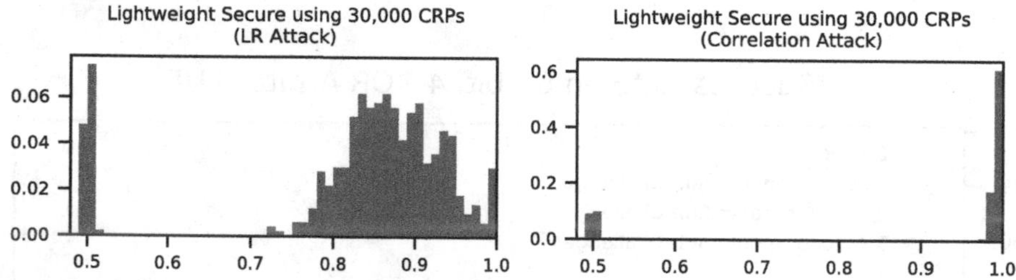

Fig. 3. Accuracy distribution for learning attempts on randomly chosen simulated 64-bit 4-XOR Lightweight Secure PUFs. Using the Logistic Regression Attack, many learning attempts end with an intermediate result, while all other input transformations studied in this work do not show such accuracies. It can be seen that using our new correlation attack, the resulting model accuracy is increased significantly over the plain LR attack.

[2] Strictly speaking, all models will have an infinite amount of local minima, as all weights in the model can be modified by a small value or scaled by a positive scalar without affecting the model's behavior. To fix above argument we can argue that additional symmetry causes the gradient descent to remain at a local minima with higher probability.

as we will show in Sect. 4.2. The approximating permutations can be observed as local minima in the logistic regression attack. On the contrary, using pseudorandom transformations, we can reduce the symmetries of f down to the minimum, hence increasing machine learning hardness and avoiding any intermediate solutions.

4 Input Transformations: Lightweight Secure

The Lightweight Secure PUF design was introduced by Majzoobi et al. [7] in 2008 before Rührmair et al. [10] published their machine-learning attacks. The design proposes an input transformation presented in two steps.

First, for the generation of the l-th sub-challenge, the master-challenge is rotated by l bits, here denoted by $d^{(l)}$. Second, the sub-challenge $c^{(l)}$ will mostly be computed by xoring bits pairwise, such that it consists of three parts with length $n/2$, 1, and $n/2-1$, respectively.

More specifically, we have

$$\begin{aligned} \left(c_1^{(l)}, \ldots, c_{n/2}^{(l)}\right) &= \left(d_1^{(l)} d_2^{(l)},\ d_3^{(l)} d_4^{(l)},\ \ldots,\ d_{n-1}^{(l)} d_n^{(l)}\right), \\ \left(c_{n/2+1}^{(l)}\right) &= \left(d_1^{(l)}\right), \\ \left(c_{n/2+2}^{(l)}, \ldots, c_n^{(l)}\right) &= \left(d_2^{(l)} d_3^{(l)},\ d_4^{(l)} d_5^{(l)},\ \ldots,\ d_{n-2}^{(l)} d_{n-1}^{(l)}\right). \end{aligned} \quad (4)$$

In this section, we will refer to the sub-challenges with $\tau^{(1)}(c), \ldots, \tau^{(k)}(c)$ and to the feature vectors they induce with $\sigma^{(1)}(c), \ldots, \sigma^{(k)}(c)$.

The transformation is chosen such that the Strict Avalanche Criterion is (almost) satisfied [7], i.e., a single bit flip in the master challenge will result in bit flips in about 50% of the elements of each *feature* vector for each arbiter chain. If 50% of the *feature* vector bits flip, then the PUF output also flips with probability 50%.

In this work, we will not consider weaker versions of the Lightweight Secure PUF with multiple output bits.

4.1 Feature Vector Correlation

In a typical machine learning attack on an XOR Arbiter PUF, we expect that a call of the LR algorithm either yields a near optimal model that has a predictive accuracy of around 99% or yields a model that performs poorly in prediction, barely exceeding an accuracy of 50%, i.e., random guessing. Interestingly, this is not the case for the Lightweight PUF, as can be observed in Fig. 3. We found that the machine learning algorithm yielded models that performed clearly better than random guessing but did not achieve the desired accuracy of around 99%.

In empirical results, we found that weight vectors of the intermediate solutions consisted mostly of a permutation of the weight values of the original PUF model. In fact, by permuting the individual weight vectors of the arbiter chains and rotating them for certain but distinct amounts, a close approximation of the original weight vectors could be constructed. Furthermore, we learned, that if weight vector $w^{(a)}$ was at position b it was rotated by π, then if $w^{(b)}$ was at position a it was rotated by π^{-1}.

To give a theoretical basis to our attack, we formalize this observation by examining the impact of swapping and rotating two different weight vectors. Let $w^{(1)}, ..., w^{(k)}$ be the weight vectors of a Lightweight Secure XOR Arbiter PUF. Our observations suggest that this PUF can be approximated when weight vectors are swapped and shifted in a characteristic way. We call the weight vectors to be swapped w and v and the corresponding input transformation functions λ and μ. Note that this argument uses feature vectors, not sub-challenges. Consider the relevant part of the product in the XOR Arbiter PUF model (cf. (3) and (4)):

$$\langle w, \lambda(c)\rangle \cdot \langle v, \mu(c)\rangle = \sum_{i,j} w_i \cdot v_j \cdot \lambda(c)_i \cdot \mu(c)_j$$

In the following, we compare this to the model where the weight vectors v and w are swapped and rotated by π and π^{-1}, respectively. That is, we replace w by $\pi^{-1}(v)$ and replace v by $\pi(w)$:

$$\begin{aligned}\langle \pi^{-1}(v), \lambda(c)\rangle \cdot \langle \pi(w), \mu(c)\rangle &= \sum_{i,j} \pi(w)_i \cdot \pi^{-1}(v)_j \cdot \mu(c)_i \cdot \lambda(c)_j \\ &= \sum_{i,j} w_i \cdot v_j \cdot \pi^{-1}(\mu(c))_i \cdot \pi(\lambda(c))_j \quad \text{(re-numbering i,j)}\end{aligned}$$

To prove that the latter is an approximation of the original model, we studied the relationship of $\pi^{-1}(\mu(c))_i \cdot \pi(\lambda(c))_j$ and $\lambda(c)_i \cdot \mu(c)_j$ and found that for most pairs i, j, we have equality with significant probability for a uniformly random master-challenge c. The higher this probability, the better is the approximation of the original model by the swapped and rotated version.

The correlation of the Lightweight Secure input transformation $\sigma^{(1)}, ..., \sigma^{(6)}$ can be measured by

$$\frac{1}{(n+1)^2} \sum_{i=1}^{n+1} \sum_{j=1}^{n+1} \Pr_c \left[\lambda(c)_i \cdot \mu(c)_j = \pi^{-1}(\mu(c))_i \cdot \pi(\lambda(c))_j\right], \tag{5}$$

where c is chosen uniformly at random. For each pair, there is exactly one rotation π which produces a significant correlation, cf Table 1.

For example, consider the 64-bit 4-XOR Lightweight Secure PUF, where we write $(\sigma^{(1)}, \sigma^{(2)}, \sigma^{(3)}, \sigma^{(4)})$ for the input transformation and denote $\sigma^{(1)}$ as λ and $\sigma^{(2)}$ as μ. If we rotate the first feature vector $\lambda(c)$ by 32, say $\pi(\lambda(c))$, and the second feature vector $\mu(c)$ by the inverse of 33 positions to the right, say $\pi^{-1}(\mu(c))$, then we have high correlation as defined by (5).

As we can see, the correlation of the feature vectors leads to the fact that an approximation of the original model can be constructed by swapping two weight vectors and rotating them accordingly. Using this concept iteratively, any permutation of the weight vectors can be achieved.

Our empirical results in Fig. 3 suggest that those partial solutions also generate local minima to which the regression algorithm converges. The combination of the information on the local minimum along with the correlation as outlined above can be used to stage an attack on the input transformation by Majzoobi et al. This must be considered a key weakness of the Lightweight Secure transformation, as our empirical attack results show.

The cause for this symmetry lies in the definition of the input transformation and in the fact that results are xored. There is a clear pattern and essentially every pair of PUFs can be exchanged by a rotated version, although the correlation decreases the further the PUF positions are apart from each other.

Table 1. Overview of correlations for a 64-bit 6-XOR Lightweight Secure Arbiter PUF. As an example, the feature vectors of the first and second arbiter chain show a correlation of 0.98 as defined in (5) with a rotation by 32 and 33 positions, respectively. Hence, the corresponding weight vectors can be swapped if they are rotated accordingly without significant change in the model accuracy.

	1	2	3	4	5	6
1	-/-	32/0.98	64/0.97	31/0.95	63/0.94	30/0.92
2	33/0.98	-/-	32/0.98	64/0.97	31/0.95	63/0.94
3	1/0.97	33/0.98	-/-	32/0.99	64/0.97	31/0.95
4	34/0.95	1/0.97	33/0.99	-/-	32/0.98	64/0.97
5	2/0.94	34/0.95	1/0.97	33/0.98	-/-	32/0.98
6	35/0.92	2/0.94	34/0.95	1/0.97	33/0.98	-/-

4.2 Improved Attack

As seen in the previous section, the LR machine learning attack on the Lightweight Secure PUF often leads to local minima that model the PUF behavior only with a limited accuracy. In this section, we show how a local minimum can be used to find a high-accuracy model.

If the logistic regression attack has found a model with an intermediate accuracy in the range of 65%–98%, we assume that the initialization values for the attack lead to a swapped and rotated version of the high-accuracy version of the weights. Instead of restarting the machine learning algorithm with new initializations until we find a high-accuracy solution and hence the correct ordering, the *correlation attack* tries to generate the correct ordering of the weights. To that end, we first generate the rotated weights for each possible permutation of the weight vectors in a brute-force manner and check their accuracy on a validation set. As a second step, the $2k$ most accurate rotated weights are used to restart the logistic regression attack and refine the weights.

Table 2. Expected time until the first success for attacks on classic XOR Arbiter PUF, Lightweight Secure XOR Arbiter PUF, and Permutation-Based XOR Arbiter PUF. An accuracy of at least 98% is considered success, all entries are based on 1000 samples. Runs with no success are marked with an asterisk (*). We acknowledge the HPC service of Freie Universität Berlin. Source code available at https://github.com/nils-wisiol/pypuf.

n	k	# CRPs	LR on classic	LR on LW secure	Correlation attack on LW secure	LR on permutation-based
64	4	12,000	0m 33s	10m 11s	0m 58s	24m 50s
64	4	30,000	0m 31s	3m 57s	0m 44s	4m 45s
64	5	300,000	7m 03s	3h 03m	11m 07s	13h 59m
64	6	1,000,000	42m 30s	8 days	1h 42m	(96h 00m)*
64	7	2,000,000	75h 07m	(20 days)*	8 days	(16 days)*
128	4	1,000,000	20m 31s	2h 53m	51m 23s	58m 38s
128	5	2,000,000	1h 35m	35h 20m	3h 17m	(16 days)*

Although the first step has run time $O(k! \cdot nk \cdot V)$ with validation set size V, this procedure can outperform the simple restarting of the LR attack (Table 2) for practical values of k, as $10! = 3\,628\,800$. Furthermore, the restarted logistic regression algorithm can use a much lower bound on the maximum number of iterations, discarding low-accuracy solutions rapidly. To achieve fast run times, we used a small validation set for the $k!$ accuracy computations. We empirically found that rotations with high initial accuracy have a higher chance to yield a high-accuracy solution, hence the ordering by initial accuracy helps speed up the attack.

More specifically, we examined the ranking of the permutation that resulted in the highest accuracy solution for 1000 instances of 64-bit 6 XOR Lightweight Secure PUFs. In most cases, the best permutation was within the first 10 candidates.

In Table 2 we have compared the expected time until first result with accuracy better than 98%, computed as the quotient of mean attack time and success probability, for attacking the classic XOR Arbiter PUF and the classic and improved attack on the Lightweight Secure Arbiter PUF. It can be seen that the Lightweight Secure PUF can be learned with much higher accuracy in less time than previously believed, with the security in some instances reduced to what the classic XOR Arbiter PUF provides. In contrast, the XOR Arbiter PUF with the permutation-based input transformation defined in Sect. 5 is considerably harder to attack and does not posses the attack surface we used in the correlation-based attack, i.e. does not show intermediate results when attacked with the Logistic Regression attack.

5 Solution

The previous sections show that input transformations have an impact on the machine learning resistance. When using the same challenges for all arbiter chains as done in the classic XOR Arbiter PUF, there are multiple equivalent solutions as the order of the weight vectors $(w^{(1)}, ..., w^{(k)})$ does not matter. Using pseudorandom sub-challenges ensures that only one order is valid and hence reduces the number of global minima in the gradient descent of the LR attack. However, it should be noted that this comes with quite some overhead in terms of area as well as power/energy since at least $k \cdot n$ registers are needed to store the pseudo random bits together with some logic to generate them. For example, Yu *et al.* [22] use a 256 bit LFSR to feed the four arbiter chains in the used 64-Stages 4-XOR Arbiter PUF. The area overhead of their 4-XOR Arbiter PUF is given by Yu *et al.*as 1024 Gate Equivalents (GE). The size of the LFSR is not provided in [22], but assuming 4.5 GE for a flip-flop, the size of a 256 stage LFSR is comparable to that of the PUF circuitry[3]. Implementing a cryptographically secure pseudorandom generator will consume even more resources.

In the Lockdown Protocol [22] the LSFR is an essential part of the authentication protocol and hence needed anyways. But for other designs, especially if larger PUF instances are used with 128 stages, a more efficient input transformation is advised as the overhead is not negligible. However, our analysis of the Lightweight Secure PUF shows that this input transformation suffers a significant weakness and must be considered insecure. The fact that feature vectors correlate in a certain way simplifies the machine learning attack to the point where no relevant advantage over the classic XOR Arbiter PUF is achieved.

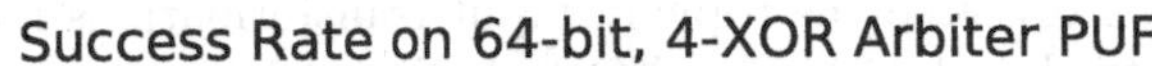

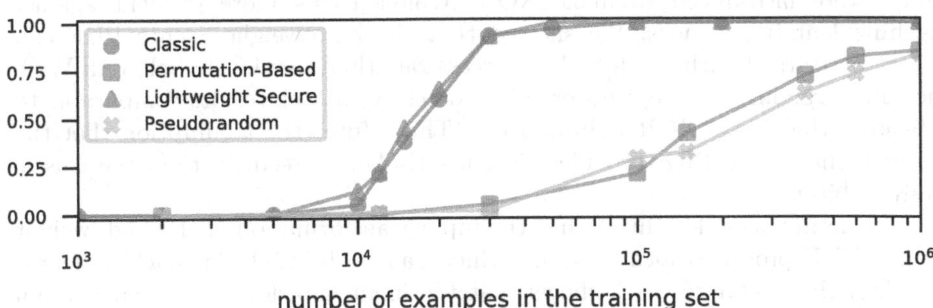

Fig. 4. Success rate of logistic regression attacks on simulated XOR Arbiter PUFs with 64-bit arbiter chains and four arbiter chains each; accuracies above 70% are considered as a success.

---

[3] Although the Gate Equivalents for a PUF circuit can be a bit misleading as PUFs need special isolated routing compared to conventional digital circuits such as LFSRs.

5.1 Permutation-Based Input Transformations

We propose an input transformation that is actually even more lightweight than the Lightweight Secure PUF solution but does not show any indication of local minima. The idea is to use k different, fix-point-free permutations $\pi_1, \ldots, \pi_k$ as sub-challenge generators[4]. We hence obtain the sub-challenges $c^{(l)} = \pi_l(c)$. As this input transformation can be implemented in wiring, no additional gate is used in the PUF design. A permutation of the challenges does not result in a permutation of the feature vectors due to the nature of the ATT. To be more precise, the multiplications in (2) ensure that if the challenge vectors are permuted, different bits are being multiplied. Therefore pairs of feature vectors do not show significant correlation according to (5) even if they are permuted. We call this family of input transformations the *permutation-based input transformations.*

We empirically confirmed that this approach does not show any of the local minima we observed for the Lightweight Secure PUF. The machine learning resistance was instead comparable to the results of pseudorandom inputs (Fig. 4), which represent and upper bound on input transformation quality as argued in Sect. 3. Without observing local minima or correlations, the attack described in Sect. 4.2 cannot be applied.

Additionally, this input transformation comes at nearly zero resource overhead. Compared to using a pseudorandom input transformation, the permutation-based transformation is more efficient in terms of area and power and is also more efficient than the input transformation proposed for the Lightweight Secure PUF.

6 Conclusion

In this paper we revisited the topic of input transformations for Arbiter PUFs, which were introduced to make XOR Arbiter PUFs more resilient against machine learning attacks. We showed that the Lightweight Secure PUF can in fact be learned with much higher success rate than previously believed. With the same training set size, we were able to achieve attack results comparable to attacking the classic XOR Arbiter PUF. This refutes the assumption that the Lightweight Secure PUF provides significantly better security than the classic XOR Arbiter PUF.

The main reason for this is that the input transformation of the Lightweight Secure PUF produces local minima which can be learned via machine learning algorithms. Our research shows that the input transformation can play an important role when determining the machine learning resistance of a PUF construct. In particular, one needs to ensure that the input transformation does not result in local minima that can be exploited using our two-stage machine

[4] Additionally, we chose the permutations such that no pair always shows the same value on the same output coordinate. The (up to seven) permutations of our 64-bit experiments can be obtained in Python with `[numpy.random.RandomState(s).permutation(64) for s in [2989, 2992, 3038, 3084, 3457, 6200, 7089]]`.

learning attack. Based on these findings we presented an alternative input transformation using fix-point-free permutations. Our results show that PUFs using this input transformation are nearly as hard to learn as pseudorandom inputs, which we argue is the most resilient input transformation in regards to machine learning attacks. The proposed design has a very low hardware-overhead as it simply consists of a fixed routing of challenge bits to the individual arbiter chains and does not feature any obvious feature vector correlations that could be used to launch an improved attack.

Finally, it should be noted that while our results focus on XOR Arbiter PUF, the results can be generalized to other constructs such as the multiplexer PUF [13] or PUF constructs not based on Arbiter PUFs such as an XOR Bistable Ring PUF [21] or XOR Voltage PUFs [19].

References

1. Becker, G.T.: The gap between promise and reality: on the insecurity of XOR arbiter PUFs. In: Güneysu, T., Handschuh, H. (eds.) CHES 2015. LNCS, vol. 9293, pp. 535–555. Springer, Heidelberg (2015). https://doi.org/10.1007/978-3-662-48324-4_27
2. Becker, G.T., Kumar, R., et al.: Active and passive side-channel attacks on delay based PUF designs. IACR Cryptology ePrint Archive **2014**, 287 (2014)
3. Chen, Q., Csaba, G., Lugli, P., Schlichtmann, U., Rührmair, U.: The bistable ring PUF: a new architecture for strong physical unclonable functions. In: 2011 IEEE International Symposium on Hardware-Oriented Security and Trust (HOST), pp. 134–141. IEEE (2011)
4. Delvaux, J., Verbauwhede, I.: Side channel modeling attacks on 65nm arbiter PUFs exploiting CMOS device noise. In: 2013 IEEE International Symposium on Hardware-Oriented Security and Trust (HOST), pp. 137–142. IEEE (2013)
5. Gassend, B., Clarke, D., Van Dijk, M., Devadas, S.: Silicon physical random functions. In: Proceedings of the 9th ACM Conference on Computer and Communications Security (CCS), pp. 148–160. ACM (2002)
6. Lim, D.: Extracting secret keys from integrated circuits. Department Electrical Engineering Computer Science, Massachusetts Institute Technology, Cambridge (2004)
7. Majzoobi, M., Koushanfar, F., Potkonjak, M.: Lightweight secure PUFs. In: IEEE/ACM International Conference on Computer-Aided Design (ICCAD 2008), pp. 670–673. IEEE (2008)
8. Nguyen, P.H., Sahoo, D.P., Chakraborty, R.S., Mukhopadhyay, D.: Security analysis of arbiter PUF and its lightweight compositions under predictability test. ACM Trans. Des. Autom. Electron. Syst. (TODAES) **22**(2), 20 (2017)
9. Rostami, M., Majzoobi, M., Koushanfar, F., Wallach, D.S., Devadas, S.: Robust and reverse-engineering resilient PUF authentication and key-exchange by substring matching. IEEE Trans. Emerg. Topics Comput. **2**(1), 37–49 (2014)
10. Rührmair, U., Sehnke, F., Sölter, J., Dror, G., Devadas, S., Schmidhuber, J.: Modeling attacks on physical unclonable functions. In: Proceedings of the 17th ACM Conference on Computer and Communications Security (CCS), pp. 237–249. ACM (2010)

11. Rührmair, U., et al.: PUF modeling attacks on simulated and silicon data. IEEE Trans. Inf. Forensics Secur. **8**(11), 1876–1891 (2013)
12. Rührmair, U., et al.: Efficient power and timing side channels for physical unclonable functions. In: Batina, L., Robshaw, M. (eds.) CHES 2014. LNCS, vol. 8731, pp. 476–492. Springer, Heidelberg (2014). https://doi.org/10.1007/978-3-662-44709-3_26
13. Sahoo, D.P., Mukhopadhyay, D., Chakraborty, R.S., Nguyen, P.H.: A multiplexer-based arbiter PUF composition with enhanced reliability and security. IEEE Trans. Comput. **67**(3), 403–417 (2018)
14. Schuster, D., Hesselbarth, R.: Evaluation of bistable ring PUFs using single layer neural networks. In: Holz, T., Ioannidis, S. (eds.) Trust 2014. LNCS, vol. 8564, pp. 101–109. Springer, Cham (2014). https://doi.org/10.1007/978-3-319-08593-7_7
15. Sölter, J.: Cryptanalysis of electrical PUFs via machine learning algorithms. M.Sc. thesis, Technische Universität München (2009)
16. Suh, G.E., Devadas, S.: Physical unclonable functions for device authentication and secret key generation. In: Proceedings of the 44th Annual Design Automation Conference (DAC), pp. 9–14. ACM (2007)
17. Tajik, S., et al.: Physical characterization of arbiter PUFs. In: Batina, L., Robshaw, M. (eds.) CHES 2014. LNCS, vol. 8731, pp. 493–509. Springer, Heidelberg (2014). https://doi.org/10.1007/978-3-662-44709-3_27
18. Tobisch, J., Becker, G.T.: On the scaling of machine learning attacks on PUFs with application to noise bifurcation. In: Mangard, S., Schaumont, P. (eds.) RFIDSec 2015. LNCS, vol. 9440, pp. 17–31. Springer, Cham (2015). https://doi.org/10.1007/978-3-319-24837-0_2
19. Vijayakumar, A., Patil, V.C., Prado, C.B., Kundu, S.: Machine learning resistant strong PUF: possible or a pipe dream? In: 2016 IEEE International Symposium on Hardware Oriented Security and Trust (HOST), pp. 19–24. IEEE (2016)
20. Wisiol, N., Margraf, M.: Why attackers lose: design and security analysis of arbitrarily large XOR arbiter PUFs. J. Cryptogr. Eng. **9**(3), 221–230 (2019). https://doi.org/10.1007/s13389-019-00204-8
21. Xu, X., Rührmair, U., Holcomb, D.E., Burleson, W.: Security evaluation and enhancement of bistable ring PUFs. In: Mangard, S., Schaumont, P. (eds.) RFIDSec 2015. LNCS, vol. 9440, pp. 3–16. Springer, Cham (2015). https://doi.org/10.1007/978-3-319-24837-0_1
22. Yu, M.D., Hiller, M., Delvaux, J., Sowell, R., Devadas, S., Verbauwhede, I.: A lockdown technique to prevent machine learning on PUFs for lightweight authentication. IEEE Trans. Multi-Scale Comput. Syst. **2**(3), 146–159 (2016)
23. Yu, M.D., Verbauwhede, I., Devadas, S., M'Raïhi, D.: A noise bifurcation architecture for linear additive physical functions. In: IEEE International Symposium on Hardware-Oriented Security and Trust (HOST), pp. 124–129. IEEE (2014)

Post-Quantum Cryptography

Improving Speed of Dilithium's Signing Procedure

Prasanna Ravi[1,2](✉), Sourav Sen Gupta[2], Anupam Chattopadhyay[1,2], and Shivam Bhasin[1]

[1] Temasek Laboratories, Nanyang Technological University, Singapore, Singapore
{prasanna.ravi,anupam,sbhasin}@ntu.edu.sg

[2] School of Computer Science and Engineering, Nanyang Technological University, Singapore, Singapore
sg.sourav@ntu.edu.sg

Abstract. Dilithium is a round 2 candidate for digital signature schemes in NIST initiative for post-quantum cryptographic schemes. Since Dilithium is built upon the "Fiat Shamir with Aborts" framework, its signing procedure performs rejection sampling of its signatures to ensure they do not leak information about the secret key. Thus, the signing procedure is iterative in nature with a number of rejected iterations, which serve as unnecessary overheads hampering its overall performance. As a first contribution, we propose an optimization that reduces the computations in the rejected iterations through *early-evaluation* of the conditional checks. This allows to perform an early detection of the rejection condition and reject a given iteration as early as possible. We also incorporate a number of standard optimizations such as *unrolling* and *inlining* to further improve the speed of the signing procedure. We incorporate and evaluate our optimizations over the software implementation of Dilithium on both the Intel Core i5-4460 and ARM Cortex-M4 CPUs. As a second contribution, we identify opportunities to present a more refined evaluation of Dilithium's signing procedure in several scenarios where pre-computations can be carried out. We also evaluate the performance of our optimizations and the memory requirements for the pre-computed intermediates in the considered scenarios. We could yield speed-ups in the range of *6%* upto *35%*, considering all the aforementioned scenarios, thus presenting the fastest software implementation of Dilithium till date.

Keywords: Dilithium · Early evaluation · *pqm4* · Digital signatures · Lattice-based cryptography · Post-quantum cryptography

1 Introduction

It has been known for quite sometime that modern public-key cryptography that is being used today, is not secure against attacks by large-scale quantum computers [13]. With continued advances in the field of quantum computing [3], it

S. Belaïd and T. Güneysu (Eds.): CARDIS 2019, LNCS 11833, pp. 57–73, 2020.
https://doi.org/10.1007/978-3-030-42068-0_4

will probably not be long before we have the world's first large scale quantum computer, that can break modern day public-key cryptography. This prompted NIST to initiate a standardization process for public-key cryptographic schemes (public-key encryption, digital signatures, and key establishment schemes) that are secure against quantum computers [11]. NIST received 69 valid submissions for the first round of the standardization process. After intense scrutiny by NIST and based on public feedback, NIST selected 26 algorithms (17 public-key encryption and 9 digital signature schemes) for the second round out of the 69 valid submissions from the first round of the standardization process. The Dilithium lattice-based signature scheme, part of the CRYSTALS (Cryptographic Suite for Algebraic Lattices) package is one of the leading second-round candidates for digital signatures [8]. Dilithium offers both good security and efficiency guarantees with its security based on the efficient Module-Learning With Errors (MLWE) problem. Thus, most if not all computations in Dilithium involve operations over polynomials in a structured cyclotomic ring that allows use of the efficient Number Theoretic Transform (NTT) for polynomial multiplication.

However, one of the main features of Dilithium is that it is built upon the well-known *Fiat-Shamir with Aborts* framework [7]. The signing procedure performs *rejection sampling* of certain intermediate variables through a number of conditional checks. This is done to ensure that the generated signatures do not leak the distribution of the secret key. Thus, the signing procedure is iterative in nature and goes through a number of rejected iterations until it outputs a valid signature. For example, the signing procedure for recommended parameter sets of Dilithium has an average repetition rate of 6.6 [8] and hence the computations performed in all except the last iteration (5.6 iterations) are just un-necessary overheads. Thus, the repetition rate severely hampers the performance of Dilithium's signing procedure.

As a *first contribution*, we propose an optimization to perform *early-evaluation* of the conditional checks, so as to perform optimal number of computations to reject an iteration. Our high-level optimizations simply involve reorganization of computations within each iteration and hence can be adopted to speed-up both SW and HW implementations. Moreover, our optimizations could also be applicable to other lattice-based schemes built upon a similar framework. We also further enhance the performance of the signing procedure through techniques such as *unrolling* and *inlining* optimizations. The proposed optimizations do not create any secret key related timing dependency. We also identified opportunities to refine the approach to evaluate the signing performance of Dilithium in certain realistic scenarios where pre-computations are possible. We mainly consider two scenarios - (1) pre-computed intermediates in case of static public-private key pairs and (2) partitioning the signing procedure in case of the randomized variant of Dilithium. Thus as a *second contribution*, we perform a detailed evaluation of the performance improvements and the memory requirements for the above mentioned scenarios. We present results for the optimized signing procedure for different scenarios on both the Intel(R) Core(TM) i5-4460 CPU and observe speed-ups of *upto 31%* across all updated parameter sets of Dilithium.

We also present the fastest software results for Dilithium on the ARM Cortex-M4F by optimizing the open-source implementation of Dilithium available in the open source *pqm4* library and observe speed-ups in the range of *6%* upto *35%*, thus demonstrating the portability of our optimizations across implementation platforms.

2 Preliminaries

Notation: Elements in the integer ring $\mathbb{Z}_q$ are denoted by regular font letters viz. $a, b \in \mathbb{Z}_q$, where q is a prime. We denote $x \xleftarrow{\$} X$ to denote sampling x uniformly in random from set X. We denote the polynomial ring $\mathbb{Z}_q[X]/\langle X^n+1\rangle$ as R_q. For an element $\mathbf{a} \in R_q$, we define $\|\mathbf{a}\|_\infty = \max_{0\leq i\leq n-1} |a(i) \pmod q|$. For a given $\eta \in \mathbb{N}$, define $S_\eta = \{a \in R_q \mid \|a\|_\infty \leq \eta\}$. Multiplication of two polynomials $\mathbf{a}, \mathbf{b} \in R_q$ is denoted as $\mathbf{a} \cdot \mathbf{b}$ or $\mathbf{ab} \in R_q$. Matrices and vectors of polynomials in R_q are referred to as *modules* and are denoted using bold letters viz. $\mathbf{a} \in R_q^{k\times l}, \mathbf{b} \in R_q^l$. Each polynomial element of module $\mathbf{b} \in R_q^l$ is denoted as $\mathbf{b}[i]$ for $i \in [0, l-1]$.

Lattice-Based Cryptography: The security of most efficient lattice-based cryptographic schemes are based on the hardness of two average case-hard problems known as the Ring-Learning With Errors problem (RLWE) [9] and the Ring-Short Integer Solutions problem (RSIS) [10]. Both these problems reduce to corresponding worst-case instances of hard problems over ideal lattices. For a public key $(\mathbf{a}, \mathbf{t}) \in (R_q, R_q)$, an RLWE attacker is asked to solve for polynomials $\mathbf{s}_1, \mathbf{s}_2 \in S_\eta$ with $\eta \ll q$ such that $\mathbf{t} = \mathbf{a} \cdot \mathbf{s}_1 + \mathbf{s}_2$. Given m uniformly random elements $\mathbf{a}[i] \in R_q$ for $i \in [0, m-1]$, an MSIS attacker is required to solve for a short non-zero vector $\mathbf{z} = (\mathbf{z}[0], \mathbf{z}[1], \ldots, \mathbf{z}[m-1]) \in S_\eta^m$ such that $\sum_i^m \mathbf{a}[i] \cdot \mathbf{z}[i] = 0 \in R_q$.

The RLWE and RSIS problems generalize to the corresponding Module-LWE (MLWE) and Module-SIS (MSIS) problems respectively, where computations are performed over matrices and vectors of polynomials in the space $R_q^{k\times\ell} = \mathbb{Z}_q^{k\times\ell}[X]/(X^n+1)$ for $k, \ell > 1$ (as opposed to R_q for their ring variants). The generalized module version of the LWE and SIS problems also provide better security guarantees compared to their corresponding ring variants. A change in security of a scheme based on MLWE or MSIS only requires to alter the module dimensions k, ℓ while keeping the underlying operating ring fixed. Thus, change in security can be easily achieved through very minimal changes in the underlying implementation.

2.1 Dilithium

The security of Dilithium is based on the MLWE and MSIS problems. While the property of indistinguishability of the public key comes from the MLWE problem, security against existential forgery under the quantum random oracle model is based on MSIS hardness assumption [8]. Based on how the ephemeral nonce in the signing procedure is generated, Dilithium comes in two variants (i.e) deterministic or probabilistic.

In the following discussion, we discuss the details of the Dilithium signature scheme with more focus on its signing procedure [8]. The signature scheme is based on the "Fiat-Shamir with Aborts" framework [7] while the scheme itself derives from the lattice-based signature scheme proposed by Bai and Galbraith [2]. The scheme operates over the base ring R_q with $n, q = (256, 8380417)$ while offering flexibility with the module parameters (k, ℓ) allowing to operate over varying dimensions $(k \times \ell)$ in four different security levels henceforth referred to as Dilithium1 (Weak), Dilithium2 (Medium), Dilithium3 (Recommended) and Dilithium4 (Very High).

Algorithm 1. Dilithium Signature scheme

Procedure Sign (sk, M)
  $\mathbf{A} \in R_q^{k\times\ell} := \mathsf{ExpandA}(\rho)$
  $\mu = \mathsf{CRH}(\mathsf{tr}\|M)$
  $\kappa = 0, (\mathbf{z}, \mathbf{h}) = \perp$
  $\rho' \in \{0,1\}^{384} := \mathsf{CRH}(K\|\mu)$(or $\rho' \leftarrow \{0,1\}^{384}$ for randomized signing)
  while $(\mathbf{z}, \mathbf{h}) = \perp$ **do**
    $\mathbf{y} \in S_{\gamma_1-1}^{\ell} := \mathsf{ExpandMask}(\rho'\|\kappa)$
    $\mathbf{w} = \mathbf{A} \cdot \mathbf{y}$
    $(\mathbf{w}_1, \mathbf{w}_0) = \mathsf{D}_q(\mathbf{w}, 2\gamma_2)$
    $\mathbf{c} \in B_{60} = H(\mu\|\mathbf{w}_1)$
    $\mathbf{z} = \mathbf{y} + \mathbf{c} \cdot \mathbf{s}_1$
    $(\mathbf{r}_1, \mathbf{r}_0) := \mathsf{D}_q(\mathbf{w} - \mathbf{c} \cdot \mathbf{s}_2, 2\gamma_2)$
    if $\|\mathbf{z}\|_\infty \geq \gamma_1 - \beta$ or $\|\mathbf{r}_0\|_\infty \geq \gamma_2 - \beta$ or $\mathbf{r}_1 \neq \mathbf{w}_1$ **then**
      $(\mathbf{z}, \mathbf{h}) = \perp$
    else
      $\mathbf{h} = \mathsf{MH}_q(-\mathbf{c} \cdot \mathbf{t}_0, \mathbf{w} - \mathbf{c} \cdot \mathbf{s}_2 + \mathbf{c} \cdot \mathbf{t}_0, 2\gamma_2)$
      if $\|\mathbf{c} \cdot \mathbf{t}_0\|_\infty \geq \gamma_2$ or $\mathsf{wt}(\mathbf{h}) > \omega$ **then**
        $(\mathbf{z}, \mathbf{h}) = \perp$
    end
    $\kappa = \kappa + 1$
  end
  return $\sigma = (\mathbf{z}, \mathbf{h}, \mathbf{c})$

Key Generation: The main operation of the key generation procedure is to generate the MLWE instance that forms the public-private key pair (pk, sk) of Dilithium. An LWE instance $\mathbf{t} = \mathbf{a} \cdot \mathbf{s}_1 + \mathbf{s}_2$ is created where $\mathbf{a} \in R_q^{k\times\ell}$ is the public parameter while the secret and error modules $\mathbf{s}_1 \in R_q^{\ell}$ and $\mathbf{s}_2 \in R_q^{k}$ are small modules sampled from S_η^ℓ and S_η^k respectively. The LWE instance is not directly output as the public key but is decomposed into $\mathbf{t}_0, \mathbf{t}_1$ such that $\mathbf{t}_0$ consists of the d lower order bits of all coefficients of $\mathbf{t}$ while $\mathbf{t}_1$ consists of its remaining higher order bits. Subsequently, $\mathbf{t}_1$ is published as part of the public key pk while $\mathbf{t}_0$ along with $\mathbf{s}_1, \mathbf{s}_2$ form part of the secret key sk.

Signing: Refer to Algorithm 1 for the signing procedure of Dilithium. The signing procedure is iterative in nature (While loop from Line 6 to 21 of Sign in Algorithm 1) with a number of conditional checks (Line 13 and 17) and it exits with a valid signature only when all the conditional checks are successfully passed. Moreover, these selective rejections in the signing procedure together ensure both security and 100% correctness of the signature scheme.

The most important component of the signing procedure (apart from the secret key) is the ephemeral nonce $\mathbf{y} \in R_q^\ell$. Knowledge of a single value of $\mathbf{y}$ or reuse of $\mathbf{y}$ for different messages leads to a trivial break of the signature scheme. Moreover, the method of generation of the ephemeral nonce $\mathbf{y}$ also determines the deterministic nature of the signature scheme. In deterministic Dilithium, $\mathbf{y} \in R_q^\ell$ is deterministically generated using the ExpandMask function which takes as inputs, the message μ to be signed, a random secret key component $K \in \{0,1\}^{256}$ and the iteration count k (Line 5 and 7). But, in case of probabilistic Dilithium, $\mathbf{y}$ is randomly generated using the same ExpandMask function but with inputs, ρ' and the iteration count k where ρ' is sampled randomly from $\{0,1\}^{384}$ (Line 5).

Once $\mathbf{y}$ is sampled, the product $\mathbf{w} = \mathbf{a} \cdot \mathbf{y} \in R_q^k$ is computed and further decomposed into $\mathbf{w}_1$ and $\mathbf{w}_0$ such that $\mathbf{w} = \mathbf{w}_1 \cdot 2\gamma_2 + \mathbf{w}_0$. Further, a sparse challenge polynomial $\mathbf{c}$ (only 60 non-zero coefficients in either ± 1) is generated by hashing together the message, ephemeral nonce and public key information. Using $\mathbf{c}$ and $\mathbf{y}$, the signer generates the primary signature component $\mathbf{z}$ as $\mathbf{z} = \mathbf{s}_1\mathbf{c} + \mathbf{y}$. Finally, a hint vector $\mathbf{h} \in R_q^k$ with coefficients in $\{0,1\}$ is generated and is also published along with $\mathbf{z}, \mathbf{c}$ as the signature. This hint vector $\mathbf{h}$ is actually used by the verifier along with the signature to recover the value of $\mathbf{w}_1$ which is used to verify the authenticity of the challenge polynomial $\mathbf{c}$. We do not discuss the verification procedure and the reader is referred to [8] for more details.

3 Early Evaluation Optimization

Referring to the Sign procedure in Algorithm 1, we provide the following terminologies for the various conditional/rejection checks. It is important to note that all these checks have to be passed together in a single iteration, in order to output a valid signature.

- $\|\mathbf{z}\|_\infty \leq \gamma_1 - \beta$: Chk_Norm($\mathbf{z}$) (Line 13 of Sign in Algorithm 1)
- $\|\mathbf{r}_0\|_\infty \leq \gamma_2 - \beta$: Chk_Norm($\mathbf{r}_0$) (Line 13)
- $\|\mathbf{c}\mathbf{t}_0\|_\infty \leq \gamma_2$: Chk_Norm($\mathbf{c}\mathbf{t}_0$) (Line 17)
- $wt(\mathbf{h}) < w$: Chk_Weight($\mathbf{h}$) (Line 17)
- $\mathbf{r}_1 \neq \mathbf{w}_1$ (Line 13)

We make a couple of observations about implementation of the rejection checks in the reference implementation of Dilithium submitted to the NIST standardization process [8]. For reference, we consider the same code snippet in Fig. 1

which contains operations corresponding to the computation of $\mathbf{z}$ followed by its corresponding rejection check $\mathsf{Chk\_Norm}(\mathbf{z})$[1].

- **Observation-1:** Out of the five rejection checks, the three rejection checks $\mathsf{Chk\_Norm}(\mathbf{z})$, $\mathsf{Chk\_Norm}(\mathbf{r}_0)$ and $\mathsf{Chk\_Norm}(\mathbf{ct}_0)$ contribute to more than 99% of the rejections in the signing procedure. They are all *infinity_norm* checks ($\mathsf{Chk\_Norm}$) over modules with multiple polynomials.

```
for(i = 0; i < L; ++i)
{
   poly_pointwise_invmontgomery(z1.vec+i , &chat , s1.vec+i);
   poly_invntt_montgomery(z2.vec+i ,z1.vec+i);
}
polyvecl_add(&z3 , &y, &z2);
polyvecl_freeze(&z ,$z3);
if(polyvecl_chknorm(&z , GAMMA1 - BETA))
    goto rej;
```

Fig. 1. C-Code snippet corresponding to computation of $\mathbf{z}$ according to the reference implementation in static single assignment form

Infinity norm checks are necessary conditions and computed one coefficient at a time. Considering $\mathsf{Chk\_Norm}(\mathbf{z})$, all individual polynomials $\mathbf{z}[i]$ for $i \in \{0, L-1\}$ of $\mathbf{z}$ are supposed to pass the check, for the complete module $\mathbf{z}$ to be considered valid. Hence, an iteration can be immediately rejected upon detecting a violation in any of the polynomials of $\mathbf{z}$. Lets assume a case where the first polynomial of $\mathbf{z}[0]$ violates $\mathsf{Chk\_Norm}(\mathbf{z})$. Though the violation can be detected just by computing the first polynomial $\mathbf{z}[0]$, analysis of the reference implementation of Dilithium revealed that all polynomials of $\mathbf{z}$ are computed before the conditional check over the whole module of $\mathbf{z}$ is performed. If $\mathbf{z}[0]$ can be computed independently and checked immediately, then one can immediately reject the iteration saving the un-necessary computations of $\mathbf{z}[1], \ldots, \mathbf{z}[L-1]$. The same applies to the other two $\mathsf{Chk\_Norm}$ conditions over $\mathbf{r}_0$ and $\mathbf{ct}_0$ in the signing procedure.

Hence, we alternately propose to *compute and check* $\mathbf{z}$ *one polynomial at a time* (instead of *one module at a time* in the reference implementation). Only if the check over a particular polynomial $\mathbf{z}[i]$ is passed, the next polynomial $\mathbf{z}[i+1]$ is computed, else the iteration is rejected immediately. We also make the following observation.

- **Observation-2:** The module $\mathbf{z}$ is computed over a series of computations ($\mathbf{z}_1 \rightarrow \mathbf{z}_2 \rightarrow \mathbf{z}_3 \rightarrow \mathbf{z}$) with each computation ($\mathsf{poly\_pointwise\_invmontgomery}$,

[1] The code snippet shown in Fig. 1 is in its static single assignment form. In the static single assignment code, the result of an operation is always written to a new variable. In the original implementation, all of $\mathbf{z}_i$ for $i = \{0, \ldots, 3\}$ refer to a single variable $\mathbf{z}$. The single assignment form is used for better illustration of our idea.

poly_invntt_montgomery, polyvecl_add and polyvecl_freeze) operating over the entire module. But, all these computations preceding the rejection check can also independently operate over single polynomials and do not have any dependency over other polynomials in the same module.

This enables us to *chain* these computations corresponding to single polynomials and compute $\mathbf{z}$ one polynomial at a time. The same technique can also be applied to the computation of $\mathbf{r}_0$ and $\mathbf{ct}_0$ pertaining to the two other rejection checks (though the computations involved are slightly different). For a better illustration, the compute chain of $\mathbf{z}$ corresponding to the original implementation can be depicted as in Eq. 1 as follows:

$$\begin{aligned}
&(\mathbf{z}_1[0] \rightarrow \mathbf{z}_1[1] \rightarrow \ldots \rightarrow \mathbf{z}_1[L-1]) \rightarrow (\mathbf{z}_2[0] \rightarrow \mathbf{z}_2[1] \rightarrow \ldots \rightarrow \mathbf{z}_2[L-1]) \rightarrow \ldots \\
&(\mathbf{z}_3[0] \rightarrow \mathbf{z}_3[1] \rightarrow \ldots \rightarrow \mathbf{z}_3[L-1]) \rightarrow (\mathbf{z}[0] \rightarrow \mathbf{z}[1] \rightarrow \ldots \rightarrow \mathbf{z}[L-1])
\end{aligned} \tag{1}$$

From Eq. 1, we can see that a particular computation is performed over every polynomial in the module before starting the next computation. But our optimized technique computes $\mathbf{z}$ according to the compute chain as depicted in Eq. 2:

$$\begin{aligned}
&(\mathbf{z}_1[0] \rightarrow \mathbf{z}_2[0] \rightarrow \mathbf{z}_3[0] \rightarrow \mathbf{z}[0]) \rightarrow (\mathbf{z}_1[1] \rightarrow \mathbf{z}_2[1] \rightarrow \mathbf{z}_3[1] \rightarrow \mathbf{z}[1]) \rightarrow \ldots \\
&(\mathbf{z}_1[2] \rightarrow \mathbf{z}_2[2] \rightarrow \mathbf{z}_3[2] \rightarrow \mathbf{z}[2]) \rightarrow \ldots \rightarrow \\
&(\mathbf{z}_1[L-1] \rightarrow \mathbf{z}_2[L-1] \rightarrow \mathbf{z}_3[L-1] \rightarrow \mathbf{z}[L-1])
\end{aligned} \tag{2}$$

In fact, the above compute chain is not always fully computed and is *halted* at the earliest possible instance as every polynomial ($\mathbf{z}[0], \ldots, \mathbf{z}[L-1]$) is immediately checked after it is computed. This is in contrast to the reference implementation where the compute chain is always fully computed before the whole of $\mathbf{z}$ is checked. Going one step further, we also observe that the set of consecutive computations including the rejection check (i.e) (polyvecl_add, polyvecl_freeze and polyvecl_chknorm) are actually point-wise operations which operate over single coefficients. Thus, it is possible to combine these consecutive operations into a single composite operation, thus bringing our optimization from the *polynomial level* down to the *coefficient level*. Refer to Fig. 2 for the code-snippet of the optimized computation of $\mathbf{z}$, wherein computations are performed *one polynomial at a time*. Furthermore, the identified consecutive point-wise operations are further fused into a single function (poly_add_freeze_chk_norm) which computes and immediately checks each coefficient before moving onto the next. These optimizations also directly apply to the other rejection checks involving $\mathbf{r}_0$ and $\mathbf{ct}_0$. We will henceforth refer to it as the *Early-Eval* optimization throughout the paper. Since it mainly works to remove un-necessary computations, we can clearly see that it will benefit serial implementations much more than parallel implementations. While we expect to observe maximum speed-up for serial implementations (HW/SW) which iterate over computations corresponding to *one polynomial at a time*, we would only observe negligible/no speed-up in *embarrassingly parallel* HW implementations which parallelize computations corresponding to all polynomials of the module.

```
for(i = 0; i < L; ++i)
{
   poly_pointwise_invmontgomery(z.vec+i, &chat, s1.vec+i);
   poly_invntt_montgomery(z.vec+i);
   if(poly_add_freeze_chk_norm(z.vec+i, z.vec+i,
      y.vec+i, GAMMA1 - BETA))
         goto rej;
}
```

Fig. 2. C-Code snippet of computation of **z** improved using our *Early-Eval* optimization

3.1 Note on Timing Attacks

Any given iteration of our signing procedure in our optimized implementation is immediately *rejected* as soon as a coefficient that violates a conditional check is computed. Thus, any adversary with access to the timing side-channel may potentially derive information about the position of the coefficient which resulted in rejection. However, the probability of a given coefficient violating the bound is independent of the secret key and thus knowledge of the position of the coefficient that resulted in rejection does not leak any exploitable information about the secret key. Thus, to the best of our knowledge, our *Early-Eval* optimization does not bring in any additional exploitable timing vulnerabilities.

3.2 Additional Optimizations

While implementing the proposed optimization on the public code of *pqm4* library, we observed some potential scope for further optimizations. Though these optimizations might be intuitively known and not necessarily novel, we included these optimizations to test the limits of speed-up that can be achieved. We observed that the reference implementation of Dilithium consists of a large number of functions which operate over single coefficients. These functions were implemented in separate files and were compiled into separate object files and hence the compiler couldn't *inline* them automatically. With these computations spanning over multiple polynomials each of degree 256, the overhead from just function calls (branch to and from the functions) in these point-wise functions are significant. Hence, we resorted to manually *inlining* all the point-wise functions used in the implementation. Though inlining doesn't result in very elegant code, it avoids the un-necessary overhead from branching to and from the function for every coefficient.

We also incorporated another standard optimization of *unrolling* the loops in all the small functions that computed over single coefficients. We limited the unroll factor to 8 for all such loops within these functions so as to maintain the readability and simplicity of the code. We henceforth refer to these optimizations as the *Impl-Level* optimizations throughout the paper. It is important to note that the *Impl-Level* optimizations are applied to all point-wise/coefficient-wise operations within the Dilithium signature scheme, while our *Early-Eval* optimizations only apply to the few operations preceding the conditional checks within the signing procedure. Though the *Impl-level* optimizations speed up all the three procedures of Dilithium (KeyGen, Sign and Verify), we limit our focus only to the performance improvements of its signing procedure.

4 Experimental Results

In this section, we perform an experimental evaluation of our optimizations over the Dilithium's signing operation on two software platforms (1) Intel Core i5 CPU and (2) ARM Cortex-M4 MCU. Our optimizations were incorporated over the updated reference implementation of Dilithium submitted to the *second* round of the ongoing NIST standardization process. It is possible to independently employ both the *Early-Eval* and *Impl-Level* optimizations and thus we present two different optimized implementations of the signing operation (Refer Table 1). While the proposed Opt-1 variant demonstrates the speed-up only due to the *Early-Eval* optimization, the Opt-2 variant demonstrates the speed-up from the combination of both the *Early-Eval* and *Impl-Level* optimizations.

Table 1. Different variants of Dilithium's signing procedure based on the employed optimizations

Variant	Optimization used
Ref	None
Opt-1	*Early-Eval*
Opt-2	*Early-Eval* & *Impl-Level*

4.1 A Refined Evaluation Approach

While experimenting with the implementation of Dilithium's signing procedure, we found that it can be further refined when considering its practical usage in certain realistic scenarios. The main factor we consider is the *cryptoperiod* of the public-private key pair. According to the NIST SP 800-57 Part-1 document on "Recommendation for Key Management", "a *cryptoperiod* is the time span during which a specific key is authorized for use by legitimate entities, or the keys for a given system will remain in effect." NIST dedicates a complete section on cryptoperiods and details on the various risk factors, consequence factors and recommendations that allows one to decide the cryptoperiod for the various keys used in any secure application. The reader is referred to Section 5.3 of the SP 800-57 document [4] for more in-depth details.

4.1.1 Precomputing Operations over the Static Public-Private Key Pair

NIST recommends that a private signature key can have a cryptoperiod of about 1–3 years at the signer's side while the public signature key used for verification could be valid for several years depending on the key size [4]. Though these are mere recommendations from NIST and not strict guidelines, considering the complexity of repeatedly refreshing key-pairs from the perspective of a key-management system, one can expect most secure applications to work with static public-private key pairs with relatively long cryptoperiods. We observed a number of operations within Dilithium's signing procedure which operate over the static public-private key pair. But, in situations where public-private key pairs are static, these operations can simply be computed once and have its results reused to avoid unnecessary overheads from performing redundant computations.

To be specific, operations such as expanding a seed into the public parameter $\mathbf{A}$, unpacking the secret key sk into its individual components and NTT operations over the secret key components $\mathbf{s}_1$, $\mathbf{s}_2$, $\mathbf{t}_0$ are redundant if the public-private key pairs are static[2]. Thus, we consider the following two scenarios for evaluation based on the cryptoperiod of the public-private key pair. We denote:

- Scenario-1: All operations are computed *online* assuming ephemeral public-private key pairs.
- Scenario-2: Certain operations are *pre-computed offline* assuming static public-private key pairs with very long cryptoperiods.

4.1.2 Partitioning the Signing Procedure

Considering the randomized variant of Dilithium's signing procedure, we observe that some more operations within the signing procedure can be computed offline, independent of the message to be signed. In particular, operations such as sampling $\mathbf{y}$ using ExpandMask (Line 7 of Sign in Algorithm 1) and computation of $\mathbf{w}_0$ and $\mathbf{w}_1$ (Lines 8 & 9) can be computed offline. If we also assume static public-private key pair, it is possible to split the signing procedure into offline and online phases. Such partitioning techniques can significantly speed-up the signing procedure in real-time applications with main focus on low-latency times. In such scenarios, computations in lines 2, 7, 8 and 9 of Sign procedure in Algorithm 1 can be performed offline assuming that the device has a large enough buffer to store all the intermediates. The remaining operations can be computed online upon knowledge of the message to be signed. In fact, Aysu *et al.* in [1] utilized the same partitioning technique in their high-performance and low-latency HW-SW co-designed implementation of the GLP lattice-based signature scheme [5]. A similar idea of partitioning was also suggested by Pöppelmann *et al.* in [12] to improve the speed of the BLISS lattice-based signature scheme. We denote:

---

[2] The authors of Dilithium also note that the above operations can be pre-computed and stored to "slightly" speed up the signing operation, but do not present any performance evaluation or the memory requirements due to the same (Refer Sec. 3.1 of [8]).

– Scenario-3: Considering the randomized variant of Dilithium, we assume all message independent operations along with operations over the static public-private secret key to be computed offline. Thus, we only evaluate the performance of online phase of the signing procedure.

4.2 Results on the Intel Core i5-4460 CPU

We first present results of our optimized implementations of Dilithium's signing procedure on the Intel Core i5-4460 CPU 3.20 GHz, compiled with gcc-4.2.1 without modifying the compiler flags set for the reference implementation. We use the average computational run-times of the signing procedure as our evaluation metric, which was obtained across 10^6 runs of the signing procedure. We tested two versions of Dilithium (i.e) (1) Dilithium-SHA that uses SHAKE from the SHA3 family as an XOF and (2) Dilithium-AES that uses AES-256 in counter mode as an XOF, across all parameter sets of Dilithium. Refer Tables 2 and 3 for a comparative performance evaluation of our optimized implementations (Opt-1 and Opt-2) against the reference implementation, in all the three identified scenarios (in terms of number of clock cycles). While we use the randomized variant of Dilithium for evaluation in Scenario-3 as stated earlier, we use the deterministic variant with the same secret key and message inputs for a direct comparative evaluation in Scenario-1 and Scenario-2.

Table 2. Comparative performance evaluation of the optimized Opt-1 implementation variant against the reference implementation of Dilithium's signing procedure on the Intel Core i5-4460 CPU. The results are reported in units of **million (10^6) clock cycles**.

Scheme	Cycles ($\times 10^6$)								
	Scenario-1			Scenario-2			Scenario-3		
	Ref	Opt-1	Imp. (%)	Ref	Opt-1	Imp. (%)	Ref	Opt-1	Imp. (%)
Dilithium1-SHA	0.904	0.833	**7.8**	0.778	0.715	**8.08**	0.365	0.303	**16.88**
Dilithium2-SHA	1.621	1.461	**9.88**	1.378	1.246	**9.57**	0.598	0.457	**23.5**
Dilithium3-SHA	2.359	2.153	**8.69**	2.042	1.838	**10.0**	0.812	0.598	**26.2**
Dilithium4-SHA	2.183	2.035	**6.77**	1.731	1.586	**8.38**	0.694	0.548	**20.95**
Dilithium1-AES	1.156	1.094	**5.33**	0.910	0.863	**5.21**	0.365	0.303	**17.01**
Dilithium2-AES	2.110	1.973	**6.919**	1.663	1.526	**8.23**	0.589	0.457	**22.4**
Dilithium3-AES	3.175	2.969	**6.498**	2.460	2.258	**8.17**	0.814	0.597	**26.5**
Dilithium4-AES	3.174	2.970	**6.414**	2.459	2.258	**8.18**	0.817	0.600	**26.5**

We first compare the runtimes of the reference implementations of the signing procedure in the three identified scenarios. Comparing Scenario-1 and Scenario-2, we observe a difference of about 13–14% in runtime for Dilithium-SHA and 20–21% for Dilithium-AES, which corresponds to the time spent on performing redundant operations over the static public-private key pair. When comparing Scenario-1 and Scenario-3, we observe a large difference of about 60% for

Dilithium-SHA and 71–72% for Dilithium-AES, which shows that a significant amount of time within each iteration is spent in sampling the ephemeral nonce $\mathbf{y}$ using XOF functions either through Keccak permutations in case of Dilithium-SHA and AES-256 in counter mode in case of Dilithium-AES. This difference also arises from computation of associated variables $\mathbf{w}_1$ and $\mathbf{w}_0$ in each iteration, but is very small when compared to the time taken from sampling $\mathbf{y}$.

We now perform a performance comparison of our optimized implementations against the reference implementations on the Intel i5-CPU, individually based on the different identified scenarios (Refer Tables 2 and 3). Considering Scenario-1, where all operations are done online, we observe a speed-up of about 6.7–9.8% and 5.3–6.9% for the Opt-1 implementation of Dilithium-SHA and Dilithium-AES respectively. But, our proposed Opt-2 variant which is additionally padded with *Impl-Level* optimizations yields a much higher speed-up of 17–21% for Dilithium-SHA and 13.5–15.7% for Dilithium-AES in Scenario-1. Considering Scenario-2, where the operations over the static public-private key pair are pre-computed, we observe improved speed-ups of about 8–10% and 5.2–8.1% for the Opt-1 implementation of Dilithium-SHA and Dilithium-AES respectively. But, our Opt-2 implementation shows an improved speed-up of about 20–23% for Dilithium-SHA and 16–20% for Dilithium-AES in Scenario-2. The improved speed-up in Scenario-2 is mainly observed due to removal of the overheads due to operations over the static public-private key pair in all the compared implementations (Ref, Opt-1, Opt-2).

Table 3. Comparative performance evaluation of the optimized implementation Opt-2 against the reference implementation of Dilithium's signing procedure on the Intel(R) Core(TM) i5-4460 CPU. The results are reported in units of **million (10^6) clock cycles**.

Scheme	Cycles ($\times 10^6$)								
	Scenario-1			Scenario-2			Scenario-3		
	Ref	Opt-2	Imp. (%)	Ref	Opt-2	Imp. (%)	Ref	Opt-2	Imp. (%)
Dilithium1-SHA	0.904	0.742	**17.8**	0.778	0.617	**20.07**	0.365	0.280	**23.2**
Dilithium2-SHA	1.621	1.281	**20.9**	1.378	1.069	**22.4**	0.598	0.424	**29.1**
Dilithium3-SHA	2.359	1.86	**21.1**	2.042	1.545	**24.3**	0.812	0.557	**31.38**
Dilithium4-SHA	2.183	1.771	**18.85**	1.731	1.320	**23.7**	0.694	0.505	**27.2**
Dilithium1-AES	1.156	0.999	**13.55**	0.910	0.758	**16.6**	0.365	0.281	**23.04**
Dilithium2-AES	2.110	1.79	**15.15**	1.663	1.341	**19.3**	0.589	0.426	**27.59**
Dilithium3-AES	3.175	2.676	**15.72**	2.460	1.966	**20.0**	0.814	0.557	**31.53**
Dilithium4-AES	3.174	2.677	**15.65**	2.459	1.966	**20.0**	0.817	0.557	**31.7**

Considering Scenario-3, where we only evaluate the online phase of the signing procedure, we observe much higher speed-ups of about 16.9–23.5% and 17.0–26.5% for the Opt-1 implementation of Dilithium-SHA and Dilithium-AES respectively. But, the more optimized Opt-2 implementation yields significant speed-ups of about 23.2–31.4% and 23.0–31.7% for Dilithium-SHA and

Dilithium-AES respectively in Scenario-3. The best speed-ups were observed in Scenario-3 because all the operations in the online phase of the signing procedure are enhanced by our optimizations. This is unlike Scenario-1 and Scenario-2, where the major computational time of the signing procedure was dominated by the XOF functions which are *unaffected* by either of our optimizations.

4.3 Results on the ARM Cortex-M4

In the following, we present results of our optimized implementations on the ARM Cortex-M4 MCU. We port our optimizations onto the publicly available implementation of Dilithium taken from the *pqm4* library [6], a benchmarking and testing framework for PQC schemes on the ARM Cortex-M4 family of microcontrollers. Our implementations were compiled with arm-none-eabi-gcc-7.2.1 with compiler flags `-O3 -mthumb -mcpu=cortex-m4 -mfloat-abi=hard -mfpu=fpv4-sp-d16` and run on the STM32F4DISCOVERY board (DUT) housing the STM32F407, ARM Cortex-M4 microcontroller. Since we observe similar if not better speed-ups for both our Opt-1 and Opt-2 implementation variants on the ARM Cortex-M4 MCU when compared to the Intel CPU, we only provide detailed evaluation of our fastest Opt-2 implementation in Table 4. These results were obtained across 10k runs of the signing procedure of Dilithium-SHA across all parameter sets. However, for the sake of completeness, we provide results for our Opt-1 variant on the recommended parameter set of Dilithium, Dilithium-3. Considering Scenario-1 for our Opt-2 variant, we observe speed-ups of about 18–20% while for Scenario-2 we observe increased speed-ups in the range of 21–24% across all parameter sets of Dilithium. As for Scenario-3, we observe a significant speed-up of about 29–35%, thus clearly demonstrating the portability and applicability of our optimization techniques across different implementation platforms. Please refer Table 5 for the code-size of our optimized implementation variants. While there is negligible increase in code-size (0.5%) for our Opt-1 variant, we observe an increased overhead of about 17.6% for our Opt-2 variant, that can be mainly attributed due to the *unrolling* optimizations.

Table 4. Performance evaluation of the reference, Opt-1 and Opt-2 implementation of Dilithium's signing procedure on the ARM Cortex-M4 MCU. The results are reported in units of **million (10^6) clock cycles**.

Scheme	Cycles ($\times 10^6$)								
	Scenario-1			Scenario-2			Scenario-3		
	Ref	Opt-1	Imp. (%)	Ref	Opt-1	Imp. (%)	Ref	Opt-1	Imp. (%)
Dilithium3-SHA	8.907	8.332	**6.45**	7.292	6.78	**7.01**	2.239	1.716	**23.35**
	Ref	Opt-2	Imp. (%)	Ref	Opt-2	Imp. (%)	Ref	Opt-2	Imp. (%)
Dilithium1-SHA	3.033	2.482	**18.16**	2.493	1.950	**21.76**	1.016	0.721	**29.08**
Dilithium2-SHA	5.761	4.632	**19.59**	4.752	3.640	**23.41**	1.630	1.085	**33.42**
Dilithium3-SHA	8.907	7.085	**20.45**	7.292	5.495	**24.64**	2.237	1.449	**35.21**
Dilithium4-SHA	8.648	7.061	**18.34**	6.283	4.733	**24.67**	1.916	1.274	**33.49**

Table 5. Comparison of code-size of the different implementation variants of Dilithium. The size of actual code, constant data and the global variables are separately tabulated as **text**, **data** and **bss** respectively. All the numbers are reported in **bytes**.

Variant	text	data	bss	Total	Overhead (%)
Ref	29696	12	8	29716	–
Opt-1	29864	12	8	29884	**0.56**
Opt-2	34912	12	8	34932	**17.6**

4.4 Memory Requirements for Scenario-2 and Scenario-3

Though we observe increased speed-ups for Scenario-2 and Scenario-3, it does come at the cost of requiring to precompute and store certain intermediate values, which consequently requires allocation of additional memory for storage. Hence, we analyze the memory requirements in both scenarios for all parameter sets of Dilithium. Considering Scenario-2, it is required to buffer the modules $\mathbf{A}$, $\mathsf{NTT}(\mathbf{s}_1)$, $\mathsf{NTT}(\mathbf{s}_2)$ and $\mathsf{NTT}(\mathbf{t}_0)$. All the coefficients of these modules occupy 23 bits and hence there are two possible ways to store them. We can either completely use 32 bits (4 bytes) to store each coefficient (wasting 9 bits for each) or we can efficiently use a compact bit-packing strategy to efficiently store the same intermediates. Readers are referred to Section 5.2 of [8] for the description of the bit-packing strategy used in Dilithium's reference implementation.

In case of Scenario-3, calculation of the memory requirement is a bit more involved, as it is required to additionally pre-compute and store the ephemeral nonce $\mathbf{y}, \mathbf{w}_0$ and $\mathbf{w}_1$ for every iteration. Since the number of iterations required to generate a signature is not known a priori, we perform an analysis of the number of repetitions observed over 10^7 runs of the signing procedure. Refer Fig. 3 for the cumulative distribution plot of the percentage of signatures passed against the minimum number of iterations to be pre-computed, for all parameter sets of Dilithium[3]. We empirically calculated the minimum number of iterations to be pre-computed so as to pass signatures according to three different success rates: 90%, 95% and 99%. Refer Table 6 for these empirically calculated minimum iteration counts for the aforementioned success rates. Based on these numbers, we also calculated the additional memory requirements for storage of $\mathbf{y}, \mathbf{w}_0$ and $\mathbf{w}_1$ required for implementations in Scenario-3.

Refer Table 6 for the total memory requirements for implementations in Scenario-2 and Scenario-3 for varying success rates across all parameter sets of Dilithium. We present the memory requirement results for both the packed and unpacked cases. As expected, memory requirements for the packed intermediates are much lesser compared to the unpacked intermediates. But, this comes at the expense of additional performance overhead of unpacking all the stored intermediates.

[3] By precomputed iterations, we do not mean computation of the complete iterations, but only computation of $\mathbf{y}, \mathbf{w}_0$ and $\mathbf{w}_1$ corresponding to those iterations.

Table 6. Memory requirements for implementations in Scenario-2 and Scenario-3 for all parameter sets of Dilithium. Both the packed and un-packed cases are considered. Memory requirements are reported in **Kilobytes**. Please note that Scenario-2 and Scenario-3 are abbreviated as Scen-2 and Scen-3 respectively.

Scheme[a]	Minimum no. of iterations			No Packing (KB)				Packing (KB)			
	90%	95%	99%	Scen-2	Scen-3			Scen-2	Scen-3		
					90%	95%	99%		90%	95%	99%
Dilithium1	9	12	18	14	86	110	158	10.1	35.9	44.6	61.8
Dilithium2	13	16	25	23	166	199	309	16.3	68.9	81.0	117.3
Dilithium3	15	19	29	34	244	300	440	24.4	102.3	123.0	174.9
Dilithium4	9	12	18	47	200	251	353	33.8	90.8	109.9	148.0

[a] The reported numbers remain the same irrespective of the utilized XOF function (AES or SHA-3).

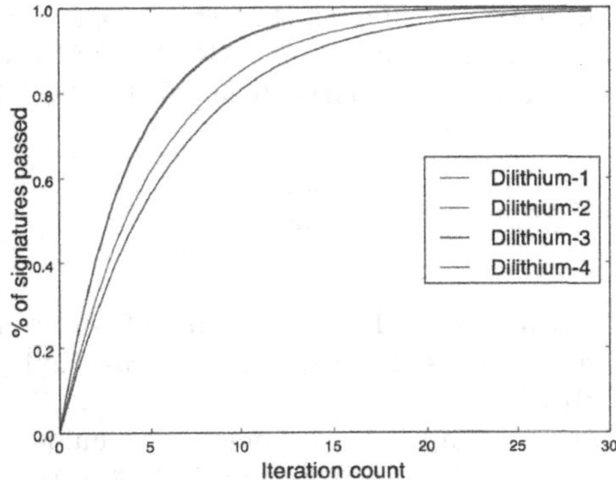

Fig. 3. Cumulative distribution plot of the percentage of signatures passed against the minimum number of iterations to be pre-computed. Please note that the curves for Dilithium1 and Dilithium4 are overlapping one-another.

It is natural to see that the memory requirements increase with increasingly secure parameter sets (i.e) from Dilithium1 to Dilithium4 due to the increase in the module's dimensions. We can clearly see that the memory requirements for Scenario-2 are much lower (14–47 KB for the packed case and 10–34 KB for the unpacked case) compared to Scenario-3 with much higher memory requirements numbering in the hundreds of KBs. The main reason being that the memory requirements for Scenario-2 only depend on the module dimensions, but memory requirements for Scenario-3 mainly depend on the repetition rate of the parameter set. This is also evident from the Table 6 that Dilithium-4 with higher module dimensions ($k, \ell = 6, 5$) but with a lower average repetition rate of 4.3 has reduced memory requirements in Scenario-3 compared to Dilithium-3 ($k, \ell = 5, 4$) with a higher average repetition rate of 6.6.

5 Conclusion

In this paper, we have presented an algorithmic optimization on Dilithium's signing procedure which reduces the computations done in the rejected iterations through early-evaluation of the conditional checks. We also incorporate a couple of standard optimization techniques such as inlining and unrolling to further improve upon the speed of the signing procedure. We also evaluate our optimizations in three different scenarios based on the possibility of performing pre-computations. We perform detailed evaluation of the performance of our optimizations and the memory requirements in the afore mentioned scenarios on the Intel Core i5-4460 CPU and the ARM Cortex-M4F MCU and reported speed-ups in the range of *6%* upto *35%*, thus demonstrating the effectiveness of our proposed optimizations.

Acknowledgment. The authors acknowledge the support from the Singapore National Research Foundation ("SOCure" grant NRF2018NCR-NCR002-0001 - www.green-ic.org/socure). This work is also partially supported by NRF TUM CREATE grant.

References

1. Aysu, A., Yuce, B., Schaumont, P.: The future of real-time security: latency-optimized lattice-based digital signatures. ACM Trans. Embedded Comput. Syst. (TECS) **14**(3), 43 (2015)
2. Bai, S., Galbraith, S.D.: An improved compression technique for signatures based on learning with errors. In: Benaloh, J. (ed.) CT-RSA 2014. LNCS, vol. 8366, pp. 28–47. Springer, Cham (2014). https://doi.org/10.1007/978-3-319-04852-9_2
3. Barends, R., et al.: Superconducting quantum circuits at the surface code threshold for fault tolerance. Nature **508**(7497), 500–503 (2014)
4. Barker, E., Barker, W., Burr, W., Polk, W., Smid, M.: Recommendation for key management part 1: general (revision 3). NIST Spec. Publ. **800**(57), 1–147 (2012)
5. Güneysu, T., Lyubashevsky, V., Pöppelmann, T.: Practical lattice-based cryptography: a signature scheme for embedded systems. In: Prouff, E., Schaumont, P. (eds.) CHES 2012. LNCS, vol. 7428, pp. 530–547. Springer, Heidelberg (2012). https://doi.org/10.1007/978-3-642-33027-8_31
6. Kannwischer, M.J., Rijneveld, J., Schwabe, P., Stoffelen, K.: PQM4: Post-quantum crypto library for the ARM Cortex-M4. https://github.com/mupq/pqm4
7. Lyubashevsky, V.: Fiat-Shamir with aborts: applications to lattice and factoring-based signatures. In: Matsui, M. (ed.) ASIACRYPT 2009. LNCS, vol. 5912, pp. 598–616. Springer, Heidelberg (2009). https://doi.org/10.1007/978-3-642-10366-7_35
8. Lyubashevsky, V., et al.: CRYSTALS-Dilithium. Technical report, National Institute of Standards and Technology (2017). https://csrc.nist.gov/Projects/Post-Quantum-Cryptography/Round-2-Submissions
9. Lyubashevsky, V., Peikert, C., Regev, O.: On ideal lattices and learning with errors over rings. J. ACM **60**(6), 43 (2013)
10. Micciancio, D.: Generalized compact knapsacks, cyclic lattices, and efficient one-way functions. Comput. Complex. **16**(4), 365–411 (2007)

11. NIST: Post-Quantum Crypto Project (2016). http://csrc.nist.gov/groups/ST/post-quantum-crypto/
12. Pöppelmann, T., Ducas, L., Güneysu, T.: Enhanced lattice-based signatures on reconfigurable hardware. In: Batina, L., Robshaw, M. (eds.) CHES 2014. LNCS, vol. 8731, pp. 353–370. Springer, Heidelberg (2014). https://doi.org/10.1007/978-3-662-44709-3_20
13. Shor, P.W.: Algorithms for quantum computation: discrete logarithms and factoring. In: 1994 Proceedings of the 35th Annual Symposium on Foundations of Computer Science, pp. 124–134. IEEE (1994)

An Efficient and Provable Masked Implementation of qTESLA

François Gérard[1(✉)] and Mélissa Rossi[2,3,4]

[1] Université libre de Bruxelles, Brussels, Belgium
fragerar@ulb.ac.be
[2] École normale supérieure, CNRS, PSL University, Paris, France
[3] Thales, Gennevilliers, France
[4] Inria, Paris, France
melissa.rossi@ens.fr

Abstract. Now that the NIST's post-quantum cryptography competition has entered in its second phase, the time has come to focus more closely on practical aspects of the candidates. While efficient implementations of the proposed schemes are somewhat included in the submission packages, certain issues like the threat of side-channel attacks are often lightly touched upon by the authors. Hence, the community is encouraged by the NIST to join the war effort to treat those peripheral, but nonetheless crucial, topics. In this paper, we study the lattice-based signature scheme qTESLA in the context of the masking countermeasure. Continuing a line of research opened by Barthe et al. at Eurocrypt 2018 with the masking of the GLP signature scheme, we extend and modify their work to mask qTESLA. Based on the work of Migliore et al. in ACNS 2019, we slightly modify the parameters to improve the masked performance while keeping the same security. The masking can be done at any order and specialized gadgets are used to get maximal efficiency at order 1. We implemented our countermeasure in the original code of the submission and performed tests at different orders to assess the feasibility of our technique.

Keywords: Lattice based signatures · Side-channels · Masking

1 Introduction

Following NIST's call for proposals a few years ago, the practical aspects of post-quantum cryptography have lately been studied more closely in the scientific literature. Many researchers tried to optimize parameters of cryptosystems to achieve reasonable practicality while still resisting state-of-the-art cryptanalysis. Once the design phase was over, a lot of implementations flourished on various platforms, proving that those cryptosystems can hope to achieve something useful outside of academia. Nevertheless, everyone is now well aware that

S. Belaïd and T. Güneysu (Eds.): CARDIS 2019, LNCS 11833, pp. 74–91, 2020.
https://doi.org/10.1007/978-3-030-42068-0_5

having a fast and correct implementation of some functionality is seldom sufficient to get a secure system. In practice, side-channel attacks should not be overlooked and the capability of a cryptosystem to be easily protected against this kind of threats may be a strong argument to decide what will be the reigning algorithm in a post-quantum world.

In this work, we focus on applying the masking countermeasure to qTESLA [1], a Fiat-Shamir lattice-based signature derived from the original work of Lyubashevsky [22]. This signature is, with Dilithium [14], one of the most recent iteration of this line of research and a candidate for the NIST's competition. In 2018, Barthe et al. [3] described and implemented a proof of concept for a masked version of an ancestor of Dilithium/qTESLA called GLP [18]. Their goal was to prove that it is possible to mask the signature procedure at any order. This work led to a concrete masked implementation of Dilithium with experimental leakage tests [23]. In the latter, Migliore *et al.* noticed that replacing the prime modulus by a power of two allows to obtain a considerably more efficient masked scheme, by a factor of 7.3 to 9 for the most timeconsuming masking operations. Our work is in the same spirit. Similarly, we slightly modify the signature and parameters to ease the addition of the countermeasure while keeping the original security. In addition, we provide a detailed proof of masking for the whole signature process taking public outputs into account. Indeed, similarly to the masking of GLP in [3], several elements of qTESLA may be securely unmasked, like, for example, the number of rejections. Besides, we propose an implementation for which we have focused on *performance and reusability*. Our masked signature implementation still keeps the property of being compatible with the original verifying procedure of qTESLA and has been directly implemented within the code of the submission. Even if we target high order masking, we also implemented specialized gadgets for order 1 masking to provide a lightweight version of the masking scheme with reasonable performance fitting nicely on embedded systems. We finally provide extensive performance data and show that the cost of provable masking can be reasonable at least for small orders. Our code is publicly available at https://github.com/fragerar/Masked_qTESLA.

Parameter Sets Removal. While this paper was under peer review, the heuristic parameter sets on which our experiments are based were removed by the qTESLA team. We emphasis that the parameters we use were *not* broken but are not part of the standardization process anymore. Furthermore, our theoretical work is somewhat oblivious to the underlying parameter set used to instanciate the signature and the code can be adapted to implement the provably-secure sets as well.

2 Preliminaries

2.1 Notations

For any integers q, n and $\mathbb{Z}_q = \mathbb{Z}/q\mathbb{Z}$, we denote by $\mathcal{R}_q$ the ring $\mathbb{Z}_q[X]/(X^n+1)$. Polynomials are written with bold lower case, e.g. $\mathbf{y} \in \mathcal{R}_q$. Note that, in our study, we do not need to introduce a notation for vectors of polynomials. Let B be an integer, we write $\mathcal{R}_{q,[B]}$ to denote the subset of polynomials in $\mathcal{R}_q$ with coefficients in $[-B, B]$. The usual norm operators are extended to polynomials by interpreting them as a vector of their coefficients. For a polynomial $\mathbf{v} = \sum_{i=0}^{n-1} v_i \cdot \mathbf{x}^i$, $||\mathbf{v}||_1 = \sum_{i=0}^{n-1} |v_i|$ and $||\mathbf{v}||_\infty = \mathsf{max}_i|v_i|$. For a modulus q and an integer x, we write $x \bmod q$ to denote the unique integer $x_{cn} \in [0, \ldots, q-1]$ such that $x_{cn} \equiv x \pmod q$. We call this integer the *canonical representative* of x modulo q. We also write $x \bmod^{\pm} q$ to denote the unique integer $x_{ct} \in (-q/2, \ldots, q/2]$ (where the lower bound is included if q is odd) such that $x_{ct} \equiv x \pmod q$. We call this integer the *centered representative* of x modulo q. For integers w, d, the function $[\cdot]_L : \mathbb{Z} \to \mathbb{Z}, w \mapsto w \bmod^{\pm} 2^d$ denotes the signed extraction of the d last bits of w. We use this function to define $[\cdot]_M : \mathbb{Z} \to \mathbb{Z}, w \mapsto (w \bmod^{\pm} q - [w]_L)/2^d$. Those two functions are extended to polynomials by applying them separately on each coefficient.

2.2 Masking

Side channel attacks are a family of cryptanalytic attacks where the adversary is able access several physical parameters of the device running the algorithm. These physical attacks include, for instance, cache attacks, simple and correlation electromagnetic analysis or fault injections. Modelling and protecting the information leaked though physical parameters has been an important research challenge since the original attack warning in [20].

The *probing model* or *ISW model* from its inventors [19] is the most studied leakage model. It has been introduced in order to theoretically define the vulnerability of implementations exposed to side-channel attacks. In a nutshell, a cryptographic implementation is N-probing secure iff any set of at most N intermediate variables is statisctically independent of the secrets. This model can be applied to practical leakages with the reduction established in [13] and tightened in [17]. The *masking* countermeasure performs computations on secret-shared data. It is the most deployed countermeasure in this landscape. Basically, each input secret x is split into $N+1$ variables $(x_i)_{0 \leq i \leq N}$ referred to as shares. N of them are generated uniformly at random whereas the last one is computed such that their combination reveals the secret value x. The integer N is called *masking order* and represents the security level of an implementation with respect to side channels. Let us introduce two types of additive combination in the following definition.

Definition 1 (Arithmetic and Boolean Masking). *A sensitive value x is shared with mod q arithmetic masking if it is split into $N+1$ shares $(x_i)_{0 \leq i \leq N}$ such that*

$$x = x_0 + \cdots + x_N \pmod q. \qquad \text{(Arithmetic masking mod } q\text{)}$$

It is shared with Boolean masking if it is split into $N+1$ shares $(x_i)_{0 \leq i \leq N}$ such that

$$x = x_0 \oplus \cdots \oplus x_N. \qquad \text{(Boolean masking)}$$

For lattice-based cryptography where most operations are linear for mod q addition, arithmetic masking seems the best choice. However, for certain operations like the randomness generation and comparisons, Boolean masking is better fit. Fortunately, some conversions exist [3,9,11] and allow to switch from one masking to another.

Proofs by Composition. To achieve N-probing security, Barthe et al. formally defined two security properties in [4], namely *non-interference* and *strong non-interference*, which (1) ease the security proofs for small gadgets (see Definition 2), and (2) allows to securely combine secure gadgets together.

Definition 2. *A (u, v)-gadget is a probabilistic algorithm that takes as inputs u shared values, and returns distributions over v-tuples of shared values.*

Definition 3. *A gadget is N-non-interfering (N-NI) iff any set of at most N observations can be perfectly simulated from at most N shares of each input.*

Definition 4. *A gadget is N-strong non-interfering (N-SNI) iff any set of at most N observations whose N_{int} observations on the internal data and N_{out} observations on the outputs can be perfectly simulated from at most N_{int} shares of each input.*

It is easy to check that N-SNI implies N-NI which implies N-probing security. The strong non-interference only appears in the proofs for subgadgets inside the signature and key generation algorithm. An additional notion was introduced in [3] to reason on the security of lattice-based schemes in which some intermediate variables may be revealed to the adversary.

Definition 5. *A gadget with public outputs X is N-non-interfering with public outputs (N-NIo) iff every set of at most N intermediate variables can be perfectly simulated with the public outputs and at most N shares of each input.*

Table 1. Parameters for qTESLA-I and qTESLA-III

Parameters	qTESLA-I	qTESLA-III	Description
n	512	1024	Dimension of the ring
q	4 205 569 $\approx 2^{22}$	8 404 993 $\approx 2^{23}$	Modulus
σ	22.93	10.2	Standard deviation
h	30	48	Nonzero entries of $\mathbf{c}$
E	1586	1147	Rejection parameter
S	1586	1233	Rejection parameter
B	$2^{20} - 1$	$2^{21} - 1$	Bound for $\mathbf{y}$
d	21	22	Bits dropped in $[\cdot]_M$

2.3 The qTESLA Signature

Let us now describe qTESLA [1], a (family of) lattice-based signature based on the RLWE problem and round 2 candidate for the NIST's post-quantum competition. The signature stems from several iterations of improvements over the original scheme of Lyubashevsky [22]. It is in fact a concrete instantiation of the scheme of Bai and Galbraith [2] over ideal lattices. Its direct contender in the competition is Dilithium [14] which is also based on this same idea of having a lattice variant of Schnorr signature. The security of Dilithium rely on problems over module lattices instead of ideal lattices, in the hope of increasing security by reducing algebraic structure, at the cost of a slight performance penalty.

To avoid overloading the paper, we will not describe in details all the subroutines and subtleties of qTESLA and sometimes simplify some aspects of the signature not required to understand our work.

Parameters
We store in Table 1 the set of selected parameters that are relevant for the rest of the paper. For the sake of practicability, we focus on the heuristic version of qTESLA in this work. More specifically, we implement our countermeasure in qTESLA-I and qTESLA-III even though the techniques we used are not specific to any parameter set.

Scheme
The key generation and signature procedures are formally recalled in Algorithms 1 and 2. They are similar to the corresponding ones in other Fiat-Shamir lattice-based signatures. We redirect the interested reader to [1] or the NIST submission [5] for a detailed description. In the following, PRF is a pseudorandom function, GenA generates a uniformly random polynomial, GaussSampler samples a polynomial according to a Gaussian distribution, CheckS and CheckE verifies that a secret polynomial does not have too large coefficients, ySampler samples a uniformly random polynomial $\mathbf{y} \in \mathcal{R}_{q,[B]}$, H is a collision resistant hash function and Enc encodes a bitstring into a sparse polynomial $\mathbf{c} \in \mathcal{R}_{q,[1]}$ with $||\mathbf{c}||_1 = h$.

3 Masked qTESLA

3.1 Masking-Friendly Design

In the process of masking qTESLA, we decided to make slight modifications in the signing procedure in order to facilitate masking. The idea is that some design elements providing small efficiency gains may be really hard to carry on to the masked version and actually do even more harm than good. Our two main modifications are the modulus which is chosen as the closest power of two of the original parameter set and the removal of the PRF to generate the polynomial $\mathbf{y}$.

Power of Two Modulus. Modular arithmetic is one of the core component of plenty of cryptographic schemes. While, in general, it is reasonably fast for any

Algorithm 1. qTESLA key generation

Result: $sk = (\mathbf{s}, \mathbf{e}, \text{seed}_a, \text{seed}_y)$, $pk = (seed_a, \mathbf{t})$

counter $\leftarrow 1$
pre-seed $\xleftarrow{r} \{0,1\}^\kappa$
$\text{seed}_{s,e,a,y} \leftarrow$ PRF(pre-seed)
$\mathbf{a} \leftarrow$ GenA(seed_a)
do
    $\mathbf{s} \leftarrow$ GaussSampler(seed_s,counter)
    counter $\leftarrow$ counter $+ 1$
while (CheckS($\mathbf{s}$) $\neq 0$)
do
    $\mathbf{e} \leftarrow$ GaussSampler(seed_e,counter)
    counter $\leftarrow$ counter $+ 1$
while (CheckE($\mathbf{e}$) $\neq 0$)
$\mathbf{t} \leftarrow \mathbf{a} \cdot \mathbf{s} + \mathbf{e} \bmod q$
$sk \leftarrow (\mathbf{s}, \mathbf{e}, \text{seed}_a, \text{seed}_y)$
$pk \leftarrow (seed_a, \mathbf{t})$
return sk, pk

Algorithm 2. qTESLA sign

Data: $sk = (\mathbf{s}, \mathbf{e}, \text{seed}_a, \text{seed}_y)$
Result: $\Sigma = (\mathbf{z}, \mathbf{c})$

counter $\leftarrow 1$
$r \xleftarrow{r} \{0,1\}^\kappa$
rand $\leftarrow$ PRF(seed_y, r, H(m))
$\mathbf{y} \leftarrow$ ySampler(rand, counter)
$\mathbf{a} \leftarrow$ GenA(seed_a)
$\mathbf{v} \leftarrow \mathbf{a} \cdot \mathbf{y} \bmod^{\pm} q$
$\mathbf{c} \leftarrow$ Enc(H($[\mathbf{v}]_M, m$))
$\mathbf{z} \leftarrow \mathbf{y} + \mathbf{s} \cdot \mathbf{c}$
if $\mathbf{z} \notin \mathcal{R}_{q,[B-S]}$ **then**
    counter $\leftarrow$ counter $+ 1$
    goto 4
end if
$\mathbf{w} \leftarrow \mathbf{v} - \mathbf{e} \cdot \mathbf{c} \bmod^{\pm} q$
if $\|[\mathbf{w}]_L\|_\infty \geq 2^{d-1} - E$
  or $\|\mathbf{w}\|_\infty \geq \lfloor q/2 \rfloor - E$ **then**
    counter $\leftarrow$ counter $+ 1$
    goto 4
end if
return $(\mathbf{z}, \mathbf{c})$

modulus (but not necessarily straightforward to do in constant time), modular arithmetic in masked form is very inefficient and it is often one of the bottlenecks in terms of running time. In [3], a gadget SecAddModp is defined to add two integers in boolean masked form modulo p. The idea is to naively perform the addition over the integers and to subtract p if the value is larger than p. While this works completely fine, the computational overhead is large in practice and avoiding those reductions would drastically enhance execution time. The ideal case is to work over $\mathbb{Z}_{2^n}$. In this case, almost no reductions are needed throughout the execution of the algorithm and, when needed, can be simply performed by applying a mask on boolean shares. The reason why working with a power of two modulus is not the standard way to instanciate lattice-based cryptography is that it removes the possibility to use the number theoretic transform (NTT) to perform efficient polynomial multiplication in $\mathcal{O}(n \log n)$. Instead, multiplication of polynomial has to be computed using the Karatsuba/Toom-Cook algorithm which is slower for parameters used in state-of-the-art algorithms. Nevertheless, in our case, not having to use the heavy SecAddModp gadget largely overshadows the penalty of switching from NTT to Karatsuba. Since modulus for both parameter sets were already close to a power of two, we rounded to the closest one, i.e. 2^{22} for qTESLA-I and 2^{23} for qTESLA-III. This modification does not change the security of the scheme. Indeed, security-wise, for the heuristic version of the scheme that we study, we need a q such that $q > 4B$[1] and the corresponding decisional LWE instance is still hard. Yet, the form of q does not impact the hardness of the problem as shown in [21] and, since q was already extremely close to a power of two for both parameters sets, the practical bit hardness of the corresponding instance is not sensibly changed.

Removal of the PRF. It is well known that in Schnorr-like signatures, a devastating attack is possible if the adversary gets two different signatures using the same $\mathbf{y}$. Indeed, they can simply compute the secret $\mathbf{s} = \frac{\mathbf{z}-\mathbf{z}'}{\mathbf{c}-\mathbf{c}'}$. While such a situation is very unlikely due to the large size of $\mathbf{y}$, a technique to create a deterministic version of the signature was introduced in [24]. The idea is to compute $\mathbf{y}$ as $\mathsf{PRF}(secret\_seed, m)$ such that each message will have a different value for $\mathbf{y}$ unless a collision is found in PRF. This modification acts as a protection against very weak entropy sources but is not necessary to the security of the signature and was not present in ancestors of qTESLA. Unfortunately, adding this determinism also enabled some side-channel attacks [8,25]. Hence, the authors of qTESLA decided to take the middle ground by keeping the deterministic design but also seeding the oracle with a fresh random value r[2].

While those small safety measures certainly make sense if they do not incur a significant performance penalty, we decided to drop it and simply sample $\mathbf{y}$ at random at the beginning of the signing procedure. The reason is twofold. First, keeping deterministic generation of $\mathbf{y}$ implied masking the hash function evaluation itself which is really inefficient if not needed and would unnecessarily complicate the masking scheme. Second, implementing a masking countermeasure is, in general, making the hypothesis that a reasonable source of randomness (or at least not weak to the point of having a nonce reuse on something as large as $\mathbf{y}$) is available to generate shares and thus can be also used for the signature itself.

3.2 Existing Gadgets

First, let us describe gadgets already existing in the literature. Since they are not part of our contribution, we decided to only recall their functionalities without formally describing them.

- SecAnd: Computes the logical and between two values given in boolean masked form, output also in boolean masked form. Order 1 algorithm: [12]. Order n algorithm [3].
- SecAdd: Computes the arithmetic add between two values given in boolean masked form, output also in boolean masked form. Order 1 algorithm: [12]. Order n algorithm [3].
- SecArithBoolModq: Converts a value in arithmetic masked form to a value in boolean masked form. Order 1 algorithm: [16]. Order n: [11]. We slightly

[1] The other condition on q in the parameters table of the submission is to enable the NTT.

[2] Note that the fault attacks is still possible in case of failure of the RNG picking r.

Algorithm 3. Absolute Value - AbsVal

Data: A boolean masking $(x_i)_{0\leq i\leq N}$ of some integer x and an integer k
Result: A boolean masking $(|x|_i)_{0\leq i\leq N}$ corresponding to the absolute value of $x \bmod^{\pm} 2^k$

$(mask_i)_{0\leq i\leq N} \leftarrow ((x_i)_{0\leq i\leq N} << (\text{RADIX} - k)) >> (\text{RADIX} - 1))$
$(x'_i)_{0\leq i\leq N} \leftarrow \mathsf{Refresh}((x_i)_{0\leq i\leq N})$
$(x_i)_{0\leq i\leq N} \leftarrow \mathsf{SecAdd}((x'_i)_{0\leq i\leq N}, (mask_i)_{0\leq i\leq N}))$
$(|x|_i)_{0\leq i\leq N} \leftarrow ((x_i)_{0\leq i\leq N} \oplus (mask_i)_{0\leq i\leq N}) \wedge (2^k - 1)$

modify it to an algorithm denoted GenSecArithBoolModq taking into account non power of two number of shares.

- SecBoolArith: Converts a value in boolean masked form to a value in arithmetic masked form. Order 1 algorithm: [16]. Order n algorithm: [9]. This gadget does not explicitly appear in the following but is used inside DataGen.
- DataGen: Takes as input an integer B and outputs a polynomial $\mathbf{y} \in \mathcal{R}_{q,[B]}$ in arithmetic masked form. Uses the boolean to arithmetic conversion.
- FullXor: Merges shares of a value in boolean masked form and output the unmasked value.
- FullAdd: Merges shares of a value in arithmetic masked form and output the unmasked value.
- Refresh: Refreshes a boolean sharing using fresh randomness [19]. We use its N-SNI version, sometimes denoted FullRefresh ([10] Algorithm 4), which is made of a succession of $N + 1$ linear refresh operations.

3.3 New Gadgets

To comply with the specifications of qTESLA, our signature scheme includes new components to be masked that were not covered or different than in [3,23]. In all the following, RADIX refers to the size of the integer datatype used to store the shares.

Absolute Value (Algorithm 3): The three checks during the signing procedure are: $\mathbf{z} \notin \mathcal{R}_{q,[B-S]}$, $||[\mathbf{w}]_L||_\infty \geq 2^{d-1} - E$ and $||\mathbf{w}||_\infty \geq \lfloor q/2 \rfloor - E$. They all involve going through individual coefficients (or their low bits) of a polynomial and checking a bound on their absolute value. In the first version of our work, we were actually making two comparisons on each signed coefficients before realizing that it was actually less intensive to explicitly compute the absolute value and do only one comparison. The gadget takes as input any integer x masked in boolean form and outputs $|x \bmod^{\pm} 2^k|$. Since computers are performing two's complement arithmetic, the absolute value of x can be computed as follows:

1. $m \leftarrow x \gg RADIX - 1$
2. $|x| \leftarrow (x + m) \oplus m$

Algorithm 4. Masked rounding - MaskedRound

Data: An arithmetic masking $(a_i)_{0 \le i \le N}$ of some integer a

Result: An integer r corresponding to the modular rounding of a

$(\text{MINUS\_Q\_HALF}_i)_{0 \le i \le N} \leftarrow (-q/2 - 1, 0, ..., 0)$

$(\text{CONST}_i)_{0 \le i \le N} \leftarrow (2^{d-1} - 1, 0, ..., 0)$

$(a'_i)_{0 \le i \le N} \leftarrow \mathsf{GenSecArithBoolModq}(a_i)_{0 \le i \le N}$

$(b_i)_{0 \le i \le N} \leftarrow \mathsf{SecAdd}((a'_i)_{0 \le i \le N}, (\text{MINUS\_Q\_HALF}_i)_{0 \le i \le N})$

$b_0 = \neg b_0$

$(b_i)_{0 \le i \le N} \leftarrow ((b_i)_{0 \le i \le N} >> \text{RADIX} - 1) << \log_2 q$

$(a'_i)_{0 \le i \le N} \leftarrow (a'_i)_{0 \le i \le N} \oplus (b_i)_{0 \le i \le N}$

$(a'_i)_{0 \le i \le N} \leftarrow \mathsf{SecAdd}((a'_i)_{0 \le i \le N}, (\text{CONST}_i)_{0 \le i \le N})$

$(a'_i)_{0 \le i \le N} \leftarrow (a'_i)_{0 \le i \le N} >> d$

return $t := \mathsf{FullXor}((a'_i)_{0 \le i \le N})$

As we work on signed integers, one can note that the $\gg$ in the first step is an arithmetic shift and actually writes the sign bit in the whole register. If x is negative then $m = -1$ (all ones in the register) and if x is positive then $m = 0$. The gadget AbsVal is using the same technique to compute $|x \bmod^{\pm} 2^k|$. The small difference is that the sign bit is in position k instead of position RADIX. This is why line 1 is moving the sign bit (modulo 2^k) in first position before extending it to the whole register to compute the mask.

Masked Rounding (Algorithm 4): In [2], a compression technique was introduced to reduce the size of the signature. It implies rounding coefficients of a polynomial. Revealing the polynomial before rounding would allow an adversary to get extra information on secret values and thus, this operation has to be done on the masked polynomial. Recall that the operation to compute is $[v]_M = (v \bmod^{\pm} q - [v]_L)/2^d$.

The first step is to compute the centered representative of v, i.e. subtract q from v if $v > q/2$. Taking advantage of our power of two modulus, this operation would be really easy to do if the centered representative was defined as the integer congruent to v in the range $[-q/2, q/2)$ since it would be equivalent to copying the qth bit of v in the most significant part, which can be performed with simple shift operations on shares. Unfortunately, the rounding function of qTESLA works with representatives in $(-q/2, q/2]$. As we wanted compatibility with the original scheme, we decided to stick with their design. Nevertheless, we were still able to exploit our power of two modulus. Indeed, in this context, switching from positive to negative representative modulo q is merely setting all the high bits to one. Hence, we subtract $q/2 + 1$ from v, extract the sign bit b and copy $\neg b$ to all the high bits of v.

The second step is the computation of $(v - [v]_L)/2^d$. We used a small trick here. Subtracting the centered representative modulo 2^d is actually equivalent to the application of a rounding to the closest multiple of 2^d with ties rounded down. Hence we first computed $v + 2^{d-1} - 1$ and dropped the d least significant bits. This is analogous to computing $\lfloor x \rceil = \lfloor x + 0.499\ldots \rfloor$ to find the closest integer to a real value.

Algorithm 5. Masked well-rounded - MaskedWR

Data: Integer $a \in \mathbb{Z}_q$ in arithmetic masked form $(a_i)_{0\leq i\leq N}$
Result: A boolean masking r of $(\|a\| \leq q/2 - E) \wedge (\|[a]_L\| \leq 2^{d-1} - E)$

$(\mathrm{SUP\_Q}_i)_{0\leq i\leq N} \leftarrow (-q/2 + E, 0, ..., 0)$
$(\mathrm{SUP\_D}_i)_{0\leq i\leq N} \leftarrow (-2^{d-1} + E, 0, ..., 0)$
$(a'_i)_{0\leq i\leq N} \leftarrow \mathsf{GenSecArithBoolModq}(a_i)_{0\leq i\leq N}$
$(x_i)_{0\leq i\leq N} \leftarrow \mathsf{AbsVal}((a'_i)_{0\leq i\leq N}, \log_2 q)$
$(x_i)_{0\leq i\leq N} \leftarrow \mathsf{SecAdd}((x_i)_{0\leq i\leq N}, (\mathrm{SUP\_Q}_i)_{0\leq i\leq N}))$
$(b_i)_{0\leq i\leq N} \leftarrow (x_i)_{0\leq i\leq N} >> (\mathrm{RADIX} - 1)$
$(a'_i)_{0\leq i\leq N} \leftarrow \mathsf{Refresh}((a'_i)_{0\leq i\leq N})$
$(a'_i)_{0\leq i\leq N} \leftarrow (a'_i)_{0\leq i\leq N} \wedge 2^d - 1$
$(y_i)_{0\leq i\leq N} \leftarrow \mathsf{AbsVal}((a'_i)_{0\leq i\leq N}, d)$
$(y_i)_{0\leq i\leq N} \leftarrow \mathsf{SecAdd}((y_i)_{0\leq i\leq N}, (\mathrm{SUP\_D}_i)_{0\leq i\leq N}))$
$(b'_i)_{0\leq i\leq N} \leftarrow (y_i)_{0\leq i\leq N} >> (\mathrm{RADIX} - 1)$
$(b_i)_{0\leq i\leq N} \leftarrow \mathsf{SecAnd}((b_i)_{0\leq i\leq N}, (b'_i)_{0\leq i\leq N})$
return $r := \mathsf{FullXor}((b_i)_{0\leq i\leq N})$

Algorithm 6. Rejection Sampling - MaskedRS

Data: A value a to check, in arithmetic masked form $(a_i)_{0\leq i\leq N}$
Result: 1 if $|a| \leq B - S$ else 0

$(\mathrm{SUP}_i)_{0\leq i\leq N} \leftarrow (-B + S - 1, 0, ..., 0)$
$(a'_i)_{0\leq i\leq N} \leftarrow \mathsf{GenSecArithBoolModq}((a_i)_{0\leq i\leq N})$
$(x_i)_{0\leq i\leq N} \leftarrow \mathsf{AbsVal}((a'_i)_{0\leq i\leq N}, \log_2 q)$
$(x_i)_{0\leq i\leq N} \leftarrow \mathsf{SecAdd}((x_i)_{0\leq i\leq N}, (\mathrm{SUP}_i)_{0\leq i\leq N})$
$(b_i)_{0\leq i\leq N} \leftarrow ((x_i)_{0\leq i\leq N} >> \mathrm{RADIX} - 1)$
return $rs := \mathsf{FullXor}((b_i)_{0\leq i\leq N})$

Masked Well-Rounded (Algorithm 5): Unlike GLP, the signature scheme can fail to verify and may have to be restarted even if the rejection sampling test has been successful. This results from the fact that the signature acts as a proof of knowledge only on the **s** part of the secret key and not on the error **e**. Nonetheless, thanks to rounding, the verifier will be able to feed correct input to the hash function if the commitment is so called 'well-rounded'. Since not well-rounded signatures would leak information on the secret key, this verification has to be performed in masked form.

The MaskedWR gadget has to perform the two checks $||[\mathbf{w}]_L||_\infty < 2^{d-1} - E$ and $||\mathbf{w}||_\infty < \lfloor q/2 \rfloor - E$. While the cost of this rather simple operation is negligible compared to polynomial multiplication in the unprotected signature, this test is fairly expensive in masked form. Indeed, it requires four comparisons in addition to the extraction of the low bits of **w**.

After trying the four comparisons method, we realized that the best strategy was actually to compute both absolute values with the AbsVal gadget. While comparisons only require one SecAdd and one shift, which is less than AbsVal, the cost of all SecAnd operations between the results of those comparisons makes our approach of computing the absolute value slightly better.

Rejection Sampling (Algorithm 6): The rejection sampling procedure consists in ensuring that the absolute value of all coefficients of a polynomial $\mathbf{z}$ are smaller than a bound B. In [3], a gadget verifying that the centered representative of a masked integer is greater than $-B$ was applied to both $\mathbf{z}$ and $-\mathbf{z}$. In [23], a less computationally intensive approach was taken: their rejection sampling gadget takes as input an arithmetic masking of a coefficient $a \in \mathbb{Z}_q$ identified by its canonical representative and check directly that either $a - B$ is negative or $a - q + B$ is positive. This can be easily done using precomputed constants $(-B-1, 0, ..., 0)$ and $(-q+B, 0, ..., 0)$. Our approach is similar but we use instead the same technique as in the MaskedWR algorithm, that is to first compute the absolute value of a and perform the masked test $||a|| \leq B$. This saves the need for a masked operation to aggregate both tests.

Algorithm 7. Masked signature

Data: message m, secret key $sk = ((\mathbf{s}_i)_{0 \leq i \leq N}, (\mathbf{e}_i)_{0 \leq i \leq N})$, seed sd
Result: Signature $(\mathbf{z}_{unmasked}, \mathbf{c})$

Let t be a byte array of size n
$\mathbf{a} \leftarrow \mathsf{GenA}(sd)$
$(\mathbf{y}_i)_{0 \leq i \leq N} \leftarrow \mathsf{DataGen}(B)$
for $i = 0, \ldots, N$ **do**
    $\mathbf{v}_i \leftarrow \mathbf{a} \cdot \mathbf{y}_i$
end for
$\mathbf{u} \leftarrow \mathsf{FullRound}((\mathbf{v}_i)_{0 \leq i \leq N})$
$\mathbf{c} \leftarrow \mathsf{Encode}(\mathsf{H}(\mathbf{u}, m))$
for $i = 0, \ldots, N$ **do**
    $\mathbf{z}_i \leftarrow \mathbf{y}_i + \mathbf{s}_i \cdot \mathbf{c}$
end for
if $rs := \mathsf{FullRS}((\mathbf{z}_i)_{0 \leq i \leq N}) = 0$ **then**
    goto 3
end if
for $i = 0, \ldots, N$ **do**
    $\mathbf{w}_i \leftarrow \mathbf{v}_i - \mathbf{e}_i \cdot \mathbf{c}$
end for
if $r := \mathsf{FullWR}((\mathbf{w}_i)_{0 \leq i \leq N}) = 0$ **then**
    goto 3
end if
$\mathbf{z}_{unmasked} \leftarrow \mathsf{FullAdd}((\mathbf{z}_i)_{0 \leq i \leq N})$
return $(\mathbf{z}_{unmasked}, \mathbf{c})$

3.4 Masked Scheme

In all signature schemes, two algorithms can leak the secret key through side channels: the key generation algorithm and the signing algorithm.

Masked Sign: The masked signature can be found in Algorithm 7. It uses the gadgets described in Sect. 3.3: the gadgets FullRS, FullWR and FullRound denote the extension of MaskedRS, MaskedWR and MaskedRound to all coefficients $j \in [0, n-1]$ of their input polynomial. Beside the removal of the PRF for $\mathbf{y}$, its structure follows closely the unmasked version of the signature.

Masked Key Generation: As the number of signature queries per private key can be high (up to 2^{64} as required by the NIST competition), whereas the key generation algorithm is typically only executed once per private key, the vulnerability of the key generation to side channel attacks is therefore less critical. We nevertheless masked the key generation algorithm using a CDT sampling. The detailed gadgets and proofs can be found in the full version of our paper [15]. The final algorithm is pretty inefficient because many comparisons are needed.

4 Proof of Masking

We first list in Table 2 all the known gadgets and new gadgets introduced together with their security properties. The techniques for proving the security properties are similar to the proof of Theorem 6. They can be found in the full version of our paper [15].

Table 2. Security properties of the known and new gadgets.

Existing gadgets			New gadgets (proofs in [15])	
Name	Property	Reference	Name	Property
SecAnd	N-NI	[3,12]	GenSecArithBoolModq	N-NI
SecAdd	N-NI	[3,12]	AbsVal	N-NI
SecArithBoolModq	N-SNI	[11,16]	MaskedRound	N-NIo
SecBoolArith	N-NI	[11,16]	FullRound	N-NIo
FullXor	N-NIo	[3]	MaskedWR	N-NIo
FullAdd	N-NIo	[3]	FullWR	N-NIo
DataGen	N-NIo	[3]	MaskedRS	N-NIo
MultAdd	N-NI	[3], denoted H^1	FullRS	N-NIo
Refresh	N-SNI	[19]		

4.1 Main Masking Theorem

In the following, we introduce a theorem that proves the N-NIo property of our masked signature algorithm. For simplicity and without losing generality, the theorem only considers one iteration for the signature: the signing algorithm outputs $\perp$ if one of the tests in Steps 13 or 19 in Algorithm 7 has failed. We also assume the security properties of Table 2. We denote by $\left(r^{(j)}\right)_{0 \leq j<n}, \left(rs^{(j)}\right)_{0 \leq j<n}$ and $\left(u^{(j)}\right)_{0 \leq j<n}$ the outputs of FullRS, FullWR and FullRound (the values for each coefficient $j \in [0, n-1]$).

Theorem 6. *Each iteration of the masked signature in Algorithm 7 is N-NIo secure with public outputs*[3]

$$\left\{ \left(r^{(j)}\right)_{0\leq j<n}, \left(rs^{(j)}\right)_{0\leq j<n}, \left(u^{(j)}\right)_{0\leq j<n} \right\}$$

(and the signature if returned).

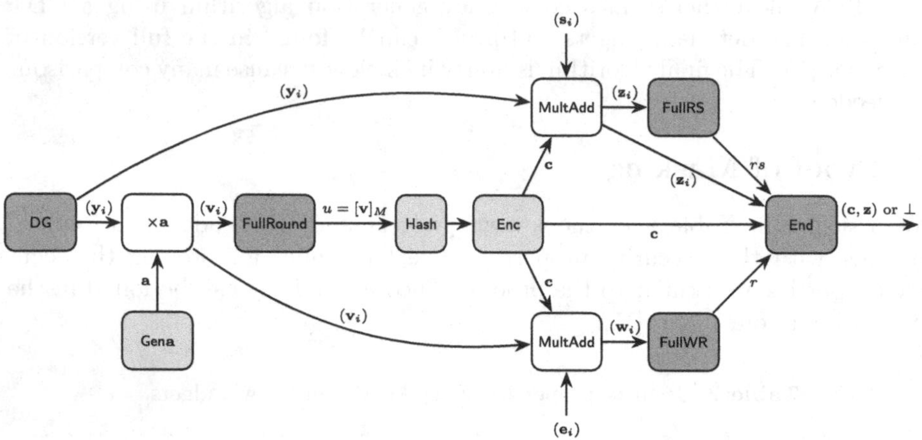

Fig. 1. Masked signature structure (The white (resp. blue, red) gadgets are proved N-NI (resp. N-NIo, unmasked)). The non sensitive element sd is ommited for clarity. (Color figure online)

Proof. The overall gadget decomposition of the signature is in Fig. 1.

Gadgets. The gadget $\times\mathbf{a}$ multiplies each share of the polynomial $\mathbf{y}$ by the public value $\mathbf{a}$. By linearity, it is N-NI. The gadget FullRound denotes the extension of the MaskedRound to all coefficients of $\mathbf{v}$ and is N-NIo. The gadget MultAdd takes $(\mathbf{y}_i)_{0\leq i\leq N}$, $(\mathbf{s}_i)_{0\leq i\leq N}$ and $\mathbf{c}$ (resp. $(\mathbf{v}_i)_{0\leq i\leq N}$, $(\mathbf{e}_i)_{0\leq i\leq N}$ and $\mathbf{c}$) and computes $(\mathbf{z}_i)_{0\leq i\leq N} = (\mathbf{y}_i)_{0\leq i\leq N} - \mathbf{c}\cdot(\mathbf{s}_i)_{0\leq i\leq N}$ (resp. $(\mathbf{w}_i)_{0\leq i\leq N} = (\mathbf{v}_i)_{0\leq i\leq N} - \mathbf{c}(\mathbf{e}_i)_{0\leq i\leq N}$). The gadget End simply outputs (FullAdd($(\mathbf{z}_i)_{0\leq i\leq N}$), $\mathbf{c}$) if rs and r are true; and $\perp$ otherwise. By the N-NIo security of FullAdd, this gadget is also N-NIo secure.

Thus, all the subgadgets involved are either N-NI secure, N-SNI secure, N-NIo secure or they do not manipulate sensitive data (see Table 2 for the recap. We prove that the final composition of all gadgets is N-NIo. We assume that an attacker has access to $\delta \leq N$ observations. Our goal is to prove that all these δ observations can be perfectly simulated with at most δ shares of $(\mathbf{s}_i)_{0\leq i\leq N}$ and $(\mathbf{e}_i)_{0\leq i\leq N}$ and the knowledge of the outputs.
In the following, we consider the following distribution of the attacker's δ observations:

[3] Here too, the number of iterations of the gadget DG is ommited as a public output.

- δ_1 observed during the computations of DG that produces shares of $(\mathbf{y}_i)_{0\le i\le N}$,
- δ_2 observed during the computations of the gadget $\times\mathbf{a}$ that produces the shares of $(\mathbf{v}_i)_{0\le i\le N}$,
- δ_3 observed during the computations of FullRound,
- δ_4 observed during the computations of the upper MultAdd gadget that produces $(\mathbf{z}_i)_{0\le i\le N}$,
- δ_5 observed during the computations of the lower MultAdd gadget that produces $(\mathbf{w}_i)_{0\le i\le N}$,
- δ_6 observed during the FullRS,
- δ_7 observed during the FullWR,
- δ_8 observed during the End.

Some observations may be done on the unmasked gadgets (GenA, Hash and Enc) but their amount will not matter during the proof. Finally, we have $\sum_{i=1}^{8} \delta_i \le \delta$.

We build the proof from right to left. The gadgets End, FullRS, FullRound and FullWR are N-NIo secure with the output $(\mathbf{z}, \mathbf{c})$ or $\perp$ (resp. $\left(rs^{(j)}\right)_{0\le j<n}$, $\left(u^{(j)}\right)_{0\le j<n}$, $\left(r^{(j)}\right)_{0\le j<n}$). As a consequence, all the observations from their call can be perfectly simulated with at most δ_8 (resp. δ_6, δ_7) shares of $\mathbf{z}$ (resp. $\mathbf{z}$, $\mathbf{w}$). For the upper MultAdd gadget, there are at most $\delta_8 + \delta_6$ observations on the outputs and δ_4 local observations. The total is still lower than δ and thus they can be simulated with at most $\delta_4 + \delta_6 + \delta_8 \le \delta$ shares of $\mathbf{y}$ and $\mathbf{s}$.

Concerning the lower MultAdd gadget, there are at most δ_7 observations on $\mathbf{w}$ and δ_5 made locally. Thus they can be simulated with at most $\delta_5 + \delta_7 \le \delta$ shares of $\mathbf{v}$ and $\mathbf{e}$.

The gadget FullRound is N-NIo so all the observations from its call can be simulated with at most δ_3 shares of $\mathbf{v}$. Thus, there are $\delta_3 + \delta_5 + \delta_7$ observations on the output of gadget $\times\mathbf{a}$. And then, they can be simulated with at most $\delta_3 + \delta_5 + \delta_7 + \delta_2$ shares of $\mathbf{y}$. Summing up all the observations of $\mathbf{y}$ gives $(\delta_3 + \delta_5 + \delta_7 + \delta_2) + (\delta_4 + \delta_6 + \delta_8) \le \delta$. This allows to conclude the proof by applying the N-NIo security of DG. All the observations on the algorithm can be perfectly simulated with at most $\delta_4 + \delta_6 + \delta_8 \le \delta$ shares of $\mathbf{s}$, $\delta_5 + \delta_7 \le \delta$ shares of $\mathbf{e}$ and the knowledge of the public outputs. □

4.2 EUF-CMA Security in the N-probing Model

We recall the EUF-CMA security in the N-probing model. For the complete game description, we refer to [3].

Definition 7. *A signature scheme is EUF-CMA-secure in the N-probing model if any PPT adversary has a negligible probability to forge a signature after a polynomial number of queries to a leaky signature oracle. By leaky signature oracle, we mean that the signature oracle will (1) update the shares of the secret key with a refresh algorithm (2) output a signature together with the leakage of the signature computation.*

Definition 8. *We denote by* (r, rs, u)*-qTESLA a variant of qTESLA where all the values*

$$\left\{\left(r^{(j)}\right)_{0\leq j<n}, \left(rs^{(j)}\right)_{0\leq j<n}, \left(u^{(j)}\right)_{0\leq j<n}\right\}$$

are outputted for each iteration during the signing algorithm.

Theorem 6 allows to reduce the EUF-CMA security in the N-probing model of our masked `qTESLA` signature at order N to the EUF-CMA security of (r, rs, u)-`qTESLA`. The security of (r, rs, u)-`qTESLA` is actually not fully supported by the security proof of `qTESLA` because the adversary is not supposed to see these values for the failed attempts of signing. However, based on the work of [3], we can prove that, under some computational assumptions, outputting $\left(u^{(j)}\right)_{0\leq j<n}$ for each iteration does not affect the security. We redirect the reader to [3] for further discussions on this issue. The values $\left\{\left(r^{(j)}\right)_{0\leq j<n}, \left(rs^{(j)}\right)_{0\leq j<n}\right\}$ correspond to the conditions of rejection, and more precisely, the positions of the coefficients of the polynomials that do not pass the rejections. Such a knowledge do not impact the security of the scheme because the rejection probability does not depend on the position of the coefficients (Table 3).

5 Practical Aspects

Our masking scheme has been implemented inside the reference code of `qTESLA` available on the repository of their project [26]. We performed benchmarks for the two parameters sets `qTESLA-I` and `qTESLA-III` on a desktop computer with and without the random number generator activated (in gadgets). The reason why we decided to switch off the RNG[4] is to show how masking schemes of this magnitude are sensitive to the speed at which the device is capable of retrieving randomness. We also tested the smaller parameter set at order 1 on a Cortex-M4 microcontroller to see how it performs on a device more realistically vulnerable to side-channel attacks. We speculate that the scaling difference between the microcontroller and the computer is due to the fact that architectural differences matter less for the masking code than for the base signature code.

Our tests with the randomness enabled were performed using xoshiro128** [6], a really fast PRNG that has been recently used to speed-up public parameters generation in a lattice-based cryptosystem [7]. One looking for real life application of our technique and believing that masking needs strong randomness would maybe want to use a cryptographically secure PRNG instead. Another option could be to expand a seed with the already available `cSHAKE` function but as we will see in the sequel, it might be pretty expensive as the number of random bytes required grows very fast with the number of shares.

The results for all individual gadgets, both parameters sets as well as number of calls to the random number generator lead to interesting considerations. We

[4] To switch the RNG off, we just set the `rand_uint32()` function to return 0.

refer to the full version of our paper [15] for more details. Our general conclusion of all these tests is that beside our much needed design change, the performances are largely dictated by the randomness generation speed and that the bottleneck gadget is the arithmetic to boolean conversion.

Table 3. Median speed of masked signature in clock cycles over 10000 executions for qTESLA-I on Intel Core i7-6700HQ running at 2.60 GHz

Masking order	Unmasked	Order 1	Order 2	Order 3	Order 4	Order 5
qTESLA-I (RNG off)	645 673	2 394 085	7 000 117	9 219 826	16 577 823	24 375 359
qTESLA-I (RNG on)	671 169	2 504 204	13 878 830	24 582 943	39 967 191	59 551 027
qTESLA-I (RNG on) Scaling	1	×4	×21	×37	×60	×89

Table 4. Median speed of masked signature in clock cycles over 1000 executions for qTESLA-I on cortex-M4 microcontroller

Masking order	Unmasked	Order 1
qTESLA-I CortexM4	11 304 025	23 519 583

As noted in [23], the power of two modulus allows to get a reasonable penalty factor for low masking orders. Without such a modification, the scheme would have been way slower. Besides, our implementation seems to outperform the masked implementation of Dilithium as given in [23]. The timing of our order 1 masking for qTESLA-I is around 1.3 ms, and our order 2 is around 7.1 ms. This result comes with no surprise because the unmasked version of qTESLA already outperformed Dilithium. However, we do not know if our optimizations on the gadgets could lead to a better performance for a masked Dilithium (Table 4).

Acknowledgements. We thank Sonia Belaïd for interesting insights about the masking proofs. We acknowledge the support of the French Programme d'Investissement d'Avenir under national project RISQ P14158. This work is also partially supported by the European Union's H2020 Programme under PROMETHEUS project (grant 780701). This research has been partially funded by ANRT under the programs CIFRE N 2016/1583.

References

1. Alkim, E., et al.: The lattice-based digital signature scheme qTESLA. Cryptology ePrint archive, report 2019/085 (2019). https://eprint.iacr.org/2019/085
2. Bai, S., Galbraith, S.D.: An improved compression technique for signatures based on learning with errors. In: Benaloh, J. (ed.) CT-RSA 2014. LNCS, vol. 8366, pp. 28–47. Springer, Cham (2014). https://doi.org/10.1007/978-3-319-04852-9_2
3. Barthe, G., et al.: Masking the GLP lattice-based signature scheme at any order. In: Nielsen, J.B., Rijmen, V. (eds.) EUROCRYPT 2018. LNCS, vol. 10821, pp. 354–384. Springer, Cham (2018). https://doi.org/10.1007/978-3-319-78375-8_12

4. Barthe, G., et al.: Strong non-interference and type-directed higher-order masking. In: Weippl, E.R., et al. (ed.) ACM CCS 2016, pp. 116–129. ACM Press, October 2016
5. Bindel, N., et al.: qTESLA. Technical report, National Institute of Standards and Technology (2017). https://csrc.nist.gov/projects/post-quantum-cryptography/round-1-submissions
6. Blackman, D., Vigna, S.: Scrambled linear pseudorandom number generators. In: CoRR abs/1805.01407 (2018). arXiv:1805.01407
7. Bos, J.W., et al.: Fly, you fool! Faster Frodo for the ARM Cortex-M4. Cryptology ePrint archive, report 2018/1116 (2018). https://eprint.iacr.org/2018/1116
8. Bruinderink, L.G., Pessl, P.: Differential fault attacks on deterministic lattice signatures. IACR Trans. Cryptograph. Hardw. Embedded Syst. **2018**(3), 21–43 (2018). https://tches.iacr.org/index.php/TCHES/article/view/7267
9. Coron, J.-S.: High-order conversion from boolean to arithmetic masking. Cryptology ePrint archive, report 2017/252 (2017). http://eprint.iacr.org/2017/252
10. Coron, J.-S.: Higher order masking of look-up tables. In: Nguyen, P.Q., Oswald, E. (eds.) EUROCRYPT 2014. LNCS, vol. 8441, pp. 441–458. Springer, Heidelberg (2014). https://doi.org/10.1007/978-3-642-55220-5_25
11. Coron, J.-S., Großschädl, J., Vadnala, P.K.: Secure conversion between boolean and arithmetic masking of any order. In: Batina, L., Robshaw, M. (eds.) CHES 2014. LNCS, vol. 8731, pp. 188–205. Springer, Heidelberg (2014). https://doi.org/10.1007/978-3-662-44709-3_11
12. Coron, J.-S., Großschädl, J., Tibouchi, M., Vadnala, P.K.: Conversion from arithmetic to boolean masking with logarithmic complexity. In: Leander, G. (ed.) FSE 2015. LNCS, vol. 9054, pp. 130–149. Springer, Heidelberg (2015). https://doi.org/10.1007/978-3-662-48116-5_7
13. Duc, A., Dziembowski, S., Faust, S.: Unifying leakage models: from probing attacks to noisy leakage. In: Nguyen, P.Q., Oswald, E. (eds.) EUROCRYPT 2014. LNCS, vol. 8441, pp. 423–440. Springer, Heidelberg (2014). https://doi.org/10.1007/978-3-642-55220-5_24
14. Ducas, L., et al.: CRYSTALS-Dilithium: a lattice-based digital signature scheme. IACR Trans. Ctyptograph. Hardw. Embedded Syst. **2018**(1), 238–268 (2018). https://tches.iacr.org/index.php/TCHES/article/view/839
15. Gérard, F., Rossi, M.: An efficient and provable masked implementation of qTESLA. Cryptology ePrint archive, report 2019/606 (2019). https://eprint.iacr.org/2019/606
16. Goubin, L.: A sound method for switching between boolean and arithmetic masking. In: Koç, Ç.K., Naccache, D., Paar, C. (eds.) CHES 2001. LNCS, vol. 2162, pp. 3–15. Springer, Heidelberg (2001). https://doi.org/10.1007/3-540-44709-1_2
17. Goudarzi, D., et al.: Unifying leakage models on a Rényi Day. Cryptology ePrint archive, report 2019/138 (2019). https://eprint.iacr.org/2019/138
18. Güneysu, T., Lyubashevsky, V., Pöppelmann, T.: Practical lattice-based cryptography: a signature scheme for embedded systems. In: Prouff, E., Schaumont, P. (eds.) CHES 2012. LNCS, vol. 7428, pp. 530–547. Springer, Heidelberg (2012). https://doi.org/10.1007/978-3-642-33027-8_31
19. Ishai, Y., Sahai, A., Wagner, D.: Private circuits: securing hardware against probing attacks. In: Boneh, D. (ed.) CRYPTO 2003. LNCS, vol. 2729, pp. 463–481. Springer, Heidelberg (2003). https://doi.org/10.1007/978-3-540-45146-4_27
20. Kocher, P.C.: Timing attacks on implementations of Diffie-Hellman, RSA, DSS, and other systems. In: Koblitz, N. (ed.) CRYPTO 1996. LNCS, vol. 1109, pp. 104–113. Springer, Heidelberg (1996). https://doi.org/10.1007/3-540-68697-5_9

21. Langlois, A., Stehlé, D.: Hardness of decision (R)LWE for any modulus. Cryptology ePrint archive, report 2012/091 (2012). http://eprint.iacr.org/2012/091
22. Lyubashevsky, V.: Lattice signatures without trapdoors. In: Pointcheval, D., Johansson, T. (eds.) EUROCRYPT 2012. LNCS, vol. 7237, pp. 738–755. Springer, Heidelberg (2012). https://doi.org/10.1007/978-3-642-29011-4_43
23. Migliore, V., et al.: Masking Dilithium: efficient implementation and side-channel evaluation. Cryptology ePrint archive, report 2019/394 (2019). https://eprint.iacr.org/2019/394
24. M'Raïhi, D., Naccache, D., Pointcheval, D., Vaudenay, S.: Computational alternatives to random number generators. In: Tavares, S., Meijer, H. (eds.) SAC 1998. LNCS, vol. 1556, pp. 72–80. Springer, Heidelberg (1999). https://doi.org/10.1007/3-540-48892-8_6
25. Poddebniak, D., et al.: Attacking deterministic signature schemes using fault attacks. Cryptology ePrint archive, report 2017/1014 (2017). http://eprint.iacr.org/2017/1014
26. qTESLA team. https://qtesla.org/

Side-Channel Analysis

Side-Channel Attacks on Blinded Scalar Multiplications Revisited

Thomas Roche[1(✉)], Laurent Imbert[2], and Victor Lomné[1]

[1] NinjaLab, Montpellier, France
thomas@ninjalab.io
[2] LIRMM, CNRS,
University of Montpellier, Montpellier, France
https://ninjalab.io

Abstract. In a series of recent articles (from 2011 to 2017), Schindler *et al.* show that exponent/scalar blinding is not as effective a countermeasure as expected against side-channel attacks targeting RSA modular exponentiation and ECC scalar multiplication. Precisely, these works demonstrate that if an attacker is able to retrieve many randomizations of the same secret, this secret can be fully recovered even when a significative proportion of the blinded secret bits are erroneous. With a focus on ECC, this paper improves the best results of Schindler *et al.* in the specific case of structured-order elliptic curves. Our results show that larger blinding material and higher error rates can be successfully handled by an attacker in practice. This study also opens new directions in this line of work by the proposal of a three-steps attack process that isolates the attack critical path (in terms of complexity and success rate) and hence eases the development of future solutions.

1 Introduction

Nowadays, all modern tamper-resistant implementations of public-key algorithms embed relatively cheap, yet very strong countermeasures based on various randomization strategies. As a consequence, single-trace horizontal attacks have gained more and more attention from the side-channel community.

Single trace horizontal attacks apply to both elliptic curve scalar multiplication and modular exponentiation (RSA). Implemented in a supervised or non-supervised setup, they provide the attacker with a randomized, or blinded scalar (resp. exponent) from the observation of a single scalar multiplication or exponentiation. Although these attacks do not yield the original scalar (resp. exponent), the disclosure of a blinded value may allow an attacker to counterfeit digital signatures or impersonate any party in a key exchange protocol.

This ultimate attack thus renders scalar (resp. exponent) randomization useless. However, it requires a very high signal-to-noise ratio to be successful in practice. Many recent publications claim successful single trace horizontal attacks on secure RSA or ECC [2,7–11,16,18]. These attacks do not usually recover

S. Belaïd and T. Güneysu (Eds.): CARDIS 2019, LNCS 11833, pp. 95–108, 2020.
https://doi.org/10.1007/978-3-030-42068-0_6

the whole blinded value. The missing bits are eventually recovered using brute-force. Therefore, the number of incorrect bits must remain relatively small for the attack to be successful. In single-trace horizontal attacks, this number of incorrect bits is dictated by the so-called bit error rate of the attack.

In this work, we consider the case where brute-forcing the incorrect bits is impracticable. We focus on ECC scalar multiplication on so-called structured-order elliptic curves (very common in Elliptic Curves Cryptography). We assume that the attacker can observe several scalar multiplications with the same long-term secret scalar but each execution uses fresh randoms for scalar blinding. A typical example of such a context occurs in the public key generation of ECC cryptosystems. The attacker requests from a device many generations of the public key corresponding to the private key securely stored inside the device. We will also assume that the scalar randomization is done following [4] by adding to the secret scalar a random multiple of the elliptic curve order.

The first paper in the literature to tackle this problem is the seminal work of Schindler and Itoh [12] which exhibits a very efficient attack (in terms of number of traces and computational effort) when small blinding factors r are used. Over the past five years, this result was improved [13], applied to specific elliptic curves [5,14] and to RSA with CRT [15]. In the present paper, we expand this line of results by suggesting several improvements that make it possible to recover scalars blinded with large random factors (>32 bits), and high bit error rates (>10%).

1.1 Preliminaries and Notations

In the following, we consider an elliptic curve defined over the finite field $\mathbb{F}_p$, with p a K-bit prime (typically $K = 256$). E denotes the order of the curve and d is the secret scalar, target of the attack. Both E and d can be represented on K bits. The term msb (resp. lsb) will be used to shorten *most* (resp. *least*) *significant bits.*

For each scalar multiplication, the scalar d is blinded by adding a random multiple of the group order, i.e. $d_\ell = d + r_\ell \times E$, where r_ℓ is an R-bit random value. The blinded scalar d_ℓ is then represented on $K + R$ bits.

The attaker observes N scalar multiplications. These N side-channel observations, called *traces*, are denoted $\{T_\ell\}_{\ell<N}$[1].

For each trace T_ℓ, the attacker's horizontal side-channel attack outputs a *noisy* blinded scalar, denoted $\tilde{d_\ell}$. For all bit index $i < K + R$, it is assumed that the probability ϵ_b for bit $\tilde{d_\ell}[i]$ to be erroneous, called *bit error rate*, is independent of both ℓ and i. Depending on the context (supervised or non-supervised horizontal attacks) ϵ_b is considered known or unknown to the attacker.

[1] A more formal notation would be $\{T_\ell\}_{\ell\in\mathbb{Z};0\leqslant\ell<N}$.

1.2 Overall Attack Process

Our attack context is the gathering of three independent steps. Our contributions are solely related to the second step and, for completeness, we briefly describe the whole attack process below.

Step 1: The attacker acquires N traces corresponding to N independent scalar multiplications and performs a horizontal attack for each of them. The output of this first step is a set of noisy blinded scalars $\{\tilde{d}_\ell\}_{\ell<N}$ together with a bit error rate ϵ_b. In the supervised setting[2] (see *e.g.* [1,2,18]) the attacker possesses a good estimation of the bit error rate ϵ_b. Given ϵ_b the attacker knows beforehand the number of acquisitions N that must be performed to have good chance of success. In the more general unsupervised setting (see *e.g.* [7–11,16]), the access to a training device is not possible. The attacker acquires as many traces as possible and induces a maximal value for ϵ_b that can be handled through the attack. In both cases, this first step provides the attacker with N noisy blinded scalars together with a gross value for ϵ_b.

Step 2: From each noisy blinded scalar $\tilde{d}_\ell$, the attacker guesses the blinding factor r_ℓ or discards the corresponding data from the attack process. The output of this filtering step is a subset $\{\tilde{d}_\ell\}_{\ell\in J}$ along with guessed blinding factors $\{r_\ell\}_{\ell\in J}$ for some $J \subset (\mathbb{Z} \cap [0, N-1])$. All r_ℓ do not have to be correct but some of them must be correctly guessed.

Step 3: The last step of the attack recovers the secret scalar d from $\{\tilde{d}_\ell\}_{\ell\in J}$ and $\{r_\ell\}_{\ell\in J}$. A powerfull *vertical* side-channel attack can be mounted on the remaining traces. Such an attack is described in [5].

1.3 Paper Organization and Contributions

This work focuses on improvements in *Step 2* in the specific case of elliptic curves whose order is close to a power of 2. Section 2 describes the previous works, namely the best known attack in this setting [14]. Our strategy and results are presented in Sect. 3. Our simulations show significant increases in the success rates for blinding factors up to $R = K/2$ compared to [14].

2 Previous Works

In [14], Schindler and Wiemers study elliptic curves with order of the form $E = 2^K \pm E_0$, where E_0 is close to $2^{K/2}$. This case is pretty common in cryptography when the base field is defined using a pseudo-Mersenne prime for efficiency reasons. Most of the EC standards are of this form, *e.g.* SEC2 curves [17], NIST curves [6].

---

[2] A learning phase is conducted prior to the attack on a similar device where scalar multiplication inputs and randoms can be chosen, *e.g.* a template building or a deep-learning training phase.

2.1 A Divide and Conquer Algorithm

Schindler and Wiemers observe that the problem of solving the N noisy blinded scalars can be done using a divide and conquer algorithm. This observation leads to a much more robust decoding algorithm than in the general case. Indeed, a blinded scalar d_ℓ with blinding factor r_ℓ can be written as follows:

$$\begin{aligned} d_\ell &= r_\ell \times E + d \\ &= r_\ell \times (2^K \pm E_0) + d \\ &= r_\ell \times 2^K + (d \pm r_\ell \times E_0) \end{aligned}$$

Hence, if $d \pm r_\ell \times E_0$ is smaller than 2^K, then the R msb of d_ℓ are exactly the R bits of r_ℓ. As a side remark, if $r_\ell \times E_0$ is smaller than d, then the most significant bits of d are not correctly masked (see *e.g.* [3]).

Now, for a given window size w, if $(d \pm r_\ell \times E_0) < 2^K$, then $d_\ell \bmod 2^w$ and $\lfloor d_\ell / 2^K \rfloor \bmod 2^w$ only involve the known w lsb of E and the unknown w lsb of d and r_ℓ. From this observation, Schindler and Wiemers (see [14]) propose an efficient algorithm to recover the secret d that comprises two phases:

- *Phase 1:* find the R lsb of d as well as the most likely values of the blinding factor r_ℓ for each noisy blinded scalar $\tilde{d}_\ell$.
- *Phase 2:* select the values r_ℓ that are the most likely to be correct and recover the full secret scalar d.

Phase 2 corresponds to step 3 of our overall attack scheme described in Sect. 1.2 and, as observed by the authors of [14], is not the critical path of the attack. In other words, if Phase 1 is successful (*i.e.* the R lsb of d are correctly found) then Phase 2 will results in recovering the full value of d with high probability.

2.2 Schindler and Wiemers' Phase 1 Algorithm

It is described in [14, Algorithm 4] along with several empirical improvments discussed in the next sections. The algorithm processes iteratively over a small sliding window of size w (typically w is 8 or 10). Each iteration consists of two main steps recalled in Algorithms 1 and 2 respectively.

In Algorithm 1, the call to EvaluateProbability($\hat{r}_\ell, \hat{d}_\ell, \tilde{d}_\ell, i, w, \epsilon_b$) computes the probability of observing $\tilde{d}_\ell$ knowing the error rate ϵ_b and the two w-bit words $\hat{r}_\ell$ and $\hat{d}_\ell$ which correspond respectively to the two w-bit words $\lfloor \tilde{d}_\ell / 2^{K+i-1} \rfloor \bmod 2^w$ and $\lfloor \tilde{d}_\ell / 2^{i-1} \rfloor \bmod 2^w$. Hence, we have:

$$\text{EvaluateProbability}(\hat{r}_\ell, \hat{d}_\ell, \tilde{d}_\ell, i, w, \epsilon_b) = \epsilon_b^h (1 - \epsilon_b)^{2w-h},$$

where

$$\begin{aligned} h = \texttt{HammingDistance}(\hat{r}_\ell, \left\lfloor \tilde{d}_\ell / 2^{K+i-1} \right\rfloor \bmod 2^w) + \\ \texttt{HammingDistance}(\hat{d}_\ell, \left\lfloor \tilde{d}_\ell / 2^{i-1} \right\rfloor \bmod 2^w) \end{aligned}$$

Parameter : Iteration i
Parameter : Window size w, bit error rate ϵ_b
Input : $\{\tilde{d}_\ell\}_{\ell<N}$: N noisy scalars
Input : $\{\tilde{r}_\ell\}_{\ell<N}$: $i-1$ lsb of the recovered blinding factors
Input : $d \bmod 2^{i-1}$: $i-1$ lsb of the recovered scalar
Output : d^*: best guess for $d \bmod 2^{w+i-1}$

$P \leftarrow$ float 1D array of size 2^w initialized with zeros;
// For each possible value of the next w bits of the secret scalar;
for $\hat{d} \leftarrow 0$ **to** $2^w - 1$ **do**
  // Prediction of the $w+i-1$ lsb of the scalar knowing the first $i-1$ bits;
  $\bar{d} \leftarrow \hat{d} \times 2^{i-1} + d \bmod 2^{i-1}$;
  // For each noisy blinded scalar;
  for $\ell \leftarrow 0$ **to** $N-1$ **do**
    // For each possible value of the next w bits of the random r_ℓ;
    for $\hat{r}_\ell \leftarrow 0$ **to** $2^w - 1$ **do**
      $\bar{r}_\ell \leftarrow \hat{r}_\ell \times 2^{i-1} + \tilde{r}_\ell$;
      // Predict $w+i-1$ lsb of d_ℓ;
      $\bar{d}_\ell \leftarrow (\bar{r}_\ell \times E + \bar{d}) \bmod 2^{w+i-1}$;
      // Define $\hat{d}_\ell$, the w msb of $\bar{d}_\ell$;
      $\hat{d}_\ell \leftarrow \lfloor \bar{d}_\ell / 2^{i-1} \rfloor$;
      // Compute the probability of observing $\tilde{d}_\ell$, knowing $\hat{d}$ blinded by $\hat{r}_\ell$;
      $p \leftarrow$ EvaluateProbability$(\hat{r}_\ell, \hat{d}_\ell, \tilde{d}_\ell, i, w, \epsilon_b)$;
      $P[\hat{d}] \leftarrow P[\hat{d}] + p$;

$d^* \leftarrow \text{argmax}(P) \times 2^{i-1} + (d \bmod 2^{i-1})$;
Return : d^*

Algorithm 1. Phase 1, Step 1 of [14, Algorithm 4]

After R iterations of Algorithms 1 and 2 the output is $d \bmod 2^R$ if everything went correctly. As stated above, this is the most critical phase in Schindler and Wiemers's algorithm. They propose two empirical approaches to improve both its efficiency and effectiveness. We will briefly present them in the next section. However, since these improvements are based on hand-picked thresholds by the authors of [14] without clear explanations on how to choose these limits (we are assuming that these thresholds must be adjusted in a case-by-case manner) we will not take them into account in our study. Nevertheless, since the improvements presented here can be applied on the core algorithms, the empirical improvements can always be added above them. We then focus on the low level algorithms and leave for future work the addition and study of these extra improvments.

2.3 Empirical Improvements

The first improvement is added to Algorithm 2 to increase the effectivness of the attack. Concretely, the authors add an estimation of the correctness of $\bar{r}_\ell$. When this estimation of correctness goes below a certain threshold, the corresponding noisy blinded scalar $\tilde{d}_\ell$ is removed from the process. The question of how to choose the threshold is not discussed in [14] but several values are proposed depending on the bit error rate ϵ_b and the iteration number i.

The second improvement is dedicated to efficiency. The algorithm cost is dominated by Step 1 (Algorithm 1), its complexity being $O(2^{2w}N)$. The authors

Parameter : Iteration i
Parameter : Window size w, bit error rate ϵ_b
Input : $\{\tilde{d}_\ell\}_{\ell<N}$: N noisy scalars
Input : $\{\tilde{r}_\ell\}_{\ell<N}$: $i-1$ lsb of the recovered blinding factors
Input : d^*: $w+i-1$ lsb of the recovered scalar from Step 1
Output : $d \bmod 2^i$
Output : $\{\tilde{r}_\ell\}_{\ell<N}$: i lsb of the recovered blinding factors

// For each noisy blinded scalar;
for $\ell \leftarrow 0$ **to** $N-1$ **do**
  $P \leftarrow$ float 1D array of size 2 initialized with zeros;
  // For each possible value of the next w bits of the random r_ℓ;
  for $\hat{r}_\ell \leftarrow 0$ **to** 2^w **do**
    $\bar{r}_\ell \leftarrow \hat{r}_\ell \times 2^{i-1} + \tilde{r}_\ell$;
    // Predict $w+i-1$ lsb of d_ℓ;
    $\bar{d}_\ell \leftarrow (\bar{r}_\ell \times E + d^*) \bmod 2^{w+i-1}$;
    // Define $\hat{d}_\ell$, the w msb of $\bar{d}_\ell$;
    $\hat{d}_\ell \leftarrow \lfloor \bar{d}_\ell / 2^{i-1} \rfloor$;
    // Compute the probability of observing $\tilde{d}_\ell$, knowing d^* blinded by $\hat{r}_\ell$;
    $p \leftarrow$ EvaluateProbability$(\hat{r}_\ell, \hat{d}_\ell, \tilde{d}_\ell, i, w, \epsilon_b)$;
    $P[\hat{r}_\ell \bmod 2] \leftarrow P[\hat{r}_\ell \bmod 2] + p$;
  $\tilde{r}_\ell \leftarrow \text{argmax}(P) \times 2^{i-1} + \tilde{r}_\ell$;
$d^* \leftarrow d^* \bmod 2^i$;
Return : $d^*, \{\tilde{r}_\ell\}_{\ell<N}$

Algorithm 2. Phase 1, Step 2 of [14, Algorithm 4]

propose to reduce the number of treated noisy blinded scalars in this step and apply the second step to all noisy blinded scalars. The idea is that, if costly, Step 1 is more robust than Step 2 and therefore does not need all the N noisy blinded scalars to correctly guess $d \bmod 2^{w+i-1}$. The authors propose, again without justification, hand-picked numbers of noisy blinded scalars to be used in Step 1 for various bit error rates ϵ_b and iteration numbers i.

The above improvements were not tested in this paper. However, one can easily see that they can be applied pretty much similarly to our algorithms with adjusted thresholds.

2.4 Some Results

It is shown in [14] that Algorithms 1 and 2 allow to correct noisy blinded scalars with large values of R, typically $\geqslant 64$ and large error rates $0.1 \leqslant \epsilon_b \leqslant 0.15$. This result is very important since before [14], a value of $R = 64$ was considered perfectly safe from a side-channel point of view.

One crucial parameter of these algorithms is the choice of the window size w since the robustness of the procedure increases with w. However, since the algorithm complexity is dominated by $O(2^{2w}N)$, w cannot be very large either. Figure 1 provides simulation results of Algorithms 1 and 2 effectivness for various values of w. It gives the average number of bits of d guessed correctly before a wrong bit appears, as a function of the number of traces N. These simulations were done with $K = 256$, $R = 64$ and $\epsilon_b = 0.15$ for curve `secp-256-k1` [17] (aka the Bitcoin's curve).

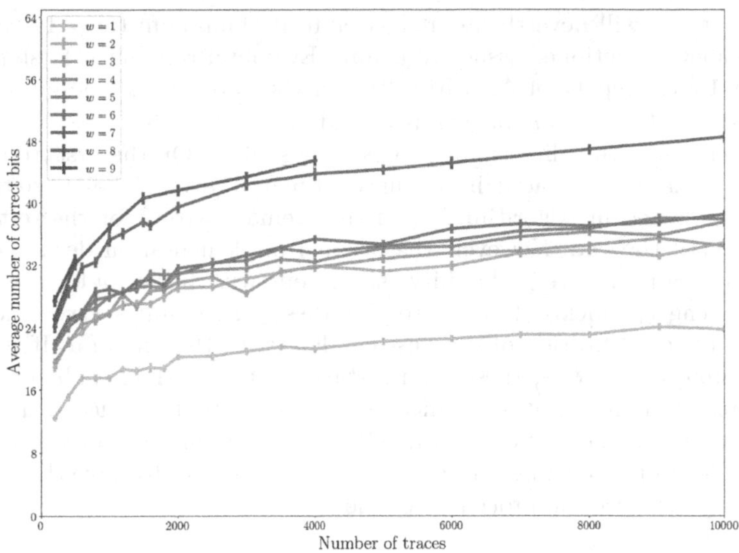

Fig. 1. Simulations for $K = 256, R = 64, \epsilon_b = 0.15$ on curve `secp-256-k1`.

In Fig. 1, we represent mean values over 50 executions of the algorithms. Standard deviations to the average results are illustrated by error bars. These simulations are extremely time consuming as w increases. This is why some results are missing for $w > 7$. This is probably why the simulation results in [14] are scattered over a few parameters. We believe that Fig. 1 provides a complementary point of view on the efficiency of the correction algorithm of [14][3]. Notably, it is interesting to remark that the impact of the window size is not regular and that window sizes ranging from 3 to 6 produce similar success rates.

We will see in next Section how the algorithms can be improved in both efficiency and effectivness.

3 Improved Algorithms

3.1 First Observations

As remarked earlier (and in [14]) w cannot be too small for the algorithm to work. The reason is that the probability estimation (from the call to EvaluateProbability() in Algorithm 1) improves as w increases. As a matter of fact, the EvaluateProbability() procedure estimates the probability of observing the noisy blinded scalar $\tilde{d}_\ell$ knowing two w-bit word predictions on two separate w-bit sections of $\tilde{d}_\ell$. Therefore, if w is too small this estimation is not good enough to distinguish good predictions from wrong ones (Fig. 1 illustrates this behaviour).

[3] Without the empirical improvements discussed in Sect. 2.3.

Our proposal will nevertheless reduce w to its minimum ($w = 1$) and cope with the above mentioned issue by calling EvaluateProbability() (step 12 of Algorithm 1 and step 12 of Algorithm 2) over the two $(w + i - 1)$-bit words $\bar{r}_\ell$ and $\bar{d}_\ell$ instead of the two w-bit words $\hat{r}_\ell$ and $\hat{d}_\ell$.

However, doing this directly has a desastrous effect. On the first iteration of Algorithm 1, many $\tilde{r}_\ell$ are actually wrongly estimated (even if they were the best candidates selected in Algorithm 2) and they remain wrong for the rest of the execution until the end. However, the original implementation deals naturally with them because future probability estimations with future w-bit predictions on these wrong $\tilde{r}_\ell$ quickly decrease to give these wrong starts lower and lower weights in the computation of the best candidate for the bits of d. If we apply our first proposal directly, these wrong starts will keep their high probability estimations for more iterations (since we now involve their successful past in the computation). These wrong starts will then create more chance to choose a wrong candidate for the guessed bit of d. We propose here to solve this problem by loosening the selection procedure of the $\tilde{r}_\ell$.

3.2 Keeping a List of the Blinding Factors Best Candidates

In a nutshell, the idea is to modify Algorithms 1 and 2 such that instead of working on a single value $\bar{r}_\ell$ (for each $\ell < N$) which is updated bit-by-bit at each iteration (step 14 of Algorithm 2), the algorithms will keep a pool of good estimates for $\tilde{r}_\ell$. Intuitively, if the list of potential candidates is large enough, it will contain the correct value of $\bar{r}_\ell$ for the current iteration. We will see that small list sizes are enough to match and exceed the original algorithm effectiveness.

3.3 Algorithms Improvements in Detail

Algorithms 3 and 4 describe in detail the full improvements. Concretely, the modifications compared to Algorithms 1 and 2 are threefold:

- the window size w is forced to its minimum ($w = 1$) and then does not appear in the algorithm anymore.
- the list of recovered blinding factors at iteration i, *i.e.* $\{\tilde{r}_\ell\}_{\ell<N}$ where the $\tilde{r}_\ell$ are defined over $i - 1$ bits, is replaced by a 2D array (denoted Lr[4]) of $N \times L$ best candidates for each $\tilde{r}_\ell$. This array is updated at each iteration of Algorithm 4. Note that during the first iterations ($i \leqslant log_2(L)$), all possible candidates are kept until the list is full.
- the probability estimation is done over t msb of $\bar{r}_\ell$ and $\bar{d}_\ell$ instead of the w msb in Algorithm 1. Note that if $t \geqslant R$, then all the bits of $\bar{r}_\ell$ and $\bar{d}_\ell$ are considered in the probability estimation at each iteration.

[4] The array Lr must be initialized to an integer array of dimension $N \times L$ with all cells initialized to -1 but the first column ($Lr[i][0]$ for all $i < N$) which must be initialized to 0.

Together, the last two changes aim at decreasing the value of w to its minimum and therefore reduce the algorithm complexity without damaging too much the algorithm success rate. The overall complexity of steps 1 and 2 becomes then $O(N \times L)$. (More precisely, Step 1 runs $4 \times N \times L$ loop iterations.)

Parameter : Iteration i
Parameter : Bit error rate ϵ_b
Parameter : Max list size L for the candidate lists of $\tilde{r}_\ell$
Parameter : Window size t: this size defines the number of msb to select for probability estimations
Input : $\{\tilde{d}_\ell\}_{\ell<N}$: N noisy scalars
Input : Lr array of dimension $N \times L$ containing, for each $\ell < N$, the L best candidates $\tilde{r}_\ell$
Input : $d \bmod 2^{i-1}$: $i-1$ lsb of the recovered scalar
Output : $d \bmod 2^i$

$P \leftarrow$ float 1D array of size 2 initialized with zeros;
`// For each possible value of the next bit of the secret scalar;`
for $\hat{d} \leftarrow 0$ **to** 1 **do**
  `// Prediction of the` i `lsb of the scalar knowing the first` $i-1$ `bits;`
  $\bar{d} \leftarrow \hat{d} \times 2^{i-1} + d \bmod 2^{i-1}$;
  `// For each noisy blinded scalar;`
  for $\ell \leftarrow 0$ **to** $N-1$ **do**
    `// For each possible value of the next bit of the random` r_ℓ`;`
    for $\hat{r}_\ell \leftarrow 0$ **to** 1 **do**
      `// For each` $\tilde{r}_\ell$ `in the list` $Lr[l]$`;`
      for $s \leftarrow 0$ **to** $L-1$ **do**
        $\tilde{r}_\ell \leftarrow Lr[l][s]$;
        if $\tilde{r}_\ell == -1$ **then**
          `// go to next` $\hat{r}_\ell$ `value;`
          Break;
        $\bar{r}_\ell \leftarrow \hat{r}_\ell \times 2^{i-1} + \tilde{r}_\ell$;
        `// Predict` $w+i-1$ `lsb of` d_ℓ`;`
        $\bar{d}_\ell \leftarrow (\bar{r}_\ell \times E + \bar{d}) \bmod 2^i$;
        `// Define` d_ℓ^t`, the` t `msb of` $\bar{d}_\ell$`;`
        $d_\ell^t \leftarrow \left\lfloor \bar{d}_\ell / 2^{max(0,i-t)} \right\rfloor$;
        `// Define` r_ℓ^t`, the` t `msb of` $\bar{r}_\ell$`;`
        $r_\ell^t \leftarrow \left\lfloor \bar{r}_\ell / 2^{max(0,i-t)} \right\rfloor$;
        `// Compute the probability of observing` $\tilde{d}_\ell$`, knowing` $\hat{d}$ `blinded by` r_ℓ^t`;`
        $p \leftarrow$ EvaluateProbability$(r_\ell^t, d_\ell^t, \tilde{d}_\ell, max(0, i-t), min(t, i), \epsilon_b)$;
        $P[\hat{d}] \leftarrow P[\hat{d}] + p$;
$d^* \leftarrow \text{argmax}(P) \times 2^{i-1} + d \bmod 2^{i-1}$;
Return : d^*

Algorithm 3. Improved Algorithm Step 1

3.4 Simulation Results and Comparisons

We conducted simulations in order to evaluate and compare the new algorithms to the original proposition of [14]. As in Fig. 1, the results give the average (over 50 tentatives) number of bits of d guessed correctly before a wrong bit appears, as a function of the number of traces N used for the attack. This number of

Parameter : Iteration i
Parameter : Bit error rate ϵ_b
Parameter : Max list size L for the candidate lists of $\tilde{r}_\ell$
Input : Lr array of dimension $N \times L$ containing, for each $\ell < N$, the L best candidates $\tilde{r}_\ell$ on $i-1$ bits
Input : d^*: i lsb of the recovered scalar from Step 1
Output : Updated Lr array with best candidates $\tilde{r}_\ell$ on i bits

// For each noisy blinded scalar;
for $\ell \leftarrow 0$ **to** $N-1$ **do**
  $lr \leftarrow$ number of loaded elements in $Lr[l]$ $(lr \leqslant L)$;
  // Create temporary list Lr_ℓ of size $2lr$;
  $Lr_\ell \leftarrow$ integer 1D array of size $2lr$;
  $P \leftarrow$ float 1D array of size $2lr$ initialized with zeros;
  // For each $\tilde{r}_\ell$ in the list $Lr[l]$;
  for $s \leftarrow 0$ **to** $lr-1$ **do**
    $\tilde{r}_\ell \leftarrow Lr[l][s]$;
    // Add the two possible values of the next bit of the blinding factor r_ℓ to the temporary list;
    $Lr_\ell[s] \leftarrow \tilde{r}_\ell$;
    $Lr_\ell[s+lr] \leftarrow 2^{i-1} + \tilde{r}_\ell$;
  if $2lr \leqslant L$ **then**
    // If Lr_ℓ is small enough, keep all $\tilde{r}_\ell$ candidates;
    $Lr[l][0 \cdots 2lr-1] \leftarrow Lr_\ell$;
  else
    // For each $\bar{r}_\ell$ in the list Lr_ℓ;
    for $s \leftarrow 0$ **to** $2lr-1$ **do**
      $\bar{r}_\ell \leftarrow Lr_\ell[s]$;
      // Predict i lsb of d_ℓ;
      $\bar{d}_\ell \leftarrow (\bar{r}_\ell \times E + d^*) \bmod 2^i$;
      // Compute the probability of observing $\tilde{d}_\ell$, knowing d^* blinded by $\bar{r}_\ell$;
      $p \leftarrow \text{EvaluateProbability}(\bar{r}_\ell, \bar{d}_\ell, \tilde{d}_\ell, 0, i, \epsilon_b)$;
      $P[s] \leftarrow p$;
    $Lr[l] \leftarrow$ best L candidates in Lr_ℓ from their probability estimations P;

Return : Lr

Algorithm 4. Improved Algorithm Step 2

correct bits are majored by R since the algorithms studied here stop when the R lsb of d are found. Apart from R and K, various parameters have an impact on the efficiency and the effectivness of the algorithms, notably:

- L: the maximum size of the best candidate pool for the blinding factors $\tilde{r}_\ell$ for each noisy blinded scalar. We recall here that the complexity of Algorithms 3 and 4 increase linearly with L;
- w: the window size, only the original algorithms are affected by w, the complexity of Algorithms 1 and 2 increase exponentially with w;
- t: the number of bits involved in the probability estimation of $\bar{r}_\ell$ and $\bar{d}_\ell$ with respect to $\tilde{d}_\ell$.

Our first simulations are conducted to find the best empirical value for t. Once t is chosen, we will focus on the parameter L and its impact on the effectiveness (compared to the original algorithm when w changes).

Recall that t has no impact on the computational cost of the algorithms, so it can be chosen freely. Figure 2 displays simulation results for the new algorithm with the parameter t taking its values in $\{6, 8, 10, 16, 24, R\}$[5] and small values for L. It appears that $t = 16$ provides better results than greater or smaller values of t in our setup ($K = 256, R = 64$).

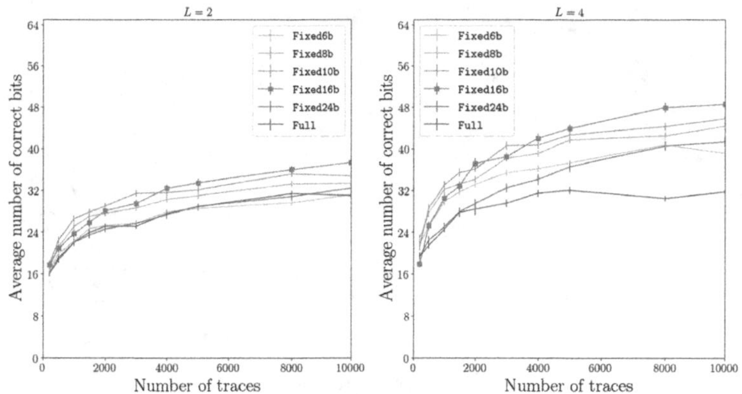

Fig. 2. Simulation results $K = 256, R = 64, \epsilon_b = 0.15$.

Figure 3 compares the original algorithm for various values of w to the new algorithm (with $t = 16$) for various values of L. From these results, we have equivalent effectivness between the original algorithm with $w = 7$ and the new algorithm with $L = 4$. However, the new algorithm is 2^{10} times more efficient than the original algorithm for these parameters. The gap of efficiency seems to increase with w and L since, for another pair of results ($w = 8$ for the original algorithm and $L = 8$ for the new algorithm) the multiplicative factor between both algorithm complexity is doubled (2^{11}) whereas the new algorithm clearly outperforms the original one. Finally, let us also remark that the new algorithm with $L > 16$ reaches the limit of 64-bit correctly recovered on average (*i.e.* a 100% success rate since 64 is the maximum number of recovered bits) in less than 10000 traces. We recall that these algorithms must reach the end with correct 64-bit lsb of d (since in our simulation we choose $R = 64$) for the overall attack to be successful.

Finally, Fig. 4 provides simulation results for $R = 64, 96, 120$ for the new algorithm ($t = 16, L = 32$) and two different bit-error-rate ($\epsilon_b = 0.15$ and $\epsilon_b = 0.13$). These results show, in accordance with original results from [14], that when elliptic curves with structured-order are used, R must be chosen strictly larger $K/2$ in practice for an effective side-channel countermeasure.

[5] For $t = R$, at iteration i, all bits of $\bar{r}_\ell$ and $\bar{d}_\ell$ are considered for probability estimation, this version is labeled "`Full`".

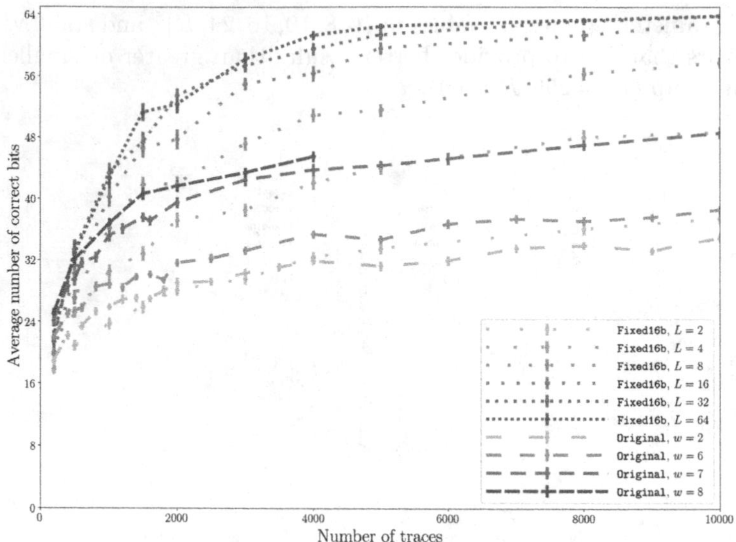

Fig. 3. Simulation results $K = 256, R = 64, \epsilon_b = 0.15$.

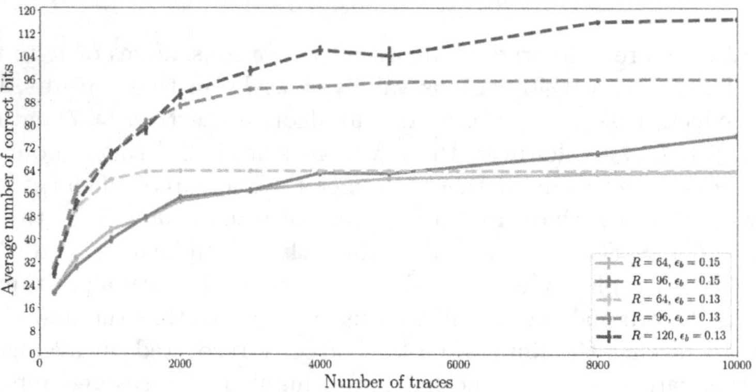

Fig. 4. Simulation $K = 256, L = 32, t = 16$.

4 Conclusion and Future Work

In this paper we exhibited algorithms to recover a secret scalar from many *noisy* blinded scalars (*e.g.* outputs of horizontal side-channel attacks over blinded scalar multiplications) when blinding factors are large and bit error rate is larger than 10%. Our propositions, in the specific case of structured-order elliptic curves, outperform the best known algorithms for these parameters.

Apart from a series of articles from Schindler *et al.* works on this topic are rather scarse in the literature. This is however a very important aspect of practical side-channel analysis over public-key cryptography and we believe there are still room for improvements. Another interesting avenue for future work is to formulate theoretic bounds on the attacker capability to recover the secret scalar given a set of *noisy* blinded scalars.

Acknowledgments. The authors would like to thank Cyril Bouvier and Bruno Grenet from the ECO group at LIRMM (https://www.lirmm.fr/eco/) for their fruitful suggestions and assistance with the cluster MESO@LR (https://meso-lr.umontpellier.fr/).

References

1. Bauer, A., Jaulmes, E., Prouff, E., Wild, J.: Horizontal and vertical side-channel attacks against secure RSA implementations. In: Dawson, E. (ed.) CT-RSA 2013. LNCS, vol. 7779, pp. 1–17. Springer, Heidelberg (2013). https://doi.org/10.1007/978-3-642-36095-4_1
2. Carbone, M., et al.: Deep learning to evaluate secure RSA implementations. IACR Trans. Cryptograph. Hardw. Embed. Syst. **2019**(2), 132–161 (2019). https://doi.org/10.13154/tches.v2019.i2.132-161
3. Ciet, M., Joye, M.: (Virtually) free randomization techniques for elliptic curve cryptography. In: Qing, S., Gollmann, D., Zhou, J. (eds.) ICICS 2003. LNCS, vol. 2836, pp. 348–359. Springer, Heidelberg (2003). https://doi.org/10.1007/978-3-540-39927-8_32
4. Coron, J.-S.: Resistance against differential power analysis for elliptic curve cryptosystems. In: Kocc, cC.K., Paar, C. (eds.) CHES 1999. LNCS, vol. 1717, pp. 292–302. Springer, Heidelberg (1999). https://doi.org/10.1007/3-540-48059-5_25
5. Feix, B., Roussellet, M., Venelli, A.: Side-channel analysis on blinded regular scalar multiplications. In: Meier, W., Mukhopadhyay, D. (eds.) INDOCRYPT 2014. LNCS, vol. 8885, pp. 3–20. Springer, Cham (2014). https://doi.org/10.1007/978-3-319-13039-2_1
6. FIPS PUB 186–3: Digital Signature Standard. National Institute of Standards and Technology, March 2006. Draft
7. Heyszl, J., Ibing, A., Mangard, S., De Santis, F., Sigl, G.: Clustering algorithms for non-profiled single-execution attacks on exponentiations. In: Francillon, A., Rohatgi, P. (eds.) CARDIS 2013. LNCS, vol. 8419, pp. 79–93. Springer, Cham (2014). https://doi.org/10.1007/978-3-319-08302-5_6
8. Järvinen, K., Balasch, J.: Single-trace side-channel attacks on scalar multiplications with precomputations. In: Lemke-Rust, K., Tunstall, M. (eds.) CARDIS 2016. LNCS, vol. 10146, pp. 137–155. Springer, Cham (2017). https://doi.org/10.1007/978-3-319-54669-8_9
9. Nascimento, E., Chmielewski, Ł.: Applying horizontal clustering side-channel attacks on embedded ECC implementations. In: Eisenbarth, T., Teglia, Y. (eds.) CARDIS 2017. LNCS, vol. 10728, pp. 213–231. Springer, Cham (2018). https://doi.org/10.1007/978-3-319-75208-2_13
10. Nascimento, E., Chmielewski, Ł., Oswald, D., Schwabe, P.: Attacking embedded ECC implementations through cmov side channels. In: Avanzi, R., Heys, H. (eds.) SAC 2016. LNCS, vol. 10532, pp. 99–119. Springer, Cham (2017). https://doi.org/10.1007/978-3-319-69453-5_6

11. Perin, G., Imbert, L., Torres, L., Maurine, P.: Attacking randomized exponentiations using unsupervised learning. In: Prouff, E. (ed.) COSADE 2014. LNCS, vol. 8622, pp. 144–160. Springer, Cham (2014). https://doi.org/10.1007/978-3-319-10175-0_11
12. Schindler, W., Itoh, K.: Exponent blinding does not always lift (partial) spa resistance to higher-level security. In: Lopez, J., Tsudik, G. (eds.) ACNS 2011. LNCS, vol. 6715, pp. 73–90. Springer, Heidelberg (2011). https://doi.org/10.1007/978-3-642-21554-4_5
13. Schindler, W., Wiemers, A.: Power attacks in the presence of exponent blinding. J. Cryptograph. Eng. **4**(4), 213–236 (2014). https://doi.org/10.1007/s13389-014-0081-y
14. Schindler, W., Wiemers, A.: Efficient Side-Channel Attacks on Scalar Blinding on Elliptic Curves with Special Structure. In: NIST Workshop on ECC Standards (2015)
15. Schindler, W., Wiemers, A.: Generic power attacks on RSA with CRT and exponent blinding: new results. J. Cryptograph. Eng. **7**(4), 255–272 (2017). https://doi.org/10.1007/s13389-016-0146-1
16. Specht, R., Heyszl, J., Kleinsteuber, M., Sigl, G.: Improving Non-profiled attacks on exponentiations based on clustering and extracting leakage from multi-channel high-resolution EM measurements. In: Mangard, S., Poschmann, A.Y. (eds.) COSADE 2014. LNCS, vol. 9064, pp. 3–19. Springer, Cham (2015). https://doi.org/10.1007/978-3-319-21476-4_1
17. Standards for Efficient Cryptography Group (SECG): SEC 2: recommended elliptic curve domain parameters. Certicom Research (2000). http://www.secg.org/collateral/sec2_final.pdf
18. Weissbart, L., Picek, S., Batina, L.: One trace is all it takes: machine learning-based side-channel attack on EdDSA. Cryptology ePrint archive, report 2019/358 (2019). https://eprint.iacr.org/2019/358

Remote Side-Channel Attacks on Heterogeneous SoC

Joseph Gravellier[1,2](✉), Jean-Max Dutertre[1], Yannick Teglia[2], Philippe Loubet Moundi[2], and Francis Olivier[2]

[1] Mines Saint-Etienne, CEA-Tech, Centre CMP, 13541 Gardanne, France
{joseph.gravellier,jean-max.dutertre}@emse.fr
[2] Thales, 13600 La Ciotat, France
{joseph.gravellier,yannick.teglia,philippe.moundi, francis.olivier}@thalesgroup.com

Abstract. Thanks to their performance and flexibility, FPGAs are increasingly adopted for hardware acceleration on various platforms such as system on chip and cloud datacenters. Their use for commercial and industrial purposes raises concern about potential hardware security threats. By getting access to the FPGA fabric, an attacker could implement malicious logic to perform remote hardware attacks. Recently, several papers demonstrated that FPGA can be used to eavesdrop or disturb the activity of resources located within and outside the chip. In a complex SoC that contains a processor and a FPGA within the same die, we experimentally demonstrate that FPGA-based voltage sensors can eavesdrop computations running on the CPU and that advanced side-channel attacks can be conducted remotely to retrieve the secret key of a symmetric crypto-algorithm.

Keywords: SoC · Remote attacks · FPGA · Time-to-digital converter · Voltage sensing · Side-channel attacks

1 Introduction

Traditionally, hardware attacks are conducted in specialized laboratory using specific heavy and expensive equipment such as oscilloscopes, probes and lasers. For these reasons, they are considered as local attacks which require direct access to the target for the attacker. Nowadays, getting a physical access to a target seems trivial, but not necessarily in the future. The multiplication of cloud services, the decentralization of computing resources and the proliferation of connected devices will progressively isolate the physical device from the user and bring a distance between the potential attacker and the victim device. Lately, the challenge behind these new constraints associated with the ever-growing complexity of system-on-chips (SoC) gave rise to a new kind of hardware attacks.

Remote hardware attacks leverage hardware vulnerabilities of distant targets to perform fault attack injection or side-channel analysis. Also known as software induced hardware attacks, they take advantage of several weaknesses such

S. Belaïd and T. Güneysu (Eds.): CARDIS 2019, LNCS 11833, pp. 109–125, 2020.
https://doi.org/10.1007/978-3-030-42068-0_7

as the combination of software & hardware reconfiguration on critical resources (Clkscrew [1]), the vulnerabilities of peripherals such as memories (Rowhammer [2]) or the micro-architectural CPU optimizations (Spectre & Meltdown [3,4] and more recently Foreshadow [5]). The trend around remote attacks relies on three main points: **feasibility**, **robustness** and **scalability**. Firstly, contrary to traditional hardware attacks, no expensive or specific equipment is required and a simple network connection with the target can be enough to perform the attack. Secondly, these attacks take advantage of hardware resources that are inherent to the target chip. This means that the vulnerability cannot be completely fixed or patched without redesigning the entire hardware resource, involving at least years of development. Finally, another asset of the remote hardware attack is its ability to be scaled up and launched on billions of connected devices simultaneously.

This work focuses on FPGA and its recent adoption in SoCs and cloud datacenters [6,7]. The presence of FPGA within connected devices and also in the cloud raises concerns about the potential associated security threats. Indeed, the FPGA provides enough flexibility and performance to replicate a complete hardware attack bench. Through the access to reconfigurable logic, an attacker can implement sensors to eavesdrop side-channel leakage induced by surrounding logic blocks and infer secret keys [8]. Glitch injectors can also be instantiated within the fabric to disturb surrounding computations [9]. The implementation of multi-user cloud FPGA was discussed in [10] and could act as a huge security backdoor if a malicious tenant starts to eavesdrop or disturb other users computations. Denial-of-service, bitstream decryption fault attack [11], crypto-algorithms side-channel [8] are some examples of threats. This paper focuses on a specific application of FGPA-based side-channel attacks. Using a heterogeneous SoC that consists in a FPGA and a CPU implemented on the same die, we carry on the work started by [12] which consists in eavesdropping CPU computation using FPGA-based voltage sensors. Our contributions are detailed below:

- The in-depth study and improvement of FPGA-based voltage sensors performances for side-channel purpose.
- The first FPGA-based side-channel attack conducted on symmetric crypto-algorithms running on the CPU core of a SoC: *Tiny AES* + *OpenSSL AES*.
- The evaluation and comparison of FPGA-based sensors with a traditional electromagnetic side-channel setup.

This paper presents an FPGA-based side-channel attack on a SoC CPU core. An iterative work is conducted from the reproduction of the actual state-of-the-art through the attack of a hardware AES to the first successful attack of a software AES. Section 2 provides the background about FPGA side-channel and the adopted threat model. Section 3 describes the global side-channel setup. Sections 4 and 5 are dedicated to the side-channel experiments conducted both on hardware and software AES. Then, Sect. 6 provides EM side-channel results conducted on the same targets for comparison purpose and discuss feasibility and countermeasures of FPGA-based side-channel attacks. Finally, Sect. 7 concludes this work.

2 Background

2.1 Power Side-Channel Attacks

Power side-channel attacks make use of the transistors switching activity leakage through voltage variations to collect information about the processes running inside a target device. Thanks to a correlation between the leakage and the data processed, a side-channel attack can be performed to retrieve cryptographic keys and secrets from a target without tampering it. By analysing power traces, an attacker can visually speculate on the different instructions performed by the device using Simple Power Analysis (SPA [13]). Advanced side-channel methods such as differential power analysis (DPA [14]) or correlation power analysis (CPA [15]) allow an attacker to infer the secret keys of cryptographic processes by correlating guessed leakage hypotheses with a set of experimental traces.

2.2 FPGA-Based Voltage Sensors

On-chip voltage fluctuations can be measured externally with an oscilloscope by connecting a shunt resistor to the power supply pads. Sometimes, though, they need to be measured internally by the chip itself to ensure good operating conditions or detect fault attacks. Analog solutions such as Analog-to-digital converters (ADC) can be used to directly measure internal voltage fluctuations. However, for the sake of area economy and cost saving, on-chip sensing solutions are generally based on digital circuits easier to implement and accurate enough to detect fine-grained voltage fluctuations. These sensors monitor propagation delay which is the time required for a signal to propagate through a logic gate [16]. This delay fluctuates with the power supply level and can be digitally estimated. Ring-oscillator based sensors [17] and Time-digital converters (TDC) [18] are the two major solutions adopted for low-cost delay monitoring. Moreover, they can easily be implemented within a FPGA fabric using available logic.

2.3 Threat Model

Our threat model addresses all the connected devices that incorporate hardware acceleration based on FPGA logic: from reconfigurable resources in cloud data centers to SoCs deployed for industrial and commercial purposes. In this context, we consider the potential implementation of malicious FPGA-based voltage sensors through cloud FPGA rental, untrusted IP insertion or access to the bitstream reconfiguration of unsecured chips. Using these sensors, an attacker could eavesdrop side-channel leakage induced by surrounding computations. In a cloud scenario, a malicious user could target the side-channel leakage of cryptographic computations conducted by other users. In SoC context, these sensors can be implemented to eavesdrop the side-channel leakage induced by the SoC surrounding logic blocks such as CPU cores or secure elements. The following work targets heterogeneous SoCs that provide both CPU and FPGA logic blocks within the same die. Our goal is to assess the feasibility of FPGA-based side-channel attacks on software crypto-algorithms running within the SoC CPU.

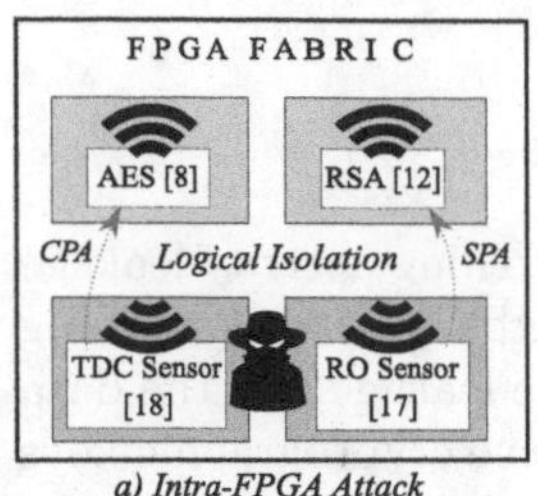

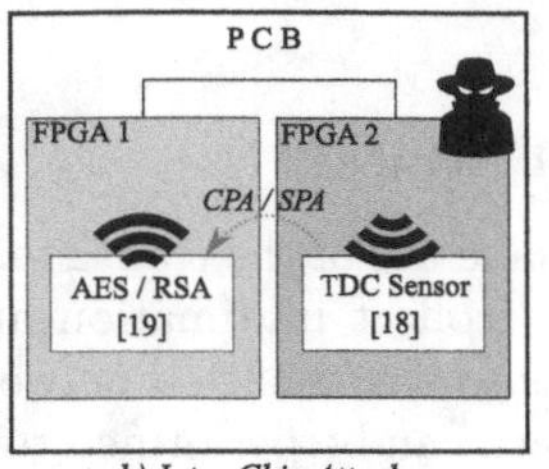

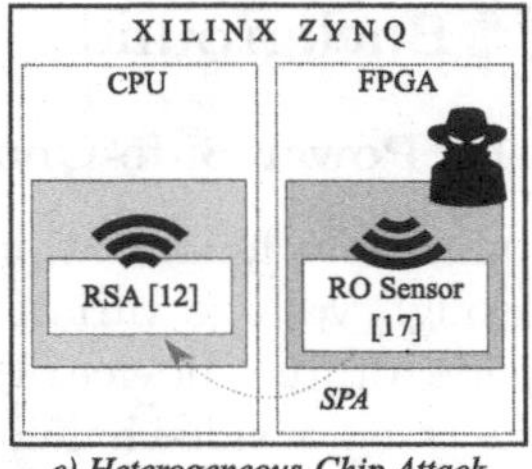

Fig. 1. Overview of FPGA-based Power Side-Channel Exploits

2.4 Related Works

Several works studying these threats were previously conducted. Although being all based on FPGA sensors they introduce three different scenarios as illustrated in Fig. 1.

(1) Intra-FPGA Attack: Remote side-channel attacks on FPGAs were introduced in 2018 [8]. The adversary model consists in a FPGA fabric shared among multiple users. Each user is protected from the others by logical isolation. Despite this protection, a malicious user can implement voltage sensors in his rented logic to monitor voltage fluctuations induced by surrounding computations. Assuming this model, the adversary is able to perform a CPA attack against a victim AES hardware module. A second exploit uses RO-based sensors to perform intra-chip SPA against a RSA hardware module [12].

(2) Inter-Chip Attack: The Inter-Chip Side-channel Attack illustrated in Fig. 1b goes a step further by proving that an untrusted chip on a PCB can sense voltage variations induced by other chips through the power distribution network. In this exploit, an adversary FPGA is able to perform a CPA attack against an AES module and a SPA attack against a RSA module running on another FPGA fabric [19].

(3) Heterogeneous Chip Attack: Xilinx Zynq technology integrates a dual core ARM processor and a FPGA fabric within the same SoC. In [12], malicious ROs were implemented in the FPGA fabric to perform a SPA against a naive square and multiply RSA algorithm running on a linux OS inside the ARM CPU core as shown in Fig. 1c.

3 Presentation of the Side-Channel Setup

3.1 Side-Channel Sensors

TDC-based sensor converts propagation delay variations induced by power supply fluctuations into digital information. Thanks to a low-cost design and a fine-grained resolution it is commonly adopted as on-chip temperature or voltage sensor: for operating control of the chip [20] as well as glitch attack detection [21]. More recently, with the rise of FPGA cloud services, some researchers

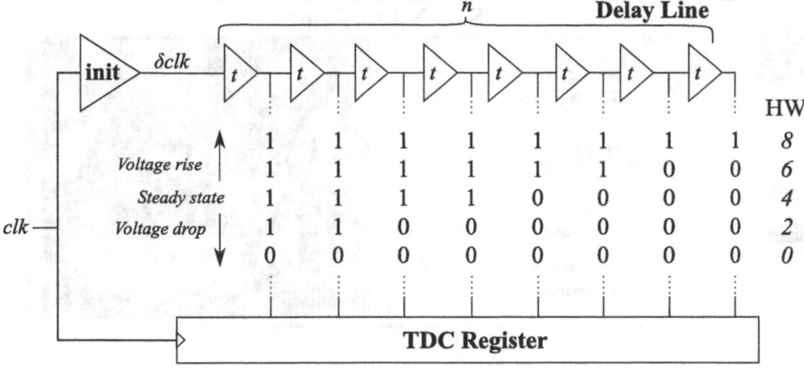

Fig. 2. Functional schematic of a TDC-based sensor. The Hamming Weight of the delay line provides an image of the actual on-chip voltage level.

started to use it to perform power side-channel attacks [8,19]. As it offers the best trade-off between achievable resolution, accuracy and sampling frequency [18,21], TDC is adopted for the experiments. As illustrated in Fig. 2, the TDC contains three main logic blocks:

- An **init** delay block whose propagation delay depends of the chip internal voltage.
- A **delay line** made of n elementary delay elements (with an individual propagation delay t) that allows fine measurement of propagation delay fluctuations.
- A **register** that captures and stores the delay line state.

A clock signal, denoted *clk*, is connected to the TDC *init* delay block input and delayed to form a δclk signal. The phase shift between *clk* and δclk signals fluctuates with the voltage variations. The *init* delay is calibrated in order to have the δclk edge inside the delay line when its state is captured by the TDC register. Then, the Hamming Weight of the stored value is computed and delivers an image of the actual voltage level inside the chip (as a thermometer code). Figure 2 illustrates the impact of voltage fluctuations on the sampled value. A voltage rise reduces the propagation delay of the *init* block. Therefore, the δclk rising edge travels faster and manages to pass more elements in the delay line. Therefore, more “1” are sampled and the Hamming Weight of the TDC register increases. A voltage drop induces the opposite behaviour by increasing the propagation delay and thus, the number of “0”. To enable fine-grained voltage sensing, the propagation delay t of the logic primitives constituting the chain needs to be as small as possible. However, a small propagation delay involves a long delay line to avoid saturation of the TDC. Therefore, there is a trade-off between quantum resolution, voltage range and area consumption. We based our experiments on an existing version of the TDC based on FPGA resources [18]. Figure 10 in appendix illustrates the schematic view of the TDC-based sensor instance designed for the experiments.

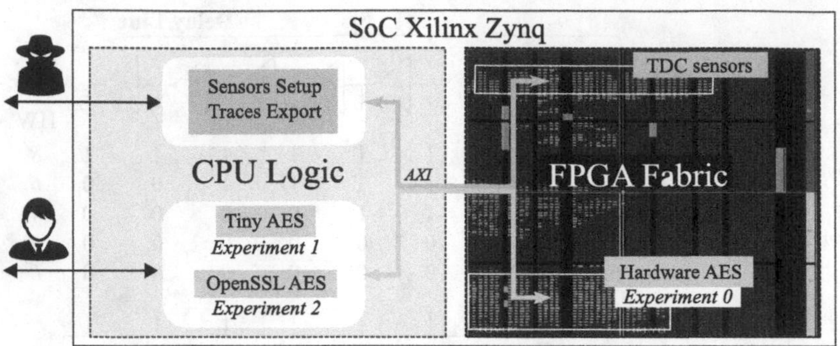

Fig. 3. Xilinx Zynq experimental side-channel setup

3.2 Side-Channel Targets

Previous work concerned with attacks on software used simple, self-written public key algorithms [12]. We propose to go a step further, by proving that freely-available (and actually deployed) symmetric crypto-algorithms are also vulnerable to FPGA-based side-channel attacks. By taking advantage of the high accuracy and performances provided by the TDC, we aim to conduct CPA attacks against AES software implementations.

This work targets one hardware AES and two software AES implementations. Each one of them implements distinct characteristics and enriches the global study. The first experiment targets a hardware AES module implemented within the FPGA fabric. The aim of this attack is the evaluation of the intrinsic device leakage and the optimization and calibration of our sensors (note that this attack was already conducted by [8]). The second and third experiments are conducted on Tiny AES [22] (*8-bit data-path*) and OpenSSL AES [23] (*32-bit data-path*). Experiments 2 and 3 represent the novelty of this publication.

3.3 Xilinx Zynq Experimental Setup

The entire side-channel setup is based on a Xilinx Zynq 7000 heterogeneous SoC that implements both FPGA (Xilinx Artix-7) and CPU (ARM Cortex-A9) on the same die. Figure 3 represents our experimental setup which is organized as follows: the Artix-7 FPGA fabric embeds 8 TDC-based sensors set to provide a sampling rate of 200 MS/s per sensor and all the logic required to store the acquired data (FIFOs). *The use of several TDCs increases the voltage fluctuation coverage area and the granularity of the overall side-channel setup. However, TDCs multiplication is limited by the voltage noise resulting from their own activity. 8 TDCs is the best trade-off found for our experiments.*

The fabric also integrates a custom hardware AES-128 module implemented for experiment purposes. The dual-core Cortex-A9 CPU is cadenced at 667 MHz and runs a bare-metal C program that implements both Tiny and OpenSSL AES. From the attacker point of view, the side-channel traces are exported through

UART for upcoming CPA computations. (*Note that in a practical scenario, CPA computation could be launched directly inside the target to reduce the amount of exported data*).

4 FPGA-Based Attack on Hardware AES

An hardware AES module is instantiated within the FPGA fabric as a preliminary test for our sensors. The attacked module has a 128-bit size for both the message and the key and encrypts data in 10 clock cycles (+1 additional cycle for the export). Figure 4 illustrates the hardware AES power consumption measured using the 8 TDCs of our test setup (their output values are added and averaged).

Side-Channel Attack: Each round transformation of the AES module ends up with the updating of a 128-bit register that temporarily stores the round state. The synchronous update of 128 flip-flops induces a strong leakage clearly visible in Fig. 4. The CPA selection function is taken as the Hamming Distance between the 9th and 10th round register values and a 8-bit assumption is made on the last round key (*last round attack* [24]). Because the data-path is 128-bit wide, the prediction suffers a 120-bit noise that might yield errors. 10,000 AES leakage traces are acquired using TDCs and a CPA side-channel attack is conducted. The usage of large set of traces progressively extracts the leakage out of the noise variance. After 4,483 traces on average, the right guess shows up. Despite the attack success, the number of traces required to retrieve the AES secret key can be significantly reduced through the calibration of the TDCs. Two side-channel setup optimizations are presented in the following paragraphs, their effect on CPA results is illustrated in Table 1.

Placement Optimization: The impact of the sensor distance from the target was already discussed in [8]. We implement it here as a preliminary side-channel optimization. Close and far setups are instantiated as depicted in Fig. 5. In the far setup (used for the previous attack), the TDCs are 80 slices distant from the AES, while in the close setup, the logical distance between them is 6 slices.

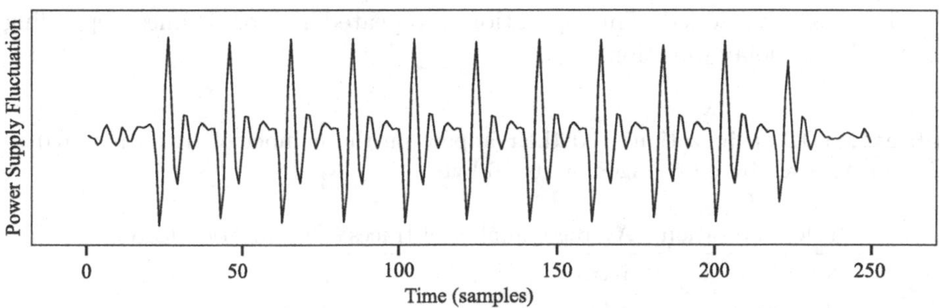

Fig. 4. Averaged power supply fluctuation resulting from 100 hardware AES encryptions. AES frequency: 10 MHz - TDCs sampling rate: 200 MS/s.

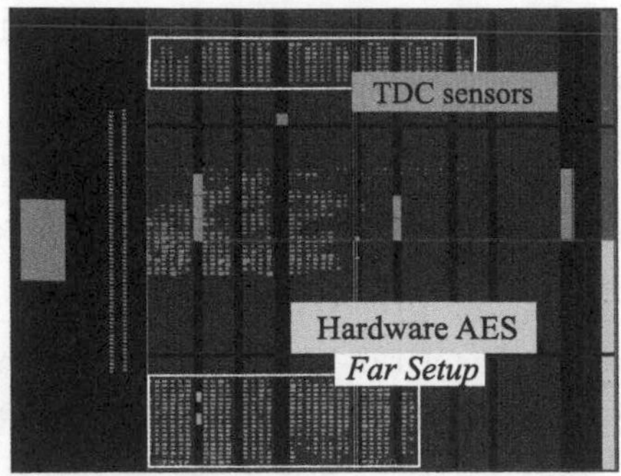

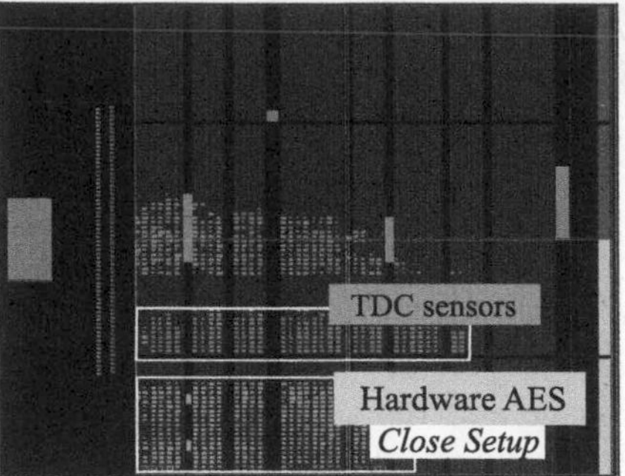

Fig. 5. Logical distance between sensors and target algorithm.

The noise induced by the logic placed between the AES and the sensors alters the valuable side-channel leakage. Reducing the distance between the sensors and the target should improve the CPA results. As illustrated in Table 1, by adopting the close setup, the number of traces required to perform the attack drops from 4,483 to 3,440.

Init Delay Optimization: Init delay of the TDC represented in Fig. 2 (and more specifically in Fig. 10 in appendix) can be dynamically configured using coarse and fine tuning. The attacker programs the dedicated logic (MUX) to modify the number of logic elements forming the path, and consequently the delay duration. The δclk edge propagation speed gets impacted by all the voltage fluctuation that occurs as it travels through the *init* delay, yielding thereby an averaging effect. This effect naturally smooths the sampled values and thus acts as a high-frequency noise filter. However, depending on its duration, it can deteriorate the accuracy of the sensor.

Through the implementation of 4 delay paths having different lengths, we are looking forward to finding the best averaging trade-off for our device. The *init* delay is increased of a half *clk* period per path. In practical terms, the *init* path size (logic elements) is progressively increased until the propagation of the δclk edge fills a half of the delay line with "1". When it is the case, a half *clk* period of delay has been added. This operation is repeated 1, 2 or 3 times depending on the chosen delay duration.

Table 1. TDC optimizations and their impact on the number of traces required to infer an AES key byte (averaged on its 16 bytes).

TDC calibration	Average number of traces	Optimization factor
No	4,483	/
Placement	3,440	1,30
Init + Placement	1,381	3,25

Experimentally, the side-channel attack results are progressively enhanced with the *init* delay path size, until it reaches 1.5 times the *clk* period. Then, it finally decreases for the last setup. As highlighted in Table 1, CPA results are significantly improved by the *init* calibration, the number of traces required to infer the secret key drops from 3,440 to 1,381 traces. Altogether, placement and *init* delay calibration divides by 3,25 the number of traces required to infer the AES secret key. This optimization is substantial for the following attacks that require a significantly larger number of side-channel traces.

5 FPGA-Based Attack on Software AES

In this section, side-channel attacks are conducted against freely available AES software implementations. The optimal setup for the attacks relies on 8 TDCs placed vertically along the left border of the fabric. According to the Zynq implemented design, this placement makes sense as it bring TDCs closer to the processing system (i.e CPU). While this paper focuses on the CPU side-channel attack feasibility, the identification of the best TDC positions and shapes need to be further investigated in future works.

5.1 Experiment 1: 8-Bit Tiny AES

The first target adopted for CPU experiments is the Tiny AES implementation available on github [22]. This small 8-bit data path AES computes each AES subfunction sequentially and processes data from the less to the most significant byte. Our experiment focuses on the AES-128 encryption, plaintexts are randomly generated and collected through UART. To make sure that the AES runs at the CPU max frequency (667 MHz), we measured the number of clock cycles elapsed during the encryption using ARM performance counters: around 26,000 clock cycles are required (39 µs). Figure 6 illustrates a full Tiny AES encryption acquired using TDCs at a sampling rate of 200 MS/s. The first 9 rounds of the AES can be easily distinguished thanks to the variation of power consumption

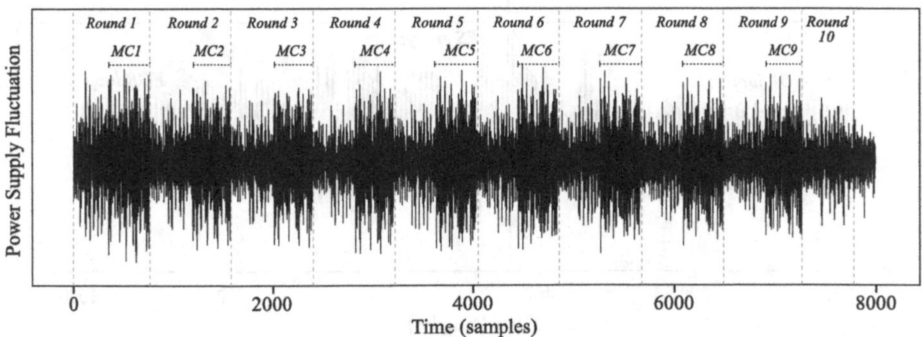

Fig. 6. Averaged power supply fluctuation resulting from 100 Tiny AES encryptions. TDC sampling rate is 200 MS/s per sensor.

between 8-bit AES subfunctions *ByteSub*, *ShiftRow* and *AddRoundKey* and the 32-bit *MixColumn* subfunction. The last AES round differs from the others as it doesn't use the *MixColumn* subfunction.

Side-Channel Attack: The side-channel leakage resulting from 8-bit AES computations has a low impact on the overall chip voltage fluctuations. The encryption measurement only covers 5 TDC quantization levels amongst the 32 possible and is thus more vulnerable to the low-frequency noise induced by the surrounding peripherals (eg: voltage regulator module 500 KHz) and physical effects (eg: temperature variations). To enhance the signal-to-noise ratio and reduce the number of traces required for the attack, we need to apply high-pass filtering on each side-channel trace. After preliminary filtering, the CPA can be conducted. The selection function chosen for the CPA is the standard Hamming Weight model of the first round *ByteSub* output: $HW[Sbox[k \oplus m]]$. The attack is a success, an average of 111,000 traces are required to infer a secret AES key byte. Despite a significant increase of the number of traces required for the attack, TDCs are still accurate enough to perform CPA against software algorithms running on our target. The side-channel performance deterioration can be explained by the greater logical distance between the FPGA-based sensors and the CPU logic and the sensibility limitation of the TDC-based sensors.

5.2 Experiment 2: 32-Bit OpenSSL AES

The OpenSSL library [23] implements a wide range of cryptographic algorithms massively used for secure channels over computer networks. In this work, we focus on the OpenSSL AES-128 that implements a 32-bit tabulated version of the AES [25]. This variant merges *Mixcolumn* and *ByteSub* subfunctions into 4 look-ups tables known as T-tables (256×32-bit). The round transformation of each input byte is directly loaded from the T-tables and thus speeds up the computation. OpenSSL cadenced at 667 MHz encrypts 128-bit of data in 2,9 µs - 13.5 faster than the Tiny AES. Figure 7 illustrates the power consumption induced by OpenSSL AES encryption.

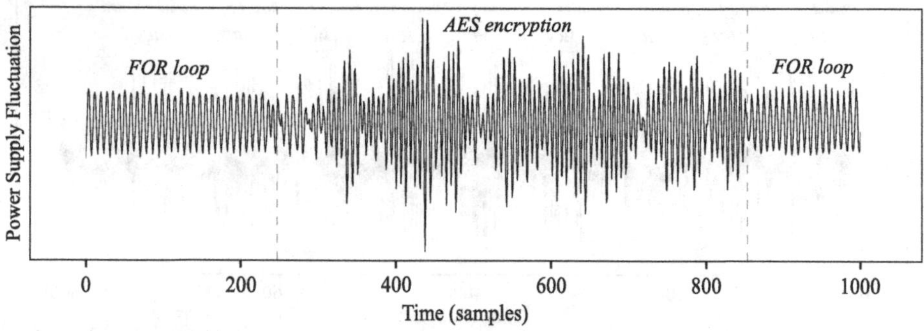

Fig. 7. Averaged power supply fluctuation resulting from 100 OpenSSL AES encryptions. TDC sampling rate is 200 MS/s per sensor.

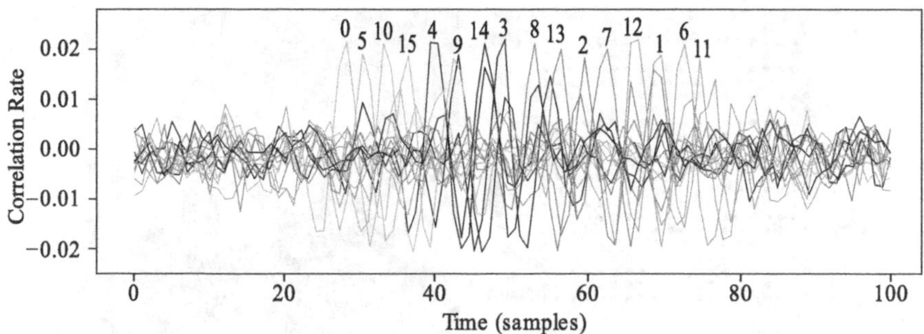

Fig. 8. Correlation rate over the time obtained for the good guess of each OpenSSL key byte. The 32-bit implementation can be recognized by observing the byte order. (Each color represent a 32-bit word) (Color figure online)

OPENSSL1: 8-bit Selection Function. The first round model $HW[Sbox[k \oplus m]]$ previously used for the Tiny AES attack works fairly well even against OpenSSL tabulated AES. According to the definition of the 4 T-tables described in [25], each table output consists in a 32-bit word $T[k_i \oplus m_i]$ in which the natural *Sbox* value relative to the input byte $k_i \oplus m_i$ has been multiplied by the *MixColumn* coefficients. For each table the natural 8-bit value of the *Sbox* appears twice in the word because two of the *Mixcolumn* coefficients equal one. Therefore, 16-bit of the 32-bit output word will leak according to the *Sbox* model. Using such a selection function, 130,000 traces are necessary for the attack to succeed.

OPENSSL2: 32-bit Selection Function. The first round model can be used to perform reverse engineering. Contrary to classic 8-bit AES which computes each AES byte from the less significant byte to the most significant, tabulated 32-bit AES computes each key byte according to the *ShiftRow* order. This order can be perceived in temporal CPA results. Figure 8 illustrates the timing correlation obtained for each right guess of the 16 AES key bytes. The byte order follows the *ShiftRow* order and betrays the presence of a tabulated AES. Thanks to this information, an attacker can slightly improve the CPA model by making a full 32-bit prediction. Instead of targeting the Hamming Weight of the *Sbox* output, the attacker adds the T-table in his selection function: $HW[T_t(k \oplus m)]$. The expected benefit is a slightly better correlation and a quicker hypotheses distinguishing. Experimentally, the average number of traces required to perform the attack drops to 87,000 which is 1.5 time less than the *Sbox* model.

This section experimentally demonstrates that FPGA-based sensors are suitable for side-channel attacks against software symmetrical algorithms. According to the selection function adopted for the experiments the number of traces required to infer the secret key fluctuates from 87,000 to 127,000. No significant distinction exists between the 8-bit Tiny AES and 32-bit OpenSSL AES attacks as they both leaks accordingly to the *Sbox* model. The attack of side-channel resistant crypto-algorithms could be considered in future works to further evaluate the potential and limitations of FPGA-based sensors.

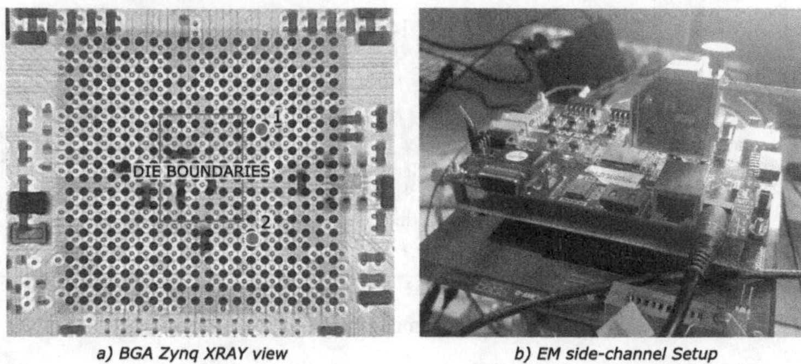

Fig. 9. On the left, a XRAY picture of the Zynq BGA package, the die is contained within the rectangle. On the right, the side-channel setup based on a langer EM probe.

6 EM Results and Discussion

To evaluate the pertinence of side-channel analysis that can be performed remotely by our TDC sensors, we challenge these results regarding classical local side-channel attacks. This section presents a performance comparison with a traditional EM side-channel setup and discusses about FPGA-based attacks feasibility and associated countermeasures.

6.1 Electromagnetic Side-Channel Attack

Figure 9b illustrates the EM setup that consists in a Langer near field microprobe connected to an oscilloscope with a 5 GS/s sampling rate and a 12-bit resolution. The probe position can be controlled using a X, Y, Z table. The signal is first amplified by a low noise amplifier (LNA), then connected to the oscilloscope. A XRAY picture of the ZYNQ7000 depicted in Fig. 9a was taken to check the die structure. Two hot-spots are represented, the first one offers the best contrast and visualisation of the hardware AES side-channel leakage, while the second one gives the best results for software AES algorithms. The electromagnetic leakage of the first round of each attacked AES is leveraged to trigger the oscilloscope. The captured samples are then extracted and used to perform a correlation electromagnetic analysis (CEMA).

CEMA is conducted against each AES studied in this work. Table 2 gathers all the results obtained with both TDCs and EM setups. Although these setups are

Table 2. Averaged number of traces required to retrieve a key byte on various AES implementations for EM and TDC side-channel setups

Setup	HAES	Tiny AES	OpenSSL 1	OpenSSL 2
EM	**1,021**	**52,438**	**106,225**	88,412
TDC	1,381	111,758	127,558	**87,422**

not based on the same physical effect, it makes sense to compare FPGA-based sensors performance. According to Table 2, the hardware AES and OpenSSL AES attacks based on TDCs require roughly as many side-channel traces than EM. This means that with only 32 quantization levels and a 200 MS/s sampling rate, TDCs provide similar results to a high performance oscilloscope. Naturally, this must be interpreted with caution as TDCs were previously calibrated and optimized for this specific device and attack scenario. Moreover, a significant difference between EM and TDCs still appears when it comes to the Tiny AES attack. As mentioned before, this has to do with the surrounding noise and the sensibility limitation of the TDCs.

This experiment aimed to demonstrate that through the calibration and optimization of our sensors, we are able to provide similar results to traditional side-channel setups. Finally, this further proves the extent of the remote hardware attack threat.

6.2 Attack Feasibility

The feasibility of FPGA-based attack on a practical scenario substantially relies on the security level provided by the target. Three major requirements need to be met to make it possible:

(1) **Medium:** The side-channel attacks conducted in this paper require the implementation of voltage sensors within a victim FPGA fabric. This can be done in cloud datacenters through the rental of reconfigurable logic, by the insertion of malicious trojan within untrusted FPGA IPs or through the direct reconfiguration of unsecured FPGA chips.

(2) **Data knowledge:** Side-channel attacks conducted against secret key algorithms such as AES require the knowledge of victim plaintexts or ciphertexts. Depending on the use case, accessing this information can be challenging for the attacker especially because each trace acquired using TDCs must match with the exact plain/cipher text used for the encryption. The feasibility is related to the opportunity for the attacker to trigger victim encryption and to retrieve plain or cipher texts.

(3) **Synchronisation:** Victim side-channel leakage needs to be dynamically detected by the sensor logic to facilitate the attack. A trigger mechanism can be implemented within the TDC to start the data storage when a large voltage undershoot occurs. However, this trigger mechanism cannot be fully reliable and sometimes get disturbed by surrounding noise induced by temperature variations or peripherals computations. Depending on the overall noise level, the attack complexity can soar. To facilitate the attack, a local clone of the targeted device can be used to adjust and calibrate the side-channel setup towards the actual remote exploit.

6.3 Countermeasures

The threat behind FPGA-based hardware attack has already been taken into account by cloud providers who assure that, for the sake of security and integrity, their FPGA resources are not shared between multiple users. However, although this protection mitigates intra-FPGA attacks, FPGA sensors can still eavesdrop computations that occur in other chips connected to the same power supply even in presence of decoupling capacitors [19]. To mitigate the threat once for all, an independent power supply should then be provided for each FPGA chip. Protecting SoCs that implement both FPGA and CPU within the same die should be more complex. The dissociation of the power sources would require the creation of two independent power distribution networks and thus increase the overall design cost. Designers should be aware of the side-channel threat and should consider it even when the device is not physically accessible by the attacker. An efficient way to prevent a crypto-algorithm from being remotely attacked is the usage of the usual side-channel countermeasures as for instance shuffling, masking, random delays or jitter.

7 Conclusion

With the massive adoption of FPGA hardware acceleration in connected systems such as SoC and cloud data centers, the eventuality of remote FPGA-based hardware attacks become more and more realistic. In this work, we demonstrated that FPGA logic instantiated within a complex SoC can be leveraged to monitor voltage fluctuations of the surrounding logic blocks and in particular that of a CPU. We conducted three experiments from the side-channel attack of a hardware AES instantiated within the FPGA logic to the attack of two software AES running on the CPU core. The first experiment was carried out on the hardware AES module. It allowed us to calibrate several parameters to improve side-channel results (init delay, position, filtering, etc.). Then we performed the first FPGA-based side-channel attacks on software AES (Tiny AES and OpenSSL AES). The side-channel leakage induced by CPU core being much weaker, the attack required a substantial increase of the number of side-channel to infer the encryption key. To evaluate the performances of our sensors, we conducted the same attack using a EM traditional setup and obtained comparable results to those achieved with TDC-based sensors. This attests the extend of the threat that unsecured FPGA SoC constitute. Finally, care must be taken when designing SoC to ensure that hardware resources cannot be maliciously used as hardware attack means.

8 Appendix

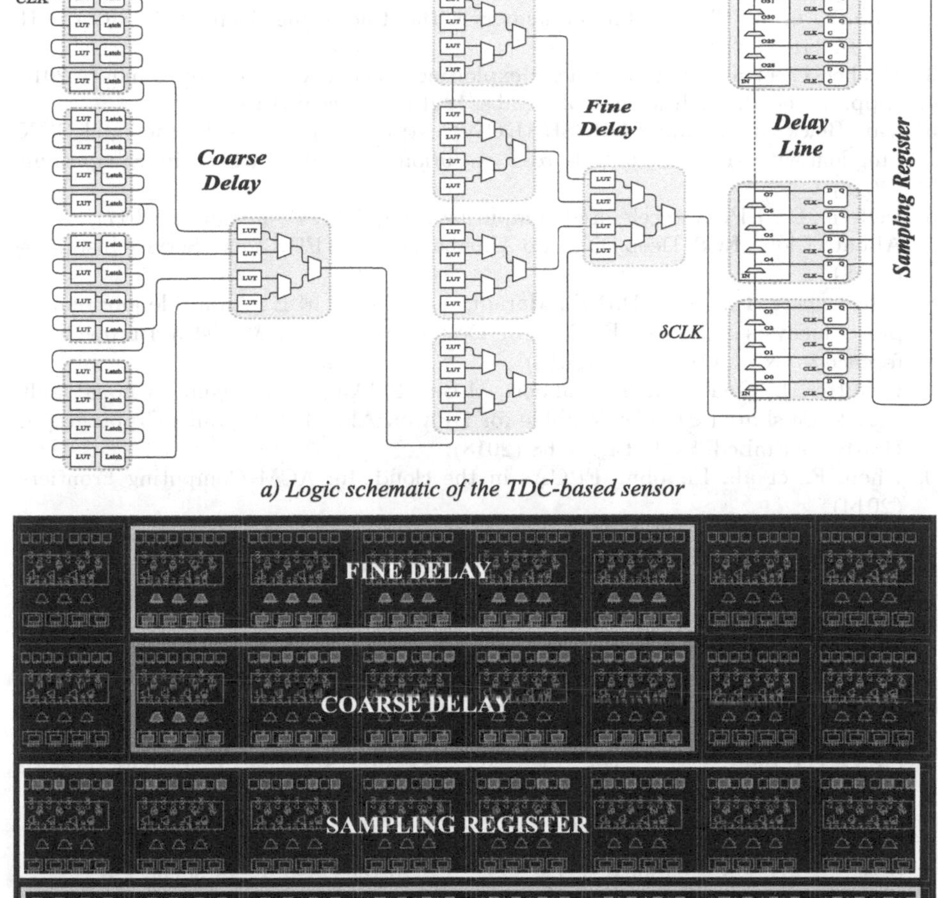

Fig. 10. Logic schematic and implemented design of one TDC-based sensor instance. Each dotted rectangle in the logic schematic represents 1 slice (26 in total). The delay line provides 32 quantization levels and a sampling rate of 200 MS/s per sensor.

References

1. Tang, A., Sethumadhavan, S., Stolfo, S.: CLKSCREW: exposing the perils of security-oblivious energy management. In: 26th USENIX Security Symposium (2017)
2. Kim, Y., et al.: Flipping bits in memory without accessing them. ACM SIGARCH **42**(3), 361–372 (2014)
3. Kocher, P., et al.: Spectre attacks: exploiting speculative execution, January 2018
4. Lipp, M., et al.: Meltdown. CoRR, abs/1801.0, January 2018
5. Van Bulck, J., et al.: FORESHADOW: extracting the keys to the intel SGX kingdom with transient out-of-order execution. In: USENIX Security Symposium (2018)
6. Pellerin, D.: FPGA accelerated computing using AWS F1 instances (2017)
7. Alibaba Cloud ECS: Deep Dive into Alibaba Cloud F3 FPGA as a Service Instances (2018)
8. Schellenberg, F., Gnad, D.R.E., Moradi, A., Tahoori, M.B.: An inside job: remote power analysis attacks on FPGAs. In: Design, Automation & Test in Europe Conference & Exhibition. IEEE (2018)
9. Krautter, J., Gnad, D.R.E., Tahoori, M.B.: FPGAhammer : remote voltage fault attacks on shared FPGAs, suitable for DFA on AES. IACR Trans. Cryptograph. Hardware Embed. Syst. **14**, 44–68 (2018)
10. Chen, F., et al.: Enabling FPGAs in the cloud. In: ACM Computing Frontiers (2014)
11. Gnad, D.R.E., Oboril, F., Tahoori, M.B.: Voltage drop-based fault attacks on FPGAs using valid bitstreams. In: 2017 27th International Conference on Field Programmable Logic and Applications, FPL 2017 (2017)
12. Zhao, M., Suh, G.E.: FPGA-based remote power side-channel attacks. In: IEEE Symposium on Security and Privacy (2018)
13. Kocher, P.C.: Timing attacks on implementations of Diffie-Hellman, RSA, DSS, and other systems. In: CRYPTO 1996 (1996)
14. Kocher, P., Jaffe, J., Jun, B.: Differential power analysis. In: Wiener, M. (ed.) CRYPTO 1999. LNCS, vol. 1666, pp. 388–397. Springer, Heidelberg (1999). https://doi.org/10.1007/3-540-48405-1_25
15. Brier, E., Clavier, C., Olivier, F.: Correlation power analysis with a leakage model. In: Joye, M., Quisquater, J.-J. (eds.) CHES 2004. LNCS, vol. 3156, pp. 16–29. Springer, Heidelberg (2004). https://doi.org/10.1007/978-3-540-28632-5_2
16. Dutertre, J.-M., Robisson, B., Tria, A., Zussa, L.: Investigation of timing constraints violation as a fault injection means. In: Design of Circuits and Integrated Systems (2012)
17. Zick, K.M., Hayes, J.P.: Low-cost sensing with ring oscillator arrays for healthier reconfigurable systems. ACM Trans. Reconfigurable Technol. Syst. **5**(1), 1–26 (2012)
18. Gnad, D.R.E., Oboril, F., Kiamehr, S., Tahoori, M.B.: An experimental evaluation and analysis of transient voltage fluctuations in FPGAs. IEEE Trans. Very Large Scale Integr. Syst. **26**(10), 1817–1830 (2018)
19. Schellenberg, F., Gnad, D.R.E., Moradi, A., Tahoori, M.B.: Remote inter-chip power analysis side-channel attacks at board-level. In: Proceedings of the International Conference on Computer-Aided Design (2018)
20. Ueno, M., Hashimoto, M., Onoye, T.: Real-time on-chip supply voltage sensor and its application to trace-based timing error localization. In: International On-Line Testing Symposium (IOLTS). IEEE, July 2015

21. Zick, K.M., Srivastav, M., Zhang, W., French, M.: Sensing nanosecond-scale voltage attacks and natural transients in FPGAs. In: ACM/SIGDA (2013)
22. Kokke: Tiny AES in C (2018)
23. OpenSSL: OpenSSL AES (2002)
24. Mestiri, H., Benhadjyoussef, N., Machhout, M., Tourki, R.: A comparative study of power consumption models for CPA attack. Int. J. Comput. Netw. Inf. Secur. **5**(3), 25 (2013)
25. Daemen, J., Rijmen, V.: The Rijndael Block Cipher (1999)

Optimal Collision Side-Channel Attacks

Cezary Glowacz[1] and Vincent Grosso[2(✉)]

[1] Telekom Security, Bonn, Germany
cezary.glowacz@t-systems.com
[2] CNRS/Laboratoire Hubert Curien, Université de Lyon, Lyon, France
vincent.grosso@univ-st-etienne.fr

Abstract. Collision side-channel attacks are effective attacks against cryptographic implementations, however, optimality and efficiency of collision side-channel attacks is an open question. In this paper, we show that collision side-channel attacks can be derived using maximum likelihood principle when the distribution of the values of the leakage function is known. This allows us to exhibit the optimal collision side-channel attack and its efficient computation. Finally, we can compute an upper bound for the success rate of the optimal post-processing strategy, and we show that our method and the optimal strategy have success rates close to each other. Attackers can benefit from our method as we present an efficient collision side-channel attack. Evaluators can benefit from our method as we present a tight upper bound for the success rate of the optimal strategy.

1 Introduction

Since the late 90's and the first side-channel attacks by Kocher, various techniques of side-channel attacks have been proposed in the literature. Side-channel attacks are attacks against cryptographic implementations, the goal of such attacks is to link a physical property (e.g. power consumption, electromagnetic radiation) of the device to some secret information used in the implementation.

The optimal manner to exploit side-channel leakages is known in general [13]. It requires knowledge of the leakage function (estimated through profiling), then the maximum likelihood distinguisher is applied. However, the profiling step is not always possible, in some context like banking the attacker may not have access to an open device. Moreover, estimation of the leakage function can be a hard task [6] and model errors can be made. For these settings where profiling is difficult or impossible, it is interesting to look at optimal non-profiled attacks.

Among non-profiled attacks, collision attacks [12] are efficient side-channel attacks. The idea of collision side-channel attacks is that the same code processing the same data should have the same impact on monitored physical properties. This allows the attacker to detect when two sensitive values are equal. From this equality, the attacker extracts a relation between two different subkeys. Repeating this strategy for different couples of subkeys she ends with a system of equations that involve all subkeys with a degree of freedom of 1. Thus the set

S. Belaïd and T. Güneysu (Eds.): CARDIS 2019, LNCS 11833, pp. 126–140, 2020.
https://doi.org/10.1007/978-3-030-42068-0_8

of potential keys is reduced to a set of computationally enumerable candidates. In a noisy leakage scenario, detecting collisions may be not directly possible. To improve the success rate of collision side-channel attacks, Bogdanov introduces a collision attack across different executions of the AES and uses Euclidean distance as a score [1]. In [2] Bogdanov suggests using binary and ternary voting to improve the detection method. Moradi et al. suggest using the Pearson correlation coefficient to detect a collision with averaging to remove a part of the measurement noise [10]. Thus every trace can be exploited for the attack. In [4] Bruneau et al. derive a collision attack from stochastic side-channel attacks. They show that the scalar product score is more adapted to multi-collisions. However, they did not give any computationally efficient manner to maximize the score for the full key.

Once the scores of each collision between two subkeys are computed the attacker needs to select an independent collision relation to recover the key. Moreover, due to noise in measurements, some equations might be incorrect. Thus performing a key recovery attack can be tricky. Several algorithms have been proposed in the literature in order to extract information from the result of collision side-channel attacks. The proposed methods are based on heuristics, e.g. LDPC decoding for the solution of Gérard and Standaert [7] or branch-and-bound for the solution of Wiemers and Klein [14]. While both approaches improve the success rate of the collision attack the status of the optimality of these methods is not known, thus leaving space for potentially more efficient exploitation of side-channel collision attacks.

Having an efficient attack is interesting for attackers and evaluation labs. Security labs are also interested in computing security margins independent of the adversarial strategy. Thus finding the adversarial best strategy is important and computing a bound for its success rate is essential for a fair evaluation. Due to the dependence among the relations in collision side-channel attacks formulating the best strategy and evaluation of security margins were an open problem.

Our Contributions. We derive optimal collision side-channel attacks when the attacker knows the distribution of the leakage function values, and the attacker has a balanced set-up of traces. Bruneau et al. [4] use other hypotheses: same leakage function φ and a white Gaussian noise with the same variance for each of the measurements. Bogdanov and Moradi et al. solutions are based on statistical tools and are not derived using the maximum likelihood principle. From our derivation of collision attacks using the maximum likelihood principle we extract an evaluation of the distinguisher in an efficient manner. We show that the success rate of this manner is in practice close to that of the optimal evaluation of the distinguisher (the optimal evaluation is computationally unfeasible). This is achieved thanks to bounding the success rate of the optimal evaluation of the distinguishers. To the best of our knowledge, it is the first time an upper bound for the first order success rate of optimal collision side-channel attacks is exhibited. We compare our method to existing techniques and show that our method achieved better performance than previous methods, and that its success rate is close to the upper bound of the success rate of optimal collision side-channel attack. We use the maximum likelihood principle for the score derivation. The experimental results show that our method for maximization of the sum of the scores is close in term of success rate to the optimal strategy (bounded thanks to the upper bound). In our case, we measure the optimality in terms of achieving the same success rate as the optimal strategy (using the exact ML distinguisher derived according to the knowledge of the probability distribution of the leakage function values).

2 Background and Model Notations

2.1 Collision Side-Channel Attacks

Collision side-channel attacks were invented to exploit the similarity between leakages of similar computations over similar data values. Collision side-channel attacks do not require profiling of the leakage or a hypothesis of the leakage model. This is one of the main differences between collision side-channel attacks and other side-channel attacks such as template attacks [5] or correlation attacks [3]. Collision side-channel attacks have been introduced as attacks against block cipher implementations in [12].

As collision attacks aim at detecting repeated code execution with the same data we target in this paper block cipher implementations that reuse the same instance of the S-box, like in several reference implementations of Present or of AES. We denote by n the input size of the S-box (e.g. $n = 8$ for AES). We denote by L the number of S-box calls in one round (e.g. $L = 16$ for AES-128).

For all $l \in \{1, \dots, L\}$ we denote by $k^{*(l)}$ the l-th secret key byte and by $k^{(l)}$ any possible l-th key byte hypothesis. We denote by $\boldsymbol{k} = (k^{(1)}, \dots, k^{(L)})$ the full key. The l-th byte of the plaintext corresponding to the q-th query is denoted by $t_q^{(l)}$ and the associated leakage is denoted by $x_q^{(l)}$. $\boldsymbol{x}^{(\cdot)}$ is the matrix with $q - th$ row corresponding to the L-variate leakage $x_q^{(1)}, ..., x_q^{(L)}$.

We assume an identical, but unknown, leakage model for all $l \in \{1, \dots, L\}$. I.e.

$$x_q^{(l)} = \varphi(t_q^{(l)} \oplus k^{*(l)}) + N,$$

where the noise N is independent among l and q and φ is a deterministic leakage function.

The goal of collision side-channel attacks is to find links among the different key bytes $k^{(l)}$. The main idea is to detect when $\varphi(t_{q_1}^{(l_1)} \oplus k^{*(l_1)}) = \varphi(t_{q_2}^{(l_2)} \oplus k^{*(l_2)})$ for $l_1, l_2 \in \{1, \dots, L\}, l_1 \neq l_2$ and some know plaintext byte $t_{q_1}^{(l_1)}, t_{q_2}^{(l_2)}$.

In this paper, we consider only the case where we have a number of measurements that is a multiple of 2^n, and for each S-box calculation, we have observed the same number of traces for each value of the plaintext. This balanced setup allows to remove the bias of the plaintext distribution and it can be easily implemented using shuffling of batches. Hence, after performing averaging over the traces $x_q^{(l)}$ with the same plaintext values $\boldsymbol{x}^{(\cdot)}$ becomes a matrix of real numbers of dimension $2^n \times L$, where the i-th row corresponds to the leakage of the plaintext $i-1$.

In the rest of the paper we consider leakage functions that are partially unknown, i.e. the leakage function values are random variables and follow some plausible probability distribution. Without knowing this distribution, we cannot figure out an optimal distinguisher using maximum likelihood principle. For the experiment part, we also consider a more classical case where the leakage function is the Hamming weight.

2.2 Stochastic and Correlation Enhanced Collision Attacks

Bruneau et al. combine flavours of collision and of stochastic side-channel attacks [4]. Contrary to previous formulations, Bruneau et al. derive the attack rather than inventing it. The derivation is based on maximizing the likelihood function stated for the full key, given the measured leakages under the assumption of the same leakage function φ for each of the executions of the S-box and of the Gaussian noise having the mean 0 and the same variance for each of the measurements.

Stochastic differential side-channel attacks [11] were introduced in order to optimize the efficiency of DPA. The key idea of stochastic DPA is to approximate the leakage function φ within a suitable vector subspace with a relatively "small" basis to be efficient.

To use a stochastic approach in the collision context Bruneau et al. consider the unknown leakage function φ as an additional part of the secret. Thus the optimization problem, i.e. maximizing the likelihood function, is not only on the key value $\boldsymbol{k}$, but also on the leakage function. The stochastic approach for the representation of the leakage function φ can be shown to be equivalent to replacing the leakage function values in the likelihood function by their estimates calculated for each key $\boldsymbol{k}$ as the arithmetic mean over l of the measured leakages $x^{(l)}_{q\oplus k^{(l)}}$. Using these estimates maximizes the likelihood function values,[1] as it is also the case when using the stochastic approach utilizing the full basis for the representation of the leakage function φ. Finally, Bruneau et al. obtain the following distinguisher:

$$\mathcal{D}_{sto.coll} = \underset{\boldsymbol{k}\in(\mathbb{F}_2^n)^L}{\operatorname{argmax}} \sum_{u\in\mathbb{F}_2^n} \frac{\left(\sum_{l=1}^{L}\sum_{q=1\ldots Q|t_q\oplus k^{(l)}=u} x_q^{(l)}\right)^2}{\sum_{l=1}^{L}\sum_{q=1\ldots Q|t_q\oplus k^{(l)}=u} 1}.$$

As the distinguisher is computed over L key bytes, the formula can be maximized over all keys only for small values L (e.g. up to 5).

[1] To see this we rewrite the $\mathcal{D}_{opt}$ from the Eq. (2) [4] in the balanced setup as

$$\mathcal{D}_{opt} = \underset{\boldsymbol{k}\in(\mathbb{F}_2^n)^L}{\operatorname{argmax}} \sum_{q=0}^{2^n-1} \left(- \left(\varphi(t_q^{(l)}) - \frac{1}{L}\sum_{l=1}^{L} x^{(l)}_{q\oplus k^{(l)}}\right)^2 + \frac{2}{L^2}\sum_{l_1=1}^{L}\sum_{l_2=l_1+1}^{L} x^{(l_1)}_{q\oplus k^{(l_1)}} \times x^{(l_2)}_{q\oplus k^{(l_2)}} \right).$$

When the data set is balanced and averaging of traces is performed we can rewrite the distinguisher as a sum of scalar products between rows of the matrix $\boldsymbol{x}^{(\cdot)}$ (re-indexed by the key). As a matter of fact, we have $\forall u \in \mathbb{F}_2^n, \forall l \in \{1, \ldots, L\} \sum_{q=0\ldots 2^n-1 | q\oplus k^{(l)}=u} 1 = L$, thus:

$$\begin{aligned}
\mathcal{D}_{sto.coll.bal} &= \underset{\boldsymbol{k}\in(\mathbb{F}_2^n)^L}{\operatorname{argmax}} \sum_{u\in\mathbb{F}_2^n} \left(\sum_{l=1}^{L} \sum_{\substack{q=0\ldots 2^n-1 \\ q\oplus k^{(l)}=u}} x_q^{(l)} \right)^2 \\
&= \underset{\boldsymbol{k}\in(\mathbb{F}_2^n)^L}{\operatorname{argmax}} \sum_{u\in\mathbb{F}_2^n} \left(\sum_{l=1}^{L} x_{u\oplus k^{(l)}}^{(l)} \right)^2 \\
&= \underset{\boldsymbol{k}\in(\mathbb{F}_2^n)^L}{\operatorname{argmax}} \sum_{u\in\mathbb{F}_2^n} \sum_{l=1}^{L} \left(x_{u\oplus k^{(l)}}^{(l)} \right)^2 + 2 \sum_{l_1=1}^{L} \sum_{l_2=l_1+1}^{L} \left(x_{u\oplus k^{(l_1)}}^{(l_1)} \times x_{u\oplus k^{(l_2)}}^{(l_2)} \right) \\
&= \underset{\boldsymbol{k}\in(\mathbb{F}_2^n)^L}{\operatorname{argmax}} \sum_{u\in\mathbb{F}_2^n} \sum_{l_1=1}^{L} \sum_{l_2=l_1+1}^{L} \left(x_{u\oplus k^{(l_1)}}^{(l_1)} \times x_{u\oplus k^{(l_2)}}^{(l_2)} \right),
\end{aligned}$$

since $\sum_{u\in\mathbb{F}_2^n} \sum_{l=1}^{L} \left(x_{u\oplus k^{(l)}}^{(l)} \right)^2$ is constant for every key.

We can notice that $\forall i \in \mathbb{F}_2^n$,

$$\begin{aligned}
&\sum_{u\in\mathbb{F}_2^n} \sum_{l=1}^{L} \sum_{l_2=l_1+1}^{L} \left(x_{u\oplus k^{(l_1)}}^{(l_1)} \times x_{u\oplus k^{(l_2)}}^{(l_2)} \right) \\
&= \sum_{u\in\mathbb{F}_2^n} \sum_{l=1}^{L} \sum_{l_2=l_1+1}^{L} \left(x_{u\oplus k^{(l_1)}\oplus i}^{(l_1)} \times x_{u\oplus k^{(l_2)}\oplus i}^{(l_2)} \right),
\end{aligned}$$

thus the keys are equivalent up to a byte i xor on every key byte, i.e.

$$\left(k^{(1)}, \ldots, k^{(L)} \right) \sim \left(k^{(1)} \oplus i, \ldots, k^{(L)} \oplus i \right).$$

Moradi et al. proposed correlation-enhanced collision attack in [10]. They average traces to reduce the impact of randomness (noise in measurement). Then, they use the correlation between every two rows of the matrix $\boldsymbol{x}^{(\cdot)}$ and for every re-indexing of the coefficients due to the differential value of any two sub-keys. To recover the full differential of the sub-keys of the key ad hoc solutions were proposed. E.g. extract a system of independent equations [10], perform a branch-and-bound on the sum of correlation coefficients [14], or use an adapted decoding technique [7].

None of these techniques based on correlation enhanced collision attack address the optimality of the approach, leaving the question about it open.

Actually, for any two key bytes we can link scalar product and correlation coefficient as:

$$\rho_{k^{(l_1)},k^{(l_2)}}\left(x^{(l_1)},x^{(l_2)}\right)$$
$$=\frac{2^n\sum_{i=0}^{2^n-1}x^{(l_1)}_{i\oplus k^{(l_2)}}\times x^{(l_2)}_{i\oplus k^{(l_2)}}-\sum_{i=0}^{2^n-1}x_i^{(l_1)}\sum_{i=0}^{2^n-1}x_i^{(l_2)}}{\sqrt{2^n\sum_{i=0}^{2^n-1}\left(x_i^{(l_1)}\right)^2-\left(\sum_{i=0}^{2^n-1}x_i^{(l_1)}\right)^2}\sqrt{2^n\sum_{i=0}^{2^n-1}\left(x_i^{(l_2)}\right)^2-\left(\sum_{i=0}^{2^n-1}x_i^{(l_2)}\right)^2}}.$$

It can be seen from the above formula that for the balanced setup the couple $k^{(l_1)},k^{(l_2)}$ that maximizes the correlation coefficient is the same that maximizes the scalar product. However, maximizing the sum of correlation coefficients or of scalar products might not give the same relation between key bytes. The reason for this is a statistical fluctuations of the factors used as weights (see the denominator in the above formula) when going from the sum of scalar products to the sum of correlation coefficients.

3 Optimal Distinguishers for Random Leakage Functions

With reference to the Eq. (4) [4] and to the previously introduced notations the maximum likelihood (ML) distinguisher can be written as:

$$\mathcal{D}_{opt}=\underset{k\in(\mathbb{F}_2^n)^L}{\operatorname{argmax}}\prod_{q=0}^{2^n-1}\prod_{l=1}^{L}f_{\sigma^2}\left(x_q^{(l)}-\varphi\left(t_q^{(l)}\oplus k^{(l)}\right)\right),$$

where f_{σ^2} denotes Gaussian distribution with the mean value 0 and the standard deviation σ. Bruneau et al. maximize D_{opt} also over the leakage function values. This approach is not sufficient for obtaining a provably optimal, i.e. one that maximizes the likelihood of the key given the measured leakage, distinguisher for the key. However, in some practical situations the attacker might have some a priori knowledge about the leakage function and using it she may try to derive an optimal distinguisher, e.g. by considering each of the leakage function values $\varphi(x)$ as random variables with some guessed distribution. Using such distinguisher maximizes the average success probability when repeating attacks while each time the leakage function values are selected according to the assumed distribution. In particular it is also expected that the attack succeeds on some actual leakage function with higher success probability than in a case of using the distinguisher $D_{sto.coll}$. This can be explained by the fact that the actual leakage function might be a kind of a typical leakage function with respect to the assumed distribution of the leakage function values and with respect to the success probability of the derived distinguisher.

We verified in case of two 8 bit wide S-boxes the higher success rate of 0.90 when using the distinguisher derived (see below) using the knowledge of the distribution of leakage function values as compared to the success rate of 0.50

when using the $D_{sto.coll.bal}$ distinguisher. The following describes the used distribution. Each leakage function φ is created randomly according to the following rule: for each $u \in \{0, \ldots, 255\}$ assign to $\varphi(u)$ a value v selected randomly from a distribution given by the following histogram:

$$H_{ex} = \left\{ \left(0, \frac{246}{256}\right), \left(1, \frac{1}{256}\right), \left(2, \frac{2}{256}\right), \left(3, \frac{3}{256}\right), \left(4, \frac{4}{256}\right) \right\},$$

where (v, p) means that the value v has the probability p of being selected. The higher success rate was also verified for some fixed leakage functions with values drawn from that distribution. Note that the example is given only to show that the $D_{sto.coll.bal}$ or equivalently $D_{sto.coll}$ distinguisher might be not optimal given additional knowledge of the distribution of the leakage function values, and thus to motivate further investigations. No other claims are made at that point.

The optimal distinguisher derived under known distribution p of leakage function values φ is given by:[2] (Any constant mask which is applied to each S-box and which does not change the distribution p has no effect on the distinguisher $D_{opt.fun.p}$).

$$D_{opt.fun.p} = \underset{k \in (\mathbb{F}_2^n)^L}{\operatorname{argmax}} \prod_{q=0}^{2^n-1} \int \left(\prod_{l=1}^{L} f_{\sigma^2}\left(x^{(l)}_{q \oplus k^{(l)}} - \varphi\right) \right) dp(\varphi),$$

where $\int \alpha(\varphi) dp(\varphi)$ means the expectation value of $\alpha(\varphi)$ given the distribution density $dp(\varphi)$ of the leakage function values.

In the example above the integral was just a sum over the values $v \in \{0, \ldots, 4\}$ and $dp(v)$ was set to the probability of the occurrence of each of the value v.

Of special practical interest is the case of Hamming weight leakages. Even without knowing the exact leakage model, it is reasonable in many situations to assume a Hamming weight leakage, and therefore the distribution of the leakage function values is binomial, e.g. it is given by the following histogram:

$$H_{bin.4} = \left\{ \left(0, \frac{1}{16}\right), \left(m, \frac{4}{16}\right), \left(m \times 2, \frac{6}{16}\right), \left(m \times 3, \frac{4}{16}\right), \left(m \times 4, \frac{1}{16}\right) \right\},$$

in case of a 4 bit wide S-box, where the m is a parameter of the distribution.

While it is straightforward to write an exact formula for the optimal distinguisher $D_{opt.fun.binomial}$ in that case, the parameters m of the leakage and the

[2] The derivation is based on the following equation with statistically independent K and ϕ

$$P(K = k | X = x) = \sum_{\varphi} \frac{P(X = x | (K = k, \phi = \varphi)) \times P(K = k) \times P(\phi = \varphi)}{P(X = x)}.$$

Without knowing the distribution $P(\phi)$ of the leakage function values we cannot figure out an optimal distinguisher using the maximum likelihood principle.

standard deviation σ of the noise are still unknown. However, later on we will use such distinguisher derived with known values of m and σ as a benchmark when comparing the success rate of the related $D_{opt.fun.gauss}$ distinguisher derived for leakage function values distributed according to Gaussian distribution. We expect similar success rates for both $D_{opt.fun.binomial}$ and $D_{opt.fun.gauss}$ because Gaussian distribution is an approximation of the binomial distribution.

The integration in the formula for $D_{opt.fun.p}$ can be performed with the standard deviation σ of the noise and dp taken as a density of Gaussian distribution with the mean m_φ and the standard deviation σ_φ. In addition to knowing that the leakage function values are drawn from a Gaussian distribution we also require a balanced set-up of traces.

The result in that case is

$$
\begin{aligned}
&D_{opt.fun.gauss}\\
&= \underset{\boldsymbol{k}\in(\mathbb{F}_2^n)^L}{\operatorname{argmax}} \prod_{q=0}^{2^n-1} \left(\int \left(\prod_{l=1}^{L} f_{\sigma^2}(x^{(l)}_{q\oplus k^{(l)}} - \varphi) \right) \times f_{\sigma_\varphi^2}(\varphi - m_\varphi) d\varphi \right)\\
&= \underset{\boldsymbol{k}\in(\mathbb{F}_2^n)^L}{\operatorname{argmax}} \prod_{q=0}^{2^n-1} \left(e^{\frac{(\sigma_\varphi^2 \times \sum_{l=1}^{L} x^{(l)}_{q\oplus k^{(l)}} + \sigma^2 \times m_\varphi)^2}{2\times\sigma^2\times\sigma_\varphi^2\times(\sigma^2 + L\times\sigma_\varphi^2)} - \frac{m_\varphi^2}{2\times\sigma_\varphi^2} - \frac{\sum_{l=1}^{L}(x^{(l)}_{q\oplus k^{(l)}})^2}{2\times\sigma^2}} \right.\\
&\left. \times \int e^{-\frac{\sigma^2 + L\times\sigma_\varphi^2}{2\times\sigma^2\times\sigma_\varphi^2}\times(\varphi - \frac{\sigma_\varphi^2\times\sum_{l=1}^{L} x^{(l)}_{q\oplus k^{(l)}} + \sigma^2\times m_\varphi}{\sigma^2 + L\times\sigma_\varphi^2})^2} d\varphi \right)\\
&= \underset{\boldsymbol{k}\in(\mathbb{F}_2^n)^L}{\operatorname{argmax}} \sum_{q=0}^{2^n-1} \left(\sigma_\varphi^2 \times \sum_{l=1}^{L} x^{(l)}_{q\oplus k^{(l)}} + \sigma^2 \times m_\varphi \right)^2\\
&= \underset{\boldsymbol{k}\in(\mathbb{F}_2^n)^L}{\operatorname{argmax}} \sum_{q=0}^{2^n-1} \sum_{l_1=1}^{L} \sum_{l_2=l_1+1}^{L} \left(x^{(l_1)}_{q\oplus k^{(l_1)}} \times x^{(l_2)}_{q\oplus k^{(l_2)}} \right).
\end{aligned}
$$

Remarkably, this special result is independent of the parameters, i.e. of the standard deviation σ of the noise, of the mean m_φ and of the standard deviation σ_φ of the leakage function values. It also shows the optimality in terms of maximum likelihood of the $D_{sto.coll.bal}$ distinguisher in case of Gaussian distributed leakage function values.

4 Optimal Evaluation of Distinguishers

The $D_{opt.fun.p}$ distinguishers require to maximize over all $\boldsymbol{k} \in (\mathbb{F}_2^n)^L$. Unfortunately, the triple sum has no structure (local maximum does not lead to global maximum), and to find the $\boldsymbol{k}$ maximizing the sums all cases need to be computed. Thus the optimal solution to recover the key using an optimal collision side-channel attack requires to compute all of the $2^{(n-1)L}$ (e.g. 2^{120} in the case of AES-128) values.[3] We present here an algorithm that aims to find the maximizing $\boldsymbol{k}$ using random space exploration by looking only at a small number of candidate keys $\boldsymbol{k}$.

4.1 Random Space Exploration

The random space exploration algorithm is described in Algorithm 1.[4]

The algorithm returns a key candidate that maximizes the sum of scalar products over the small set of key candidates we explore. Hence, the algorithm tries to find the maximizing key $\boldsymbol{k}$ of the $D_{opt.fun.gauss}$ distinguisher. We note that the term $\sum_{j=1}^{s-1} s(l_j, l_s, \delta \oplus k^{(l_j)})$ in step 14: results in matching the leakage of S-box l_s with a kind of template given by the sum of the leakages of the S-boxes l_1 to $l_{(s-1)}$. If the guess for the keys $k^{(l_1)}$ to $k^{(l_{s-1})}$ is correct, that template converges for larger values of s to the true leakage function value and the chance to recover the correct key k_s increases with greater s. Actually this observation could already have been the starting point for designing the algorithm. Another design idea was based on the observation, that when having a set of different pairs of S-boxes there is a good chance to have one pair for which the correct key can be found. This pair then results in a better template for matching the leakage of the third S-box, and so on.

The cost of the proposed algorithm is modest in terms of memory, we just need to store the maximum key. In terms of time, the algorithm is also efficient and it has a running time $O(L \times 2^n \times max\_tries)$.

We also use a modified version of the Algorithm 1 for the evaluation of the $D_{opt.fun.binomial}$ distinguisher, i.e. for finding its maximizing key $\boldsymbol{k}$. First, the algorithm receives as input the full matrix $\boldsymbol{x}^{(\cdot)}$, and the modification consists also of replacing in line 9:

$$Sum = max_{\delta} \left(s(l_1, l_2, \delta) \right)$$

[3] The minus 1 comes from the equivalence of the keys when xor-ing any fixed value with each subkey.

[4] The random space exploration algorithm can be seen as a repeated execution of the Wiemers' and Klein's algorithm variant 1 with $W = 1$, the details of the algorithm are given in [14]. While the algorithm of Wiemers and Klein was designed for entropy reduction of collision attacks, the target of the random space exploration algorithm was to enable the investigation of the limits of success rates for collision attacks. To sum up, the differences between the Wiemers' and Klein's algorithm and the random space exploration algorithm are:

- the repetition of the execution of variant 1 with $W = 1$ instead of one run with $W > 1$,
- randomized order of S-boxes on each run instead of the fixed order,
- the output of only one candidate instead of a list of $W > 1$ candidates,
- the use of $D_{opt.fun.gauss}$ distinguisher instead of a sum of correlation coefficients.

Algorithm 1. Random space exploration

1: **Input:** The $\frac{L(L-1)}{2}$ lists of 2^n scalar products $s(l_1, l_2, \delta) = \sum_{q=0}^{2^n-1} x_q^{(l_1)} \times x_{q\oplus\delta}^{(l_2)}$
2: **Output:** A key candidate $\boldsymbol{k}$
3: **Notation:** $\overset{\$}{\leftarrow}$ means we pick a value in the set on the right randomly following a uniform distribution
4: $Max = -\infty$
5: **for** $1 \leq try \leq max\_tries$ **do**
6: $\quad l_1 \overset{\$}{\leftarrow} \{1, \ldots, L\}$
7: $\quad ktmp^{(l_1)} = 0$
8: $\quad l_2 \overset{\$}{\leftarrow} \{1, \ldots, L\} \backslash \{l_1\}$
9: $\quad Sum = max_\delta(s(l_1, l_2, \delta))$
10: $\quad ktmp^{(l_2)} = \text{argmax}_\delta(s(l_1, l_2, \delta))$
11: $\quad$ **for** $3 \leq s \leq L$ **do**
12: $\quad\quad l_s \overset{\$}{\leftarrow} \{1, \ldots, L\} \backslash \{l_1, \ldots, l_{s-1}\}$
13: $\quad\quad$ **for** $0 \leq \delta \leq 2^n$ **do**
14: $\quad\quad\quad Current(\delta) = Sum + \sum_{j=1}^{s-1} s(l_j, l_s, \delta \oplus ktmp^{(l_j)})$
15: $\quad\quad$ **end for**
16: $\quad\quad Sum = max_\delta(Current(\delta))$
17: $\quad\quad ktmp^{(l_s)} = \text{argmax}_\delta(Current(\delta))$
18: $\quad$ **end for**
19: $\quad$ **if** $Sum > Max$ **then**
20: $\quad\quad \boldsymbol{k} = \boldsymbol{ktmp}$
21: $\quad\quad Max = Sum$
22: $\quad$ **end if**
23: **end for**
24: **return** $\boldsymbol{k}$

by

$$Sum = max_\delta \left(\sum_{q=1}^{2^n-1} log \left(\int f_{\sigma^2} \left(x_{q\oplus k^{(l_1)}}^{(l_1)} - \varphi \right) \times f_{\sigma^2} \left(x_{q\oplus\delta}^{(l_2)} - \varphi \right) dp(\varphi) \right) \right)$$

and in line 14:

$$Current(\delta) = Sum + \sum_{j=1}^{s-1} s \left(l_j, l_s, \delta \oplus k^{(l_j)} \right)$$

by

$$Current(\delta) = \sum_{q=1}^{2^n-1} log \left(\int f_{\sigma^2} \left(x_{q\oplus\delta}^{(l_s)} - \varphi \right) \times \prod_{j=1}^{s-1} f_{\sigma^2} \left(x_{q\oplus k^{(l_j)}}^{(l_j)} - \varphi \right) dp(\varphi) \right),$$

where $\int \alpha(\varphi) dp(\varphi)$ means the expectation value of $\alpha(\varphi)$ given the distribution density $p(\varphi)$ of the variable φ. Here the distribution density $p(\varphi)$ is the binomial distribution of the n-bit Hamming weights and the integral is effectively a sum (see also Sect. 3).

4.2 Upper Bound for the Success Rate

Interestingly, in an evaluation setup the random space exploration can also be used to find an upper bound for the success rate of the optimal exploration, i.e. the one that recovers the key by computing the maximum of the distinguisher over all $2^{(n-1)L}$ key candidates. As a matter of fact, in the evaluation setup the correct key $\boldsymbol{k}^*$ is known, thus the score

$$S_{\boldsymbol{k}^*} = \sum_{u \in \mathbb{F}_2^n} \sum_{l=1}^{L} \sum_{l_2=l_1+1}^{L} \left(x^{(l_1)}_{u \oplus k^{*(l_1)}} \times x^{(l_2)}_{u \oplus k^{*(l_2)}} \right)$$

is also known. According to the Max value (see line 21:, Algorithm 1) which we find in random space after reaching line 23: we have two cases:

1. $S_{\boldsymbol{k}^*} < Max$, in that case, we know that the optimal exploration, and our random space exploration, will fail. They both output a candidate key that has a higher score than the actual key.
2. $S_{\boldsymbol{k}^*} \geq Max$, in that case, the optimal exploration might find the right key.

Thus, in the evaluation setup, we can count the number of times the case 2 happens and this way obtain an upper bound for the success rate of the optimal exploration. This upper bound can be computed with almost no overhead, we just need to additionally return the value Max in Algorithm 1. To the best of our knowledge, it is the first time an upper bound for the first-order success rate of optimal collision side-channel attack can be computed.

The value of the parameter *max_tries* (see line 5:, Algorithm 1) of the attack plays a role in the attack phase and also in the evaluation step. Higher values of *max_tries* result in higher success rates of the attack and in lower calculated upper bound values.

We will also calculate the upper bound for the success rate of the modified Algorithm 1 for the evaluation of the $D_{opt.fun.binomial}$ distinguisher using a method similar to the method described above.

5 Simulation Results

We present the upper bounds for success rates of collision side-channel attacks, and we compare our method to these upper bounds and to the previous methods in terms of success rate. We choose to evaluate the method using simulation to highlight the differences between the methods without being blurred by slight modifications of the leakage function according to key byte used [7]. For collision side-channel attacks we compare:

- our method presented in Algorithm 1 (labelled 'Prop.') using the distinguisher $D_{opt.fun.gauss}$ (labelled 'scalar') and using the $D_{opt.fun.binomial}$ distinguisher (labelled 'binomial') with *max_tries* $= 128$ (labelled '128 tries') and with *max_tries* $= 2^{13}$ (labelled '2^{13} tries'), and upper bounds (denoted 'UB') computed along the success rates;

- variant 1 of Wiemers' and Klein's algorithm [14] (labelled 'Wiemers') with $W = 128^5$ and using the sum of correlation coefficients (labelled 'corre.') and its modification using the sum of scalar products (labelled 'scalar'). Among all solutions in B_{16} we kept only the maximum to have only one solution to test as for the other solutions;[6]
- Gérard's and Standaert's solution [7] (labelled 'Best Gérard') with normalized correlation, we use six loops of message passing, that is greater that two times the graph's diameter.[7]

For a reference, we also plot template attacks (labelled 'Template'), which in case of the simulation are optimal profiled attacks.

We consider attacks on 16 key bytes, i.e. $L = 16$ and $n = 8$, similar to the AES case. We assume that the attacker has an access to a balanced set of traces. She observes each plaintext byte the same number of times, thanks to averaging she can just use 2^8 plaintexts per S-box. We utilize the balanced setup, and instead of varying the number of traces, we increase or decrease the variance of the white Gaussian noise in our simulations.

For the leakage function we consider two cases. The first case is the setting corresponding to derivation in Sect. 3, i.e. the distribution of the leakage function values is 8 bit binomial (labelled 'rand. leak')[8]. As the second case we consider Hamming weight (HW) leakage of the output of the AES S-box (labelled 'HW leak').

We compute all success rates based on 2500 experiments. This results in a value of standard deviation of estimated success rates less then 0.01.

In Fig. 1, we plot results for the proposed method given in Algorithm 1 using the distinguishers $D_{opt.fun.gauss}$ and $D_{opt.fun.binomial}$ and for the previous methods applied to the same set of data. We can make several observations from the figure.

- For success rates greater than 0.90 the upper bound and the success rate of the Algorithm 1 are close to each other for small value of *max_tries*, i.e. 128. For example, with $\sigma^2 = 11$ and random leakage function values, the success rates are 0.9064 for the upper bound and 0.8956 for Algorithm 1 when using the

[5] Algorithm 1 with *max_tries* = 128 and the variant 1 of Wiemers' and Klein's algorithm with $W = 128$ visit almost the same number of nodes of the search tree/trees. These settings allow meaningful performance comparison of the two algorithms.

[6] In our experiments using only the highest ranked solution or testing of all solutions has a small impact on the success rate of the method.

[7] In our experiments this setting provides the highest success rate compared to the other methods described in the paper of Gérard and Standaert, i.e. Euclidean distance vs. correlation coefficient and normalization vs. Bayesian extension. The Bayesian extension is a boost for score combination, but its derivation uses Fisher transform that is an asymptotic tool. Thus, the Bayesian extension can be counterproductive for attacks which use a small number of traces like 2^8.

[8] In more details, for each experiment we draw a new leakage function φ randomly according to the following rule: for each $u \in \{0, ..., 255\}$ assign to $\varphi(u)$ a value selected randomly according to the binomial distribution of 8-bit Hamming weights.

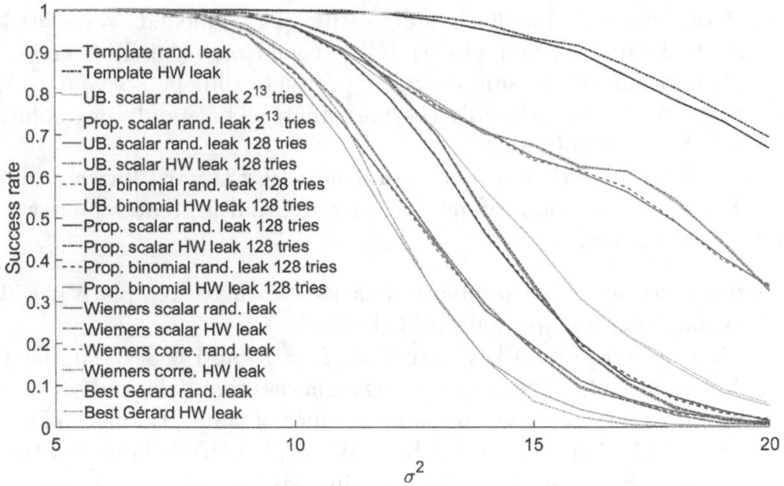

Fig. 1. Upper bounds and success rates of different techniques.

$D_{opt.fun.binomial}$ distinguisher, and the success rates are 0.9068 for the upper bound and 0.8924 for Algorithm 1 when using the $D_{opt.fun.gauss}$ distinguisher. In the same scenario for Gérard's and Standaert's solution the success rate is 0.6832, and for Wiemers' and Klein's solution the success rates are: 0.7284 using the sum of correlation coefficients and 0.7292 using the sum of scalar products.[9,10]

- For larger values of the parameter *max_tries*, i.e. 2^{13}, the distance between the upper bound and the success rate is small for all noise levels. In our experiments performed using the $D_{opt.fun.gauss}$ distinguisher and Algorithm 1 we obtained a maximum distance of 0.0088 between the upper bound and the actual success rate for $\sigma^2 = 18$.
- The use of the distinguisher $D_{opt.fun.gauss}$ instead of the optimal distinguisher $D_{opt.fun.binomial}$ has only a very small impact on the upper bound and on the success rate of the collision side-channel attacks performed using Algorithm 1.
- The Hamming weight of the output of the AES S-box seems to lead only to a bit higher success rates than the average success rate over random leakage

[9] When testing all elements in B_{16} we obtain respectively success rates 0.7808 and 0.7824.

[10] Wiemers and Klein give in [14] an approximate lower bound value of 1.2 for $\tau = \frac{b-a}{\sigma_c}$ for the variant 2 of their algorithm in the special case of the remaining entropy value of 0. This bound is also valid when the distinguisher $D_{opt.fun.gauss}$ is used. We calculated the means a and b and the variance σ_c^2 of the scalar products $c_{l_1,l_2}(k^{(l_1)}, k^{(l_2)}) = \sum_{q=0}^{255}(x^{(l_1)}_{q\oplus k^{(l_1)}} \times x^{(l_2)}_{q\oplus k^{(l_2)}})$ for AES-128, Hamming weight leakage and noise variance σ^2. Using $\delta = k^{(l_1)} \oplus k^{(l_2)}$, $a(\delta) \in [3978, 4192]$ for all $\delta \neq 0$, $b = a(0) = 4608$, $\sigma_c^2 = \sigma^2(2b + 256\sigma^2)$, and $\tau = 1.2$ we obtained for the variance σ^2 values from 10.2 for $a = 4192$ to 19.4 for $a = 3978$. Already the smaller of these approximate values does not agree with our upper bound.

function values with binomial distribution. This indicates that the AES S-box Hamming weight leakage can be considered as a kind of typical leakage function for the set of random leakage function values with binomial distribution.
- There exist a gap between success rates of template attacks and the upper bounds for success rate of collision side-channel attacks. This gap cannot be closed.

6 Summary

Our results provide new insights on collision side-channel attacks. We derive optimal distinguishers for collision side-channel attacks and a computationally efficient algorithm for the evaluation of these distinguishers. The developed evaluation algorithm can also be applied to Bruneau et al. [4] to make their attack computationally feasible for large values of L. The proposed solution offers better results than all previous solutions in terms of success rate. Our approach provides an upper bound for the success rate of collision side-channel attacks. We show experimentally that we are able to reach this upper bound for the optimal distinguishers. This result demonstrates the optimality of our approach to collision side-channel attacks.

As a future work one may try to look at higher-order success rate of collision side-channel attacks. To improve the post-processing of collision side-channel attacks in that case, it might be worth to describe the problem as a dependent knapsack problem, as it was proposed for divide and conquer strategy [9]. Another direction is to look at collision side-channel attacks for higher-order leakage. The correlation collision side-channel attack exploits only first order leakages.

Acknowledgments. The authors thank Wolfgang Thumser, Telekom Security for fruitful discussions on the notion of optimality of collision side-channel attacks.

References

1. Bogdanov, A.: Improved side-channel collision attacks on AES. In: Adams, C., Miri, A., Wiener, M. (eds.) SAC 2007. LNCS, vol. 4876, pp. 84–95. Springer, Heidelberg (2007). https://doi.org/10.1007/978-3-540-77360-3_6
2. Bogdanov, A.: Multiple-differential side-channel collision attacks on AES. In: Oswald, E., Rohatgi, P. (eds.) CHES 2008. LNCS, vol. 5154, pp. 30–44. Springer, Heidelberg (2008). https://doi.org/10.1007/978-3-540-85053-3_3
3. Brier, E., Clavier, C., Olivier, F.: Correlation power analysis with a leakage model. In: Joye, M., Quisquater, J.-J. (eds.) CHES 2004. LNCS, vol. 3156, pp. 16–29. Springer, Heidelberg (2004). https://doi.org/10.1007/978-3-540-28632-5_2
4. Bruneau, N., Carlet, C., Guilley, S., Heuser, A., Prouff, E., Rioul, O.: Stochastic collision attack. IEEE Trans. Inform. Forensics Secur. **12**(9), 2090–2104 (2017). https://doi.org/10.1109/TIFS.2017.2697401
5. Chari, S., Rao, J.R., Rohatgi, P.: Template attacks. In: Kaliski, B.S., Koç, K., Paar, C. (eds.) CHES 2002. LNCS, vol. 2523, pp. 13–28. Springer, Heidelberg (2003). https://doi.org/10.1007/3-540-36400-5_3

6. Durvaux, F., Standaert, F.-X., Veyrat-Charvillon, N.: How to certify the leakage of a chip? In: Nguyen, P.Q., Oswald, E. (eds.) EUROCRYPT 2014. LNCS, vol. 8441, pp. 459–476. Springer, Heidelberg (2014). https://doi.org/10.1007/978-3-642-55220-5_26
7. Gérard, B., Standaert, F.: Unified and optimized linear collision attacks and their application in a non-profiled setting: extended version. J. Cryptogr. Eng. **3**(1), 45–58 (2013). https://doi.org/10.1007/s13389-013-0051-9
8. Joye, M., Quisquater, J.-J. (eds.): CHES 2004. LNCS, vol. 3156. Springer, Heidelberg (2004). https://doi.org/10.1007/b99451
9. Martin, D.P., O'Connell, J.F., Oswald, E., Stam, M.: Counting keys in parallel after a side channel attack. In: Iwata, T., Cheon, J.H. (eds.) ASIACRYPT 2015, Part II. LNCS, vol. 9453, pp. 313–337. Springer, Heidelberg (2015). https://doi.org/10.1007/978-3-662-48800-3_13
10. Moradi, A., Mischke, O., Eisenbarth, T.: Correlation-enhanced power analysis collision attack. In: Mangard, S., Standaert, F.-X. (eds.) CHES 2010. LNCS, vol. 6225, pp. 125–139. Springer, Heidelberg (2010). https://doi.org/10.1007/978-3-642-15031-9_9
11. Schindler, W., Lemke, K., Paar, C.: A stochastic model for differential side channel cryptanalysis. In: Rao, J.R., Sunar, B. (eds.) CHES 2005. LNCS, vol. 3659, pp. 30–46. Springer, Heidelberg (2005). https://doi.org/10.1007/11545262_3
12. Schramm, K., Leander, G., Felke, P., Paar, C.: A collision-attack on AES. In: Joye, M., Quisquater, J.-J. (eds.) CHES 2004. LNCS, vol. 3156, pp. 163–175. Springer, Heidelberg (2004). https://doi.org/10.1007/978-3-540-28632-5_12
13. Standaert, F.-X., Malkin, T.G., Yung, M.: A unified framework for the analysis of side-channel key recovery attacks. In: Joux, A. (ed.) EUROCRYPT 2009. LNCS, vol. 5479, pp. 443–461. Springer, Heidelberg (2009). https://doi.org/10.1007/978-3-642-01001-9_26
14. Wiemers, A., Klein, D.: Entropy reduction for the correlation-enhanced power analysis collision attack. In: Inomata, A., Yasuda, K. (eds.) IWSEC 2018. LNCS, vol. 11049, pp. 51–67. Springer, Cham (2018). https://doi.org/10.1007/978-3-319-97916-8_4

Microarchitectural Attacks

A Bit-Level Approach to Side Channel Based Disassembling

Valence Cristiani, Maxime Lecomte, and Thomas Hiscock(✉)

Univ. Grenoble Alpes, CEA, LETI, MINATEC Campus, 38054 Grenoble, France
{valence.cristiani,maxime.lecomte,thomas.hiscock}@cea.fr

Abstract. Side-Channel Based Disassembling (SCBD) is a powerful application of side-channel analysis that allows recovering instructions executed by a processor from its physical leakages, such as the electromagnetic field (EM) emitted by the chip. These attacks directly compromise code confidentiality, but they can also reveal to an adversary many critical information on the system's internals. In this work, we propose a new approach for SCBD that directly focuses the bit encoding of an instruction using local EM leakage. We exploit a very precise bit-level leakage model and derive from it new algorithms that aim at recovering the actual bit values. We also propose strategies to automate the complex tasks of finding the best EM probe positions and combining them to improve results. On a PIC16 target, our method succeed in recovering the bits of an instruction with an average rate of 99,41% per bit. Compared to the state of the art, our disassembler is easier to train, recovers more information about instructions than just opcode and requires almost no modifications to target other processor architectures. Thus, this kind of disassemblers might become a threat to more complex processors, where side-channel disassembling has not been proved to be feasible yet.

Keywords: Side-channel analysis · Reverse engineering · Hardware security · Leakage analysis

1 Introduction

Side-Channel Based Disassembling (SCBD) is the task of recovering instructions executed by a device based on its physical signature, known as side-channel leakages. For more than two decades many techniques and tools have been developed to extract secrets from sources such as timing variations [7], power consumption [6], electromagnetic field [15] (EM), acoustic noise [4] and many others. While side-channel analysis research is primarily concerned with the security of cryptographic primitives, there is also an active research on SCBD [3,10,13,18]. Indeed an accurate quantification of the instruction leakage is a very useful security indicator for many systems. Obviously, SCBD is a direct threat to code intellectual property, which can be a requirement for manufacturers that put lots of efforts into the development of an algorithm. The instruction stream can also

S. Belaïd and T. Güneysu (Eds.): CARDIS 2019, LNCS 11833, pp. 143–158, 2020.
https://doi.org/10.1007/978-3-030-42068-0_9

reveal sensible code regions such as block ciphers or function entries. Such information can be exploited by an attacker to drive more specific attacks such as fault injections. Interestingly, SCBD can also be used as a non-intrusive malware detection mechanism [11].

The SCBD task can be regarded as a supervised machine learning classification problem, where a side-channel trace has to be associated to a sequence of executed instructions. The natural approach is to divide the global trace into instruction traces correctly labeled. These traces will then feed a learning algorithm in order to build a classifier able to make accurate predictions on the instructions that corresponds to an attack trace. However, training such a classifier is difficult in practice, as many target-specific knowledge is required to create a model. Furthermore, with complex processor architectures and deep pipelines, the switching noise generated by other activities in the core becomes preponderant. A proper randomization of all of these surrounding elements requires a huge amount of data, as well as complex profiling code snippets. Thus, while the opcode classification approach proved to work on small microcontrollers [13,18] it is unlikely that it would scale to more complex processors.

Contributions. In this work, we propose an alternative approach to SCBD that overcome these issues. The core idea is to create a classifier directly on the bits that encode the instructions. This approach requires almost no assumptions on the target architecture, as in any processor, the bits of the instructions are transferred from memory to the processor and then manipulated, which may introduce leakages that can be exploited. Furthermore, the training is greatly simplified: the profiling can be performed on random code snippets, and by construction a bit-level approach allows having more training data available per class. We also show how exploiting very local leakages and combining EM measured at different positions greatly improves the accuracy.

Through this paper, we detail the construction of a bit-level SCBD (Sect. 3) and evaluate its performances on a PIC16F microcontroller (Sects. 4 and 5). We manage to get an average of 99.41% recognition rate per bit which leads to an opcode recognition rate as efficient as current state of the art. However, our disassembler recovers much more information encoded in the instructions (literal values, register numbers, etc.). These results suggest that the bit-level approach proposed is worth considering for SCBD on more complex cores.

2 Background

2.1 Structure of a Side-Channel Disassembler

The high-level structure of a side-channel disassembler as a supervised machine learning classification task is shown in Fig. 1. During a *profiling phase*, the attacker has access to a clone of the target device on which he can run arbitrary programs. He then collects side-channel data, such as the EM field, during the execution of several profiling code snippets in order to train a classifier. During the *attack phase*, the classifier is applied on unknown traces to predict and recover instructions. An attack trace usually contains many instructions, thus a preliminary step is required to divide the trace of a program into individual instruction traces. On small devices, instructions have a constant execution time, hence a fixed-size windows is enough to extract instructions. But with complex cores this operation may require a more advanced strategy.

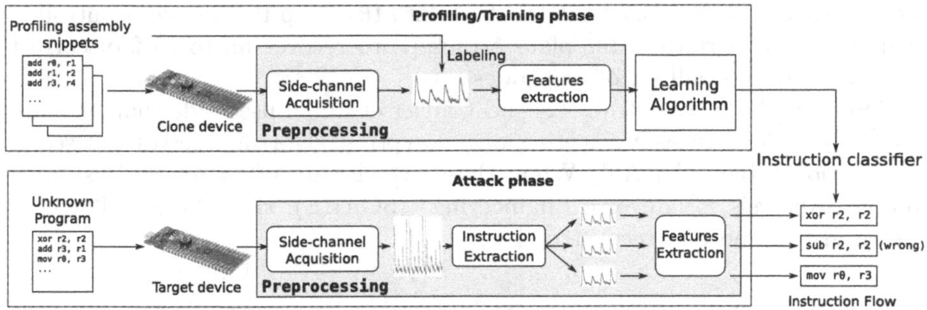

Fig. 1. High level architecture of a side-channel disassembler

The goal of a classifier is to associate a class $c \in \mathcal{C}$ to a trace $\boldsymbol{x}$ (a realization of a random variable $\boldsymbol{X}$) of p samples. In an opcode-based classifier $\mathcal{C}$ is the set of opcodes of the target architecture, for example $\mathcal{C} = \{\texttt{add}, \texttt{xor}, \texttt{load}, \dots\}$. The template attack (TA) of Chari et al. [1], used by most opcode-based classifiers [3,13,18] build an estimation of $\Pr(\boldsymbol{X} \mid C = c)$ during the profiling phase which is then used in the attack phase to compute $\Pr(C = c \mid \boldsymbol{X})$ thanks to Bayes' theorem. Given an unknown instruction trace $\boldsymbol{x}$, an attacker selects the class that maximizes $\Pr(C = c \mid \boldsymbol{X} = \boldsymbol{x})$. The TA models the per-class probability density $\Pr(\boldsymbol{X} \mid C = c)$ as a multivariate Gaussian distribution denoted $\mathcal{N}(\boldsymbol{\mu}_c, \boldsymbol{\Sigma}_c)$, where $\boldsymbol{\mu}_c$ is the mean vector and $\boldsymbol{\Sigma}_c$ the covariance matrix of the distribution. For each class c, the profiling phase infers the parameters $\boldsymbol{\mu}_c$, $\boldsymbol{\Sigma}_c$ from a set of observations $(\boldsymbol{x}_c)$ using classical statistical estimators. Due to its proximity with the quadratic discriminant analysis (QDA) technique in the machine learning field, we use the terms QDA and TA interchangeably.

However, not all samples in a trace contain relevant information. A common practice is to apply feature extraction techniques to reduce the computational cost of the attack. In a nutshell, these techniques transform a trace of p samples into a trace of d samples (with $d \ll p$) while preserving -hopefully- most of the information. Both the training and the attack phases are performed in this reduced feature space. The most common feature extraction techniques include the Principal Component Analysis (PCA) and Linear Discriminant analysis (LDA).

2.2 Related Work

Early Side-Channel Based Reverse Engineering. The use of side-channel analysis for software reverse engineering was first suggested by Quisquarter et al. [16] in 2002, who described an instruction classifier based on a neural network. Unfortunately, they did not provide experimental results. A leakage analysis on a Java card by Vermoen et al. [19] proved that some instructions (Java bytecodes) could be identified in a power trace, but they did not propose an instruction recovery algorithm. In his master thesis, Goldback [5] constructed a very detailed power leakage model of a 8-bit Microchip PIC16 microcontroller. He managed to perform a template attack [1] to recover up to 75% of correct instructions on a small set of 4 opcodes.

Concurrently, Novak et al. [12] and Clavier et al. [2] used side-channel analysis to perform reverse-engineering on encryption algorithms involving secret permutation tables (A3/A8). While these attacks are often referred as "Side Channel Analysis for Reverse Engineering" (SCARE), they do not allow any kind of instruction flow reconstruction.

Side-Channel Based Disassembly. The first real side-channel based disassembler was described by Eisenbarth et al. [3] in 2010. They constructed an opcode classifier using a template attack. Thanks to Hidden Markov Models they managed to exploit prior knowledge on instruction distribution and improve the accuracy of their disassembler by a few percents. On a PIC16 micronconroller using power consumption, they managed to get a 70% recognition rate on test data and 40% on real programs. Strobel et al. [18] also described an opcode-based side-channel disassembler, working on EM. They concluded that EM contains much more information than power consumption and managed to get 90% recognition rate on real programs and 95% on test programs. Msgna et al. [10] constructed an instruction classifier based on a k-Nearest Neighbors (k-NN) algorithm. They reported a 100% instruction recognition on 35 instructions of an ATMega163 microcontroller. However, this classifier was not evaluated on real programs and [18] could not reproduce their results. Park et al. [13] constructed a SCBD on a ATMega328P exploiting knowledge of the hardware used by each instruction. They reported a 99.03% recognition rate thanks to advanced noise reduction preprocessing techniques (based on discrete wavelet transforms) and a hierarchical classification as suggested by McCann et al. [8,9].

3 Construction of a Bit-Level Side-Channel Disassembler

3.1 Challenges of Bit-Level Instruction Recovery

Processor instructions are usually encoded as a binary word (denoted $\mathcal{I}$ for the rest of this paper) of 8 up to 128 bits which contains information such as the opcode, registers and literal values used in the instructions. Our approach consists in attacking bits of $\mathcal{I}$ independently, which requires to train a distinct classifier for each bit of the instruction. Although this idea sounds pretty straightforward, it comes with viability questions that we discuss hereafter.

Distinguishing bit level variations, which impact consumption in a very tiny manner, requires a high signal to noise ratio. More than this, each bit should have its own leakage characteristics, otherwise, distinguishing for example the 2-digits binary words `01` and `10` would not be possible. As explained in Sect. 3.4, we suggest using EM with multiple probe positions to exploit local leakage and thus, increase chances of detecting such leakage differences between bits.

Another problem is that we suggest to attack independently some bits whose impact on the physical quantities measured are not independent. Small groups of bits of $\mathcal{I}$ are sometimes only interpretable as a whole and not separately. To address this issue, we propose to analyze only the part of the trace that corresponds to the fetching of the instruction, totally ignoring the actual execution of the instruction. While this may be interpreted as a loss of information, this drastically reduces the dependencies between the bits on the power consumption. In other words, we only analyze the update of the instruction register and not its actual execution behavior.

3.2 Leakage Model and Classification

A leakage model for individual bits of the instructions has to be selected in order to derive the set of classes $\mathcal{C}$ of the bit classifiers. The most common models are the Hamming Weight and Hamming distance models which at the bit level, respectively estimate the leakage as the bit value and as the bit toggle. A more accurate model known as the "signed Hamming distance" (SHD), introduced in [14] states that with precise electromagnetic measurements, the direction of the bit toggle can also be distinguished.

Based on these observations, we selected a leakage model with 3 possible target events at a given time for each bit: the bit stayed constant, it switched from 0 to 1 or switched from 1 to 0. We denote $\mathcal{T} = \{constant, 0 \rightarrow 1, 1 \rightarrow 0\}$ the set of these transitions. Following the formalism introduced in Sect. 2.1, for each bit of the instruction a classifier with $\mathcal{C} = \mathcal{T}$ is created. It combines LDA for feature extraction and QDA for the actual classification. The training phase can be done on random instructions, with correctly labeled bit transitions, which greatly simplifies the process. Then, for an observed sequence of N instructions, the classifier is applied to all the instructions successively, and yields a finite sequence of pair: $\mathbf{T} = (t_n, p_n)_{1 \leq n \leq N}$ of bit transition associated with its probability.

3.3 From Signed Hamming Distance to Bit Values

The sequence $\mathbf{T}$ still needs to be transformed into a sequence of bit values. However, finding the optimal bit sequence is not straightforward, as each bit prediction influences the predictions for other bits. We propose a simple algorithm that perform this task. The sequence $\mathbf{T}$ generated by the classifier is given as input to the $\texttt{FindBits}_{\texttt{Left}}$ function (shown in Algorithm 1) which maintains a state bit (b_s) and updates its value according to the transitions encountered. In case of 0 → 1 or 1 → 0, the current state bit is set to the transition final value. When no transition occurred, the current bit value is kept. The algorithm also computes a confidence in the bit value returned (p_s in Algorithm 1). This value is overwritten on a bit toggle, but is decreased when a constant transition is taken. Intuitively, we should be less confident in a constant transition as we take the precedent value as output, which could also be wrong. We explored different strategies to update p_s in this case. Based on our experiments, an efficient one is to multiply p_s by the confidence of the actual transition. This confidence value is useful for comparing different predictions for the same bit.

Algorithm 1. $\texttt{FindBits}_{\texttt{Left}}$ (see comments for $\texttt{FindBits}_{\texttt{Right}}$)

Input: **T**, a sequence of transitions with their probability
Output: **B**, a sequence of bit values with their confidence

B ← empty sequence
$b_s \leftarrow 0$
$p_s \leftarrow 0$

for $(t\,,p) \in \mathbf{T}$ **do** `/* In a right scan: iterate in reverse order */`
  if $t \in \{0 \rightarrow 1,\ 1 \rightarrow 0\}$ **then**
    $p_s \leftarrow p$
    $b_s \leftarrow$ final value of t `/* And use the initial value of` t `instead */`
  else
    $p_s \leftarrow p_s \times p$
  Append $(p_s,\ b_s)$ to **B**
end
return B

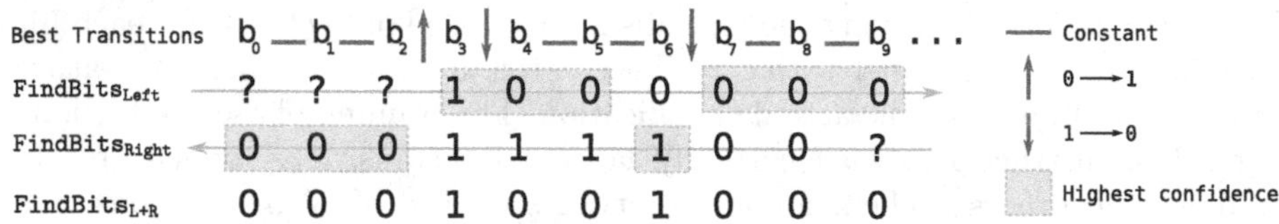

Fig. 2. Example of the different bit recovery algorithms proposed

Indeed, a transition reveals information about both the initial value and the final value. The $\texttt{FindBits}_{\texttt{Left}}$ procedure only uses the final value so far. Thus, a possible improvement is to tweak this function and define $\texttt{FindBits}_{\texttt{Right}}$ which perform the same algorithm in reverse order to exploit the information on the initial value. The right scan works the same way as the left scan but uses the initial value of the transition as the current bit value instead of the final value. The improved algorithm, denoted $\texttt{FindBits}_{L+R}$, runs both versions of $\texttt{FindBits}$, align the two output sequences so that the nth element of each sequence corresponds to the same bit transition, and compare the two sequences selecting the bit value with the highest confidence. An example of this algorithm is shown in Fig. 2. We notice that by construction $\texttt{FindBits}_{\texttt{Left}}$ and $\texttt{FindBits}_{\texttt{Right}}$ cannot give output until the first bit toggle encountered. From the previous algorithms the success rate (SR) of our classifier is defined as the number of correct bit predictions divided by the number of instructions.

3.4 Exploiting Local Information

Our classification uses EM field as input data rather than power consumption. Indeed, EM field with a careful probe positioning allows capturing very local effects such as single bit leakages. As we attack each bit of $\mathcal{I}$ independently, the best positions are likely to be different between the bits.

Choosing the Best Positions. The ideal approach to select the best probe position would be to exhaustively walk a grid of $n \times m$ positions above the circuit, run the attack on each position and select the one with the highest SR. However, this strategy can quickly become too expensive in terms of computations. For example, even a small 20×20 grid leads to 400 different positions. In our case, the longest part of the attack is the feature extraction (LDA). In order to speed up the cartography we perform the attack on a very reduced set of k points of interest (PoI). It can be viewed as an additional feature extraction step performed before the LDA during the cartography. This PoI extraction transforms the input traces ($\boldsymbol{x}_i$) of p samples into $k \ll p$ dimensional vectors ($\boldsymbol{x}'_i$). We choose to keep the k samples $\boldsymbol{x}(t)$ that maximize the Mean Difference (MD):

$$MD(t) = \sum_{\substack{c_1, c_2 \in \mathcal{I}, \\ c_1 \neq c_2}} \left| \mathrm{E}[\boldsymbol{X}(t) \mid C = c_1] - \mathrm{E}[\boldsymbol{X}(t) \mid C = c_2] \right|$$

Choosing the value of k can be done empirically observing the evolution of the SR as k decreases, at some fixed positions. Although the SRs may be lower with this additional step, we assume that this should not drastically change the ranking of the positions. Once the best positions has been found, the actual attack can be run with either a higher value of k or without the PoI extraction.

Combining Different Positions. In a previous work, Strobel et al. [18] combined EM traces acquired from different positions by concatenating them before the features extraction. However, finding the best combination of positions (which maximise the SR for instance) is hard in practice due to an exponential-size search space. We propose a simple greedy algorithm (see Algorithm 2) that searches a good subset of positions to attack one bit. In a nutshell, the algorithm builds iteratively a set $\mathcal{P}$ of best positions. At each iteration, the algorithm attempts to add each one of the remaining positions to $\mathcal{P}$. The one that improves the most the SR is added to $\mathcal{P}$. The algorithm may exit earlier if the success rate does not improve enough (this threshold is defined by ϵ).

Algorithm 2. FindPos

Input: M, a list of EM measurements at different positions in a set $\mathcal{G}$
Output: $\mathcal{P} \subset \mathcal{G}$, a subset of positions to be combined

```
/* The SR(P,M) function concatenates EM data at positions P, runs
   the attack, computes and returns the SR */
```

$\mathcal{P} \leftarrow \{\}$
for $step \leftarrow 0$ **to** $step_{max}$ **do**
    $best \leftarrow \arg\max_{pos \in \mathcal{G} \setminus \mathcal{P}} SR(\mathcal{P} \cup \{pos\}, \mathbf{M})$
    if $|SR(\mathcal{P}, \mathbf{M}) - SR(\mathcal{P} \cup \{best\}, \mathbf{M})| < \epsilon$ **then return** $\mathcal{P}$
    $\mathcal{P} \leftarrow \mathcal{P} \cup best$
end
return $\mathcal{P}$

4 Leakage Analysis of the PIC16F

4.1 Overview of the PIC16F

Our experiments are conducted on a PIC16F15376 Microchip microcontroller from the MPLAB Xpress evaluation board. Besides being ubiquitous in embedded systems, this family of PIC microcontrollers is a common reference in the SCBD literature [3,5,18] and allows a fair comparison of our results. The PIC16F15376 has around 50 instructions which are encoded on 14 bits. A typical instruction contains from 3 to 6 bits that are used to match the instruction (the opcode in some sense). The remaining bits encode the arguments of the instruction such as a control bits, source/destination registers or literal values.

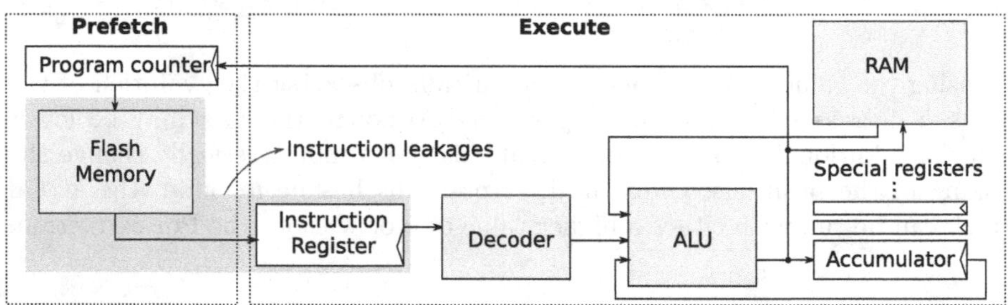

Fig. 3. Architecture of the PIC16F

Architecture. A simplified internal architecture of the PIC16F is depicted on Fig. 3. Excluding jumps, all instructions require 4 clock cycles to complete. During the execution of an instruction, the next one is prefetched from FLASH memory, thus this processor has a 2-stage pipeline: prefetch and execution. The instruction bit leakages are most likely to be caused by this prefetching and the instruction register activity. Jump instructions require 4 additional clock cycles to be executed but can be regarded as the actual instruction followed by a **nop**. This dummy instruction is actually only used to refill the pipeline after the jump and our disassembler always detect it as a **nop**.

Side-Channel Behavior. A taste of EM and power side-channel traces obtained during the execution of 3 instructions are shown in Fig. 4. Both were acquired using the measurement setup described in Sect. 4.2. We stress that in all of the experiments, the PIC16 is clocked at 20 Mhz, except for Fig. 4 where the clock was reduced to 1 MHz to distinguish power peaks (at 20 Mhz, the power curve is flat). The 4 execution cycles are clearly visible on the traces. As expected, the EM behavior is much more local: some peaks have different amplitudes and small temporal shifts based on the probe position.

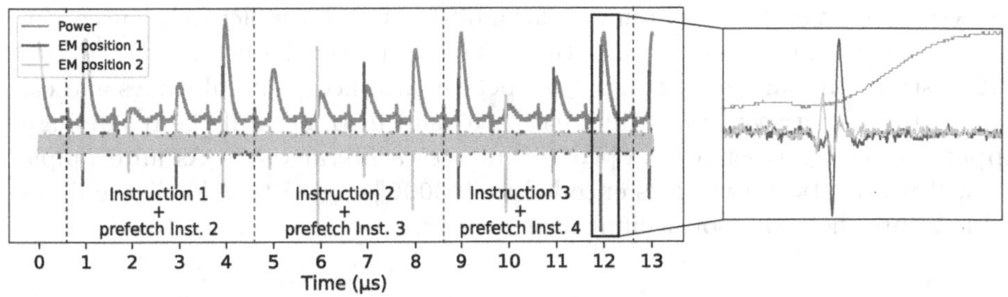

Fig. 4. Power and EM field measured during the execution of 3 instructions.

4.2 Our Experimental Setup

Our experimental setup is presented in Fig. 5. We acquire the near field electromagnetic emanations of the PIC16F through an EM Langer probe, an ICR HH 100 27 with a bandwidth of 6 GHz. The probe is placed over the IC package without any depackaging, at less than 500 μm from the package thanks to a high precision motorized XYZ table. The probe is connected through a low-noise amplifier to a digital oscilloscope (DSO) from Rohde & Schwarz (RTO 2024) which has a bandwidth of 2 GHz and a sample rate set to 10 GS/s. The PIC is clocked by an external reference set at 20 MHz. A GPIO of the PIC is used to synchronize the oscilloscope acquisition with the computation.

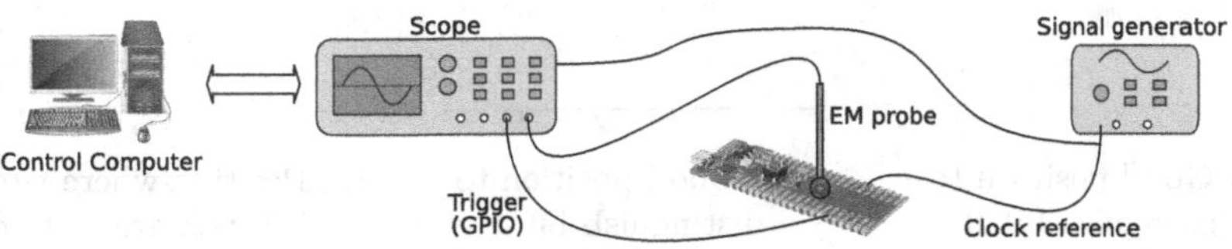

Fig. 5. Experimental setup

With these settings, the 4 clock cycles of an instruction last for 200 ns and represents 2000 samples of the oscilloscope. A typical trace may span over several milliseconds and is made of thousands of instructions. To avoid synchronization issues, the clock of the PIC is generated by a signal generator (FI5350GA) which is also connected to the reference clock of the DSO. This setup ensures that the PIC and the DSO stay synchronized and that no post processing is required to divide a trace into individual instructions.

4.3 Study of Single Bit Leakages

This section presents three experimental results which confirm that there exists probe positions where (1) single bit leakages actually occur, (2) each bit influences the EM field independently from other bits and (3) the SHD leakage model suggested in Sect. 3.2 is appropriate. These experiments are seen as pre-attack analysis to validate the requirements for a bit-level disassembler to be successful. For concision and simplicity, only the behavior of the 8 lower bits of $\mathcal{I}$ (14-bit PIC instructions) are analyzed. These specific bits encode literal values and can be set to an arbitrary value still creating a valid instruction if the remaining 6 upper bits of $\mathcal{I}$ are set to an opcode that uses a literal value. As an example, we will use `movlw k` (which is encoded as $\texttt{110000}\|k_{\text{base }2}$) that loads the literal value `k` into the processor accumulator register.

Leakage Differences Between Bits. To demonstrate that single bit leakages are distinguishable, we perform Welch's t-test [17] between traces of `movlw 0` and `movlw` 2^j, with $0 \leq j \leq 7$. This test evaluates whether there are significant differences on traces when a single bit of the instruction changes. In the profiling code, a `nop` (encoded with fourteen 0 s) is placed before each `movlw` instruction, so that the test works for any leakage model. The t-test is performed on all 400 probe positions of a square (2 mm × 2 mm) grid (20 × 20) centered over the chip. Many probe positions with a successful t-tests (that goes over a threshold of 4.5) were found, which means that the SNR in our setup is good enough to detect single bit variations. Figure 6a and b show respectively positions where a t-test for $j = 0$ and for $j = 4$ are very different from the others. Intuitively, these two positions may bring useful information to determine respectively the value of bit

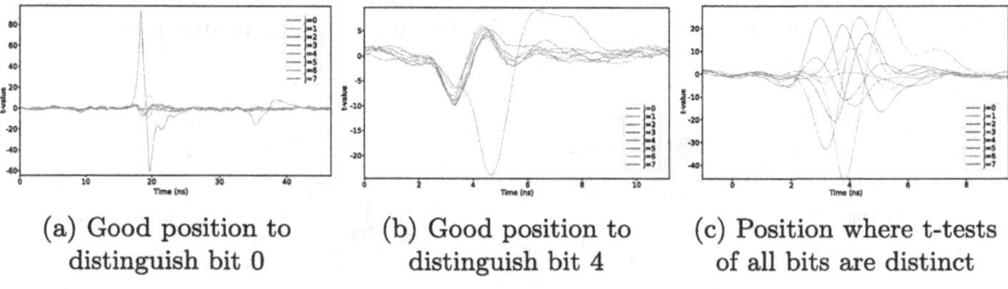

(a) Good position to distinguish bit 0 (b) Good position to distinguish bit 4 (c) Position where t-tests of all bits are distinct

Fig. 6. Single bit T-Tests results at different positions

0 and bit 4 of $\mathcal{I}$. Figure 6c shows a position where all t-tests are distinct from each other. The same experiment was performed with other literal instructions such as `addlw` or `xor` and gave similar results.

Leakage Independence of Bits. The second experiment aims at verifying that each bit of $\mathcal{I}$ contributes independently to the EM field. We use the notation $\mathcal{L}(\texttt{movlw k})$ to denote the measured EM field during the prefetching of the instruction `movlw k` (as in the previous experiment, a `nop` is prepended to each instruction). In our setup, $\mathcal{L}(\cdot)$ returns a 2000-dimensional vector, as the prefetching last for one instruction. To model the leakage strictly caused by an 8 bits literal value we define the leakage function $\mathcal{L}_{literal}$ simply by:

$$\mathcal{L}_{literal}(\texttt{k}) = \mathcal{L}(\texttt{movlw k}) - \mathcal{L}(\texttt{movlw 0})$$

If the leakage of bits are independent, one would expect that the leakages of individual bits can be summed to obtain the leakage of a given word, formally for any subset J of $\{0, 1, 2, 3, 4, 5, 6, 7\}$, one should have:

$$\sum_{j \in J} \mathcal{L}_{literal}(2^j) = \mathcal{L}_{literal}\left(\sum_{j \in J} 2^j\right)$$

We verified this equation empirically for some of the probe positions found in the previous experiments. Figure 7 shows an example where $J = \{0, 1, 2, 3, 4, 5, 6, 7\}$. All the small amplitude curves represent the leakage function $\mathcal{L}_{literal}(2^j)$ for $0 \leq j \leq 7$. The dark and light blue lines represent respectively the sum of all the individual leakages and the leakage of 255 which is equal to $\sum_{j=0}^{7} 2^j$. These two lines clearly seem to match. One could argue that this experiment is not enough to really show that each bit contributes independently to the global leakage. However, it still increases our confidence in the feasibility of the attack.

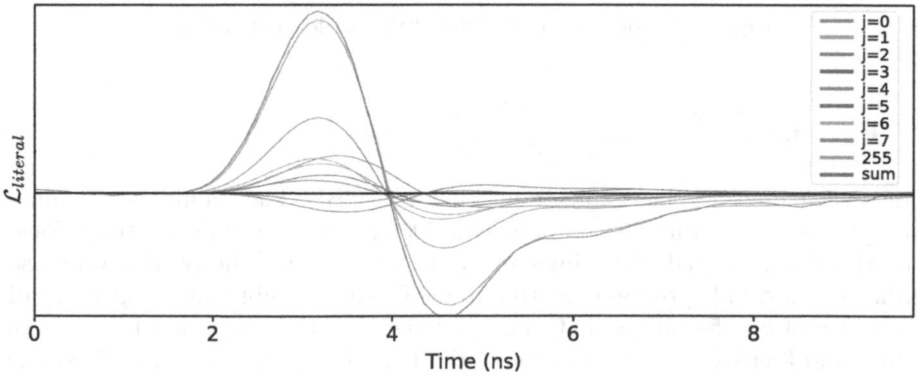

Fig. 7. Leakage independence (Color figure online)

Leakage Model. All experiments presented so far analyzed the fetching of instructions preceded by a nop, so that the results are agnostic to the leakage model. To confirm that the signed Hamming distance is an appropriate model, we choose some of the probe positions with high t-test associated to one particular bit of $\mathcal{I}$. Then, we analyzed the leakages in terms of transitions of this bit (all the other bits being constant). Figure 8 shows the EM traces for multiple transitions of the bit 0. This clearly illustrates that the three classes from the SHD model create a good partitioning of traces.

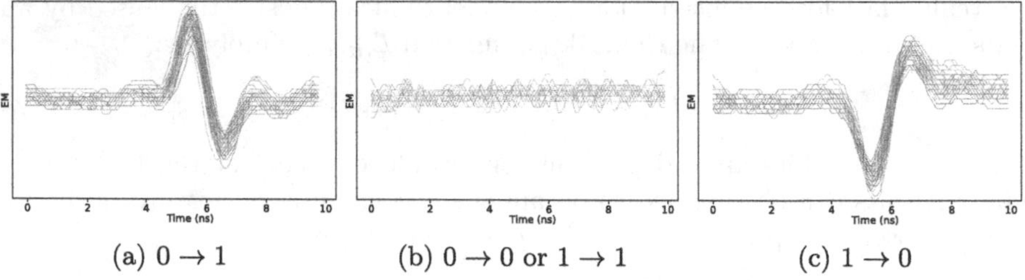

(a) $0 \to 1$ (b) $0 \to 0$ or $1 \to 1$ (c) $1 \to 0$

Fig. 8. EM traces grouped according to the transition of bit 0

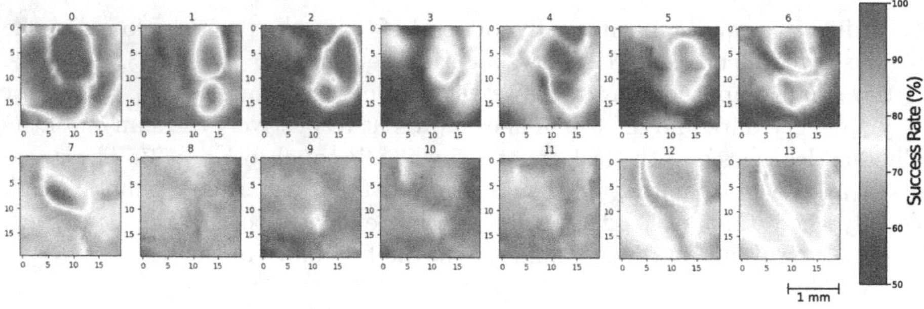

Fig. 9. Cartography of the SR of the bit-level classifiers

5 Evaluation

This section presents the results of our bit-level SCBD. The training and evaluation phases use two different sets made of 2000 random valid instructions. Each acquisition is averaged 1000 times to improve the SNR. The results were also confirmed on simple programs written in C. The disassembler first applies a PoI extraction of $k = 50$ points that maximize the MD, then applies a LDA to the results and keeps 2 components. Then, the fourteen QDA-based classifiers, one for each bit of $\mathcal{I}$, are applied to recover the 1999 bit transitions among the 3 transition classes $\mathcal{T}$ introduced in Sect. 3.2. Finally, the algorithms described in Sect. 3.3 are applied to recover the 1999 corresponding bit values.

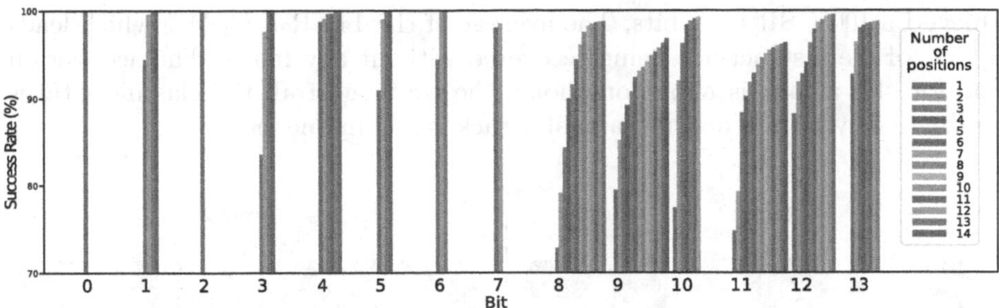

Fig. 10. Evolution of the success rate by adding new positions

5.1 Mono-Spatial Attack

The attack was first conducted for each bit on each of the 20 × 20 grid (400 positions) that was used for our leakage analysis. The SR of the attack (using the $\texttt{FindBits}_{L+R}$ algorithm) on all the grid and for each bit is shown in Fig. 9 (a Gaussian interpolation has been applied to the raw data). Surprisingly, each bit has its own spatial signature: the "hot areas", where the attack has a better success rate, strongly depend on the bit. The best success rates obtained for each bit are given in Table 1. The $\texttt{FindBits}_{L+R}$ algorithm slightly improves the accuracy of the attack. While most bits are recovered with a high accuracy, a few (bits 8, 9, 10, 11), hardly get above 80%. These results can be improved by combining measurements from multiple positions.

Table 1. Success rate at the best probe position for each bit

Bit	0	1	2	3	4	5	6	7	8	9	10	11	12	13
$\texttt{FindBits}_{\texttt{Left}}$	100	94.1	99.2	83.1	97.0	90.7	93.5	97.4	71.8	78.6	75.9	72.8	88.7	92.0
$\texttt{FindBits}_{L+R}$	100	94.8	99.5	85.7	98.2	93.1	94.6	97.9	74.5	80.6	78.7	74.2	90.9	93.5

5.2 Multi-spatial Attack

We evaluate the multi-position attack described in Sect. 3.4 by collecting and combining data from up to 14 positions using Algorithm 2. Figure 10 shows how adding more positions affects the SR of each bit. Note that for a given bit, we stop collecting new positions when the SR improvement is too low. These results show that the low SR of some bits in the mono-spatial case (bits 8 to 11) can be brought up to 97% and more with several additional positions. Once the best position combination has been found it is still possible to increase the number of sample kept by the PoI extraction: Table 2 shows the SR of a multi-spatial attack where the number of PoI is higher ($k = 400$). All the SR are above 98.4%, we achieved a 100% SR for 6 bits. The average of the 14 SR is 99.41% which leads to 95% of the instructions being recovered without any faults. The acquisition time for this attack is about one hour, the training of all the classifiers takes approximately 30 min and the actual attack is instantaneous.

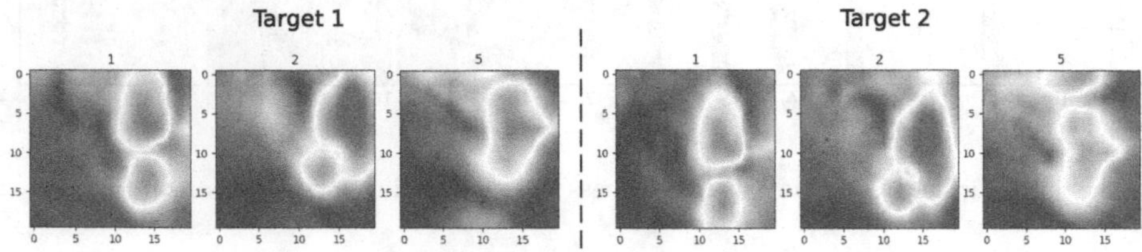

Fig. 11. Leakage cartography for two different devices (same scale as Fig. 9)

Table 2. Success rate for a multi-spatial attack

Bit	0	1	2	3	4	5	6	7	8	9	10	11	12	13
Success rate	100	100	100	100	99.8	100	100	98.5	98.6	98.9	99.3	98.4	99.6	98.7
Used positions	1	4	1	4	6	4	3	2	13	14	7	14	11	8

5.3 Template Portability

In a realistic context, the training phase would be performed on a clone of the target. This introduces the risk of overfitting on the clone device characteristics. Our first attempt to port the attack was no exception to the rule: applying our classifier to a different target completely failed. However, the SR cartography for two different targets shown in Fig. 9 reveal clear similarities, which suggests that the attacks behave almost the same on the two targets. More precisely the SR cartography shown in Fig. 11 is almost the same but shifted by a constant vector of norm around 300 µm. We successfully conducted an attack between the two target with roughly the same SR as in the mono-target case simply by shifting all the probe position at the acquisition time on the second circuit. In a real attack scenario, we argue that the shift vector could be brute-forced (until a high SR is reached) by attacking a known sequence of instructions such as the boot code.

6 Conclusion and Further Work

In this work, we described a new kind of side-channel disassembler that uses bit-level classifiers to recover instructions from non-invasive EM measurements. This approach requires a very precise experimental setup to discriminate small bits variations in traces, especially on very a low-power device like a PIC16F microcontroller. Fortunately, the algorithms proposed in this paper can fully automate the recovering process. Furthermore, we observed that the disassembler is portable between different chips of the same family, which makes this kind of attacks truly realistic. A bit-level instruction disassembler is a huge gain in terms of genericity. The training process is greatly simplified compared to an opcode classifier because it can be performed on random binaries instead of carefully crafted assembly snippets. We demonstrated that such a disassembler achieve good recognition rate, with an average success rate of 99.41% on a bit level and 95% on the full 14-bits instruction. This result may be improved by exploiting prior knowledge on the program such as instruction transition probability, invalid opcode, etc.

It seems that our approach can be extended to recover other valuable information from processors such as runtime register values. Moreover, this work opens interesting perspectives regarding the side-channel disassembling on pipelined processors, which remains an open problem. Future work will aim at validating our approach on more complex processors.

Acknowledgments. The authors would like to thanks the reviewers for their helpful comments. This work was funded thanks to the French national program "Programme d'Investissement d'Avenir IRT Nanoelec" ANR-10-AIRT-05.

References

1. Chari, S., Rao, J.R., Rohatgi, P.: Template attacks. In: Kaliski, B.S., Koç, K., Paar, C. (eds.) CHES 2002. LNCS, vol. 2523, pp. 13–28. Springer, Heidelberg (2003). https://doi.org/10.1007/3-540-36400-5_3
2. Clavier, C.: Side channel analysis for reverse engineering (SCARE), an improved attack against a secret A3/A8 GSM algorithm (2004)
3. Eisenbarth, T., Paar, C., Weghenkel, B.: Building a side channel based disassembler. In: Gavrilova, M.L., Tan, C.J.K., Moreno, E.D. (eds.) Transactions on Computational Science X. LNCS, vol. 6340, pp. 78–99. Springer, Heidelberg (2010). https://doi.org/10.1007/978-3-642-17499-5_4
4. Genkin, D., Shamir, A., Tromer, E.: RSA key extraction via low-bandwidth acoustic cryptanalysis. In: Garay, J.A., Gennaro, R. (eds.) CRYPTO 2014. LNCS, vol. 8616, pp. 444–461. Springer, Heidelberg (2014). https://doi.org/10.1007/978-3-662-44371-2_25
5. Goldack, M., Paar, I.C.: Side-channel based reverse engineering for microcontrollers. Master's thesis, Ruhr-Universität Bochum, Germany (2008)
6. Kocher, P., Jaffe, J., Jun, B.: Differential power analysis. In: Wiener, M. (ed.) CRYPTO 1999. LNCS, vol. 1666, pp. 388–397. Springer, Heidelberg (1999). https://doi.org/10.1007/3-540-48405-1_25
7. Kocher, P.C.: Timing attacks on implementations of Diffie-Hellman, RSA, DSS, and other systems. In: Koblitz, N. (ed.) CRYPTO 1996. LNCS, vol. 1109, pp. 104–113. Springer, Heidelberg (1996). https://doi.org/10.1007/3-540-68697-5_9
8. McCann, D., Oswald, E., Whitnall, C.: Towards practical tools for side channel aware software engineering: 'grey box' modelling for instruction leakages. In: USENIX Security Symposium (2017)

9. McCann, D., Whitnall, C., Oswald, E.: ELMO: emulating leaks for the ARM Cortex-M0 without access to a side channel lab. IACR Cryptology ePrint Archive (2016)
10. Msgna, M., Markantonakis, K., Mayes, K.: Precise instruction-level side channel profiling of embedded processors. In: Huang, X., Zhou, J. (eds.) ISPEC 2014. LNCS, vol. 8434, pp. 129–143. Springer, Cham (2014). https://doi.org/10.1007/978-3-319-06320-1_11
11. Msgna, M., Markantonakis, K., Naccache, D., Mayes, K.: Verifying software integrity in embedded systems: a side channel approach. In: Prouff, E. (ed.) COSADE 2014. LNCS, vol. 8622, pp. 261–280. Springer, Cham (2014). https://doi.org/10.1007/978-3-319-10175-0_18
12. Novak, R.: Side-channel based reverse engineering of secret algorithms. In: Proceedings of the Electrotechnical and Computer Science Conference (2003)
13. Park, J., Xu, X., Jin, Y., Forte, D., Tehranipoor, M.: Power-based side-channel instruction-level disassembler. In: Design Automation Conference (2018)
14. Peeters, E., Standaert, F.X., Quisquater, J.J.: Power and electromagnetic analysis: improved model, consequences and comparisons. VLSI J. **40**, 52–60 (2007)
15. Quisquater, J.-J., Samyde, D.: ElectroMagnetic Analysis (EMA): measures and counter-measures for smart cards. In: Attali, I., Jensen, T. (eds.) E-smart 2001. LNCS, vol. 2140, pp. 200–210. Springer, Heidelberg (2001). https://doi.org/10.1007/3-540-45418-7_17
16. Quisquater, J.J., Samyde, D.: Automatic code recognition for smart cards using a kohonen neural network. In: Proceedings of the Smart Card Research and Advanced Application Conference (2002)
17. Schneider, T., Moradi, A.: Leakage assessment methodology. In: Güneysu, T., Handschuh, H. (eds.) CHES 2015. LNCS, vol. 9293, pp. 495–513. Springer, Heidelberg (2015). https://doi.org/10.1007/978-3-662-48324-4_25
18. Strobel, D., Bache, F., Oswald, D., Schellenberg, F., Paar, C.: SCANDALee: a side-channel-based disassembler using local electromagnetic emanations. In: Proceedings of the Design, Automation & Test in Europe Conference & Exhibition (2015)
19. Vermoen, D., Witteman, M., Gaydadjiev, G.N.: Reverse engineering Java card applets using power analysis. In: Sauveron, D., Markantonakis, K., Bilas, A., Quisquater, J.-J. (eds.) WISTP 2007. LNCS, vol. 4462, pp. 138–149. Springer, Heidelberg (2007). https://doi.org/10.1007/978-3-540-72354-7_12

CCCiCC: A Cross-Core Cache-Independent Covert Channel on AMD Family 15h CPUs

Carl-Daniel Hailfinger[1,2(✉)], Kerstin Lemke-Rust[1], and Christof Paar[3]

[1] Bonn-Rhein-Sieg University of Applied Sciences, Sankt Augustin, Germany
Kerstin.Lemke-Rust@h-brs.de

[2] Horst-Görtz Institute, Ruhr University Bochum, Bochum, Germany
Carl-Daniel.Hailfinger@rub.de

[3] Max Planck Institute for Cyber Security and Privacy, Bochum, Germany
Christof.Paar@rub.de

Abstract. Spectre and similar microarchitectural attacks have recently caused a major paradigm shift in hardware and software development to restrict attacker-controlled speculative execution and microarchitectural sampling. So far, research has focused on cache interaction, instruction scheduling, microarchitectural sampling and speculative side effects, whereas instruction decoding research has been notably absent. We disclose two cross-core covert channels on multiple AMD processor generations (Family 15h) spanning from Bulldozer to Excavator with partial applicability to Zen.

In this work, cross-core instruction decoding and synchronization interactions are explored as a source of information leakage on these processors to yield multiple cache-independent covert channels in a non-SMT environment. In contrast to other attacks, we do not rely on memory interaction nor on speculative execution. None of the existing mitigations in the Linux kernel and processor microcode against transient execution attacks have any measurable effect on the CCCiCC covert channels. To the best of our knowledge, this is not fixable with a microcode update since any updated instruction would also become usable for signaling.

Keywords: Covert channel · Multithreaded and multicore architecture · AMD Family 15h · Instruction scheduling · CPUID instruction · Cache-independent · Cross-core · Information hiding

1 Introduction

Microarchitectural attacks lately have come into focus due to their ability to exploit even formally proven software and even if that software has been specifically hardened against some side-channel attacks. Some recently discovered side-channel attacks like Spectre-STL [11,15] can not be hardened against purely in software, but rather some processor behaviour has to be changed through

S. Belaïd and T. Güneysu (Eds.): CARDIS 2019, LNCS 11833, pp. 159–175, 2020.
https://doi.org/10.1007/978-3-030-42068-0_10

microcode updates or other means. Especially for high-performance general purpose processors, the design focus has been on speed improvements through various microarchitectural optimizations like speculative execution at the expense of exposing leakage effects of those optimizations. As such, using those leakage effects as a side-channel or a covert channel has become a viable attack option and mitigating this leakage is either costly from a performance perspective or even impossible in certain scenarios.

A *covert channel* is a hidden information channel that requires a co-operation between the sender and receiver of information. Typically, one process with access to security sensitive information acts as the sender and one process without access to sensitive information acts as the receiver. The information channel is also built upon timing, power, or memory characteristics of an implementation.

Shared hardware resources can be used as side-channels and covert channels, both for non-persistent [24] resources as well as persistent [10] resources. Due to the increasing complexity of modern processor microarchitectures and the interaction between different microarchitectural features, mitigating direct information leakage effects as well as indirect effects is getting progressively harder. Recent research has shown that even if side-channel mitigations are in place, indirect side effects still can be exploited in some cases [10].

Attacks using cache side effects of code execution (without taking speculation into account) [18,22,23] have been known since 2002, and cache timing effects were already mentioned in the context of timing analysis on cryptographic implementations in 1996 [13]. In 2018, attacks using microarchitectural side effects based on speculative execution were published: The Spectre [12] and Meltdown [14] attacks both focus on disclosing otherwise inaccessible memory content via side-channel. The proof of concept implementations for various Spectre variants rely on memory related leakage effects, specifically through cache, as the channel of choice for exfiltrating data. Mitigation efforts so far have focused mostly on reducing or eliminating speculation in vulnerable contexts as well as limiting the effect of speculation on the memory subsystem [5,9,15].

Other classes of side and covert channels are based on properties of further microarchitecture components besides the memory architecture. Among them, one class of side-channels is based on the execution engine itself. We use the term cache-independent for these kinds of side and covert channels. The execution engine can be used both as a leakage source as well as a possible information exfiltration channel.

In this work, we present two covert channel attack vectors, one using the shared instruction decoder in multicore AMD Family 15h "Piledriver" microprocessors without simultaneous multithreading (SMT) as well as another vector with lower bandwidth working on the AMD Family 15h "Steamroller" microprocessors. Our new CCCiCC attacks are capable of enabling an information channel using differences of instruction decoding speed that are caused by using micro-coded instructions (CPUID, RCL) which are blocking the instruction decoder for prolonged periods as well as using a serializing instruction (CPUID) which influences instruction scheduling even across modules. CCCiCC thus belong to the class of attacks against non-persistent shared hardware resources.

In contrast to PortSmash [4] and SMoTherSpectre [3], CCCiCC v1 works across cores as long as the instruction decoder is shared. CCCiCC v2 does not need a shared instruction decoder and relies on cross-module serializing effects instead. To the best of our knowledge, resource contention in the instruction decoder as well as instruction serialization effects in the instruction scheduler have not yet been analyzed from an information leakage perspective.

2 Background

2.1 Microarchitecture

Both AMD and Intel offer x86 processors in which multiple threads share execution units to improve utilization of those units. Intel processors are offered without and with SMT (called "Hyper-Threading") where each core has one instruction decoder, one instruction scheduler and one execution engine which are shared among two threads in the multithreading case. AMD processors with the Zen microarchitecture are offered with and without SMT. For both AMD and Intel implementations of SMT, each core shares all of its resources among two threads if multithreading is enabled. For AMD Family 15h (Fam15h) processors ("Bulldozer", "Piledriver", "Steamroller" and "Excavator" variants of the Family 15h microarchitecture) the terminology and the implementation are a bit different. These processors are a special case among x86 processors since they have a hybrid design combining some aspects of multithreading with a multicore architecture. A Fam15h processor is built from one or more modules hosting two cores each. The two cores of each module share some resources (L1 instruction cache, L2 cache, instruction fetching, floating point and vector execution units), but other resources (L1 data cache, integer execution unit and pipelines) are not shared among cores, yielding a design which can neither be classified as pure multicore nor pure multithreaded. Figure 1 shows a simplified version of the architecture diagram of two-core Fam15h Piledriver/Steamroller modules. The Fam15h "Steamroller" microarchitecture variant has one dedicated instruction decoder per core, whereas the other Fam15h microarchitecture variants share the instruction decoder between both cores of a module [2]. The Fam15h "Steamroller" also has a loop buffer after the instruction decoder. Each Fam15h core can run one thread, making it a total of two threads per module. In contrast, each core hosting a pair of threads in the Intel Sandy Bridge microarchitecture from the same era has a shared L1 data cache and shared integer execution units [20]. As such, the design of AMD Family 15h "cores" resembles the usual definition of cores more closely than the definition of threads.

Some x86 instructions are able to influence instruction scheduling, but only the CPUID instruction is both unprivileged and documented to serialize execution flow. Additionally, some microcoded instructions (CPUID, RCL) on AMD Family 15h take more than one clock cycle to decode. Depending on the microarchitectural implementation, this serialization effect and the decoding delay can be observed on other cores through a reduction in the number of executed instructions per time and/or subtle changes in timing measurement. Using

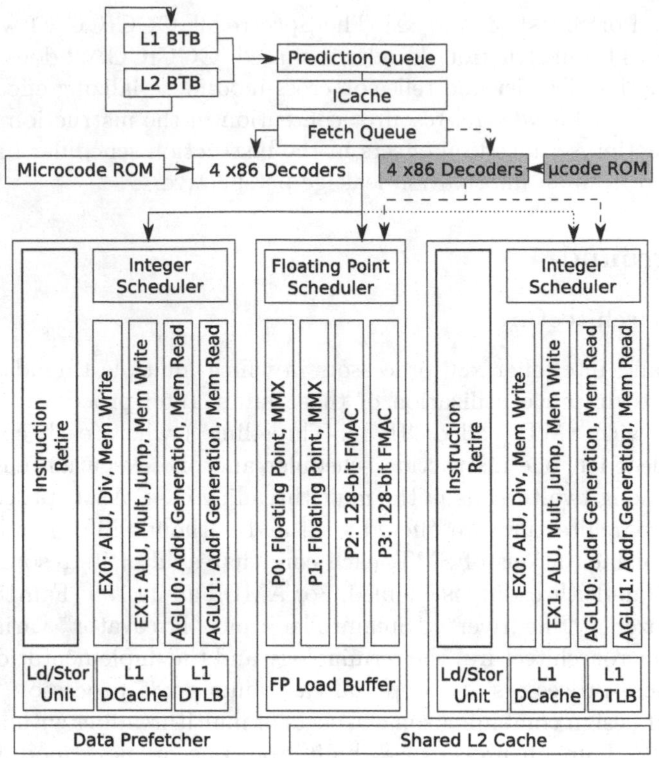

Fig. 1. Architecture diagram of a two-core module of the AMD Family 15h Piledriver (straight/dotted lines) and Steamroller (straight/ dashed lines) microarchitecture [16]

CPUID or RCL in userspace does not trap to the operating system kernel and does not access any memory. CPUID does not use any execution unit. As such, CPUID and RCL combine stealthy behaviour with desirable leakage effects. Our implementation of abusing CPUID and RCL execution to establish a cross-core covert channel yields a throughput-based covert channel on an AMD Family 15h "Piledriver" A6-4400M processor and a noise-based covert channel on an AMD Family 15h "Steamroller" A10-7800 processor. Each covert channel type yields more than 1 Mbit/s bandwidth.

2.2 Processing of an Instruction in AMD Family 15h Piledriver CPUs

For the purposes of this paper, L1 and L2 branch target buffers as well as the prediction queue and the instruction cache have no impact on the attack except to keep the instruction fetch queue full.

An instruction is first fetched from L1 instruction cache and then fed to the instruction decoder. The instruction decoder is alternating between serving each of the cores at a rate of one switch per clock cycle. In the absence of contention, each core will be serviced every other cycle. The instruction decoder can decode up to four instructions per clock cycle to RISC-style macro-ops subject to the following constraints: Four instructions generating one macro-op each or three instructions generating 2/1/1 macro-ops or two instructions generating two macro-ops each or a single instruction generating three or more macro-ops. There is a limit of four generated macro-ops per clock cycle. Any instruction generating more than four macro-ops will block the instruction decoder in subsequent clock cycles until all macro-ops for the instruction are generated. Table 1 (left part) shows the decoder interactions between NOPs as well as the decoder interactions between CPUID and NOPs on a Fam15h Piledriver microarchitecture. Table 1 (right part) shows the same interactions on a Fam15h Steamroller microarchitecture. Whereas microcoded instructions with more than 4 macro-ops on Piledriver (Table 1 (left part)) have a noticeable impact on instruction throughput of the other same-module core due to aforementioned resource contention, this scenario does not apply to Steamroller (Table 1 (right part)) because the instruction decoder is not shared between cores. Instructions which generate at least three macro-ops per instruction are using microcode [2]. Instructions like NOP, FNOP and FWAIT as well as some 128-bit register renaming operations are resolved immediately without being scheduled [7]. Some pairs of macro-ops are fused to reduce the number of macro-ops being scheduled. The macro-ops are passed to one of the out-of-order schedulers matching the type of the instruction (e.g. integer) where they are broken down into micro-ops. The micro-ops are either sent to one of the associated execution units (e.g. EX0), resolved in the register file (e.g. register-to-register moves), or resolved directly (e.g. NOP). The scheduler and execution unit for floating point is shared between cores, whereas integer scheduler and execution unit are private to each core [16].

The Fam15h "Steamroller" microarchitecture variant adds a dedicated instruction decoder per core as well as an additional macro-op queue after the instruction decoder for tight loop acceleration compared to Fam15h "Piledriver".

3 Related Work on Cache-Independent Information Leakage

Since this paper focuses on cache/memory-independent attacks, the various attacks revealing memory contents via side-channel (e.g. various Spectre variants) and attacks on cache implementations are out of scope. Other attacks such as LazyFP [21] indeed exploit the execution engine, specifically the time window between speculative execution and a subsequent fault after the CPU detects that the data accessed speculatively should not have been accessed. The branch target buffer and return stack buffer attacks are also execution engine attacks and rely strongly on speculative execution. An overview of various related classes of transient execution attacks and defenses can be found in [5]. Microarchitectural non-cache leakage effects and non-speculative interactions between instructions on x86 architectures were first explored systematically by Fogh in

Table 1. Instruction decoder behaviour for Fam15h Piledriver A6-4400M (left) and Fam15h Steamroller A10-7800 (right)

Clock cycle no.	Decoded instructions core 0 (sender)	Decoded instructions core 1 (receiver)
0	4x NOP	<inactive>
1	<inactive>	4x NOP
2	4x NOP	<inactive>
3	<inactive>	4x NOP
4	CPUID	<inactive>
5	<cont'd>	**<blocked>**
6	<cont'd>	<inactive>
7	<cont'd>	**<blocked>**
8	<cont'd>	<inactive>
9	<cont'd>	**<blocked>**
10	<cont'd>	<inactive>
11	<cont'd>	**<blocked>**
12	<cont'd>	<inactive>
13	<cont'd>	**<blocked>**
14	<cont'd>	<inactive>
15	<inactive>	4x NOP
16	CPUID	<inactive>

Clock cycle no.	Decoded instructions core 0 (sender)	Decoded instructions core 1 (receiver)
0	4x NOP	4x NOP
1	4x NOP	4x NOP
2	CPUID	4x NOP
3	<cont'd>	4x NOP
4	<cont'd>	4x NOP
5	<cont'd>	4x NOP
6	<cont'd>	4x NOP
7	<cont'd>	4x NOP
8	<cont'd>	4x NOP
9	<cont'd>	4x NOP
10	<cont'd>	4x NOP
11	<cont'd>	4x NOP
12	<cont'd>	4x NOP
13	CPUID	4x NOP
14	<cont'd>	4x NOP
15	<cont'd>	4x NOP
16	<cont'd>	4x NOP

the seminal work "Covert Shotgun – Automatically finding SMT covert channels" [8]. Covert shotgun works by running blocks of identical instructions in one thread and another block of identical instructions in another thread on the same core. The execution time of each block of instructions is measured. Instructions are selected such that the measurement is performed for each possible valid instruction pair. If the execution time for any given instruction A running on one thread differs based on which instruction is executed on another thread on the same core, instruction A can be used as the receiving side of a side-channel where blocks of the instructions causing differing execution time are executed on the sending side. Since AMD Family 15h processors are not using classical multithreading, but rather a multicore setup with some shared resources among core pairs in a multithreading-inspired design [16], they pose an interesting way to research processors with limited execution contention points outside classical SMT. A special case of contention between two threads accessing the same execution unit was presented in "Cheap hardware parallelism implies cheap security" [1] where the integer multiplier shared between threads on the same core was exploited. PortSmash [4] builds on Covert Shotgun and generalizates the Cheap Hardware Parallelism attack to determine execution time based on contention for each execution unit (and associated ports) and uses execution time differences to determine execution unit usage on the other thread of the same core. This allows the attacker to discern code execution patterns down to a level of instruction classes running on the other thread of the same core. In case of a data dependent instruction flow where the instruction classes differ for the possible executed instruction sequences, the attacker is able to reconstruct the data on which the instruction flow depends. As an example, PortSmash demonstrates the feasibility of the attack to recover an ECC P-384 private key from OpenSSL 1.1.0h. Although the PortSmash authors mention that their method depends on the SMT feature of a CPU, it is also partially applicable to Fam15h core pairs, but limited to the shared floating point and vector execution units. Since Fam15h integer units are not shared, PortSmash can't be applied against them. SMoTherSpectre [3] similarly builds on Covert Shotgun, but port contention is used as a covert channel combined with branch target injection (BTI, also known as Spectre V2) [12] to yield a cache-independent side-channel for speculatively executed code. However, due to the nature of PortSmash and SMoTherSpectre, both can be mitigated by disabling SMT. The random number generator in modern CPUs is also a shared resource which can be used as a non-cache covert channel [6]. Timing variations dependent on the time elapsed since previous AVX2 instructions are used as a side or covert channel gadget in NetSpectre [19] both in a speculative and non-speculative context, but they are limited to same-core attacks.

4 Our Cache-Independent Covert Channels on AMD Family 15h

4.1 CCCiCC v1: Instruction Decoder Throughput

The instruction decoder has not yet been a target for resource contention attacks, but it presents a prime opportunity to learn about instruction types executed by another core on the same processor module without having to resort to creating execution unit contention, making the attack harder to detect. Although instruction decoder contention may be indirectly measurable via execution unit throughput, the scheduler and pipelines between the decoder and the various execution units introduce undesirable additional effects which may completely mask the small changes in instruction decoder throughput per core. We therefore chose to measure instruction decoder throughput with instructions documented as not to get passed to any execution unit. Among the usable instructions for this case are NOP, FNOP and FWAIT [2]. NOP has the advantage over FNOP of being a single-byte instruction, maximizing the load on the instruction decoder. FNOP would serve the purpose as well, but it has a prefix and the number of prefixed instructions being serviced in the decoder is limited. FWAIT has the undesirable effect of triggering any pending floating point exceptions and will not be used here.

To establish a covert channel, we desire to block the instruction decoder as long as possible on the core of the sender side to increase the magnitude of throughput differences on the receiver side. Both the Piledriver and Steamroller microarchitecture can decode instructions up to a limit of four generated macro-ops per clock cycle, using any combination of instructions generating one or two macro-ops per instruction is not going to block the instruction decoder for the next cycle. To block decoding in subsequent clock cycles, the sending side has to use microcoded instructions which generate at least three macro-ops per instruction [2]. In the AMD 15h Family, the CPUID instruction generates between 38 and 64 macro-ops [7], therefore blocking the instruction decoder for 10 to 16 cycles. The RCL instruction is a close second and generates 17 macro-ops, blocking the instruction decoder for 5 cycles. Both instructions cause a detectable decoding slowdown on the other core of the Piledriver CPU chosen for this experiment, with the effect of CPUID being slightly more pronounced. In a virtualized scenario, using RCL would be preferable over CPUID because the former can not be trapped by a hypervisor. As opposed to CPUID, the slow-down effect of RCL does not scale linearly with the measurement length, but rather keeps a constant difference. To signal the opposite state, the instruction decoder has to be fed instructions which will complete decoding in a single clock cycle and which will not have any impact on the decoder in the following clock cycle. To rule out any possible slowdowns or other interactions from the instruction scheduler, pipelines and execution units, we pick the same NOP instruction which is also used for throughput measurement on the receiving side. Experimentally, NOP has been replaced with the INC instruction, and there have been no observable differences in measurements between NOP and INC.

To rule out other cross-core interactions on Family 15h processors, the same covert channel attack with CPUID/RCL vs. NOP/INC is performed against a Steamroller CPU which is mostly identical to a Piledriver CPU except for a per-core instruction decoder. The covert channel mentioned above based on decoder throughput does not work on a Steamroller CPU, confirming that the sharing of the instruction decoder is the actual point of contention.

4.2 CCCiCC v2: Timing Measurement Noise

However, a surprising result on Steamroller CPUs is that CPUID and RCL differ in their cross-core effect. Due to the non-shared instruction decoder, neither instruction should have a cross-core effect. RCL is indeed indistinguishable from NOP/INC, but CPUID changes the throughput measurements on the other core by introducing a small amount of noise. The only explanation for this is the serializing/synchronizing effect of CPUID. AMD has hinted in the past that CPUID at least serializes the core on which CPUID is executed. We noticed that the serializing effect on Steamroller CPUs was strong enough to be detected not only on the other core of the same module, but even on a core of another module, making this new serialization based covert channel suitable even in a scenario without shared resources and even in scenarios with all variants of multithreading disabled. The cross-module bandwidth of the noise-based covert channel is lower than the cross-core same-module bandwidth of the same channel.

4.3 Implementation

Setup. The x86 architecture offers various time sources with different precisions, among them RTC, PIT, PM Clock, APIC Timer, HPET, performance counters and TSC (Time Stamp Counter). The only high-precision low-overhead time source accessible from unprivileged code is reading the TSC with the RDTSC or RDTSCP instructions. Although RDTSC can also be blocked for userspace programs, the Linux kernel so far has not implemented that particular mechanism. The TSC is a per-core counter guaranteed to be monotonically increasing, and recent processors use the CPU base clock for counting clock cycles regardless of the current clock speed. There is a pitfall if the RDTSC instruction is used: The CPU may reorder RDTSC relative to the instructions before and after it. Intel recommends combining CPUID with RDTSC [17] to have a barrier in both directions for cycle-accurate measurements. The RDTSCP instruction is guaranteed to be executed after all preceding instructions, but it may be executed after instructions following it. Our measurements are performed back-to-back, and each RDTSCP instruction acts as a barrier for the previous RDTSCP instruction. Any measurement errors will thus be averaged out over time. Since RDTSCP is the best option available, we opt for using RDTSCP. Alternative implementations using the Linux interfaces gettimeofday() and clock_getttime() have been tested to work well and will continue to work even in cases where RDTSC/RDTSCP is blocked, but their resolution and overhead does reduce the usable bandwidth of the channel.

The environments used for measurement are a machine with an AMD A6-4400M 2-core 1-module Piledriver CPU running at 2700 MHz and for comparison another machine with an AMD A10-7800 4-core 2-module Steamroller CPU running at 3500 MHz. A third machine with an AMD Ryzen 5 1600 with SMT running at 3200 MHz is employed to check the applicability of the results on a more recent microarchitecture. All three machines run Ubuntu 18.04.2 Desktop with Linux kernel 4.18 and all current microcode updates as of 2019-07-01 installed. The operating system is installed for the x86-64 architecture. The measurement code can run both in 32-bit and 64-bit mode, no significant differences have been observed between these modes. To reduce noise, the sender thread is pinned to core 0, whereas the receiver is pinned to core 1. Both the taskset as well as the cset utilities can be used for core pinning with comparable results. The system had some noise during the measurements because a default installation of Ubuntu desktop including drivers and various daemons was active to reflect real world usage. To increase precision further at the cost of being less representative of the real world, we could consider enabling CPU isolation, disabling the scheduler for the core doing measurements and quieting various interrupt sources, although none were needed for our experiments. Further noise can be introduced by running office software, e.g. word processors, but such CPU usage generally occurs for a roughly fixed time after each keystroke and will be low unless the user is typing. A strong source of noise is browsing the web because most websites use active content, which tends to put varying load with unpredictable timing on the CPU.

To prevent CPU frequency scaling and thermal throttling interactions, the core running the sender code as well as the core running the measurement code were primed by running NOP loops for a few seconds before the covert channel was established. For comparison, some of the tests were repeated after fixing the

CPU at maximum non-turbo frequency with the utility cpufreq-set and after disabling automatic frequency turbo boosting through /sys/devices/system/cpu/cpufreq/boost. This cross-check under more controlled conditions yielded identical results, showing that the priming process caused the CPU to run at the maximum non-turbo frequency. CPU temperature was monitored to detect any thermal throttling and CPU fans were set to maximum speed. No thermal throttling except for the prevention of turbo boost was observed.

On the sending side, the code for blocking the instruction decoder is a tight loop of CPUID or RCL instructions, and the code for freeing the instruction decoder is a tight loop containing 1 NOP or INC instruction. Running a tight loop of CPUID/RCL on the sending side is associated with the value 0, and the tight loop of 1 NOP/INC is associated with the value of 1. On the receiving side, the code for measuring decoder throughput is a RDTSCP instruction followed by a tight loop containing 16 NOP instructions followed by a RDTSCP instruction. Loops containing fewer NOP instructions on the receiving side have a lower signal-to-noise ratio, and loops containing more NOP instructions have the same problem. The difference of the values returned by the two RDTSCP instructions is the elapsed time in base clock cycles.

4.4 Throughput Measurements

Due to the way the measurement code is written, all measurements include the constant cost for one RDTSCP instruction as well as two MOV instructions. Each measurement was repeated 100,000 times in a tight loop. The measurements were grouped by value and counted. The values comprising the 90th percentile of the most common measurements are listed in Tables 2 and 3. On the sending side, the number of loops was tuned to take exactly one period (bit) of the signal, yielding three different values for CPUID, RCL, and NOP/INC.

Table 2 shows the number of clock cycles per measurement for the Piledriver CPU. The timing difference between measurements on core 1 while running CPUID or NOP on core 0 start getting significant above 10 loops. In the case of 1 and 10 loops, the difference for core 1 run times is between 0 and 3 clock cycles. In contrast to that, the case of 100 loops has a run time difference of 319 or 311 clock cycles, suggesting a nonlinear relation between number of loops and run time difference at least for a low number of loops. For the case of 1000 loops, the run time difference is 3253 clock cycles, which is roughly proportional to the difference for 100 loops. The tests with 100 and 10000 loops have a so far unexplained anomaly which results in measurement values alternating between the two values listed in the corresponding cell of Table 1. Overall, tests with more than 10 loops show a consistent run time difference between runs where core 0 executes CPUID or NOP. The throughput tests were also repeated with RCL instead of CPUID on core 0. The corresponding number of clock cycles for more than 10 loops measured on core 1 were slightly higher than for CPUID, but still substantially lower than for NOP/INC. RCL has two advantages over CPUID in this scenario: slightly less noise during measurement and being undetectable even when a hypervisor is running.

Table 2. Clock cycles per measurement, Piledriver A6-4400M

Loops on core 1	Clock cycles on core 1 (CPUID on core 0)	Clock cycles on core 1 (NOP/INC on core 0)	Difference
1	88 (99.8%)	89 (51.2%), 90 (47.1%)	1, 2
10	129 (99.7%)	129 (49.9%), 132 (49.9%)	0, 3
11	134 (99.8%)	137 (99.6%)	3
12	138 (99.9%)	148 (99.9%)	10
20	174 (99.6%)	220 (99.9%)	46
100	627 (47.0%), 635 (47.0%)	946 (99.9%)	319, 311
1000	5793 (90.8%)	9046 (99.6%)	3253
10000	57327 (49.4%), 58235 (46.9%)	90046 (98.8%)	32719, 31811

Multiple values in a cell indicate that multiple values occurred during measurements

Table 3. Clock cycles per measurement, Steamroller A10-7800

Loops on core 1	Clock cycles on core 1 (CPUID on core 0)	Clock cycles on core 1 (NOP/INC/RCL on core 0)	Difference
1	119 (33.3%), 121 (33.0%), 122 (33.0%)	119 (99.9%)	0, 2, 3
10	161 (62.4%), 170 (29.2%)	160 (99.9%)	1, 10
100	592 (40.1%), 593 (39.8%), 599 (19.7%)	592 (99.9%)	0, 1, 7
1000	5092 (20.4%), 5093 (59.4%), 5099 (19.7%)	5092 (97.8%)	0, 1, 7
10000	50092 (41.0%), 50093 (37.7%), 50097 (18.7%)	50092 (98.7%)	0, 1, 5

Multiple values in a cell indicate that multiple values occurred during measurements

The best raw bit error rate after decoding of a 1 MHz RCL/INC signal with 11 loops on the receiver side on the "Steamroller" A6-4400M was $1.7 * 10^-3$. Using 10 loops or less on the receiver side often resulted in decoding failure. Increasing the number of loops substantially increased the bit error rate because the number of samples per bit approached 1.

The receiver runs all measurements back-to-back. The number of samples per second thus depends on the measurement overhead per sample as well as the number of loops per sample as well as the instructions inside the loop. There is an additional constraint on the number of loops to measure any difference in execution times. Subsect. 4.5 has an example of the number of clock cycles per measurement. With the current measurement implementation in the above example, the upper limit of sampling frequency is 18.8 MHz. The number of samples per bit can be calculated by dividing the sampling frequency by the bit rate. The bit rates in this paper were chosen arbitrarily to yield low error rates. Experimentally, we tried a 10 Mbit/s bit rate for CCCiCCv1, but the error rate approached 30%. A measurement implementation with less error checks experimentally achieved a sampling frequency of ~25 MHz.

Table 3 shows clock cycle measurements for the Steamroller CPU. Although there is a slight variability for the measurements in case of running CPUID on core 0, the absolute difference between measurements for 100, 1000 and 10000 loops varies between 0 and 7 cycles, making this a decidedly non-proportional relation likely to be caused by one-off effects of each measurement. Each measurement has a fixed and a variable component. The variable component is the number of loop iterations per measurement and thus also the execution of the instructions part of the loop. The fixed component is the RDTSCP instruction terminating one measurement and starting another as well as potentially the first iteration of the loop. Since the Steamroller CPU does not have a shared instruction decoder, an instruction decoder contention with the instructions in the loop can be ruled out and only the timing measurement code itself can be the culprit.

The difference between Tables 2 and 3 shows how architectural changes like unsharing an instruction decoder can drastically change speed measurements and code interdependencies in a processor.

4.5 From Instruction Throughput to Covert Channel

The measurements on the receiving side of a covert channel need to fulfill two primary criteria: 1. Signal reconstruction has to be possible and 2. The data rate should be maximized.

Obviously, there are real-world problems such as sender or receiver being scheduled away, processes (e.g. web browsers) consuming background CPU cycles and most importantly figuring out when to start listening. If the receiver process is temporarily halted by the scheduler, this is reflected in the RDTSC measurements and the exact duration of the pause can be calculated from the difference of the previous and current RDTSC measurement. Background CPU activity introduces noise, but unless a website is causing the browser to continuously execute javascript, the noise level in the measurements only has a minor impact on reconstructing the signal. If the sender process is halted by the scheduler, the receiver process will not be able to measure this directly. The test data in these experiments usually had a 16-bit preamble of alternating bits followed by a sequence number followed by a constant-length payload. A trivial implementation of the receiver will discard all input until the preamble has been received successfully. The received sequence number can then be compared to the expected sequence number. Any difference can be attributed to one of three reasons: Sender halted, receiver halted, or noise. The preamble and sequence number make synchronization and detection of an active sender trivially easy at a frame level. The detected signal edges at the preamble can be used to synchronize the clock of the decoder. The decoding approach used in this paper depends on oversampling and calculating the number of bits from the observed length of a given run of a constant signal level, synchronizing at every edge resulting from a level change. Scheduling interaction with the receiver in the middle of a packet can by detected through RDTSC changes during each single sample measurement, and from the elapsed time the receiver can calculate the number of bits possibly missed. The sender being scheduled away during a packet can happen for two reasons: A hardware interrupt takes priority, and the timeslice of the sender process is elapsed. Depending on the settings in the Linux kernel, the timeslice of a process will be scheduled between 100 and 1000 Hz, with no interruption if no competing requests for the same processor thread are pending. The number of possible scheduling events during a single packet for each of receiver and sender are thus low and experimentation did not yet yield any result above 1. The number of frames affected by scheduling events varies with overall system load, but on an mostly idle system the rate was below 1% on average. Detection and compensation of such scheduling events for the sender side could be accomplished on the receiver side by changing the packet format, either by incorporating a constant trailer or by incorporating an error correcting code somewhere in the packet. An error correcting code would also allow to eliminate any bit errors resulting from noise. We discarded any data inside a frame from the point the signal deteriorated, foregoing an error correction.

Error detection and noise handling are substantially more difficult for low-amplitude noise-based channels compared to the throughput-based channel. Actively browsing the web introduced enough noise to increase the error rate in the throughput-based channel, but it even prevented synchronization for the noise-based channels during most measurements.

With the data from Table 2, measuring the timing of 11 loops is sufficient to reliably distinguish between states with a signal level difference of 2.2%. The timing of 12 loops has a stronger signal level difference of 6.8%, but a 5.3% lower sampling rate on average. Given the goal of having a real-world environment, the stronger signal level difference is chosen to deal with possible noise sources. With an average of $(138 + 148)/2 = 143$ clock cycles per sample at a base clock of 2700 MHz in the CPU, a theoretical maximum sampling rate of 18.8 MHz is possible. The current implementation reaches a slightly variable sampling rate around 9 MHz. The sampling rate varies because each measurement of a constant code block takes more or less time depending on the instruction decoder contention and there is no compensatory delay after shorter measurements.

For Fig. 2 on Piledriver shows the measurements while a repeating bit pattern of 0101001000 is being sent at a rate of 1 MHz. The 0 bit is a tight loop of CPUID and the 1 bit is a tight loop of NOP. Notable are two types of artifacts resulting from an implementation choice of the sender side: The slightly increased values at boundaries between bits are an implementation artifact resulting from a call and stack frame setup necessary for every bit sent as well as stack frame teardown and call return. Both the CPUID loop and the NOP loop are assembler functions

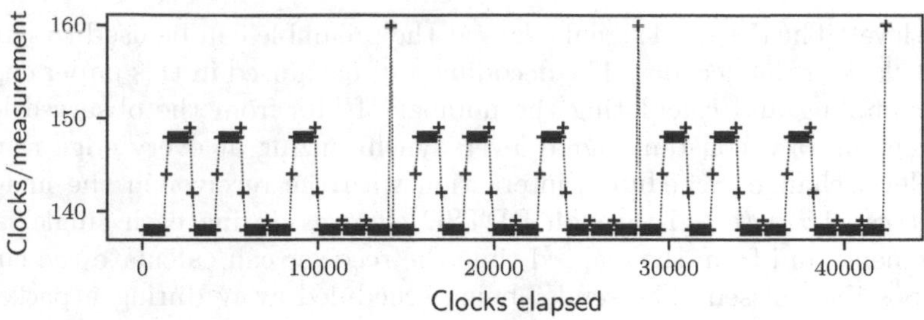

Fig. 2. CCCiCCv1 Throughput-based signal, Piledriver core 0 → 1 (same module), pattern 0101001000, 1 Mbit/s, 12 loops/measurement

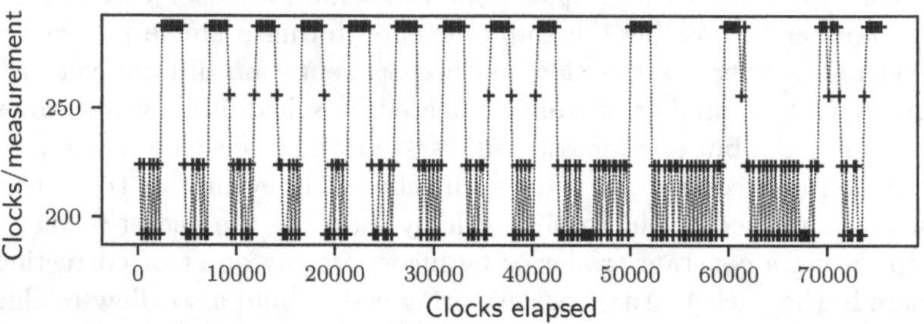

Fig. 3. CCCiCCv1 Throughput-based signal, Ryzen thread 0 → 1 (same core), pattern 0101010101010101010001000100010 1, 1 Mbit/s, 40 loops/measurement

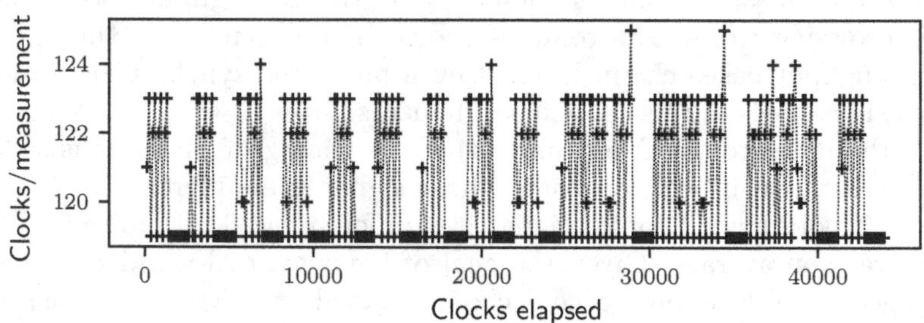

Fig. 4. CCCiCCv2 Noise-based signal, Steamroller core 0 → 1 (same module), pattern 01010101010101010100010001000101, 1 Mbit/s, 1 loop/measurement

which are called from the C code of the sender implementation. The strongly increased values at pattern start are an implementation artifact associated with an outer loop in the C code implementing the pattern repetition and loading patterns from memory. The signal is clearly visible in Fig. 2 without filtering or other postprocessing and suggests that a frequency increase on the sender side is possible.

Figure 3 shows the measurements on an AMD Ryzen 5 1600 between thread 0 and thread 1 on the same core. The Ryzen (Zen) architecture is the successor of the Family 15h architecture with two threads per core and without subdivision

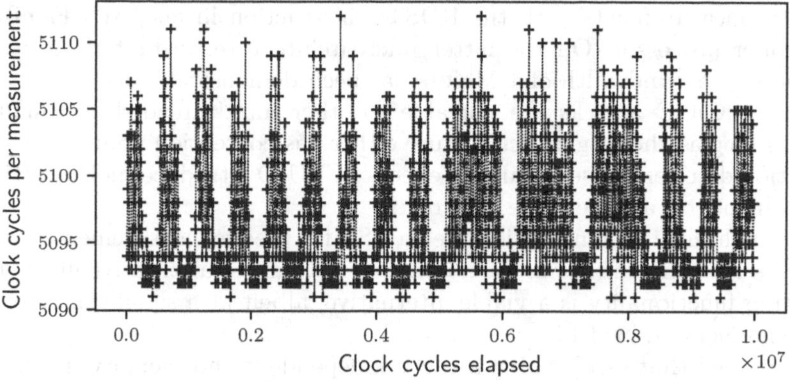

Fig. 5. CCCiCCv2 Noise-based signal, Steamroller core 0 → 3 (different module), pattern 0101010101010101010001000100101, 10 kbit/s, 1000 loops/measurement

into modules. It has one instruction decoder per core, shared between threads. As expected, the throughput-based channel caused by instruction decoder contention only works between threads on the same core. We were unable to confirm the presence of a covert channel between different cores on this AMD Ryzen platform.

Figure 4 demonstrates the RDTSC measurement noise caused by the execution of the CPUID instruction on Steamroller. The noise is clearly discernible from the noise-free time regions. The Figure shows a bit pattern transmitted from core 0 to core 1 on the same module. Table 3 has statistics on this channel.

Closely related is Fig. 5 which shows the same noise-based covert channel on Steamroller, but from core 0 to core 3 on different modules. The cross-module covert channel has a lower bandwidth of only 10 kbit/s, but it is available even if all variants of multithreading and all variants of cores with shared execution resources are disabled, i.e. even if there is only one thread per module active. There is an additional unidentified source of constant low-amplitude noise in these measurements. Compared to Fig. 4, the amplitude of the noise caused by CPUID is a bit larger. One possible explanation is that the same-module cross-core serialization only has to serialize one non-sender core, the cross-module serialization will serialize both cores of the non-sender module, yielding a longer delay until serialization is complete.

5 Summary

We presented two new high-bandwidth covert channels exploiting timing information of a non-persistent shared hardware resource. The first covert channel CCCiCC v1 is based on variations in throughput of the shared instruction decoder in an AMD Family 15h Piledriver processor. On this microarchitecture, we managed to transfer data with a covert channel at 1 Mbit/s rate. The second covert channel CCCiCC v2 is based on the presence and absence of noise in timing measurements with the RDSTC instruction in an AMD Family 15h Steamroller processor. On the latter microarchitecture, instantiating a covert channel with a bandwidth of 1 Mbit/s has been demonstrated as well.

Our CCCiCC attacks are portable to other multithreaded and multicore CPUs as long as the target architecture either has contention points in a shared instruction decoder or the serializing effect of CPUID introduces noise in RDTSC measurements on another core or thread.

Although this implementation used a TSC for precise measurements, preliminary tests have shown that in the absence of TSC access alternative unprivileged OS timing functionality is a viable alternative, albeit at a significantly reduced covert channel bandwidth.

We showed that establishing a cache-independent and memory-independent covert channel is not limited to SMT architectures, but it also can work for clustered and other shared-decoder multicore and multithreading setups as well as pure multicore setups without shared resources.

Mitigation options depend on whether the covert channel is to be prevented entirely or if a bandwidth reduction is sufficient. Removing access to precise timers enables a bandwidth reduction, whereas restricting execution to one core per processor module eliminates the throughput-based covert channel completely. For the noise-based covert channel between different modules on "Steamroller", there are only two methods to eliminate the covert channel: Enabling virtualization and trapping all CPUID instructions which is impossible in a non-virtualized setup, and running at most one concurrent process on the CPU which results in a massive slowdown.

AMD has been notified by us in a responsible disclosure process. Full proof-of-concept code including a self-synchronizing decoder for the receiver side is available at https://github.com/emsec/CCCiCC.

References

1. Acıiçmez, O., Seifert, J.P.: Cheap hardware parallelism implies cheap security. In: Workshop on Fault Diagnosis and Tolerance in Cryptography (FDTC 2007), pp. 80–91. IEEE (2007)
2. AMD: Software Optimization Guide for AMD Family 15h Processors (2014). https://www.amd.com/system/files/TechDocs/47414_15h_sw_opt_guide.pdf
3. Bhattacharyya, A., et al.: SMoTherSpectre: exploiting speculative execution through port contention. arXiv preprint arXiv:1903.01843 (2019)
4. Cabrera Aldaya, A., Brumley, B.B., ul Hassan, S., Pereida García, C., Tuveri, N.: Port Contention for Fun and Profit. Cryptology ePrint Archive, Report 2018/1060 (2018). https://eprint.iacr.org/2018/1060
5. Canella, C., et al.: A systematic evaluation of transient execution attacks and defenses. arXiv preprint arXiv:1811.05441 (2018)
6. Evtyushkin, D., Ponomarev, D.: Covert channels through random number generator: mechanisms, capacity estimation and mitigations. In: Proceedings of the 2016 ACM SIGSAC Conference on Computer and Communications Security, pp. 843–857. ACM (2016)

7. Fog, A.: Instruction tables: lists of instruction latencies, throughputs and micro-operation breakdowns for Intel, AMD and VIA CPUs (2018). https://www.agner.org/optimize/instruction_tables.pdf
8. Fogh, A.: Covert Shotgun: automatically finding SMT covert channels (2016). https://cyber.wtf/2016/09/27/covert-shotgun/
9. Ge, Q., Yarom, Y., Cock, D., Heiser, G.: A survey of microarchitectural timing attacks and countermeasures on contemporary hardware. J. Cryptogr. Eng. **8**(1), 1–27 (2018)
10. Gras, B., Razavi, K., Bos, H., Giuffrida, C.: Translation leak-aside buffer: defeating cache side-channel protections with TLB attacks. In: 27th USENIX Security Symposium, SEC 2018, pp. 955–972. USENIX Association, Berkeley (2018)
11. Horn, J.: Speculative execution, variant 4: speculative store bypass (2018). https://bugs.chromium.org/p/project-zero/issues/detail?id=1528
12. Kocher, P., et al.: Spectre attacks: exploiting speculative execution. arXiv preprint arXiv:1801.01203 (2018)
13. Kocher, P.C.: Timing attacks on implementations of diffie-hellman, RSA, DSS, and other systems. In: Koblitz, N. (ed.) CRYPTO 1996. LNCS, vol. 1109, pp. 104–113. Springer, Heidelberg (1996). https://doi.org/10.1007/3-540-68697-5_9
14. Lipp, M., et al.: Meltdown: reading kernel memory from user space. In: 27th USENIX Security Symposium, pp. 973–990 (2018)
15. Mcilroy, R., Sevcik, J., Tebbi, T., Titzer, B.L., Verwaest, T.: Spectre is here to stay: an analysis of side-channels and speculative execution. arXiv preprint arXiv:1902.05178 (2019)
16. Nussbaum, S.: AMD trinity APU. In: 2012 IEEE Hot Chips 24 Symposium (HCS), pp. 1–40. IEEE (2012)
17. Paoloni, G.: How to benchmark code execution times on Intel IA-32 and IA-64 instruction set architectures. Intel Corporation, p. 123 (2010)
18. Percival, C.: Cache Missing for Fun and Profit (2005)
19. Schwarz, M., Schwarzl, M., Lipp, M., Masters, J., Gruss, D.: NetSpectre: read arbitrary memory over network. In: Sako, K., Schneider, S., Ryan, P.Y.A. (eds.) ESORICS 2019. LNCS, vol. 11735, pp. 279–299. Springer, Cham (2019). https://doi.org/10.1007/978-3-030-29959-0_14
20. Shimpi, A.L.: Intel's Sandy Bridge Architecture Exposed (2010). https://www.anandtech.com/print/3922/intels-sandy-bridge-architecture-exposed
21. Stecklina, J., Prescher, T.: LazyFP: leaking FPU register state using microarchitectural side-channels. arXiv preprint arXiv:1806.07480 (2018)
22. Tsunoo, Y.: Crypt-analysis of block ciphers implemented on computers with cache. In: Proceedings ISITA2002, October 2002
23. Tsunoo, Y., Saito, T., Suzaki, T., Shigeri, M., Miyauchi, H.: Cryptanalysis of DES implemented on computers with cache. In: Walter, C.D., Koç, Ç.K., Paar, C. (eds.) CHES 2003. LNCS, vol. 2779, pp. 62–76. Springer, Heidelberg (2003). https://doi.org/10.1007/978-3-540-45238-6_6
24. Wang, Z., Lee, R.B.: Covert and side channels due to processor architecture. In: Proceedings of the 22nd Annual Computer Security Applications Conference, ACSAC 2006, pp. 473–482. IEEE Computer Society, Washington (2006)

Design Considerations for EM Pulse Fault Injection

Arthur Beckers[1(✉)], Masahiro Kinugawa[2], Yuichi Hayashi[3], Daisuke Fujimoto[3], Josep Balasch[1], Benedikt Gierlichs[1], and Ingrid Verbauwhede[1]

[1] imec-COSIC KU Leuven, Leuven, Belgium
{arthur.beckers,josep.balasch,benedikt.gierlichs, ingrid.verbauwhede}@esat.kuleuven.be
[2] National Institute of Technology (KOSEN), Sendai College, Sendai, Japan
kinugawa@sendai-nct.ac.jp
[3] Nara Institute of Science and Technology, Ikoma, Japan
{yu-ichi,fujimoto}@is.naist.jp

Abstract. Electromagnetic-fault injection (EM-FI) setups are appealing since they can be made at a low cost, achieve relatively high spatial resolutions, and avoid the need of tampering with the PCB or packaging of the target. In this paper we first sketch the importance of understanding the pulse characteristics of a pulse injection setup in order to successfully mount an attack. We then look into the different components that make up an EM-pulse setup and demonstrate their impact on the pulse shape. The different components are then assembled to form an EM-pulse injection setup. The effectiveness of the setup and how different design decisions impact the outcome of a fault injection campaign are demonstrated on a 32-bit ARM microcontroller.

Keywords: EM fault attack · Probe design · EM-FI setup

1 Introduction

Since the introduction of the Bellcore attack by Boneh et al. [3] many different fault injection methods have been developed [2]. These fault injection methods are often classified according to their invasiveness and locality. Techniques such as clock and voltage glitching introduce global faults into the chip, but do not require tampering with the chip package or the chip itself. Therefore they are labeled as non-invasive and global. On the other side of the spectrum, optical fault injection [12] is a (semi-)invasive technique that requires line of sight to the target IC. In return, it can achieve high locality and potentially affect only a few transistors.

EM-fault injection [11] can be situated somewhere in between. It involves exposing the target IC to a pulsed or continuous E or H-field, or a combination of both. The injected field couples with the wiring of the IC, inducing voltage and current fluctuations inside the device. Since the EM-field can propagate through

S. Belaïd and T. Güneysu (Eds.): CARDIS 2019, LNCS 11833, pp. 176–192, 2020.
https://doi.org/10.1007/978-3-030-42068-0_11

the package of the IC, the method can be labeled as non invasive. In some situations, however, removing the package might be beneficial. It can increase the resolution of the attack and the field strength received by the IC. This makes EM-FI applicable also in (semi-)invasive settings. If the spatial dimensions of the injected field are sufficiently small compared to the size of the IC, only a smaller portion of the IC is affected. This gives EM-fault injection a certain degree of locality. Alternatively, EM-FI can achieve global effects by targeting bonding wires or PCB traces. This can be seen as a "contactless" voltage or clock glitching.

Related Work. EM-FI comes in two variants. One can either inject a continuous (harmonic) EM-wave or a single EM pulse. In this work we focus on the latter. More specifically, we investigate how different design decisions impact the pulse shape generated by an EM-pulse generator. In a previous work by R. Omarouayache et al. [9] a detailed study was done on how different probe parameters impact the size and shape of the generated magnetic field. The authors investigated the effect of different parameters by simulating the probes using a 3D EM simulator. In this work, we take their design recommendations into account and perform empirical testing of various probes when integrated into a complete EM-pulse injection setup.

Setups to perform EM-pulse injection have been described in the academic literature [7]. Most works use experimental setups around commercial high-voltage pulse generators, capable of generating pulses up to 500 V and 5 ns width. Using such a setup, Ordas et al. [10] compare different type of handmade injectors (flat, sharp, crescent) when targeting an FPGA platform. Alternative designs include the BADFET by Cui and Housley [4] and the setup designed by Balasch et al. [1]. The former uses a similar circuitry as the one described in this paper, storing the energy released over the EM probe in a capacitor bank, but use rather large probes in the order of centimeters. The latter setup uses a different approach, in which the energy released to the EM probe is stored in a large inductor.

In addition to academic literature, there exist several commercial solutions available for EM-FI such as the NewAE's ChipSHOUTER[1], Riscure's EM-FI Transient Probe[2] or Langer EMV's ICI Set[3]. For most of these setups, the circuitry used for pulse generation is not public information. The only commercial solution for which the circuit diagram is available is the ChipSHOUTER, which uses a similar approach to the one we use in this work.

Contributions. The goal of this work is not to propose a new EM-FI setup and compare it to existing solutions. Rather differently, we aim to investigate how different components of an EM-pulse injection setup impact the shape of the generated pulse. We start by studying the impact of the probe design parameters. For this, we propose a measurement method based on a microstrip line to

1 http://store.newae.com/chipshouter-kit.
2 https://getquote.riscure.com/en/quote/2101068/em-fi-transient-probe.htm.
3 https://www.langer-emv.de/en/category/ic-side-channel-analysis/94.

measure spatial and temporal characteristics of the probes. After the different parameters that impact the pulse shape are established, we describe a set of design guidelines by building an EM-pulse fault injection setup and demonstrating its effectiveness on a 32-bit microcontroller.

2 Challenge

Building an EM-pulse injection setup is conceptually simple. One needs to interface a pulse generator with an injection probe. Both components are commercially available, or they can be constructed. In any case, the shape of the generated EM pulse is determined by the choice of these components. In turn, the success rate of a fault injection campaign depends strongly on the characteristics of the pulse. Thus correctly tailoring the pulse parameters to the target device might have a significant impact on the outcome of a fault injection campaign. If we have a setup capable of generating small pulse widths, we can for example target individual instructions at high clock frequencies. Or if we have a larger pulse width, we might fault multiple instructions simultaneously.

Fault models for EM-fault injection have been described by Ordas et al. [10] for FPGAs and by Moro et al. [8] for microcontrollers. Both studies conclude that EM-pulse injection causes violations of the setup and hold times of the IC. Therefore pulses must be injected around a clock edge in order to be effective. The voltage and current fluctuations caused by the EM-pulse result in an incorrect sampling of the data at the input of a flip-flop during the setup or hold time. How these induced voltages and currents propagate through a particular IC requires extensive testing or detailed EM-simulations. This aspect has been recently investigated by Dumont et al. [5], which model the interactions between EM probes, EM pulses and ICs to gain understanding on the occurrence of EM faults.

Intuitively, we can abstract the concept to the following: an IC will be faulted if a clock edge occurs when voltage and current fluctuations exceed a certain threshold. The time window ($t_{sensitive}$) during which the induced voltage and current fluctuations persist on the device, depends on a multitude of parameters. $t_{sensitive}$ can, for instance, be enlarged by increasing the pulse width, by injecting multiple pulses in rapid succession, or by increasing the size of the injected field. The ratio between the time window during which we can fault an operation and the clock period (t_{clock}) determines whether we affect one or multiple clock cycles. We call this ratio the fault sensitivity ratio (FSR) expressed as $FSR = t_{sensitive}/t_{clock}$. If the FSR is larger than 1, one can fault multiple clock cycles simultaneously. If the FSR is smaller than 1, one is able to fault a single clock cycle. The time $t_{sensitive}$ is determined by both the target device and the EM-FI pulse characteristics, as illustrated in Fig. 1. The value $t_{sensitive}$ equals the sum of the setup and hold time of the device plus the pulse width. This is a simplification of the actual fault mechanism, but it gives a good intuition on how different pulse characteristics influence the outcome of EM-pulse injection. In practice, a per device study should be done to investigate how $t_{sensitive}$ relates

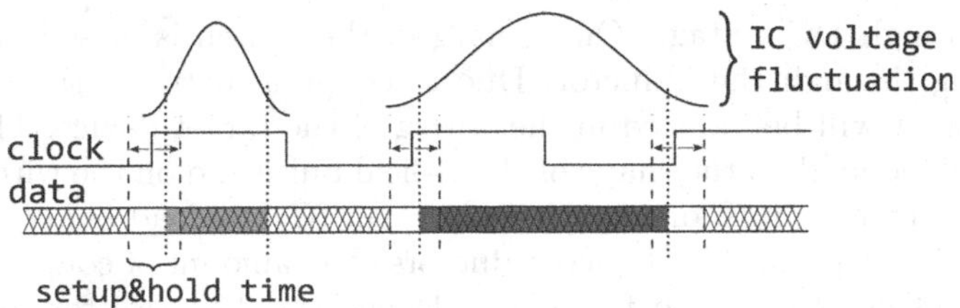

Fig. 1. Illustration of the fault sensitivity ratio (FSR).

to the pulse shape. The value t_{clock} on the other hand is fixed by the clock frequency of the target device, which may not be controllable by an adversary. By changing the pulse characteristics, we can thus tune the FSR depending on the application. A high FSR might for instance be desired when a device is profiled for its sensitivity to EM-pulse injection, while an FSR lower than 1 might be preferable when performing an attack.

3 Probe Design

In this section we examine the impact different probe parameters have on the pulse characteristics. In what follows we only consider H-field probes, although in theory also E-field probes could be used for performing EM-fault injection. H-field probes are commonly constructed by winding conductive wiring around either an air or ferrite core, thus forming a solenoid. The pulses generated by an EM-FI setup generally have a rise-time in the nanosecond range. We are thus operating in the near-field since the probes are commonly placed within a few centimeters of the target device. Different relations apply when the probes have a higher rise time or are placed further away from the target.

3.1 Near-Field Coupling

In the near-field region, currents induced into a target device are the result of coupling between probe and device. Generally, the pulse generator can be modeled as a charge capacitor in combination with a switching element. An EM-pulse is generated by discharging the capacitor through the injection probe. This model is equivalent to an RLC circuit if we assume an ideal switch. A diagram of such a circuit can be seen in Fig. 2. Before pulse injection, the capacitor is

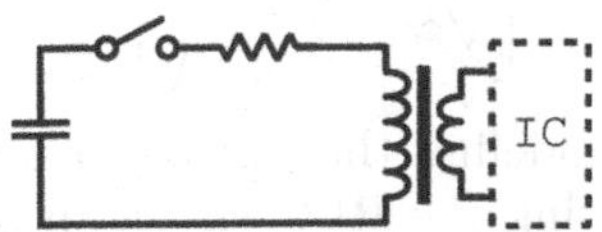

Fig. 2. Model of EM-pulse injection circuit.

charged to a high DC voltage. Once charged, the switch is closed and current starts flowing through the inductor. Due to coupling between the IC and the probe, a current will be induced in the wiring of the target device. The amount of current will depend on the shape of the H-field pulse and on the wire geometry of the target device. Thus, once placed above an IC, the load seen by the pulse generator will be that of the coupled inductors. The amount of coupling between the probe and device will be frequency dependent. The resistor in the RLC model combines both the parasitic resistance of the probe and resistance added for damping the response.

By solving the differential equation of the RLC circuit we can get a basic understanding of how different parameters influence the pulse shape. There are three possible solutions to the differential equation depending on the damping of the RLC circuit. Ideally we would like our EM-injection setup to be critically damped. Over-damping would increase our pulse width, while under-damping will result in ringing. The different current equations to resulting from the differential equation can be found in Appendix A. Since the magnetic field generated by the probe is proportional to the current flowing through it, we can derive some of the pulse characteristics from the current equations (Appendix A).

The rise time, peak amplitude and pulse width will be determined by the resistance, the initial voltage over the capacitor and the probe inductance. The resistance and the initial voltage are two parameters which can generally be chosen freely by the designer. The inductance on the other hand is determined by the probe geometry. Equation 1 gives the inductance of an ideal solenoid. Here k is the relative permeability, μ_0 is the permeability of free space, N is the number of windings, A is the loop area and l is the length of the solenoid. The actual probe will have a different inductance because of parasitics, saturation of the ferrite core, etc. but the equation gives us the basic relationship between the different variables that make up the probe inductance.

$$L = \frac{k\mu_0 N^2 A}{l} \tag{1}$$

The size of the magnetic field at the center line of the solenoid resulting from the current flowing through the probe is given by Eq. 2. Here r is the radius of the probe and z is the distance along its axis. The bottom of the solenoid is situated at $z = 0$ while the top is located at $z = l$. From Eqs. 1 and 4 we can see that the size of the magnetic field is inversely proportional to the inductance of the probe. By varying the different parameters we can tune the pulse characteristics to our needs.

$$B = \frac{k\mu_0 N}{2l} I \left[\frac{z}{\sqrt{z^2 + r^2}} - \frac{z - l}{\sqrt{(z - l)^2 + r^2}} \right] \tag{2}$$

Another approach for modeling the impact of different parameters on the generated field is by simulating the RLC circuit in SPICE, which allows for a more accurate modeling of the circuit.

3.2 Experimental Validation

In order to confirm that the theoretical relations from the previous section hold, we performed experimental measurements on solenoid probes with different winding geometries. To this end, we built a test setup similar to the circuit in Fig. 2. Instead of an ideal switch, we used a gas discharge tube with a breakdown voltage of 370 V. This component is selected because of its high rise time and small parasitics, which makes its behaviour similar to that of an ideal switch. For our experiments, the capacitor was connected to a 400 V power supply through a current limiting resistor of 1 MΩ. Once the capacitor voltage reaches 370 V, breakdown occurs and a current flows through the probe generating a magnetic pulse. Our test setup is shown in Fig. 3.

The evaluated probes were made with ferrite rods produced by Fair-Rite[4]. The windings around the ferrite core were made using enameled wire with a thickness of 150 μm. We only used rods, and no other special geometries such as sharpened tips were tested. These special geometries could however improve the magnetic field characteristics as observed in [9]. The default configuration of our evaluation board has a 47 pF charge capacitor, a probe with 2 windings and a 2 mm ferrite core.

For the probe evaluation we used a 50 Ω microstrip line to measure the H-field pulse. It was made from a 0.3 mm thick dual sided FR-4 substrate with a copper thickness of 18 μm and dielectric constant of 4.7. The resulting width of the microstrip line was 0.532 mm for a 50 Ω line. At either end, the microstrip line was terminated by a 50 Ω impedance. The PCB dimensions were 14 cm wide and 24 cm long. The board was chosen to be as thin as possible to have a narrow 50 Ω stripline, which is beneficial for measuring the spatial resolution. The length of the board was chosen as large as practically feasible, in order to have a larger temporal separation between the reflection that might occur due to small impedance mismatches and the actual pulse. In order to measure the response of the probe, we mounted the evaluation board on a stepper table with a 15 μm step size. The probe was placed on top of the PCB and moved perpendicular to the microstrip line. The theoretical result of a microstrip line measurement for an H-field pulse are shown in Fig. 4. When the centerline of the probe is placed on top of the middle of the microstrip line the measured field will be zero, since the magnetic field to either side of the microstrip line will be equal. Once the probe is moved away from the center of the microstrip line, a net magnetic field will be measured and the peak amplitude of the response will increase up to the point Re. At the point Re, we measure the maximal peak amplitude response Am of the probe. When time domain responses are given for a probe, they are taken at the point Re. The distance between the middle of the microstrip line and Re is also taken as a measure for the resolution of the probe.

The microstrip line was chosen as measurement method since besides the temporal characteristics of the probe it can also be used to evaluate its spatial

[4] https://www.fair-rite.com/products/engineering-kits/?kit=21558.

Fig. 3. Gas discharge tube based EM-probe evaluation circuit.

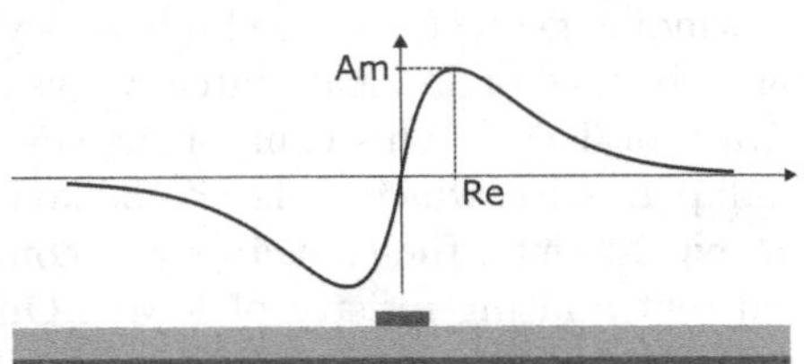

Fig. 4. Microstrip line response.

resolution. An alternative method is to use loop antennas, but these can not capture the spatial resolution of the probe. In order to determine the minimal field strength required to fault the intended target, it should be mounted on a test board and profiled for its EM-pulse sensitivity. However, this approach has its limitations for probe characterization. First, the result will not only depend on the probe characteristics but also depend heavily on the used target IC. And second, spatial resolution might be hard to establish using an IC as profiling device given that the induced currents might propagate through the entire IC depending on the internal routing. Therefore we opted to use a microstrip line as evaluation method. It should be noted however, that when an IC is targeted the frequency dependency of the coupling between probe and IC might give significant performance differences between different probes. Ideally, the transfer characteristic of an IC should first be measured and the probe should be designed accordingly. This is however outside the scope of this work.

3.3 Results

In what follows we experimentally analyze the influence several parameters in the design have on the pulse shape. All measurements are done using a Tektronix DPO7040C scope with 25 GS/s sample rate and a 6 GHz bandwidth. The input impedance of the scope is set to 50 Ω.

Ferrite Material. When large magnetic fields are induced into ferrite materials they will saturate. This saturation causes them to behave non-linearly, which makes simulating the impact of the chosen ferrite on the pulse shape difficult unless exact data is delivered by the manufacturer. The pulse shape was measured using three different ferrite materials made by the same manufacturer. They are all marketed for RF applications. The tree materials have a different frequency rating and permeability. The permeability of the first ferrite material, material 78 is 2000 H/m and has its pole at 1 MHz. The second material,

material 61 has a permeability of 110 H/m and has its pole at 20 MHz. Lastly, material 67 has a permeability of 40 H/m and a pole at 100 MHz. The probe responses for each material are depicted in Fig. 5. The plot clearly shows that the used ferrite material has a significant impact on the pulse response, e.g. the pulse magnitude of material 61 is more than 50% larger than material 67. In the rest of our experiments we use material 67. Although the pulse has the smallest amplitude response, the material is designed to operate at high frequencies making it unlikely to be the limiting factor for the rise time of our probe.

Number of Windings. The inductance is expected to rise quadratically with the number of windings. Thus according to Eq. 5, we expect the pulse amplitude to decrease with the number of windings. Since also the damping of the circuit depends on the inductance, we further expect the pulse width to increase with the number of windings. The magnetic field however linearly increases with the number of windings and thus compensates slightly for the decrease in current amplitude. Figure 6 shows the pulse response measured at position *Re* for variations in the number of windings. It behaves as expected.

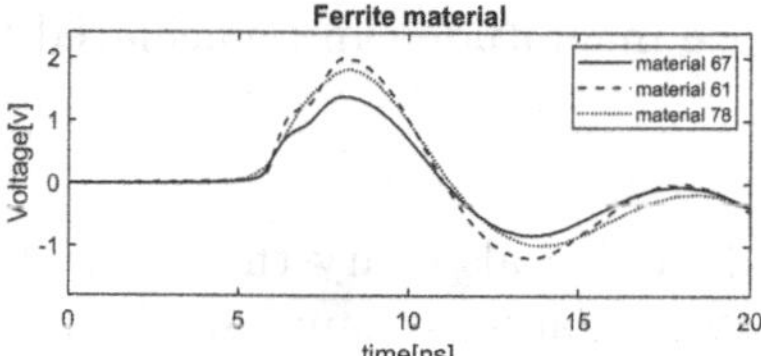

Fig. 5. Pulse response for different ferrite materials.

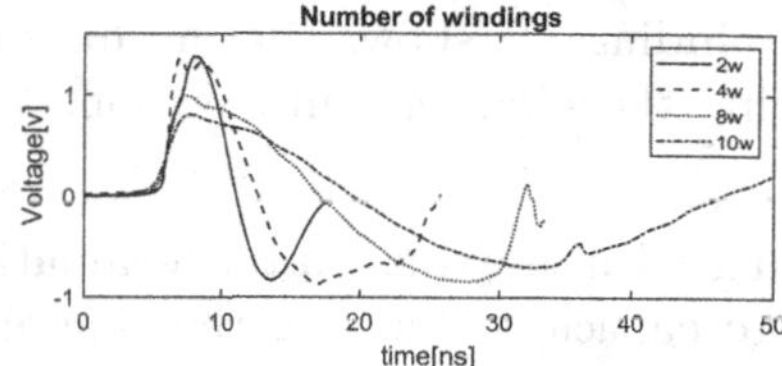

Fig. 6. Pulse response for different number of windings.

Core Diameter. Increasing the core diameter will reduce the amplitude of the pulse, since both the inductance (Eq. 1) and magnetic field (Eq. 2) depend on the solenoid radius. In this experiment we are however more interested in the probe resolution. We varied the probe diameter and measured the spatial characteristics of the probe. The results can be seen in Fig. 7. As shown in the plot, the distance between the peak amplitudes *Re* varies linearly with the probe diameter. Note that for our experiments we used rather large probe diameters, ranging from 1 to 4 mm. These diameters were chosen out of practical considerations, being one of the few sets commercially available. Using a probe with a large diameter to target an IC might not be ideal, since the current induced in the IC is proportional to the magnetic field difference around the wiring.

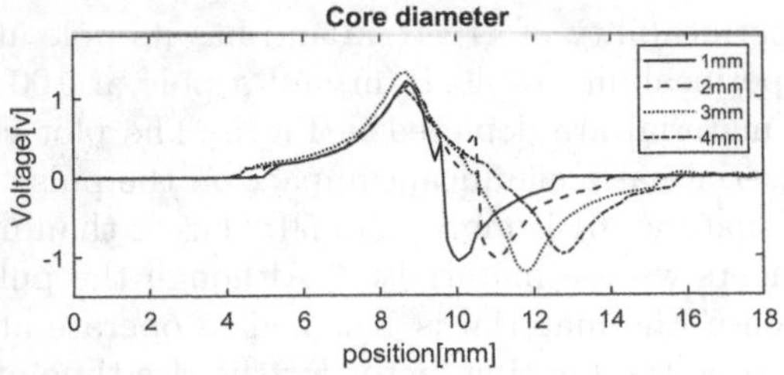

Fig. 7. Pulse response for different solenoid diameters.

Winding Geometry. A final probe parameter which can be varied is the length of the solenoid. There are two strategies which can be employed. Either the wire thickness can be reduced or windings can be overlapped. Reducing the wire thickness increases the resistance of the wire. The increased resistance usually does not pose a problem since some resistance is needed to dampen the pulse. The increased resistance however increases the risk of burning through the wiring due to the high current flowing through it. Figure 8 shows the response for a probe with 10 windings placed next to each other, and that of a probe with two layers of 5 windings. It shows that an increase in pulse magnitude can be achieved by altering the winding configuration.

Charge Capacitor. In our evaluation board we can also vary the size of the charge capacitor. Varying the charge capacitor emulates a change in the pulse generator design. In Fig. 9 the measured pulses for a varying capacitance can be seen.

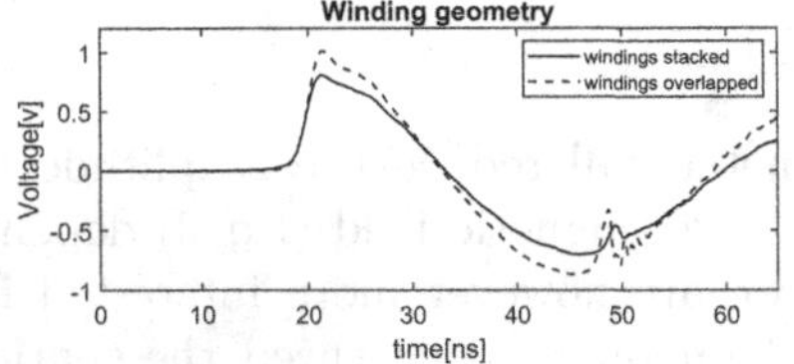

Fig. 8. Pulse response for different winding geometries.

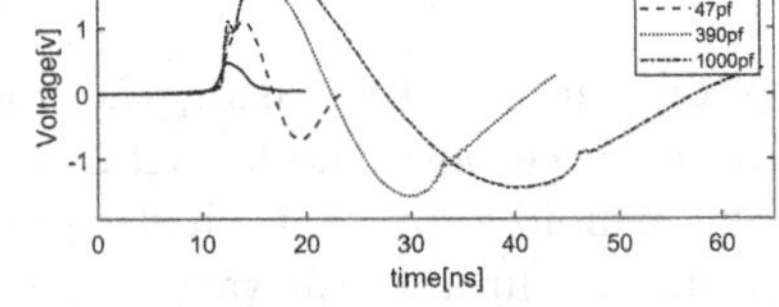

Fig. 9. Pulse response for different charge capacitors.

4 Pulse Generator

The main requirement for an EM-FI pulse generator is to produce a large current pulse with a fast rise time. Currents flowing through the probe are usually in the tens of amperes. In order to obtain a good temporal resolution, the rise time should be in the nanoseconds range. In the remainder of the paper we will restrict ourselves to a pulse generator design based on the RLC-circuit introduced in Fig. 2. Some adaptations to the circuit have to be made for it to become a functional EM-pulse generator. For instance, the ideal switch will have to be replaced and a power supply will have to be added to the design. Since the pulses needed for EM-pulse injection are generally in the nanoseconds range, the parasitics of the different discrete components can start dominating. Therefore components with good high frequency characteristics should be selected. Components with long lead wires should for instance be avoided, since the parasitic inductance of the leads will reduce the bandwidth of the pulse.

Note that off-the-shelf components such as RF power amplifiers or high voltage pulse generators are usually designed to drive a resistive 50 Ω load. EM-probes however have a different impedance which might result in a reduced efficiency of the amplifier or pulse generator. Therefore extra matching circuitry might have to be added to prevent damage to the equipment or to make sure the generated pulse matches the expectations.

4.1 Switching Element

When designing an RLC-based pulse generator different switching elements can be used. The most common switching element is a MOSFET, but also other semiconductor devices such as IGBTs or bipolar transistors in regular operation or in avalanche mode could be used. Besides semiconductor devices, one could also use dielectric breakdown devices such as a spark gap based switch. MOSFETs, and to a lesser extent IGBTs, are the preferred switching elements for EM-pulse setups. They tolerate high voltages and currents while providing a reasonable switching speed. One of the major drawbacks are the large parasitic capacitances of these components. A faster switching element, such as a bipolar transistor, could be used for better rise times. However, bipolar transistors can usually not tolerate the high currents and voltages required to generate a sufficiently large magnetic field. Biasing a bipolar transistor into its avalanche breakdown region might give us the best of both worlds: fast switching speeds and low parasitics, while being able to tolerate high voltages and currents. The drawback however is that we can only operate in this avalache region for a small voltage window.

When selecting the switching component care has to be taken that the parasitics do not start dominating the setup. For instance it is not uncommon for MOSFETs and IGBTs to have an output capacitance which is larger than 1000 pf. These devices do not only have large output capacitances, but also have significant input capacitance. Therefore a good input driving circuit is required to have a good turn on characteristics.

4.2 Pulse Delay and Jitter

Fault injection inherently requires a delay element in order to time the attack properly. From previous work [8,10] we know that often devices can only be faulted with EM-FI when the injected pulse causes a violation of either the setup or hold time. If we have a narrow pulse width and a low clock frequency, it might occur that we only have a 10 ns window ($t_{sensitive}$) around the clock edge during which we can inject faults. This puts a lower bound on the resolution of our delay element. Too much jitter will reduce the success rate of the pulse injection campaign. Even if the delay is set properly, a portion of the injected pulses will fall outside $t_{sensitive}$. With a large $t_{sensitive}$ the jitter and delay requirements can be relaxed. For our experiments in Sect. 5 we use an Agilent 33250 A signal generator as delay element. An alternative would be to use an FPGA development board as a triggering device.

4.3 Power Supply

The power supply needs to be able to provide a sufficiently high DC voltage. From Eq. 4 we can see that the current through the probe relates linearly to the voltage across the charge capacitor. The amount of current the power supply can deliver in combination with the size of the charge capacitor will determine the period between consecutive EM-pulse injections. High voltage DC power supplies can be purchased or build for around 20 Euros in the form of a Cockcroft–Walton generator. As a last remark, note that a good decoupling between the EM-FI setup and the rest of the environment is required. Otherwise, coupling between the EM-pulses might interfere with sensitive auxiliary equipment such as oscilloscopes. The decoupling can be achieved by minimizing the parasitic EM emissions from the EM-injection setup by placing decoupling capacitors on the different power supply rails, placing bulk capacitors close to the MOSFET and MOSFET driver and using shielded cables or twisted wire pairs to connect the different components. On the target side, coupling can be minimized by reducing the overall wire length and by using shielded cables, where possible.

5 Example Design

In this section we describe an example setup for EM pulse injection based on an RLC circuit with a MOSFET as switching element. This is by no means an optimal setup, but rather a use case tailored to the principles described in the paper. Our goal is to build a platform capable of generating 10 ns pulses, with the goal of targeting individual clock cycles in microcontrollers running at a frequency of 100 MHz.

5.1 EM Pulse Injection Platform

A circuit diagram of the EM-FI setup, including both pulse generator and probe, is shown in Fig. 10. As switching element (`M1`), we select an IPA80R280P7 MOSFET from Infineon Technologies. This is an n-channel MOSFET with a fast rise-time and relatively low output capacitance. It can tolerate a V_{ds} up to 800 V and a maximal pulsed drain current of 45 A. The MOSFET also has integrated ESD protection in the form of a Zener diode which is crucial in order to prevent damage to the MOSFET. Once the capacitor is discharged through `L1` there will be a flyback voltage across the inductor. The flyback voltage will result in a negative V_{DS}, which has to be protected against. We opted to not put a flyback diode directly across `L1` but instead to rely on the build in Zener diode of the MOSFET.

The IPA80R280P7 is driven by a Microchip MIC4422 low side MOSFET driver (`X1`). The jitter introduced by the MOSFET and driver combination amounts to 0.43 ns. The delay between the rising edge of the `TRIG` signal and pulse generation is 56 ns. A current limiting resistor (`R2`) is inserted at the source terminal of the MOSFET. This resistor serves as a safety mechanism to ensure the current never exceeds the maximal current rating of the MOSFET. In our case, the gate voltage during the *on* state is fixed to 12 V and the $V_{GS(th)}$ of the MOSFET is 3 V. Choosing the resistor to be 0.22 Ω, the current through the MOSFET will not exceed 40 A since the voltage across `R2` will reduce V_{GS}, turning off the MOSFET if the current exceeds 40 A. Increasing the value of `R2` and thus limiting the current through the MOSFET would also allow us to generate square pulses. The PCB design for the EM-pulse generator is shown in Fig. 11 and its corresponding schematic in Appendix B. The layout of the PCB is important not only to reduce the parasitics, but also to prevent undesired coupling or hotspots due to excessive heat generation. The main focus during PCB layout should be the high current RLC loop, which should be kept as small as possible. The cost of assembling the entire design is around 40 Euro.

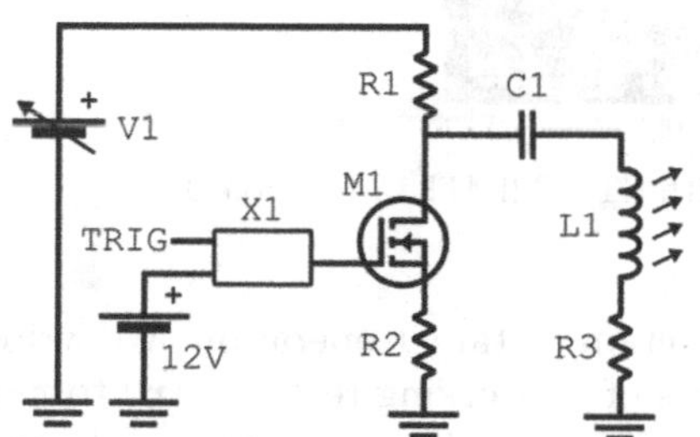

Fig. 10. Circuit diagram of EM pulse injection setup.

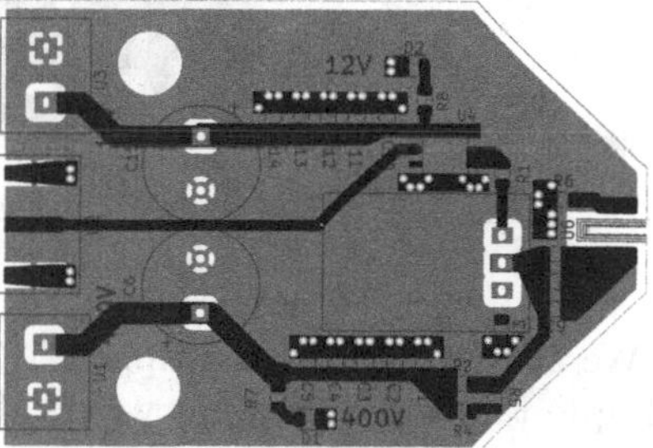

Fig. 11. EM-pulse injector PCB.

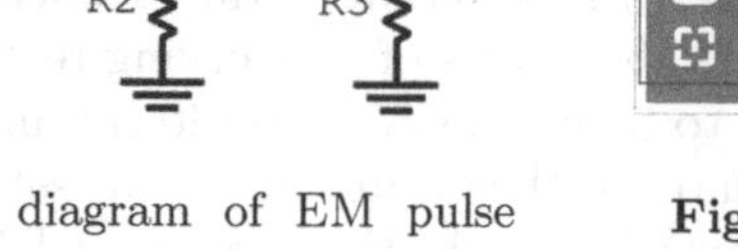

The second component in our example design is the probe. In order to obtain a good spatial resolution, we select a ferrite rod with a 750 μm diameter and 4 windings. The number of windings could be reduced in case the setup does not achieve the desired 10 ns pulse width. The inductance `L1` of the probe can be estimated using Eq. 1, or directly measured using an impedance meter. Knowing the inductance of the probe helps us with the choice of capacitor `C1`. Since we opt to build a setup that is slightly overdamped, the choice of capacitor size impacts the pulse width and amplitude. By modeling the circuit in SPICE, we estimated that a 1000 pF capacitor for `C1` would yield the desired 10 ns pulse width. With these parameters, however, the circuit turns out to be underdamped. Therefore we add a 10 Ω resistor R3 in order to achieve a slight overdamped response. After assembling the setup a pulse width of 12 ns was measured. Lowering the capacitance C1 and adjusting R3 finally enabled us to obtain the desired 10 ns pulse width.

5.2 Experimental Results

We target an STM32F411 from ST Microelectronics mounted on a NUCLEO-F411RE development board. This is a 32-bit ARM Cortex-M4 microcontroller featuring a three-stage pipeline. Its maximal frequency of 100 MHz makes it perfectly suitable for our experiments. The board is positioned on an XYZ stepper table such that the EM probe can be placed on top of the IC. Our experiments are performed in a non-invasive setting, e.g. without exposing the die of the chip (Fig. 12).

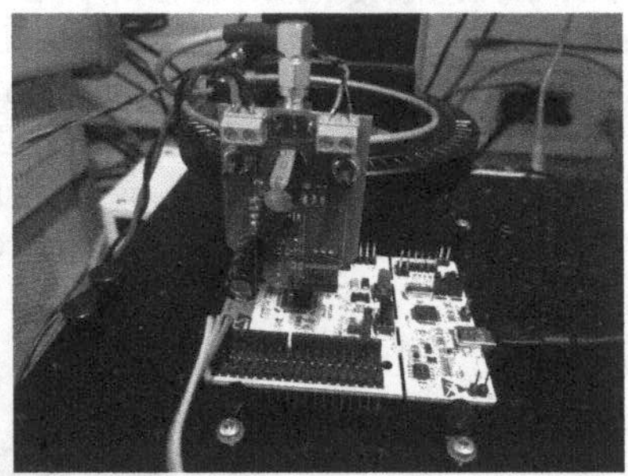

Fig. 12. EM-fault injection setup with STM32F411 target board.

We select the store multiple (`STM`) instruction as target operation. We write a simple target routine that writes the values of 10 working registers (`r0` to `r9`) to memory. The values are fixed to 0x55555555. This alternating string of ones and zeros is chosen to accommodate for the occurrence of bit set, bit reset or bit flip faults. Using a `GPIO` trigger for synchronization, we inject EM pulses during the writing stage of `STM`. Two sets of experiments are performed with different damping ratios. For the first experiment, a 10 Ω resistor is chosen for R3 making the EM-pulse critically damped. For the second experiment, R3 contains a 1 Ω resistor that makes the EM-pulse underdamped. All other parameters such as the probe, power supply voltage, injection location and timing are kept constant for both sets of experiments. The resulting pulse shapes for both the critically damped and underdamped case can be seen in Fig. 13a and b. After scanning the entire chip surface for sensitive areas, we selected a location with a high success rate. EM-pulses were injected in this region over a time period of 100 ns, with 1 ns steps.

When injecting pulses with the critically damped setup, we can fault individual writes to memory as can be seen in Fig. 13c. The X-axis corresponds to the register written to memory, while the Y-axis corresponds to the timing. An orange square indicates a fault was injected into the `STM` instruction while storing a particular register. At every step in time, 100 pulses were injected into the target. The plot clearly shows that the critically damped configuration of the setup allows to target individual writes to memory. Converting the setup to an underdamped configuration results in the fault map from Fig. 13d. We can still in some occasions target individual instructions, but also multiple instruction faults occur. This effect can be linked to the FSR described in Sect. 2. In the critically damped case, we have a single pulse with a 10 ns pulse width. It is likely that the voltage and current fluctuations only persist for a portion of this pulse width, and therefore we can target individual clock cycles. In the underdamped case however, we have multiple harmonic oscillations after the first pulse increasing the $t_{sensitive}$ and thus faulting multiple instructions simultaneously.

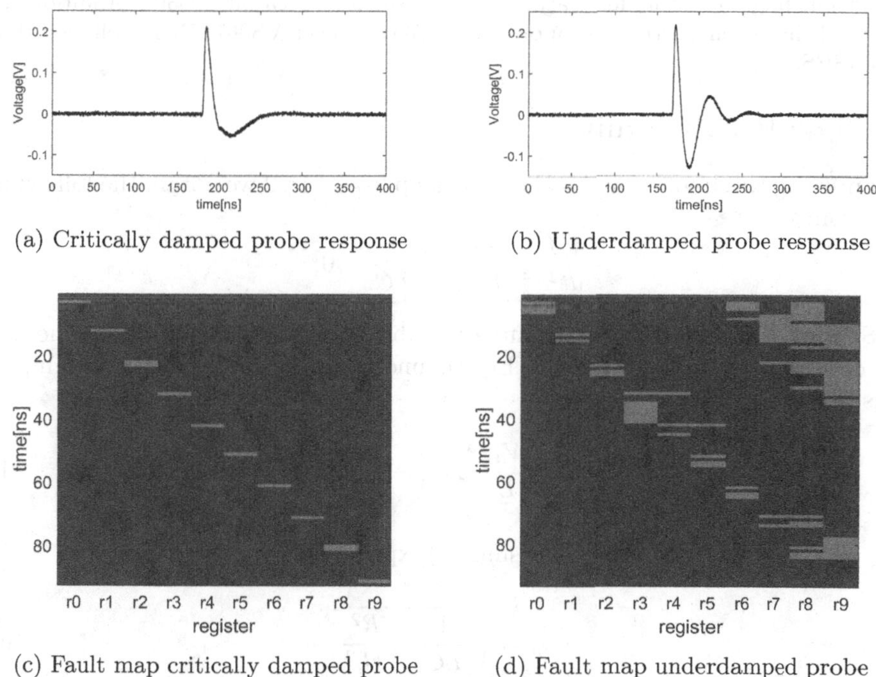

(a) Critically damped probe response (b) Underdamped probe response

(c) Fault map critically damped probe (d) Fault map underdamped probe

Fig. 13. EM-pulse injection results on the STM32F411 processor

Note that our experimental evaluation considers only the injection of a single pulse per campaign, which models an adversary capable of injecting one fault per cryptographic execution. If an adversary aims to inject multiple faults per execution, then the pulse frequency becomes a relevant design aspect. The time between consecutive pulses in our setup can be approximated by $4R1(C1 + C_{parasitic})$. The size of R1 is dependent on the drive strength of V1. The more current that can be supplied by V1, the lower we can set R1.

6 Conclusions

In this work we show that no special circuitry or equipment is needed to build a quality EM-pulse injection setup. However, a good understanding on how the different building blocks and design parameters impact the final pulse shape is important and not often discussed in the literature. Our study provides some guidelines supported by experimental results, and shows that a good tuning of the EM-pulse setup to the target device is critical for the success rate of an EM-pulse injection campaign.

Acknowledgment. This work was supported in part by the Research Council KU Leuven C1 on Security and Privacy for Cyber-Physical Systems and the Internet of Things with contract number C16/15/058 and through the Horizon 2020 research and innovation programme under Cathedral ERC Advanced Grant 695305. Additionally this work has been partially supported by FWO project VS06717N in collaboration with JSPS.

A The RLC Circuit

By applying Kirchhoff's law to the RLC loop from Fig. 2 we obtain the following equation:

$$\frac{d^2I}{dt^2} + \frac{R}{L}\frac{dI}{dt} + \frac{I}{LC} = 0, \tag{3}$$

Solving this equation yields three possible solutions depending on whether the circuit is critically damped (Eq. 4), underdamped (Eq. 5) or overdamped (Eqs. 7 and 8).

$$I = \frac{V_0}{L} t \exp\left(-\frac{R}{2L}t\right) \tag{4}$$

$$I = \frac{V_0}{L\omega_d} \sin(\omega_d t) \exp\left(-\frac{R}{2L}t\right) \tag{5}$$

$$\omega_d = \sqrt{\frac{1}{LC} - \frac{R^2}{4L^2}} \tag{6}$$

$$I = \frac{V_0}{(s_1 - s_2)L} \left[\exp(s_1 t) - \exp(s_2 t)\right] \tag{7}$$

$$s_1, s_2 = -\frac{R}{2L} \pm \sqrt{\left(\frac{R}{2L}\right)^2 - \frac{1}{LC}} \tag{8}$$

The solutions to the simple series RLC circuit can be found in nearly every physics textbook, see for instance [6].

B EM-Pulse Injection Circuit - Schematic

See Fig. 14.

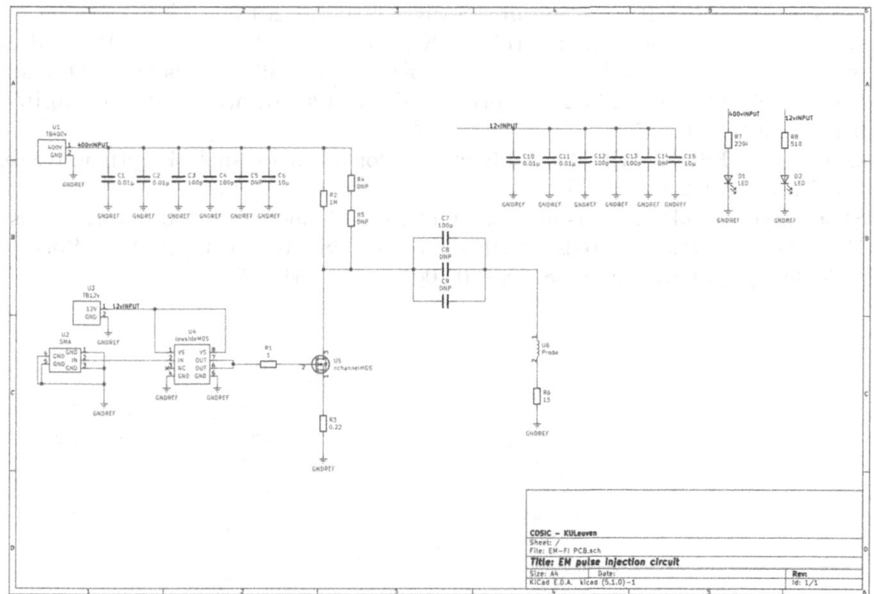

Fig. 14. EM-pulse injector schematic.

References

1. Balasch, J., Arumi, D., Manich, S.: Design and validation of a platform for electromagnetic fault injection. In: DCIS 2017, pp. 1–6. IEEE (2017)
2. Bar-El, H., Choukri, H., Naccache, D., Tunstall, M., Whelan, C.: The sorcerer's apprentice guide to fault attacks. Proc. IEEE **94**(2), 370–382 (2006)
3. Boneh, D., DeMillo, R.A., Lipton, R.J.: On the importance of checking cryptographic protocols for faults. In: Fumy, W. (ed.) EUROCRYPT 1997. LNCS, vol. 1233, pp. 37–51. Springer, Heidelberg (1997). https://doi.org/10.1007/3-540-69053-0_4
4. Cui, A., Housley, R.: BADFET: defeating modern secure boot using second-order pulsed electromagnetic fault injection. In: 11th USENIX Workshop on Offensive Technologies (WOOT 2017). USENIX Association, Vancouver (2017)
5. Dumont, M., Lisart, M., Maurine, P.: Electromagnetic fault injection: how faults occur. In: FDTC 2019, pp. 9–16. IEEE (2019)
6. Giancoli, D.C.: Physics: Principles with Applications. Pearson, Boston (2014)
7. Maurine, P.: Techniques for EM fault injection: equipments and experimental results. In: FDTC 2012, pp. 3–4 (2012)

8. Moro, N., Dehbaoui, A., Heydemann, K., Robisson, B., Encrenaz, E.: Electromagnetic fault injection: towards a fault model on a 32-bit microcontroller. In: Fischer, W., Schmidt, J. (eds.) FDTC 2013, pp. 77–88. IEEE (2013)
9. Omarouayache, R., Raoult, J., Jarrix, S., Chusseau, L., Maurine, P.: Magnetic microprobe design for EM fault attack. In: Catrysse, J., Pissoort, D. (eds.) EMC 2013, pp. 949–954. IEEE Computer Society, Brugge (2013)
10. Ordas, S., Guillaume-Sage, L., Tobich, K., Dutertre, J.-M., Maurine, P.: Evidence of a larger EM-induced fault model. In: Joye, M., Moradi, A. (eds.) CARDIS 2014. LNCS, vol. 8968, pp. 245–259. Springer, Cham (2015). https://doi.org/10.1007/978-3-319-16763-3_15
11. Quisquater, J.J., Samyde, D.: Eddy current for magnetic analysis with active sensor. In: Esmart 2002 (2002)
12. Skorobogatov, S.P., Anderson, R.J.: Optical fault induction attacks. In: Kaliski, B.S., Koç, K., Paar, C. (eds.) CHES 2002. LNCS, vol. 2523, pp. 2–12. Springer, Heidelberg (2003). https://doi.org/10.1007/3-540-36400-5_2

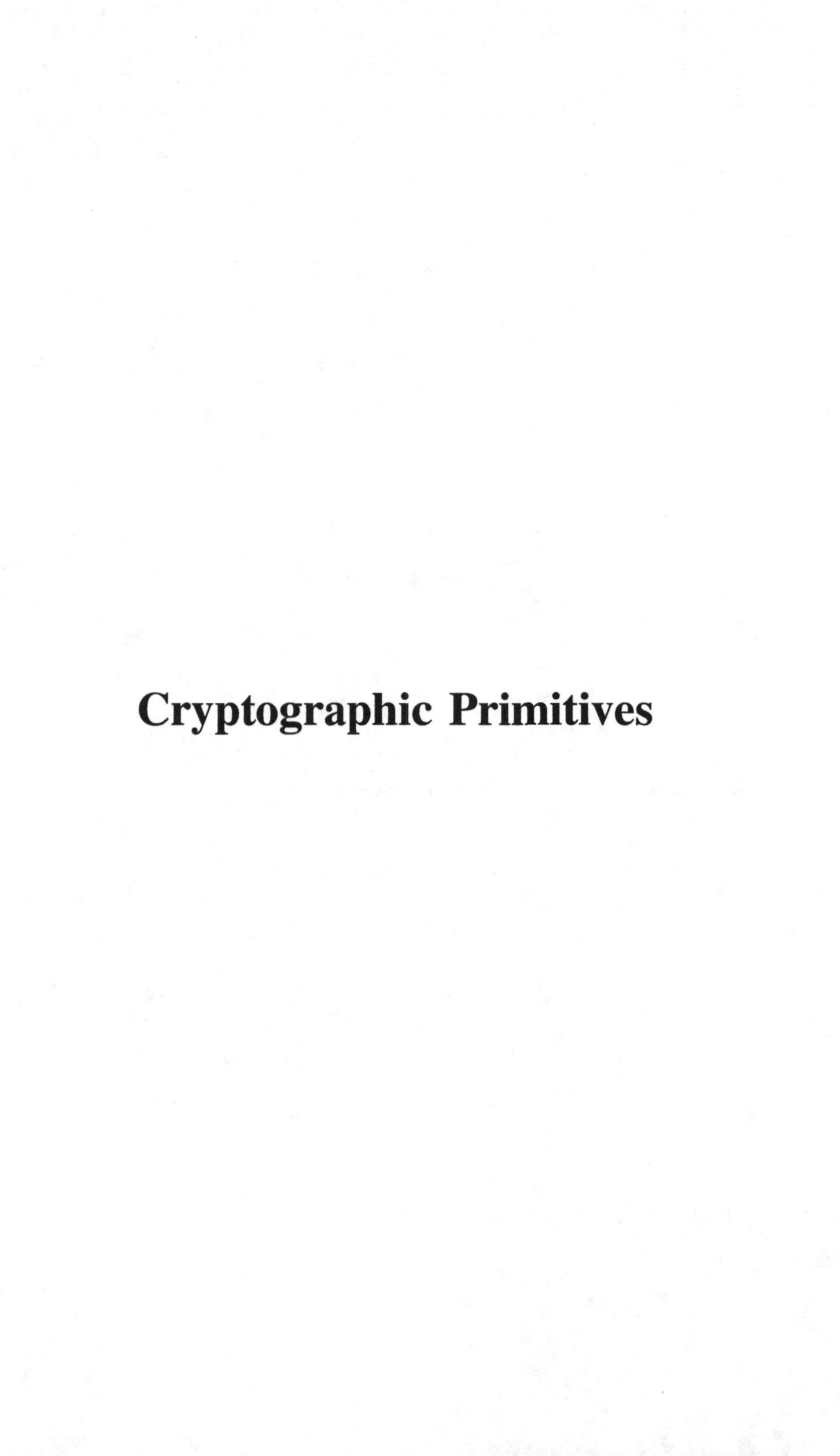

Cryptographic Primitives

Lightweight MACs from Universal Hash Functions

Sébastien Duval[1,2,3](✉) and Gaëtan Leurent[1]

[1] Inria, Paris, France
[2] Sorbonne Universités, Paris, France
[3] UCLouvain, Louvain-la-Neuve, Belgium
s.duval@uclouvain.be

Abstract. Lightweight cryptography is a topic of growing importance, with the goal to secure the communication of low-end devices that are not powerful enough to use conventional cryptography. There have been many recent proposals of lightweight block ciphers, but comparatively few results on lightweight Message Authentication Codes (MACs).

Therefore, this paper focuses on lightweight MACs. We review some existing constructions, and revisit the choices made in mainstream MACs with a focus on lightweight cryptography. We consider MACs based on universal hash functions, because they offer information theoretic security, can be implemented efficiently and are widely used in conventional cryptography. However, many constructions used in practice (such as GMAC or Poly1305-AES) follow the Wegman-Carter-Shoup construction, which is only secure up to 2^{64} queries with a 128-bit state.

We point out that there are simple solutions to reach security beyond the birthday bound, and we propose a concrete instantiation, MAC611, reaching 61-bit security with a 61-bit universal hash function. We wrote an optimized implementation on two ARM micro-controllers, and we obtain very good performances on the Cortex-M4, at only 3.7 c/B for long messages, and less than one thousand cycles for short messages.

Keywords: Lightweight cryptography · Micro-controller · MAC · Almost universal hash functions · Beyond-birthday-bound security

1 Introduction

Message Authentication Codes (MACs) are important cryptographic primitives, used to authenticate messages. A MAC is a short tag computed by the sender from the message and a key, and verified by the receiver with the same key.

In this paper, we focus on MAC algorithms for constrained environments. This is a field of growing importance, due to the increasing number of small communicating objects, such as contactless smart cards, wireless sensors, mobile phones, and Internet of Thing devices. In particular, we have seen that many of these devices use weak cryptography (*e.g.* MIFARE Crypto-1, KeeLoq), due to hardware limitations. To solve this issue, the academic community has designed

S. Belaïd and T. Güneysu (Eds.): CARDIS 2019, LNCS 11833, pp. 195–215, 2020.
https://doi.org/10.1007/978-3-030-42068-0_12

new algorithms for constrained environments, creating the field of lightweight cryptography. There is now a large number of block ciphers optimized for constrained environments and some of them have been standardized (PRESENT [9] in ISO/IEC 29192, HIGHT [19] in ISO/IEC 18033-3, KASUMI in UMTS). Recently, the NIST has started a standardization effort for lightweight cryptography[1], which shows that the field is gaining importance. However, there are still few options for modes of operation for these lightweight block ciphers and lightweight MACs; a recent survey [5] lists 117 lightweight cryptographic algorithms, including just 3 MACs.

MAC Constructions. MAC algorithms can be built in many different ways: from block ciphers (CBC-MAC [15], OMAC, PMAC), from hash functions (HMAC), or from scratch like Pelican MAC, or Chaskey. These constructions are deterministic, which makes them vulnerable against a generic forgery attack using collisions in the internal state, due to Preneel and van Oorschot [29]. Therefore, they only achieve security up to the birthday bound, *i.e.* when the amount of data authenticated with a single key is bounded by $2^{n/2}$, with n the state size.

When using a lightweight block cipher with a blocksize of $n = 64$ bits, this is typically insufficient. One way to increase the security is to use a larger internal state. Indeed, several modes have been proposed recently using a $2n$-bit internal state with an n-bit block cipher (*e.g.* `SUM-ECBC` [34], `3kf9` [35], `PMAC+` [13]).

Another way to avoid Preneel and van Oorschot's attack is to make the MAC not deterministic, using a *nonce*, a unique value provided by the user (in practice, the nonce is usually a counter). An important example of nonce-based MAC is the Wegman-Carter construction [33] which authenticates a message M using a nonce N as:

$$\mathrm{WC}[H,F]_{k_1,k_2}(M,N) = H_{k_1}(M) \oplus F_{k_2}(N),$$

with H a family of XOR universal hash functions, and F a PRF. This construction is widely deployed in schemes such as GMAC [24] and Poly1305 [3].

Lightweight MACs. While MACs seem to be an important primitive for lightweight cryptography, few constructions have been optimized for constrained environments. Notable exceptions are the ARX based Chaskey [27] and SipHash [1]. Chaskey is optimized for 32-bit micro-controllers with very good software performances, while SipHash targets 64-bit processors but should also have good performances on micro-controllers. TuLP [18] is another lightweight dedicated MAC, based on the PRESENT round function. It uses a small 64-bit state, but suffers from collision issues after 2^{32} blocks of data.

Another recent proposal is LightMAC [23], a mode for block-cipher-based MAC with a security bound independent of the message length, making it more usable with a small block size (but the security is still limited to $2^{n/2}$ queries). Lightweight hash functions such as QUARK [2] or SPONGENT [8] can also be used to build a MAC (*e.g.* using HMAC), but using a dedicated MAC is typically more efficient (in particular, hash functions require a larger internal state).

[1] https://csrc.nist.gov/projects/lightweight-cryptography.

Our Results. In this paper we study the design of lightweight MACs, optimized for software implementation on micro-controllers. To improve performance, we use a small state size of n bits for the bulk of the computation, with a nonce-based MAC to reach a security of 2^n. We focus on constructions based on universal hash functions in the style of Wegman and Carter. Universal hash functions only require statistical security, rather than computational security, which usually makes them cheaper to implement.

We note that practical MACs based on universal hash functions such as GMAC and Poly1305-AES only have security up to $2^{n/2}$ queries (the birthday bound) but simple tweaks can increase the security to 2^n queries. Additionnally, we improve the security proofs of some composition results in case some components are permutations, which improves in particular the security proof of a proposal by Minematsu and Tsunoo [26] using a reduced block cipher.

We then design a concrete instantiation, MAC611. We use a small state of roughly 64 bits with a beyond-birthday-secure mode, which allows for a faster primitive than GMAC and Poly1305-AES, with a similar data limit of roughly 2^{64} queries. Moreover, our construction can tolerate some repetition of nonces, while GMAC and Poly1305-AES fail catastrophically in this case. Nonce-misuse resistance is particularly relevant for lightweight cryptography, because the state of a device can sometimes be reset by an adversary.

MAC611 requires one block cipher call for the setup, just one multiplication $(\bmod 2^{61}-1)$ per message block, and one block cipher for the finalization, making it efficient both for short and long messages. Finally, we have implemented MAC611 on two Cortex-M micro-controllers to compare the performance with other MAC algorithms. Our results show that MAC611 is extremely efficient (Table 2), making it a promising construction for micro-controllers.

Organization of the Paper. We first review the previous literature on MAC constructions from universal hash functions in Sect. 2, and concrete constructions of universal hash functions in Sect. 3. In Sect. 4, we show that the security proof of some composition results can be improved when the underlying components are permutations. In Sect. 5, we set to build a MAC function optimized for micro-controllers. We compare the existing choices for implementing a universal hash function and turning it into a MAC, and propose a concrete construction based on polynomial evaluation in a small field in Sect. 6.

2 MAC Constructions from Universal Hash Functions

Universal hash functions were introduced by Carter and Wegman in 1977 [10] and are now used in many MAC constructions and security proofs. The idea is to hash the message then encrypt the result. The original encryption was a one-time-pad, which was then replaced by a counter-mode encryption. Such constructions are used in GMAC, the authentication part of GCM [24], and in Poly1305 [3], two of the most widely used schemes in TLS today. Many constructions exist to build efficient universal hash functions, and turn them into secure MACs. We sum up the main ones in the following.

2.1 Universal Hash Functions

There are several related definitions of universal and almost universal hash functions. In general a (almost) universal hash function H is a family of functions (denoted as $h \in H$, or $H_k \in H$ to emphasize the key) such that a fixed pair of inputs has a low collision probability for a randomly chosen element of the family. In the following, we denote the cardinality of set H as $|H|$. We define almost universal hash functions as:

Definition 1 (ε-AU). *A family $H : A \to B$ is ε-almost universal if:*

$$\forall m \neq m' \in A, |\{h \in H : h(m) = h(m')\}| \leq \varepsilon |H|$$

To handle any output difference rather than only collisions, one can use almost XOR universal hash functions:

Definition 2 (ε-AXU). *A family $H : A \to B$ is ε-almost XOR universal if:*

$$\forall m \neq m' \in A, \forall d \in B, \ |\{h \in H : h(m) \oplus h(m') = d\}| \leq \varepsilon |H|$$

If H is ε-AXU, it is also ε-AU, and we can further define an ε-AU family $G : A \times B \to B$ as follows:

$$G = \{(m_1, m_2) \mapsto h(m_1) \oplus m_2 : h \in H\}$$

Definition 3 (ε-ASU). *A family $H : A \to B$ is ε-almost strongly universal if:*

$$\begin{cases} \forall m \in A, \ \forall t \in B, \ |\{h \in H : h(m) = t\}| = |H|/|B| \\ \forall m \neq m' \in A, \ \forall t, t' \in B, \ |\{h \in H : h(m) = t, h(m') = t'\}| \leq \varepsilon |H|/|B| \end{cases}$$

If $H : A \to B$ is ε-ASU then H is also ε-AU.

2.2 MAC Algorithms

The security of a MAC algorithm is defined as an upper bound on the success probability of an adversary that tries to forge a valid tag. Formally, we consider an adversary $\mathcal{A}$ with oracle access to the MAC algorithm F; the adversary must output a message and tag pair, and succeeds if the message has not been queried to the oracle, and the tag is valid. Many constructions have been proposed to build a MAC out of a (almost) universal hash function. In the following bounds, we denote the output size of the universal hash function and the tag size as n.

Wegman-Carter. The seminal work by Wegman and Carter [33] introduced the following MAC, using an ε-AXU family of hash functions H and a PRF F. If nonces are unique, this construction reaches n-bit security:

$$\mathrm{WC}[H, F]_{k_1, k_2}(M, N) = H_{k_1}(M) \oplus F_{k_2}(N),$$
$$\mathbf{Adv}^{\mathrm{MAC}}_{\mathrm{WC}[H,F]} \leq \mathbf{Adv}^{\mathrm{PRF}}_{F} + \varepsilon + 2^{-n}.$$

Wegman-Carter-Shoup. In many concrete instantiations (GMAC [24], Poly1305-AES [3]), the PRF is instantiated with a block cipher E, following the Wegman-Carter-Shoup construction [31]. The security can be analyzed using the PRF-PRP switching lemma ($\mathbf{Adv}_E^{\mathrm{PRF}} \leq \mathbf{Adv}_E^{\mathrm{PRP}} + \frac{q^2}{2^n}$), but this adds a birthday term $q^2/2^n$ to the bound:

$$\mathrm{WCS}[H,E]_{k_1,k_2}(M,N) = H_{k_1}(M) \oplus E_{k_2}(N),$$

$$\mathbf{Adv}_{\mathrm{WCS}[H,E]}^{\mathrm{MAC}} \leq \mathbf{Adv}_E^{\mathrm{PRP}} + \tfrac{q^2}{2^n} + \varepsilon + 2^{-n}.$$

The proof can be improved by looking directly at the MAC security (instead of the PRF security) [4,31], but it is still limited by the birthday bound. Indeed, there is a forgery attack with roughly $\sqrt{n}2^{n/2}$ short queries [21,22,28].

Therefore the use of the nonce in WCS fails to increase the security compared to a deterministic MAC, but makes the construction more fragile (nonce repetion can leak the hash key).

Hash and PRF: $F(H(M))$. Alternatively, the hash and PRF construction builds a deterministic MAC from an ε-AU family H. It is analyzed in [7]:

$$\mathrm{HF}[H,F]_{k_1,k_2}(M,N) = F_{k_2}(H_{k_1}(M)),$$

$$\mathbf{Adv}_{\mathrm{HF}[H,F]}^{\mathrm{MAC}} \leq \mathbf{Adv}_F^{\mathrm{PRF}} + q^2\varepsilon/2 + 2^{-n}.$$

WMAC: $F(H(M) \,\|\, N)$. Some constructions allow to combine the n-bit security with nonces, and the birthday security when nonces are repeated. In particular, if a $2n$-bit PRF is available, one can use the construction introduced by UMAC [7] and later analyzed as WMAC [6] with an ε-AU function. This construction was analyzed in [7] assuming that the nonces are always distinct:

$$\mathrm{WMAC}[H,F]_{k_1,k_2}(M,N) = F_{k_2}(H_{k_1}(M) \parallel N),$$

$$\mathbf{Adv}_{\mathrm{HFN}[H,F]}^{\mathrm{MAC}} \leq \mathbf{Adv}_F^{\mathrm{PRF}} + \varepsilon + 2^{-n}.$$

EWCDM. Cogliati and Seurin have recently proposed a construction with similar security using only an n-bit block cipher and an ε-AXU function [11]. A later work by Mennink and Neves [25] proved security up to 2^n:

$$\mathrm{EWCDM}[H,E]_{k_1,k_2,k_3}(M,N) = E_{k_3}\big(H_{k_1}(M) \oplus E_{k_2}(N) \oplus N\big),$$

$$\mathbf{Adv}_{\mathrm{EWCDM}[H,E]}^{\mathrm{MAC}} \leq \mathbf{Adv}_F^{\mathrm{PRP}} + q/2^n + q^2\varepsilon/2^n + 2^{-n}.$$

3 Construction of Universal Hash Functions

We now review previous results on the construction of universal hash functions.

3.1 Constructions for Short Messages

Some crucial AU/AXU families use multiplication by a secret key in a field $\mathbb{F}$:

$$H_1 : \mathbb{F} \to \mathbb{F} = \{m \mapsto m \times k : k \in \mathbb{F}\} \qquad \text{is XOR universal;} \tag{1}$$

$$H_2 : \mathbb{F} \times \mathbb{F} \to \mathbb{F} = \{m_1, m_2 \mapsto m_1 \times k + m_2 : k \in \mathbb{F}\} \qquad \text{is universal.} \tag{2}$$

Polynomial Hashing [14]. In order to hash a long message with a single key, these constructions can be generalized to polynomial hashing. The input message is interpreted as a polynomial, and evaluated on the secret key:

$$H : \mathbb{F}^\ell \to \mathbb{F} = \{m_1, m_2, \dots m_\ell \mapsto \sum_{i=1}^{\ell} m_i \times k^i : k \in \mathbb{F}\}.$$

The family H with messages of length ℓ is $\ell\varepsilon$-AXU. Practical MACs like GMAC and Poly1305 use this construction with different choices of the field $\mathbb{F}$.

Using Reduced Block Ciphers [26]. Instead of multiplications, one can use reduced block ciphers. For instance, the exact MEDP of 4-round AES from [20] shows that it is ε-AXU with $\varepsilon \approx 1.18 \cdot 2^{-110}$ (if the round keys are independent).

$$H : \{0,1\}^n \to \{0,1\}^n = \{m \mapsto E_k(m) : k \in \{0,1\}^n\} \qquad \text{is } \varepsilon\text{-AXU.} \tag{3}$$

This construction has been used by Minematsu and Tsunoo to build an AES-based MAC faster than CBC-MAC [26].

3.2 Composition and Extension

To accept long messages, composition and domain extension can be used. We will focus here on the composition of (almost) universal hash functions.
Composition [32]. Let $H_1 : A \to B$ and $H_2 : B \to C$. Consider $G : A \to C$ as:

$$G = \{m \mapsto (h_2(h_1(m))) : h_1 \in H_1, h_2 \in H_2\}.$$

We have the following results:

- If H_1 is ε_1-AU and H_2 is ε_2-AU, then G is ε-AU, with $\varepsilon = \varepsilon_1 + \varepsilon_2 - \varepsilon_1\varepsilon_2$.
- If H_1 is ε_1-AU and H_2 is ε_2-ASU, then G is ε-ASU, with $\varepsilon = \varepsilon_1 + \varepsilon_2 - \varepsilon_1\varepsilon_2$.
- If H_1 is ε_1-AU and H_2 is ε_2-AXU, then G is ε-AXU, with $\varepsilon = \varepsilon_1 + \varepsilon_2 - \varepsilon_1\varepsilon_2$.

If H_1 and H_2 are compressive, their composition G will compress incrementally. The last two results can be used to compose an efficient ε-AU function and a stronger ε-AXU or ε-ASU, to build an efficient ε-AXU or ε-ASU function.

Domain Extension by Composition. Building an AU family with arbitrary input domain from a fixed-length compressing AU family can be done in a Merkle-Damgård style:

Let $H_1 : A_1 \to B_1$ and $H_2 : A_2 \times B_1 \to B_2$ be ε_1-AU and ε_2-AU, respectively. We define the iteration of H_1 and H_2, $H : A_1 \times A_2 \to B_2$ as follows:

$$H = \{(m_1, m_2) \mapsto h_2(m_2, h_1(m_1)) : h_1 \in H_1, h_2 \in H_2\}$$

Using the previous results, we can prove that H is ε-AU with $\varepsilon = \varepsilon_1 + \varepsilon_2 - \varepsilon_1\varepsilon_2 \leq \varepsilon_1 + \varepsilon_2$ because it is the composition of H_1' and H_2, where H_1' is also ε_1-AU:

$$H_1' : A_1 \times A_2 \to A_2 \times B_2 = \{(m_1, m_2) \mapsto (m_2, h_1(m_1)) : h_1 \in H_1\}.$$

Moreover, if H_2 is ε_2-AXU (resp. ε_2-ASU), then H is also ε-AXU (resp. ε-ASU).

This result can easily be extended to the iteration of three or more functions. In particular, it can be used to iterate a single ε-AU function $H : B \times A \to B$, to build the ℓ-th iterate $H^\ell : B \times A^\ell \to B$ with ℓ independent keys; H^ℓ is $\ell\varepsilon$-AU. In particular, this construction is used in [26].

4 Improved Bounds with Permutations

We can improve the security bound of the iteration of two AU hash functions (following the construction of Sect. 3.2) in the special case where the second function is a permutation when the first input is fixed.

We show that with this extra condition, the iteration of two ε-AU functions is ε-AU, while it is only ε'-AU with $\varepsilon' = 2\varepsilon - \varepsilon^2$ in general.

Theorem 1. *Let $H_1 : A_1 \to B_1$ be ε_1-AU and $H_2 : A_2 \times B_1 \to B_2$.*
Consider $G : A_1 \times A_2 \to B_2$ defined as

$$G = \{(m_1, m_2) \mapsto h_2(m_2, h_1(m_1)) : h_1 \in H_1, h_2 \in H_2\}.$$

If $x \mapsto h_2(m, x)$ is a permutation for all $h_2 \in H_2$ and all $m \in A_2$, then:

- *If H_2 is ε_2-AU, then G is $\max\{\varepsilon_1, \varepsilon_2\}$-AU,*
- *If H_2 is ε_2-AXU, then G is $\max\{\varepsilon_1, \varepsilon_2\}$-AXU,*
- *If H_2 is ε_2-ASU, then G is $\max\{\varepsilon_1, \varepsilon_2\}$-ASU.*

In particular, we can improve the security bound of PC-MAC from Minematsu and Tsunoo [26]. PC-MAC repeats d iterations of reduced-round AES with independent keys (typically, $d = 15$), with a security bound of:

$$\mathbf{Adv}^{\text{PRF}}_{\text{PC-MAC}}(q) \leq \mathbf{Adv}^{\text{PRP}}_{E_K}(\rho q + c) + \frac{2.5(\rho q + c)^2}{2^n} + (d\varepsilon_{dp} + \varepsilon_{sdp})\frac{q^2}{2},$$

with q queries of maximum length ρ, and c is roughly equal to a small constant times d. With our results, we can replace the term $d\varepsilon_{dp}$ by ε_{dp}:

$$\mathbf{Adv}^{\text{PRF}}_{\text{PC-MAC}}(q) \leq \mathbf{Adv}^{\text{PRP}}_{E_K}(\rho q + c) + \frac{2.5(\rho q + c)^2}{2^n} + (\varepsilon_{dp} + \varepsilon_{sdp})\frac{q^2}{2}.$$

Proof. **Case 1:** *AU* $\Rightarrow$ *AU***.** We denote $N = \#\{(h_1, h_2) \in H_1 \times H_2 : h_2(m_2, h_1(m_1)) = h_2(m_2', h_1(m_1'))\}$ for a fixed message pair $(m_1 \| m_2, m_1' \| m_2')$. We want to prove that: $N \leq \max\{\varepsilon_1, \varepsilon_2\} \times |H_1| \times |H_2|$.
If $m_2 = m_2'$ (and thus $m_1 \neq m_1'$), we write:

$$\begin{aligned} N &= \sum_{h_2 \in H_2} \#\{h_1 \in H_1 : h_2(m_2, h_1(m_1)) = h_2(m_2, h_1(m_1'))\} \\ &= \sum_{h_2 \in H_2} \#\{h_1 \in H_1 : h_1(m_1) = h_1(m_1')\} \quad \text{since } x \mapsto h_2(m_2, x) \text{ is a permutation} \\ &\leq \sum_{h_2 \in H_2} \varepsilon_1 \times |H_1| = \varepsilon_1 \times |H_1| \times |H_2|. \end{aligned}$$

If $m_2 \neq m_2'$, we write:

$$\begin{aligned} N &= \sum_{h_1 \in H_1} \#\{h_2 \in H_2 : h_2(m_2, h_1(m_1)) = h_2(m_2', h_1(m_1'))\} \\ &\leq \sum_{h_1 \in H_1} \varepsilon_2 \times |H_2| = \varepsilon_2 \times |H_1| \times |H_2|. \end{aligned}$$

We used that $h_1(m_1)$ and $h_1(m_1')$ are fixed values for eached fixed h_1 and $m_2 \neq m_2'$.

In the end, we get that G is $\max\{\varepsilon_1, \varepsilon_2\}$-*AU*.

Case 2: *AXU* $\Rightarrow$ *AXU***.** We denote $N = \#\{(h_1, h_2) \in H_1 \times H_2 : h_2(m_2, h_1(m_1)) \oplus h_2(m_2', h_1(m_1')) = d\}$ for a fixed message pair $(m_1 \| m_2, m_1' \| m_2')$ and a fixed $d \in B_2$. We want to prove that $N \leq \max\{\varepsilon_1, \varepsilon_2\} \times |H_1| \times |H_2|$. The complicated case is collision ($d = 0$), because collision can either occur in h_1 or in h_2. Using the *AU* case, we get that when $d = 0$, $N \leq \max\{\varepsilon_1, \varepsilon_2\} \times |H_1| \times |H_2|$.
Otherwise, $d \neq 0$. Therefore $(m_2, h_1(m_1)) \neq (m_2', h_1(m_1'))$, and we simply write:

$$\begin{aligned} N &= \sum_{h_1 \in H_1} \#\{h_2 \in H_2 : h_2(m_2, h_1(m_1)) \oplus h_2(m_2', h_1(m_1')) = d\} \\ &\leq \sum_{h_1 \in H_1} \varepsilon_2 \times |H_2| = \varepsilon_2 \times |H_1| \times |H_2|. \end{aligned}$$

Case 3: *ASU* $\Rightarrow$ *ASU***.** First, we have to show that H is balanced. For fixed messages m_1, m_2, and a fixed $y \in B_2$, we have:

$$\begin{aligned} M &= \#\{(h_1, h_2) \in H_1 \times H_2 : h_2(m_2, h_1(m_1)) = y\} \\ &= \sum_{h_1 \in H_1} \#\{h_2 \in H_2 : h_2(m_2, h_1(m_1)) = y\} \\ &\leq \sum_{h_1 \in H_1} |H_2|/|B_2| = |H_1| \times |H_2|/|B_2|. \end{aligned}$$

We denote $N = \#\{(h_1, h_2) \in H_1 \times H_2 \ : \ h_2(m_2, h_1(m_1)) = y,\ h_2(m'_2, h_1(m'_1)) = y'\}$ for a fixed message pair $(m_1 \| m_2, m'_1 \| m'_2)$ and fixed $y, y' \in B_2$. We want to prove that $N \leq \max\{\varepsilon_1, \varepsilon_2\} \times |H_1| \times |H_2|$.
Similarly to the *AXU* proof, the complicated case is collision ($y = y'$), because collision can either occur in h_1 or in h_2. Using the *AU* case, we get that when $y = y'$, $N \leq \max\{\varepsilon_1, \varepsilon_2\} \times |H_1| \times |H_2|$.
Otherwise, $y \neq y'$. Therefore $(m_2, h_1(m_1)) \neq (m'_2, h_1(m'_1))$, and we simply write:

$$\begin{aligned} N &= \#\{(h_1, h_2) \in H_1 \times H_2 \ : \ h_2(m_2, h_1(m_1)) = y,\ h_2(m'_2, h_1(m'_1)) = y'\} \\ &= \sum_{h_1 \in H_1} \#\{h_2 \in H_2 \ : \ h_2(m_2, h_1(m_1)) = y,\ h_2(m'_2, h_1(m'_1)) = y'\} \\ &\leq \sum_{h_1 \in H_1} \varepsilon_2 \times |H_2| = \varepsilon_2 \times |H_1| \times |H_2|. \end{aligned}$$

Again, we use that, for fixed h_1, $h_1(m_1)$ and $h_1(m'_1)$ are fixed values. □

5 Instantiating a Lightweight MAC

We now consider the construction of a lightweight MAC with a small state, in order to reach good performance on 32-bit micro-controllers. Following Sect. 2, we use the WMAC construction $F(H(M) \parallel N)$ with a 61-bit universal hash function, and a 128-bit block cipher[2], in order to reach a data limit of 2^{61} queries. The main downside of WMAC compared to Wegman-Carter is that the block cipher cannot be evaluated in parallel with the hash function, but this hardly matters for micro-controller implementations.

An important part of this work consists in the implementation and optimization of our algorithm, MAC611, on two 32-bit micro-controllers.

We ran benchmarks to explore design choices and compare with existing MACs. We used two micro-controllers: an FRDM-KL46Z board with a Cortex-M0+ micro-controller and an FRDM-K64F board with a Cortex-M4 micro-controller. The Cortex-M0+ is very limited, while the Cortex-M4 is slightly more powerful, with more RAM, and more instructions.

5.1 Choice of Universal Hash Function: XPoly

We focus on AU families based on field arithmetics, which offer trade-offs between key size and security. Over a field $\mathbb{F}$, the two main options are:

Polynomial hashing [14]**:** $H_k : m_1, \dots m_\ell \mapsto \sum_{i=1}^{\ell} m_i \times k^{\ell+1-i}$
H_k is an $\ell\varepsilon$-AXU family using a single field element as key, with $\varepsilon = 1/|\mathbb{F}|$.

---

[2] Unfortunately, we did not find a good 64-bit block cipher with an efficient implementation on micro-controllers to use in EWCDM.

Dot product [16]: $H_{k_1,\dots k_\ell} : m_1, \dots m_\ell \mapsto \sum_{i=1}^{\ell} m_i \times k_i$
$H_{k_1,\dots k_\ell}$ is an ε-AXU family using ℓ field elements as key, with $\varepsilon = 1/|\mathbb{F}|$.

In particular, the factor ℓ in the security of polynomial hashing leads to a class of weak keys for GMAC [30].

To balance security and key size, we propose two constructions using polynomial hashing, with independent subkeys k_i for every chunk of λ blocks of message. We denote $P[m]$ the polynomial whose coefficients are given by message m. The function is typically evaluated using Horner's rule, with a single multiplication and addition per message block:

$$P[m](k) = \sum_{i=1}^{\ell} m_i \times k^{\ell+1-i} = (((\cdots((m_1 \times k)+m_2) \times k \cdots)+m_{\ell-1}) \times k+m_\ell) \times k .$$

Sum of Polynomials. One option is to sum independent polynomials:

$$H_{k_1,\dots,k_\ell} : m_1, \dots m_{\ell\lambda} \mapsto \sum_{i=1}^{\ell} P[m_{1+\lambda(i-1)}, \dots, m_{\lambda i}](k_i) = \sum_{i=1}^{\ell} \sum_{j=1}^{\lambda} m_{\lambda(i-1)+j} \times k_i^{\lambda+1-j}$$

Since the polynomial hashes are $\lambda\varepsilon$-AXU, this construction is also a $\lambda\varepsilon$-AXU family, using the analysis of [10, Proposition 8].

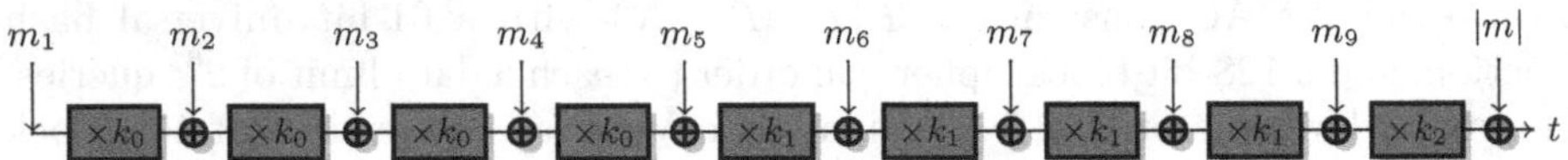

Fig. 1. XPoly: universal hashing based on composition of polynomials (with $\lambda = 4$).

Composition of Polynomials. Alternatively, we can build a $\lambda\varepsilon$-AU family with the composition result of Theorem 1, using $\lambda\varepsilon$-AU functions defined from polynomial hashing: $H_i : m_1, \dots m_\ell, m_{\ell+1} \mapsto P[m_1, \dots m_\ell](k_i) \oplus m_{\ell+1}$:

$$\mathrm{XPoly1}_{k_1,\dots,k_\ell} : m_1, \dots m_{\ell\lambda} \mapsto \sum_{i=1}^{\ell} \sum_{j=1}^{\lambda} m_{\lambda(i-1)+j} \times \prod_{u=\lambda(i-1)+j}^{\ell\lambda-1} k_{\lceil u/\lambda \rceil}$$

We still implement the construction with Horner's rule, changing the subkey every λ blocks (see Fig. 1). The composition has a smaller state than the sum of polynomials, therefore we use composition for our design.

The parameter λ offers a trade-off between security and key length. The key length is linear in the message size, but we can use a PRF to stretch a master key into sub-keys for each chunk, with $k_i = F_k(i)$. If λ is not too small, the time taken to derive the keys can be kept small.

For a practical MAC, we need a universal hash function family that can process messages of different lengths. To achieve this, we first pad the message with zeroes to a full block, we append a block with an encoding of the message length (the number of bytes), and we process the padded message through XPoly1. We denote this construction as XPoly: $\mathsf{XPoly}(m) = \mathrm{XPoly1}(\mathrm{pad}(m) \parallel |m|)$; this family is $2\lambda\varepsilon$-AU, with $\varepsilon = 1/|\mathbb{F}|$.

5.2 Choice of Field and Multiplication

We now have to choose a field to define our universal hash function. This is an important choice because the field multiplication is the main operation in XPoly. There are two kinds of fields that can be used for efficient implementations: fields $\mathbb{F}_p$ defined modulo a prime number p close to 2^{64} or 2^{128} (as used in Poly1305), and binary fields such as $\mathbb{F}_{2^{64}}$ and $\mathbb{F}_{2^{128}}$ (like GMAC).

Table-Based Implementations. Since the multiplication by a fixed key is a linear operation, it can be implemented using precomputed tables. For instance, if we precompute $\mu_i = 2^i \times k$ for $0 \leq i < n$, we can decompose an element $x \in \mathbb{F}$ as $x = \sum_{0 \leq i < n} x_i \times 2^i$ (where x_i is just the i-th bit of x), and use:

$$x \times k = \sum_{0 \leq i < n} x_i \times 2^i \times k = \sum_{0 \leq i < n} x_i \times \mu_i.$$

In particular, in a binary field, the sum is just an XOR. More generally, we can precompute multiplication tables for several consecutive bits. If we divide x into t-bit chunks and precompute tables of 2^t entries for each chunk, we just need n/t table accesses and $n/t - 1$ sums to evaluate the product $x \times k$.

Table 1. Benchmarks for universal hashing in various fields. We report timing in cycles/bytes for the multiplication (to account for the difference in field size), and the number of cycles needed to build the tables.

Field	Implem.	Mem.	Cortex-M0+		Cortex-M4	
			mul (c/B)	table (c)	mul (c/B)	table (c)
$\mathbb{F}_{2^{128}}$	1-bit chunks	4kB	148	3984	128	2756
	4-bit chunks	8 kB	48	16992	35	10918
	8-bit chunks	64 kB	-	-	19	104922
$\mathbb{F}_{2^{64}}$	1-bit chunks	1kB	91	1440	85	1131
	4-bit chunks	2 kB	21	6144	19	3769
	8-bit chunks	16 kB	12	53184	11	40142
$\mathbb{F}_{2^{128}}$	GMAC	256 B	95	?	53	?
$\mathbb{F}_{2^{61}-1}$	MAC611	–	19	–	3.7	–
$\mathbb{F}_{2^{130}-5}$	Poly1305	–	94	–	5	–

Benchmarks. We wrote table-based implementations of multiplication in a binary field in C and assembly, using several chunk sizes (1 bit, 4 bits, and 8 bits), and we give benchmarks results in Table 1. Note that we could not implement multiplication in $\mathbb{F}_{2^{128}}$ with 8-bit chunks on the Cortex-M0+ because the tables do not fit in the RAM of this small micro-controller.

For reference, we also benchmarked the OpenSSL implementations of GMAC (multiplication in $\mathbb{F}_{2^{128}}$), which includes ARM assembly that can run on the Cortex-M4 (but not on the Cortex-M0+). It uses a single table with chunks of 4 bits (256 bytes of memory).

As expected, our benchmarks show that multiplication in a small field is more efficient (the cost of the multiplication is quadratic), and table-based implementation can be quite fast on micro-controllers, using some memory for the tables. In particular, multiplication over $\mathbb{F}_{2^{64}}$ using 4-bit or 8-bit chunks is competitive with Chaskey.

Using the Multiplier. Alternatively, multiplication in fields defined modulo a prime can be implemented efficiently using the integer multiplier of the processor. This is useful for servers using different keys with several clients, since accessing tables would often incur cache misses [3].

To evaluate the speed of prime field multiplication, we benchmarked the OpenSSL implementations of Poly1305 (multiplication in $\mathbb{F}_{2^{130}-5}$), which uses assembly on the Cortex-M4, and C code on the Cortex-M0+. On the Cortex-M4, this is much faster than a table based multiplication, with just 5 c/B. Indeed, the Cortex-M4 has a fast multiplier and a well written implementation of the multiplication in a prime field can be very fast (but bad implementations can be much slower...).

Algorithm 1. MAC611

Parameters: E is Noekeon, $\lambda = 1024$
Input: K, M, N
  Divide M into 7-byte blocks m_i (with zero-padding)
  $x \leftarrow 0$
  for $1 \leq i \leq |M|$ **do**
    if $i \bmod \lambda = 1$ **then**
      $h \leftarrow T64(E_K(0 \,\|\, (i-1)/\lambda)) \bmod 2^{61} - 1$
    $x \leftarrow (x + m_i) \times h \bmod 2^{61} - 1$
  $x \leftarrow x + \mathsf{bytelen}(M)$
  return $T64\left(E_K(2^{63} + x \,\|\, N)\right)$

Since prime field multiplications can also be implemented with tables if needed, we decided to use a prime field for our construction. We wrote optimized assembly implementations of the multiplication in $\mathbb{F}_{2^{61}-1}$ (because we target the 64-bit security level). As detailed in Sect. 6.1, we achieved very good results, with just 3.7 c/B on the Cortex-M4 and 19 c/B on the Cortex-M0+ (without using any tables). Therefore, we use the field $\mathbb{F}_{2^{61}-1}$ for our construction.

6 A Concrete Instantiation: MAC611

We can now define a concrete MAC construction based on our analysis, and compare its performance with other MAC constructions. As explained above, we use the XPoly universal hash function with $\lambda = 1024$ over the field $\mathbb{F}_{2^{61}-1}$. Since the field has less than 2^{64} elements, we cut the message into blocks m_i of 56 bits (*i.e.* 7 bytes).

For the finalization of the MAC construction, we considered various choices for the PRF, and we decided to use Noekeon [12], a 128-bit block cipher with very efficient implementations on micro-controllers. Therefore, we use the construction $F(H(M) \parallel N)$ from WMAC: we concatenate the 64-bit hash and a 64-bit nonce, encrypt them, and truncate the output to 64 bits (we denote the first 64 bits of variable a by $T64(a)$). We also use Noekeon to derive the subkeys used in XPoly from the block-cipher key, by encrypting a counter and truncating then reducing the output modulo $2^{61} - 1$: $k_i = T64(\text{Noekeon}(0 \parallel i)) \bmod 2^{61} - 1$.

Since the output of XPoly is a field element, we take the representative h between 0 and $2^{61} - 2$, and we compute the MAC as $F(2^{63} + h \parallel N)$. This ensures a domain separation between the block-cipher calls for the key-derivation and for the finalization.

6.1 Implementation Details

The choice of the field allows for very efficient implementations on processors or micro-controllers with a fast integer multiplier, but table-based implementations are also possible when there is no multiplier or a very slow one. More precisely, elements of the field are stored as an unsigned 64-bit integer, and the field operations are implemented as follows[3]:

Modular reduction can be implemented very efficiently, by just computing `(x>>61) + (x&0x1fffffffffffffff)` (in C notation). This is a partial reduction with output between 0 and $2^{61} + 6$ (for x a 64-bit unsigned integer), but this range is small enough to reuse the output for further operations.

Modular addition is implemented with an integer addition. A modular reduction is rarely needed, since the result of the addition is usually smaller than 2^{64} (in the easiest case, we add a partially reduced operand in $[0, 2^{61} + 6]$ and a message block in $[0, 2^{56} - 1]$, so that the output fits in 62 bits).

Modular multiplication is implemented with an integer multiplication (with roughly 64-bit inputs and 128-bit output) followed by a modular reduction. We suggest implementation strategies for several micro-controllers.

On Cortex-M4 (armv7-M) we can multiply two 32-bit inputs and get a 64-bit

[3] The code is available at: https://github.com/Cryptosaurus/MAC611.

product in a single cycle. The 64-bit multiplication uses 4 such multiplications and few additions. The full multiplication (including a partial reduction) takes just 14 cycles. The output range is slightly larger than the input range, so we need a reduction after a few multiplications.
On Cortex-M0+ (armv6-M) we can only get a 32-bit product from the multiplication of two 32-bit inputs. Therefore, a naive implementation takes 16 multiplication instructions. Instead, we implement a 32-bit multiplication with 64-bit output using 4 multiplication instructions, and use Karatsuba's algorithm to implement a 62-bit multiplication (with 124-bit output) using three 32-bit multiplications (we first write the input in base 2^{31} to avoid overflow when adding two values). The full multiplication (including a partial reduction) takes around 100 cycles on our Cortex-M0+, with a single cycle multiplier.
Finally, some Cortex-M0+ take 32 cycles for a 32-bit product. It is then quicker to use a table-based implementation (with table entries between 0 and $2^{61} - 1$, we can add eight values without overflow). This implementation takes around 100 cycles on our Cortex-M0+, but requires 16 MB of memory.

Benchmarks Results. Table 2 shows benchmark results of MAC611 with various message lengths, and a comparison with other primitives. For comparison, we use

Table 2. Performance comparison on Cortex micro-controllers (BC denotes the block cipher, which is set Noekeon in all benchmarks). Note that OpenSSL implementations are not optimized for code size or memory usage.

Algorithm	Implem.	Code size (bytes)			Mem (B)		Speed (cycles)			
		MAC	BC	Tot.	Stack	State	56B	896B	7168B	Long
Cortex-M0+										
MAC611	Small	542	636	1178	196	40	7.6k	42.3k	306k	42 c/B
	Fast	3064	692	3765	104	40	4.4k	21.4k	138k	19 c/B
	Tables (16kB)	1420	692	2112	108	16k	4.4k	22.2k	228k	27 c/B
Poly1305	OpenSSL (0s)	1480	636	2116	364	288	12.1k	93.0k	705k	98 c/B
	OpenSSL (03)	3148	692	3840	236	288	9.5k	87.0k	672k	93 c/B
GMAC	OpenSSL (0s)	2148	636	2784	156	440	14.9k	109k	823k	114 c/B
	OpenSSL (03)	3388	692	4080	180	440	11.2k	89.2k	677k	94 c/B
Chaskey-12	B. Haase	916	–	916	48	48	1.5k	12.5k	96k	13 c/B
CBC-MAC	OpenSSL (0s)	388	636	1024	148	64	24.4k	271k	2110k	291 c/B
	OpenSSL (03)	820	692	1512	116	64	14.1k	153k	1180k	164 c/B
Cortex-M4										
MAC611	Small	842	348	1190	136	40	1243	4243	28k	3.7 c/B
	Fast	1064	3724	4788	76	40	1038	4038	27k	3.7 c/B
Poly1305	OpenSSL	900	348	1248	104	288	1631	5446	36k	4.9 c/B
GMAC	OpenSSL	2190	348	2538	168	440	5758	49598	381k	53 c/B
Chaskey-12	C Ref (03)	1084	–	1084	96	48	888	7488	58k	8.1 c/B
CBC-MAC	OpenSSL (0s)	380	348	728	120	64	4851	50066	385k	53 c/B
	OpenSSL (03)	828	3724	4552	76	64	4011	40486	310k	43 c/B

several standard MACs from OpenSSL, with Noekeon as the underlying block cipher: Poly1305, GMAC (as a part of GCM), and CBC-MAC (as a part of CCM). On the Cortex-M4, this includes optimized assembly code for Poly1305, GMAC and Noekeon. For Chaskey, we use the reference C implementation on the Cortex-M4, and an assembly implementation from B. Haase[4] optimized for the Cortex-M0+.

MAC611 is faster that all the primitives tested on the Cortex-M4, with less than one thousand cycles for short messages, and only 3.7 c/B for long messages. On the Cortex-M0+, Chaskey is the fastest with 14 c/B, but MAC611 is a close second with 19 c/B. MAC611 is also faster than Wegman-Carter MACs GMAC and Poly1305 thanks to the use of a smaller field.

When a crypto accelerator is available, standard based constructions such as AES-CBC-MAC or GMAC could be faster, but given the very good performance of MAC611, this is not always the case. For instance, presentation slides of the ST32L4[5], a Cortex-M4 with a crypto core, show that it takes 67 cycles per block for GMAC (4.2 c/B), and 206 cycles per block for AES-CBC-MAC (12.9 c/B).

We compare the security of the primitives in Sect. 6.3.

6.2 Choice of the Parameter λ

We used the benchmark results in Table 1 to choose a value of the parameter λ, such that the subkey derivation and the construction of the multiplication tables (in case of a table-based implementation) have a limited impact on performance. In a 64-bit field, the time spent building the tables corresponds to roughly 500 multiplications in the worst case. Therefore, we chose $\lambda = 1024$, so that the key derivation is amortized over 1024 blocks for long messages. For short messages, we precompute the key k_1 (and the corresponding table if needed), so that rekeying is not needed for messages smaller than λ blocks (*i.e.* 8 kB).

In terms of security, the next section shows that the impact of λ is quite limited: the advantage of an attacker with negligible data increases by a factor λ, but when the attacker uses a large amount of data (which is necessary to reach a higher success probability), the advantage does not increase with λ.

6.3 Security Bounds

Let us derive the security of MAC611. Denote $n = 64$ the output size, q the number of queries, and ρ the maximum query length. For the finalization and subkey derivation, we use a truncated block cipher with 128-bit input and 64-bit output $E' : x \in \{0,1\}^{2n} \mapsto T64(E(x))$. Therefore, there are better security bounds than the PRP-PRF switching lemma: we can use the analysis of [17, Eq. (2.5)], with $\mathbf{Adv}_{E'}^{\mathrm{PRF}}(q) \leq \mathbf{Adv}_{E}^{\mathrm{PRP}}(q) + \frac{q}{2^{3n/2}}$.

[4] http://mouha.be/wp-content/uploads/chaskey_cortex_m0.zip.

[5] http://www.st.com/resource/en/product_training/stm32l4_security_aes.pdf.

Consider first $\mathsf{MAC611}^\$$, defined with uniform independent subkeys in $\mathbb{F}_{2^{61}-1}$. From the previous results, XPoly is $\frac{2\lambda}{|\mathbb{F}|}$-$AU$. When the nonces are unique, the security proof from WMAC gives: $\mathbf{Adv}^{\text{MAC}}_{\mathsf{MAC611}^\$}(q) \leq \mathbf{Adv}^{\text{PRF}}_{E'}(q) + \frac{2\lambda}{|\mathbb{F}|} + \frac{1}{2^n}$.

We now consider the actual MAC611, *i.e.* with subkeys $k_i = T64(E(i\|0))$ mod $2^{61}-1$, $1 \leq i \leq \frac{\rho}{\lambda}$. The modular reduction to $\mathbb{F}_{2^{61}-1}$ introduces a small bias: $\delta = \frac{1}{2}\sum\left|p_i - \frac{1}{2^{61}-1}\right| = \frac{1}{2}\cdot 8 \cdot \frac{1}{2^{61}-1} \approx 2^{-62}$. Therefore:

$$\begin{aligned}\mathbf{Adv}^{\text{MAC}}_{\mathsf{MAC611}}(q) &\leq \mathbf{Adv}^{\text{MAC}}_{\mathsf{MAC611}^\$}(q) + \mathbf{Adv}^{\text{PRF}}_{E'}\left(\tfrac{\rho}{\lambda}\right) + \delta \\ &\leq \mathbf{Adv}^{\text{PRP}}_{E}\left(q + \tfrac{\rho}{\lambda}\right) + \tfrac{q+\rho/\lambda}{2^{96}} + \tfrac{5}{2^{64}} + \tfrac{2\lambda}{2^{61}-1}.\end{aligned}$$

In particular, the maximum advantage of a nonce-respecting adversary is roughly $2^{-n/2} = 2^{-32}$, even with $q = 2^{64}$ queries of $\rho = 2^{64}$ blocks. In Appendix A, we compare this bound with the security of Wegman-Carter-Shoup constructions such as GMAC. If the nonces are reused, the analysis of Hash-then-PRF gives:

$$\begin{aligned}\mathbf{Adv}^{\text{NM-MAC}}_{\mathsf{MAC611}}(q) &\leq \mathbf{Adv}^{\text{PRP}}_{E}\left(q + \tfrac{\rho}{\lambda}\right) + \tfrac{q+\lambda/\rho}{2^{3n/2}} + \delta + \tfrac{1}{2^n} + \tfrac{q^2}{|\mathbb{F}|} \\ &\leq \mathbf{Adv}^{\text{PRP}}_{E}\left(q + \tfrac{\rho}{\lambda}\right) + \tfrac{q+\lambda/\rho}{2^{96}} + \tfrac{5}{2^{64}} + \tfrac{q^2}{2^{61}-1}.\end{aligned}$$

Security Level. Comparing the security of MAC611, GMAC, CBC-MAC, Poly1305-AES and Chaskey is difficult, because security cannot be reduced to a single number. As a rough comparison, we can say that all these algorithms have a security level of (roughly) 64 bits, because they are broken by a forgery attack with about 2^{64} time and data. On the other hand, Chacha20-Poly1305 offers a significantly higher security than the previous algorithms, because it uses the one-time MAC construction (it is secure up to 2^{106} operations).

More precisely, the success rate of an attacker depends on the number of queries q and the maximum query length ρ, as shown in Appendix A. While all these algorithms are secure up to roughly 2^{64} queries, the success rate of an attacker with a small amount of data is higher against MAC611 than against the other constructions, due to the small state size.

These bounds also depend on how the algorithm is used: on the one hand the security of GMAC, CBC-MAC, Poly1305-AES and Chaskey increases if rekeying is consistently used, but on the other hand the security of GMAC and Poly1305-AES is completely lost if nonces are misused.

Conclusion

In this work we revisit MAC algorithms based on universal hash functions in the context of lightweight cryptography. We give improved results on the composition of universal hash functions, and design a concrete MAC, MAC611. Our construction uses a universal hash function on 61 bits, combined with the WMAC construction to obtain security up to roughly 2^{61} operations.

We demonstrate the good performance of this construction with fast micro-controller implementations using the on-board multiplier. On a Cortex-M4 micro-controller, we need less than one thousand cycles for small messages, and only 3.7 cycles per byte for long messages. This is significantly faster than alternative constructions like Chaskey, GMAC, CBC-MAC, or Poly1305.

Acknowledgments. The work of Sébastien Duval has been funded in parts by the European Commission through the H2020 project 731591 (acronym REASSURE).

A Comparison of Security Bounds

We can compare the maximum advantage of an adversary against MAC611, GMAC, CBC-MAC, Chakey, and LightMAC [23], as a function of the number of queries, for various query lengths. We have the following bounds:

$$\mathbf{Adv}^{\mathrm{MAC}}_{\mathsf{MAC611}}(q) \leq \mathbf{Adv}^{\mathrm{PRP}}_{E}\left(q + \tfrac{\rho}{\lambda}\right) + \tfrac{q+\rho/\lambda}{2^{3n/2}} + \tfrac{1}{2^n} + \tfrac{2\lambda}{|\mathbb{F}|} + \delta \qquad \text{with } n = 64$$

$$\mathbf{Adv}^{\mathrm{MAC}}_{\mathrm{Chaskey}}(q) \leq \frac{3(q\rho)^2 + 2q\rho t}{2^n} \qquad \text{with } n = 128$$

$$\mathbf{Adv}^{\mathrm{MAC}}_{\mathsf{LightMAC}}(q) \leq \mathbf{Adv}^{\mathrm{PRP}}_{E}(q\rho) + \left(1 + \frac{2}{2^{n/2}-1} + \frac{1}{(2^{n/2}-1)^2}\right)\frac{q^2}{2^n} \qquad \text{with } n = 64$$

$$\mathbf{Adv}^{\mathrm{MAC}}_{\mathrm{GMAC}}(q) \leq \mathbf{Adv}^{\mathrm{PRP}}_{\mathrm{AES}}(q) + \tfrac{\rho}{2^n}\left(1 - \tfrac{q}{2^n}\right)^{-\frac{q+1}{2}} \qquad \text{with } n = 128$$

$$\mathbf{Adv}^{\mathrm{MAC}}_{\mathrm{CBC\text{-}MAC}}(q) \leq \mathbf{Adv}^{\mathrm{PRP}}_{\mathrm{AES}}(q) + \tfrac{\rho^2 q^2}{2^{n-1}} \qquad \text{with } n = 128$$

The bounds for Poly1305-AES are essentially the same as for GMAC. Note that the bound for Chaskey involves the time t of the attacker; in the following we assume that the time and data of the attacker are the same, *i.e.* $t = q\rho$.

We compare all the bounds in Fig. 2.

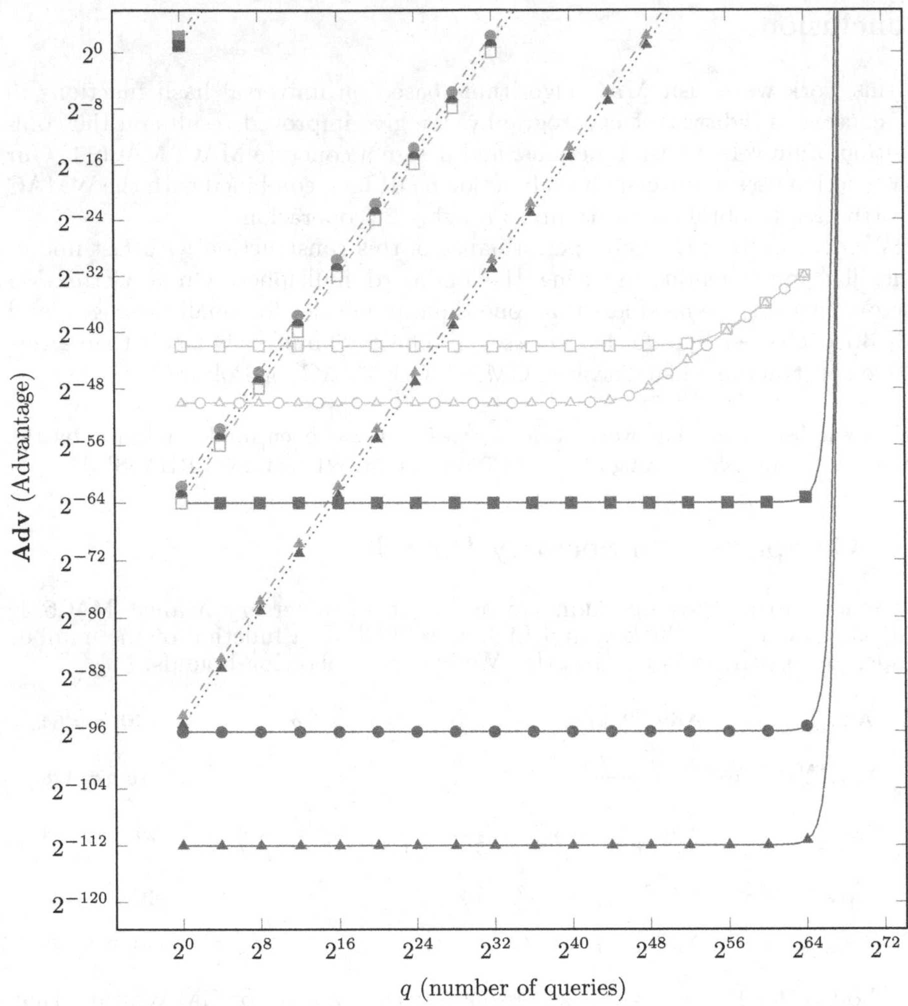

Fig. 2. Security bound for several MAC constructions

References

1. Aumasson, J.-P., Bernstein, D.J.: SipHash: a fast short-input PRF. In: Galbraith, S., Nandi, M. (eds.) INDOCRYPT 2012. LNCS, vol. 7668, pp. 489–508. Springer, Heidelberg (2012). https://doi.org/10.1007/978-3-642-34931-7_28
2. Aumasson, J.P., Henzen, L., Meier, W., Naya-Plasencia, M.: Quark: a lightweight hash. J. Cryptol. **26**(2), 313–339 (2013)
3. Bernstein, D.J.: The Poly1305-AES message-authentication code. In: Gilbert, H., Handschuh, H. (eds.) FSE 2005. LNCS, vol. 3557, pp. 32–49. Springer, Heidelberg (2005). https://doi.org/10.1007/11502760_3
4. Bernstein, D.J.: Stronger security bounds for Wegman-Carter-Shoup authenticators. In: Cramer, R. (ed.) EUROCRYPT 2005. LNCS, vol. 3494, pp. 164–180. Springer, Heidelberg (2005). https://doi.org/10.1007/11426639_10
5. Biryukov, A., Perrin, L.: State of the art in lightweight symmetric cryptography. Cryptology ePrint Archive, Report 2017/511 (2017). http://eprint.iacr.org/2017/511
6. Black, J., Cochran, M.: MAC reforgeability. In: Dunkelman, O. (ed.) FSE 2009. LNCS, vol. 5665, pp. 345–362. Springer, Heidelberg (2009). https://doi.org/10.1007/978-3-642-03317-9_21
7. Black, J., Halevi, S., Krawczyk, H., Krovetz, T., Rogaway, P.: UMAC: fast and secure message authentication. In: Wiener, M. (ed.) CRYPTO 1999. LNCS, vol. 1666, pp. 216–233. Springer, Heidelberg (1999). https://doi.org/10.1007/3-540-48405-1_14
8. Bogdanov, A., Knežević, M., Leander, G., Toz, D., Varıcı, K., Verbauwhede, I.: SPONGENT: a lightweight hash function. In: Preneel, B., Takagi, T. (eds.) CHES 2011. LNCS, vol. 6917, pp. 312–325. Springer, Heidelberg (2011). https://doi.org/10.1007/978-3-642-23951-9_21
9. Bogdanov, A., et al.: PRESENT: an ultra-lightweight block cipher. In: Paillier, P., Verbauwhede, I. (eds.) CHES 2007. LNCS, vol. 4727, pp. 450–466. Springer, Heidelberg (2007). https://doi.org/10.1007/978-3-540-74735-2_31
10. Carter, J.L., Wegman, M.N.: Universal classes of hash functions. In: Proceedings of the Ninth Annual ACM Symposium on Theory of Computing, pp. 106–112. ACM (1977)
11. Cogliati, B., Seurin, Y.: EWCDM: an efficient, beyond-birthday secure, nonce-misuse resistant MAC. In: Robshaw, M., Katz, J. (eds.) CRYPTO 2016. LNCS, vol. 9814, pp. 121–149. Springer, Heidelberg (2016). https://doi.org/10.1007/978-3-662-53018-4_5
12. Daemen, J., Peeters, M., Van Assche, G., Rijmen, V.: Nessie proposal: NOEKEON. In: First Open NESSIE Workshop (2000)
13. Datta, N., Dutta, A., Nandi, M., Paul, G., Zhang, L.: Single key variant of PMAC_Plus. IACR Trans. Symm. Cryptol. **2017**(4), 268–305 (2017)
14. Dietzfelbinger, M., Gil, J., Matias, Y., Pippenger, N.: Polynomial hash functions are reliable. In: Kuich, W. (ed.) ICALP 1992. LNCS, vol. 623, pp. 235–246. Springer, Heidelberg (1992). https://doi.org/10.1007/3-540-55719-9_77
15. Computer data authentication: National Bureau of Standards, NIST FIPS PUB 113. U.S, Department of Commerce (1985)
16. Gilbert, E.N., MacWilliams, F.J., Sloane, N.J.: Codes which detect deception. Bell Labs Tech. J. **53**(3), 405–424 (1974)
17. Gilboa, S., Gueron, S., Morris, B.: How many queries are needed to distinguish a truncated random permutation from a random function? J. Cryptol. **31**(1), 162–171 (2018)

18. Gong, Z., Hartel, P.H., Nikova, S., Tang, S., Zhu, B.: Tulp: a family of lightweight message authentication codes for body sensor networks. J. Comput. Sci. Technol. **29**(1), 53–68 (2014)
19. Hong, D., et al.: HIGHT: a new block cipher suitable for low-resource device. In: Goubin, L., Matsui, M. (eds.) CHES 2006. LNCS, vol. 4249, pp. 46–59. Springer, Heidelberg (2006). https://doi.org/10.1007/11894063_4
20. Keliher, L., Sui, J.: Exact maximum expected differential and linear probability for two-round advanced encryption standard. IET Inf. Secur. **1**(2), 53–57 (2007)
21. Leurent, G., Sibleyras, F.: The missing difference problem, and its applications to counter mode encryption. In: Nielsen, J.B., Rijmen, V. (eds.) EUROCRYPT 2018. LNCS, vol. 10821, pp. 745–770. Springer, Cham (2018). https://doi.org/10.1007/978-3-319-78375-8_24
22. Luykx, A., Preneel, B.: Optimal forgeries against polynomial-based MACs and GCM. In: Nielsen, J.B., Rijmen, V. (eds.) EUROCRYPT 2018. LNCS, vol. 10820, pp. 445–467. Springer, Cham (2018). https://doi.org/10.1007/978-3-319-78381-9_17
23. Luykx, A., Preneel, B., Tischhauser, E., Yasuda, K.: A MAC mode for lightweight block ciphers. In: Peyrin, T. (ed.) FSE 2016. LNCS, vol. 9783, pp. 43–59. Springer, Heidelberg (2016). https://doi.org/10.1007/978-3-662-52993-5_3
24. McGrew, D.A., Viega, J.: The security and performance of the Galois/counter mode (GCM) of operation. In: Canteaut, A., Viswanathan, K. (eds.) INDOCRYPT 2004. LNCS, vol. 3348, pp. 343–355. Springer, Heidelberg (2004). https://doi.org/10.1007/978-3-540-30556-9_27
25. Mennink, B., Neves, S.: Encrypted Davies-Meyer and its dual: towards optimal security using mirror theory. In: Katz, J., Shacham, H. (eds.) CRYPTO 2017. LNCS, vol. 10403, pp. 556–583. Springer, Cham (2017). https://doi.org/10.1007/978-3-319-63697-9_19
26. Minematsu, K., Tsunoo, Y.: Provably secure MACs from differentially-uniform permutations and AES-based implementations. In: Robshaw, M. (ed.) FSE 2006. LNCS, vol. 4047, pp. 226–241. Springer, Heidelberg (2006). https://doi.org/10.1007/11799313_15
27. Mouha, N., Mennink, B., Van Herrewege, A., Watanabe, D., Preneel, B., Verbauwhede, I.: Chaskey: an efficient MAC algorithm for 32-bit microcontrollers. In: Joux, A., Youssef, A. (eds.) SAC 2014. LNCS, vol. 8781, pp. 306–323. Springer, Cham (2014). https://doi.org/10.1007/978-3-319-13051-4_19
28. Nandi, M.: Bernstein bound on WCS is tight. In: Shacham, H., Boldyreva, A. (eds.) CRYPTO 2018. LNCS, vol. 10992, pp. 213–238. Springer, Cham (2018). https://doi.org/10.1007/978-3-319-96881-0_8
29. Preneel, B., van Oorschot, P.C.: MDx-MAC and building fast MACs from hash functions. In: Coppersmith, D. (ed.) CRYPTO 1995. LNCS, vol. 963, pp. 1–14. Springer, Heidelberg (1995). https://doi.org/10.1007/3-540-44750-4_1
30. Procter, G., Cid, C.: On weak keys and forgery attacks against polynomial-based MAC schemes. In: Moriai, S. (ed.) FSE 2013. LNCS, vol. 8424, pp. 287–304. Springer, Heidelberg (2014). https://doi.org/10.1007/978-3-662-43933-3_15
31. Shoup, V.: On fast and provably secure message authentication based on universal hashing. In: Koblitz, N. (ed.) CRYPTO 1996. LNCS, vol. 1109, pp. 313–328. Springer, Heidelberg (1996). https://doi.org/10.1007/3-540-68697-5_24
32. Stinson, D.R.: Universal hashing and authentication codes. In: Feigenbaum, J. (ed.) CRYPTO 1991. LNCS, vol. 576, pp. 74–85. Springer, Heidelberg (1992). https://doi.org/10.1007/3-540-46766-1_5

33. Wegman, M.N., Carter, L.: New hash functions and their use in authentication and set equality. J. Comput. Syst. Sci. **22**, 265–279 (1981)
34. Yasuda, K.: The sum of CBC MACs is a secure PRF. In: Pieprzyk, J. (ed.) CT-RSA 2010. LNCS, vol. 5985, pp. 366–381. Springer, Heidelberg (2010). https://doi.org/10.1007/978-3-642-11925-5_25
35. Zhang, L., Wu, W., Sui, H., Wang, P.: 3kf9: enhancing 3GPP-MAC beyond the birthday bound. In: Wang, X., Sako, K. (eds.) ASIACRYPT 2012. LNCS, vol. 7658, pp. 296–312. Springer, Heidelberg (2012). https://doi.org/10.1007/978-3-642-34961-4_19

FELICS-AEAD: Benchmarking of Lightweight Authenticated Encryption Algorithms

Luan Cardoso dos Santos(✉), Johann Großschädl, and Alex Biryukov

CSC and SnT, University of Luxembourg,
6, Avenue de la Fonte, 4364 Esch-sur-Alzette, Luxembourg
{luan.cardoso,johann.groszschaedl,alex.biryukov}@uni.lu

Abstract. Cryptographic algorithms that can simultaneously provide both encryption and authentication play an increasingly important role in modern security architectures and protocols (e.g. TLS v1.3). Dozens of authenticated encryption systems have been designed in the past five years, which has initiated a large body of research in cryptanalysis. The interest in authenticated encryption has further risen after the National Institute of Standards and Technology (NIST) announced an initiative to standardize "lightweight" authenticated ciphers and hash functions that are suitable for resource-constrained devices. However, while there already exist some cryptanalytic results on these recent designs, little is known about their performance, especially when they are executed on small 8, 16, and 32-bit microcontrollers. In this paper, we introduce an open-source benchmarking tool suite for a fair and consistent evaluation of Authenticated Encryption with Associated Data (AEAD) algorithms written in C or assembly language for 8-bit AVR, 16-bit MSP430, and 32-bit ARM Cortex-M3 platforms. The tool suite is an extension of the FELICS benchmarking framework and provides a new AEAD-specific low-level API that allows users to collect very fine-grained and detailed results for execution time, RAM consumption, and binary code size in a highly automated fashion. FELICS-AEAD comes with two pre-defined evaluation scenarios, which were developed to resemble security-critical operations commonly carried out by real IoT applications to ensure the benchmarks are meaningful in practice. We tested the AEAD tool suite using five authenticated encryption algorithms, namely AES-GCM and the CAESAR candidates ACORN, ASCON, Ketje-Jr, and NORX, and present some preliminary results.

Keywords: Internet of Things · Lightweight cryptography · Authenticated Encryption · Application Program Interface · Evaluation scenario

1 Introduction

An Authenticated Encryption (AE) algorithm can be loosely defined as a symmetric cryptographic algorithm that is capable to (simultaneously) assure the

S. Belaïd and T. Güneysu (Eds.): CARDIS 2019, LNCS 11833, pp. 216–233, 2020.
https://doi.org/10.1007/978-3-030-42068-0_13

confidentiality *and* authenticity of data [3,11]. A special form of AE, known as *Authenticated Encryption with Associated Data (AEAD)*, allows a part of the data to remain unencrypted, while still all data gets authenticated. The notion of AEAD was first formalized by Rogaway [14] in 2002 and has applications in such areas as network packet encryption where the header (which contains the destination address) needs to be readable by routers, but should nonetheless be authenticated and integrity-protected. An AEAD algorithm takes a quadruple of the form (M, A, K, N) as input and outputs a tuple (C, T), where M is the message to be encrypted and authenticated, A is the associated data that gets authenticated only (but not encrypted), K is the secret key, N is a nonce, C is the ciphertext, and T is an authentication tag. Conversely, the decryption uses (C, A, K, N, T) as input and outputs the original message M if T is valid, or an error symbol $\perp$ otherwise. The two essential security goals an AEAD algorithm has to achieve are confidentiality and authenticity; a mathematically rigorous definition of both was given by Rogaway [14]. Informally, confidentiality means that a passive adversary with access to C and T should not be able to deduce any information about M, except of its length. Authenticity generally refers to the ability to thwart forgery attacks, which means an active adversary should have a very low success probability when attempting to fabricate a (C, T)-tuple that the decrypting party will verify as authentic.

Initially, AEAD schemes were created by combining a block cipher in some mode of operation with a Message Authentication Code (MAC) algorithm. A clear disadvantage of this approach is the necessity of having two different primitives and requiring two passes over the message. Modern constructions use a different approach, where a single algorithm is able to deliver authenticated encryption, with a single pass over the message. In recent years, the cryptographic community has shown great interest in AEAD because of the CAESAR competition and the NIST call for lightweight primitives. CAESAR (short for Competition for Authenticated Encryption: Security, Applicability, and Robustness) is an already finished competition whose objective was to select a portfolio of AEAD algorithms. It followed the spirit of previous cryptographic competitions, such as the one that yielded the now omnipresent block cipher AES. In 2018, the NIST officially announced the initiation of a process to solicit, evaluate, and standardize lightweight cryptographic algorithms—namely AEAD schemes and hash functions—that are suitable for constrained environments where the current standards can not provide acceptable performance. The motivation behind this initiative is the emergence of more and more application domains where constrained devices are interconnected to form the so-called Internet of Things (IoT). Security and privacy are extremely important in the IoT, but cannot always be provided by the currently standardized cryptosystems. This is because the severe constraints under which present (and future) IoT devices are expected to operate were not anticipated 20–25 years ago when many of the current NIST standards (e.g. AES, SHA-2) were designed.

Motivation and Research Needs. In response to NIST's call for proposals for lightweight AEAD algorithms and hash functions, a total of 57 candidates were submitted by March 29, 2019. These candidates are currently evaluated in an open process taking various criteria into account, which include besides security (i.e. resistance against known cryptanalytic attacks) also practical aspects like performance and resource requirements (e.g. silicon area, memory footprint, code size) when implemented in hardware and software [13]. The NIST anticipates an initial (i.e. first-round) evaluation period of about six months to filter out candidates with obvious weaknesses and narrow the candidate pool for a more careful study and analysis in a second round. In total, the NIST estimates a duration of two to four years until the publication of a first draft standard and emphasizes that "the success of the lightweight crypto standardization process relies on the efforts of the researchers from the cryptographic community that provide security, implementation, and performance analysis of the candidates"[1]. Most papers introducing a new AEAD algorithm report some kind of results of some kind of performance evaluation on some kind of platform using some kind of implementation. Unfortunately, these results are usually not suitable for a comparison of the efficiency of two or more algorithms since it is not easily possible to take differences in the characteristics of the target platforms or differences in the simulation/measurement conditions into account. There is a need for a way to compare performance figures for many algorithms consistently and fairly so that designers and implementers of IoT applications can make better decisions regarding which algorithm is the most suitable one under a given set of efficiency requirements and resource constraints.

In the course of the CAESAR competition, the eBACS framework [4] was used for the bechmarking of the submitted AEAD algorithms. However, the original eBACS tools only support 64-bit Intel/AMD processors and high-end ARM models, mostly from the Cortex-A series, whereas many IoT devices are equipped with low-end microcontrollers, e.g. 8-bit AVR ATmega, 16-bit TI MSP430, or 32-bit ARM Cortex-M. These microcontrollers are optimized for small silicon area and low power consumption, which means they have totally different characteristics than their 64-bit counterparts. These differences manifest not only in the word size, but also the instruction set, the size of the register file, the latency of individual instructions, the degree of instruction-level parallelism, and many other aspects. For example, 64-bit Intel or ARM processors have a register space of 128 bytes (or even more when taking vector registers into account), whereas the MSP430 platform (which lies at the opposite end of the spectrum) provides 24 bytes altogether. Furthermore, most 8 and 16-bit microcontrollers can only execute shifts or rotations at a rate of one bit per cycle, whereas more powerful processors are capable to perform n-bit shifts/rotations in a single cycle. For all these reasons, benchmarking results generated with eBACS are of little use when it comes to the evaluation of AEAD algorithms on microcontrollers.

[1] See https://csrc.nist.gov/projects/lightweight-cryptography/round-1-candidates (accessed 2019-07-15).

Aims and Contributions of This Paper. The present paper addresses the research needs identified above and puts forward a proposal for the benchmarking of lightweight AEAD algorithms. Our proposal aims to answer two basic questions that generally arise in the context of software benchmarking of cryptographic algorithms. The first question relates to the Application Program Interface (API) that implementations of a candidate algorithms have to follow to ensure a fair and consistent evaluation. We will argue in Subsect. 2.2 that, for the purpose of benchmarking, it makes sense to use a low-level API sense since it allows one to obtain more fine-grained results compared to a high-level API consisting of just the functions `encrypt` and `decrypt`. Furthermore, we introduce an API containing seven low-level functions, which we consider well suited for the benchmarking of AEAD algorithms. The second issue concerns the question of how to measure the execution time and other metrics of interest, which includes aspects like the length of the message M and the length of the associated data A. More concretely, how should the length-ratio of M and A be to get meaningful results? We will try to answer these questions in Subsect. 2.1 through the definition of so-called evaluation scenarios that aim to mimic security-related operations commonly carried out by "real" IoT devices. More concretely, these scenarios are inspired by the need for AEAD operations in two networking protocols with relevance for the IoT, namely IEEE 802.15.4 (the most common PHY/MAC-layer protocol for low-rate wireless networks) and IPv6.

We implemented both the low-level API for AEAD and the evaluation scenarios in the form of an extension to the well-known and widely-used FELICS (Fair Evaluation of Lightweight Cryptographic Systems) framework [7]. FELICS was originally created to support the collection benchmarking results for (lightweight) block ciphers on three embedded platforms: 8-bit AVR, 16-bit MSP430, and 32-bit ARM Cortex-M3. The full source code of FELICS is available under GPLv3 to increase the transparency and reproducibility of benchmarking results. Besides execution time, FELICS is also capable to determine the binary size and RAM footprint on the three currently supported platforms. The framework is modular, built on well documented and free compilers and tools, which allows easy extension of functionality and integration of new microcontroller platforms and evaluation scenarios. We tested the extended FELICS toolsuite using optimized C implementations of five AEAD algorithms (namely AES-GCM, ACORN, ASCON, Ketje-Jr, and NORX) that adhere to our low-level API. These tests confirm that FELICS-AEAD works properly and is able to collect large amounts of benchmarking results in an efficient and highly-automated fashion. An analysis of the collected benchmarking results for these five algorithms allows us to draw some conclusions about how basic design decisions like the organization of the "state" (i.e. whether the state is processed at a granularity of 32-bit words or 64-bit words) affect the performance on small microcontrollers.

2 The FELICS Framework and Its AEAD Extension

FELICS – ***F**air **E**valuation of **L**ightweight **C**ryptographic **S**ystems* – is a free and open source framework that assesses the efficiency of C and assembly implementations of lightweight cryptographic primitives on embedded devices. Following a modular design philosophy, the framework can easily be extended to accommodate new metrics, evaluation scenarios, and devices. FELICS is the core of an effort to increase the transparency in the analysis of lightweight algorithms' performances and aims to facilitate a fair comparison of a large number of candidates. Figure 1 gives an overview of the structure and main components of the FELICS framework.

2.1 Overview of Modules

FELICS is written in C, but also includes Bash and Python scripts. The framework was designed to work on Linux and allows the benchmarking of C and assembly implementations of cryptographic primitives that follow a set of predefined requirements. C was chosen because of its continuing popularity in the IoT and the fact that most reference implementations are written in this language. Furthermore, C code is highly portable, which is an important asset since there is no single dominating platform in the IoT. However, FELICS also supports the benchmarking of platform specific Assembler implementations to eliminate the impact of the compiler's ability (or inability) for code optimization. Hand-crafted Assembler code can take architecture-specific optimizations into account and has the potential to significantly outperform compiled C code.

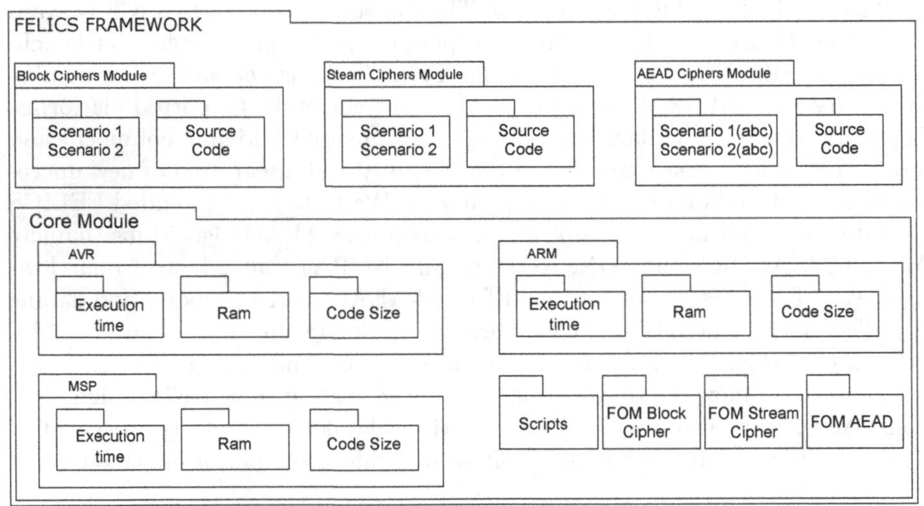

Fig. 1. Modular structure of the FELICS benchmarking framework.

Core Module. The Core module, as the name implies, is the main part of the framework, and provides the tools necessary to collect the metrics for each of the supported devices. This module aims to facilitate the integration of new target devices and new metrics. Collection of metrics can be done individually or in batch mode. Beyond metrics collection, the Core also defines modules to debug and evaluate ciphers in a PC, mainly to aid in the implementation and integration process of new ciphers by the framework's users. A Python script for processing the generated CSV files and to assemble a ranking of candidates based on a so-called Figure-Of-Merit (FOM) is also present (see [8] for details).

Authenticated Encryption Module. This module allows the evaluation of lightweight AEAD ciphers. To allow the framework to extract the metrics, each cipher's implementation must follow the defined API.

A template for implementation, as well as implementations of identity ciphers, are provided with the module and can be used as a guide to help new users to integrate new implementations. The complete rules and step-by-step integration guide for cipher implementations can be found in the `README` file in the example cipher.

The framework supports cipher evaluation based on scenarios. Scenarios implement common real-world use cases, with practical relevance for IoT, with the main objective of generating realistic benchmark results that are meaningful in the real world. The current scenarios in the AEAD module of FELICS are divided into three main groups:

- **Debug and verification Scenario:** Also called Scenario 0, is mainly used for debugging purposes. It operates over a single block of input and allows the implementers to check their implementations on known test vectors.
- **IEEE 802.15.4 Scenarios:** These scenarios are based on the security needs of data communication in wireless sensor networks and other IoT applications using the IEEE 802.15.4 MAC/PHY-layer protocol. The maximum frame size of IEEE 802.15.4 is 127 bytes; the length of the header depends on various factors, such as the format of the source and destination addresses, but can not exceed 25 bytes. This leaves (at least) 102 bytes as frame payload. IEEE 802.15.4 supports three kinds of security services, namely (i) "Encryption Only" with AES in counter mode, (ii) "Authentication Only" with AES-CBC-MAC producing a MAC of either 32, 64, or 128 bits, and (iii) "Authenticated Encryption" using AES-CCM with the same MAC lengths.
    - **Scenario 1a:** Encryption of 102 bytes of data.
    - **Scenario 1b:** Authentication of 86 bytes of payload and 25 bytes of header. This scenario assumes that 16 bytes of payload are reserved to write the authentication tag.
    - **Scenario 1c:** Authenticated encryption of 86 bytes of payload and 25 bytes of header (which is authenticated but not encrypted). As with Scenario 1b, the authentication tag has a length of 16 bytes.
- **IPv6 Scenarios:** These scenarios are based on the use cases of IPv6 frames, as defined in RFC 2460. The MTU of IPv6 is at least 1280 bytes and the

header has a fixed length of 40 bytes. Based on experiments with the Network Simulator NS-3, we found that the following message and associated data lengths serve as good representatives for real-world scenarios.

- **Scenario 2a:** Encryption of 1240 bytes of data.
- **Scenario 2b:** Authentication of 1224 bytes of payload and 40 bytes of header.
- **Scenario 2c:** Authenticated encryption of 1224 bytes of payload and 40 bytes of header.

The IEEE 802.15.4 and IPv6 scenarios differ not only in the amount of data to be protected (127 bytes vs 1280 bytes), but also in the relation of data-length of AD-length. In the former case, the AD/D ratio is 0.29, whereas in the latter case the AD-length is negligible in relation to the D-length.

2.2 API for Authenticated Encryption

The FELICS API aims to offer a generic and well-specified interface for the most common operations performed by an AEAD algorithm. Different from other frameworks, the FELICS API is composed of seven low-level functions. While this may introduce difficulties for certain implementation techniques (e.g. bitslicing), the low-level API gives the framework more flexibility and allows one to obtain more fine-grained benchmarking results. Such fine-grained results can be useful, for example, when one wants to analyze *why* a given AEAD algorithm is more or less efficient and its competitors. Our seven functions are described below and their prototypes are given in Listing 1.

- `Initialize`: This function receives as parameters pointers to the algorithm's state, key, and nonce, and should execute the cipher's initialization procedures.
- `ProcessAssocData`: This function receives as parameters a pointer to the state, a byte stream of associated data, as well as its length.
- `ProcessPlaintext`: This function receives as parameters a pointer to the state, a byte stream of data, as well as the length of plaintext and ciphertext. The ciphertext should overwrite the plaintext.
- `ProcessCiphertext`: This function receives as parameters a pointer to the state, a byte stream of data, as well as the length of plaintext and ciphertext. The plaintext should overwrite the ciphertext.
- `Finalize`: This function receives as parameters pointers to the state and key, and executes the finalization steps on the internal state, preparing it for the authentication tag generation.
- `GenerateTag`: This functions receives as parameters a pointer to the internal state and the authentication tag and should write the appropriate information on the authentication tag.
- `VerifyTag`: This function received two pointers to authentication tags, and compare both. Returns `(int)(1)` if the tags match, and `(int)(0)` otherwise.

Listing 1. Function prototypes of the low-level AEAD API.

```
void Initialize(uint8_t *state, const uint8_t *key,
     const uint8_t *nonce);
void ProcessAssocData(uint8_t *state, uint8_t *assocData,
     size_t assocDataLen);
void ProcessPlaintext(uint8_t *state, uint8_t *message,
     size_t messageLen);
void ProcessCiphertext(uint8_t *state, uint8_t *message,
     size_t messageLen);
void Finalize(uint8_t *state, uint8_t *key);
void GenerateTag(uint8_t *state, uint8_t *tag);
int  VerifyTag(uint8_t *state, uint8_t *tag);
```

NIST specified a high-level API consisting of two functions (namely `aead_encrypt` and `aead_decrypt`), which submitters of AEAD candidates had to follow when they developed the (mandatory) reference implementation and an (optional) optimized implementation. While such a high-level API is convenient for software developers using AEAD algorithms, it is not necessarily a good choice for collecting benchmarking results, especially in Scenario 0. This is probably best explained taking the block-cipher benchmarks from [9] as example. Similar to AEAD, one can benchmark block ciphers using either a high-level or a low-level API. The former consists of generic functions for encrypting/decrypting of an arbitrary amount of data using a specified mode operation. On the other hand, the low-level API consists of two functions for each encryption and decryption, one to encrypt/decrypt a single block, and one to perform the encrytion/decryption key schedule. In order to minimize the overall development effort, the high-level functions can simply be implemented as wrappers over the low-level functions. However, using the low-level API for benchmarking in Scenario 0 makes certain properties of ciphers more apparent than the high-level API. For example, RC5 is extremely fast, but has a very costly key schedule, which becomes immediately evident with benchmarking results obtained with the low-level API. Therefore, RC5 is unattractive for scenarios where the amount of data to be encrypted or decrypted is small. This information is not so directly obvious when benchmarking results are generated with the high-level API.

2.3 Target Devices and Evaluation Metrics

For this framework, three widely used microcontrollers were chosen as representatives of the most used 8, 16, and 32-bit platforms used in the IoT. These microcontrollers have been optimized for small area and low power consumption. Their main characteristics are summarized in Table 1 and a brief description of each will follow on the next paragraphs.

The **AVR ATMega 128** is a microcontroller manufactured by Atmel, featuring 32 8-bit registers (`R0` - `R31`) with single clock access time. Six of those

Table 1. Key characteristics of the target microcontrollers.

Characteristic	AVR	MSP	ARM
CPU	8-bit RISC	16-bit RISC	32-bit RISC
Frequency	16 MHz	8 MHz	84 MHz
Registers	32	16	21
Architecture	Harvard	Von Neumann	Havard
Flash	128 KB	48 KB	512 KB
SRAM	4 KB	10 KB	96 KB
Supply voltage	4.6–5.5 V	1.8–3.6 V	1.6–3.6 V

registers can also be used as 16-bit indirect address pointers for data space. The instructions are executed within a two-stage, single-level pipeline, with most of its 133 instructions requiring a single cycle to execute. AVR processors are based on a modified Harvard architecture, where program and data are stored in separate physical memory regions in different physical addresses. Regarding memory, the ATmega128 comes with 128 KB Flash amd 4 KB SRAM.

The **MSP430F1611** microcontroller is a RISC CPU produced by Texas Instruments. It follows a Von Neumann architecture, and features 16 registers, with 12 being general purpose. Operations over registers take one clock cycle, while the other instructions depend on its format and addressing mode used. Memory wise, the MSP430 has one shared address space for special function registers, peripherals, RAM and FLASH. It has 48 KB of Flash and 10 KB of SRAM. Typical applications include medical devices and smart meters.

The 32-bit **Atmel SAM3X8 Cortex M3** is a RISC CPU that executes the Thumb-2 instruction set. This processor has a three-level pipeline and 13 general-purpose registers. It features 512 KB of Flash and 96 KB of SRAM divided into two banks of 64 KB and 32 KB. The Cortex-M3 is specially designed to achieve high performance in power-sensitive embedded applications, such as microcontrollers, automotive and industrial controllers, wireless networking, and others. This processor runs at a maximum frequency of 84 MHz.

For cipher evaluation, three metrics are used: Execution time, RAM usage, and code size. These metrics were chosen because they outline the main characteristics of the implementations. Secondary metrics, such as energy consumption were not included mainly due to being closely related to the basic metrics.

Execution time consists in measuring the number of cycles necessary to execute a given operation. This metric is extracted by using either a cycle-accurate simulator a development board. Extraction of cycle-counter uses AVRORA [15] for the AVR processor, and `MSPDebug` [2] for MSP. Extraction of cycle counter on ARM is done via the automatic insertion of code to read ARM's system time registers. One important detail regarding ARM's measurements is that there may exist variations in the extracted numbers, due to different instructions being generated at compilation time and memory alignment of test data.

RAM consumption is a combination of stack and data requirements. The stack consumption describes the maximum amount of RAM used to store local variables and return addresses after interruptions and system calls. The data requirement represents the static RAM usage and is given by the size of the constants stored in the device's RAM. Static RAM consumption is measured using the GNU `size` tool. The stack consumption is measured using a `gdb` client and the target simulator or development board.

Code size is measured in bytes and quantifies the amount of storage an operation or evaluation scenario occupies in the non-volatile memory of the target device. It is measured using the GNU `size` tool on the appropriate object files. To obtain the overall code size, the framework simply sums the size of the `text` and `data` sections, which contain, respectively, the executable instructions generated by the compiler and the static variables that are initialized with a non-zero value.

Figure of Merit. Due to space limitations, normally only a subset of data can be correctly shown in publications. To aid in the classifications of the evaluated ciphers, FELICS introduces the *Figure-of-Merit* (FOM), that can be used to rank the analyzed ciphers. For each implementation i and platform d, a performance indicator p_{i_d} that aggregates the metrics from M = {execution time, RAM consumption, code size} as

$$p_{i,d} = \sum_{m \in M} w_m \frac{v_{i,d,m}}{\min_i(v_{i,d,m})}$$

where $v_{i,d,m}$ is the value of the metric m for the implementation i on the platform p; and w_m is the relative weight for the metric m, with $w_m = 1$ by default for all platforms. Then, for each cipher and the selected set of best implementations i_{AVR}, i_{MSP}, and i_{ARM} (one for each platform) the FOM is calculated as the average performance indicator across the three platforms:

$$\text{FOM}(i_{AVR}, i_{MSP}, i_{ARM}) = \frac{p_{i_{AVR}} + p_{i_{MSP}} + p_{i_{ARM}}}{3}$$

3 Analyzed AEAD Algorithms

In this section, we briefly describe the ciphers implemented in FELICS, as an example and initial work for the framework. These ciphers were chosen for their relevance in the context of IoT and lightweight cryptography, as well for being part of an ongoing effort of standardizing AEAD schemes.

ACORN. Acorn is an AEAD scheme created by Hongjun Wu, and finalist of the CAESAR competition. It features a stream-cipher-like construction based on six concatenated linear feedback shift registers. The cipher's design benefits lightweight hardware implementations since the processing can be done in a bitwise fashion [17].

Table 2. Parameters of the evaluated ciphers, in bits.

Cipher	Block	Key	Nonce	State	Tag
NORX	384	128	128	512	128
ACORN	1	128	128	293	128
Ketje-Jr	16	128	48	200	128
ASCON	64	128	128	320	128
AES-GCM	128	128	96	1824	128

AES-GCM. The Galois/Counter mode is a mode of operation for 128-bit block ciphers, widely used together with the AES block cipher for its efficiency and performance. GCM is used in MACSec Ethernet Security, IEEE 802.11ad wireless protocols, Fibre Channel security protocols, and is also included in the NSA Suite B Cryptography, as well as various other software [12].

ASCON. Ascon is a family of AEAD ciphers, finalist of the CAESAR competition. It was designed by Christoph Dobraunig et al. in 2014. The main goal of ASCON is to achieve a very low memory footprint, both in hardware and software implementations, and still provide an adequate combination of security, speed, and size, with focus on the last. ASCON is based on the Sponge Design, being similar to SpongeWrap and MonkeyDuplex constructions [10].

Ketje. Ketje is a family of four AEAD algorithms, aimed to memory-constrained devices and that strongly relies on nonce uniqueness for security. It was designed by Guido Bertoni et al. and is a third-round candidate of the CAESAR competition. Ketje is based on a reduced round version of Keccak, over a MonkeyDuplex and MonkeyWrap constructions [5].

NORX. NORX is a family of AEAD ciphers created by Jean-Philippe Aumasson et al. in 2014. NORX supports associated data both as header and trailer. The algorithm also supports arbitrary parallelism in the payload processing step and is optimized for hardware and software implementations, with a specially SIMD friendly construction. NORX is based on ChaCha's permutation, with the integer addition replaced by an ARX approximation, which –according to the designers– allows simplified cryptanalysis and improves hardware efficiency [1].

4 Preliminary Results

Using the FELICS extension for authenticated encryption described in Sect. 2, we benchmarked optimized C implementations of the five AEAD algorithms on three platforms and for two evaluation scenarios plus Scenario 0, which is mainly

Table 3. Results for Scenario 1 (IEEE 802.15.4). For each platform and each cipher, the best implementation results are reported. The code size and memory consumption are specified for the whole scenario (and not just the AEAD algorithm alone), which includes the 127-byte IEEE 802.15.4 frame to be encrypted and/or authenticated. The smaller the Figure-of-merit, the better is the implementation of a cipher.

Cipher		AVR			MSP			ARM			FOM
		Size	Mem	Time	Size	Mem	Time	Size	Mem	Time	
NORX	S1a	4702	214	135640	3992	214	66738	1474	214	17227	4.3
	S1b	3936	223	90728	3482	223	53035	1148	223	10089	4.0
	S1c	5028	207	124062	4216	207	75727	1634	207	16685	4.5
ASCON	S1a	3734	190	519420	5656	190	599643	1712	190	80316	9.4
	S1b	3734	199	340671	5656	199	395564	1712	199	52958	8.9
	S1c	3734	183	534908	5656	183	619523	1712	183	83118	9.4
Ketje-Jr	S1a	5156	165	290446	6248	165	346867	3564	165	138867	9.4
	S1b	5156	174	211749	6248	174	254923	3564	174	99490	9.8
	S1c	5156	158	311949	6248	158	372720	3564	158	148381	9.7
ACORN	S1a	3292	191	337818	3170	191	456972	1954	191	191869	10.0
	S1b	3292	200	408914	3170	200	551501	1954	200	236235	15.7
	S1c	3292	184	464381	3170	184	626192	1954	184	267168	12.5
AES-GCM	S1a	6578	374	889573	6798	374	2137251	6096	374	1086449	41.5
	S1b	5944	383	447505	6782	383	1150450	6028	383	565606	34.0
	S1c	6578	367	975184	6798	367	2369572	6096	367	1197073	44.6

for debugging and verification. Table 2 summarizes the main characteristics of the specific variants of the AEAD algorithms we implemented.

The FELICS framework allows ranking all these implementations according to their execution time, RAM footprint, or code size in any scenario on any platform. Table 3 summarizes the results of Scenario 1, which is inspired by the need for security in the IEEE 802.15.4 protocol. This scenario actually consists of three sub-scenarios with different operations and slightly different lengths of the data to be encrypted and/or authenticated. However, all three sub-scenarios have in common that the amount of data is relatively small, namely between 86 and 102 bytes, due to the 127-byte MTU – maximum transmission unit – of the IEEE 802.15.4 protocol. If associated data is processed, its length is roughly one fourth of the data-length. Concretely, in Sub-scenario 1a ("encryption only"), 102 bytes of data are encrypted, whereas in Sub-scenario 1b ("authentication only") the size of the data is 86 bytes and the size of the associated data is 25 bytes. Finally, in Scenario 1c ("authenticated encryption") 86 bytes of data are encrypted and $86 + 25 = 111$ bytes are authenticated. NORX is the clear winner in all three sub-scenarios, followed by ASCON and Ketje-Jr, which perform very similar in all three sub-scenarios. However, the FOM score of the latter two algorithms is more than twice higher than that of NORX.

Table 4. Results for Scenario 2 (IPv6). For each platform and each cipher, the best implementation results are reported. The code size and memory consumption are specified for the whole scenario (and not just the AEAD algorithm alone), which includes the 1280-byte IPv6 packet to be encrypted and/or authenticated. The smaller the Figure-of-merit, the better is the implementation of a cipher.

Cipher		AVR			MSP			ARM			FOM
		Size	Mem	Time	Size	Mem	Time	Size	Mem	Time	
NORX	S2a	4702	1376	800313	3992	1376	501290	1474	1376	109933	4.1
	S2b	3936	1376	424601	3482	1376	246263	1148	1376	46113	3.7
	S2c	5028	1376	814467	4216	1376	508728	1634	1376	111361	4.2
ASCON	S2a	3292	1353	1811457	3170	1353	2454962	1954	1353	1013715	8.5
	S2b	3292	1353	1136110	3170	1353	1541295	1954	1353	644411	10.5
	S2c	3292	1353	1916720	3170	1353	2595469	1954	1353	1077068	8.7
Ketje-Jr	S2a	5156	1327	3026956	6248	1327	3623707	3564	1327	1481660	12.6
	S2b	5156	1327	1527941	6248	1327	1860262	3564	1327	751536	13.3
	S2c	5156	1327	3007966	6248	1327	3601416	3564	1327	1471405	12.5
ACORN	S2a	3734	1352	6174633	5656	1352	7109127	1712	1352	947367	13.9
	S2b	3734	1352	3146041	5656	1352	3619665	1712	1352	479574	14.2
	S2c	3734	1352	6112583	5656	1352	7039689	1712	1352	938358	13.6
AES-GCM	S2a	6578	1536	9807655	6798	1536	23748153	6096	1536	12036393	64.4
	S2b	5944	1536	3526008	6782	1536	9531538	6028	1536	4564667	54.2
	S2c	6578	1536	9812008	6798	1536	23796554	6096	1536	12050336	63.6

Finally, Table 4 shows the results of Scenario 2, which deals with security for the IPv6 protocol. This scenario is again split into three sub-scenarios, similar to the sub-scenarios in the context of IEEE 802.15.4 described above. However, the amount of data to be encrypted is much larger, around 1200 bytes, while the amount of associated data is relatively small; more concretely, the ratio between data and associated data is roughly 30:1. Again, NORX is the clear winner in all three sub-scenarios, followed by ASCON and Ketje-Jr. However, compared to the IEEE 802.15.4 scenarios, the difference between ASCON and Ketje-Jr is much bigger. Similar to before, the FOM score of NORX is significantly better than that of the runner-up ASCON.

It is interesting to observe that NORX is in both scenarios speed-wise much better than the other candidates. NORX outperforms its CAESAR competitors by a factor of at least two; in some extreme cases, NORX is even five times faster than the second-best algorithm. This significant difference begs for more analysis and raises the question of what design decisions make an AEAD algorithm efficient (or inefficient) on small microcontroller platforms. However, this question is difficult to answer since the efficiency of AEAD designs depends on many different factors, some of which are architecture-independent, i.e. affect the performance on 8, 16, 32, and 64-bit platforms similarly, whereas others are architecture-dependent in the sense that they impact the performance across platforms differently. An example of the latter is the organization of the state, i.e. whether the state is processed at a granularity of 32-bit words or 64-bit words. The benchmarked version of NORX processes the state in 32-bit words, whereas ASCON, ACORN, and Ketje-Jr operate on 64-bit words. Organizing the state in 64-bit quantities is the natural choice for designs aiming at high performance on Intel/AMD and 64-bit ARM processors as it allows one to exploit the full word-size of these processors, but may lead to suboptimal performance on smaller microcontroller platforms, which is due to three reasons.

First, C compilers for 8-bit AVR and 16-bit MSP microcontrollers (e.g. `mspgcc`) are, in general, not very good at handling 64-bit words (i.e. operands of type `uint64_t`). We assume this is because outside cryptography there are very few application domains where a programmer really needs a 64-bit integer on an 8 or 16-bit microcontroller. NORX128 uses 32-bit words, which seems to make it much easier for a C compiler to generate efficient code than for the other CAESAR candidates that process 64-bit words. The second reason is the small register space of 8 and 16-bit microcontrollers. For example, the MSP430 architecture comes with only twelve 16-bit general-purpose registers, which means it would theoretically be possible to hold three 64-bit words in the register file. However, in practice, this is not the case since always one or two registers are needed for temporary results and often also one register has to be set to 0. Therefore, it can be expected that no more than two 64-bit words can be kept in registers at any time, but it may be possible to accommodate five 32-bit words when the cipher's state is organized in 32-bit words. Finally, the third reason why 64-bit words can entail suboptimal performance is ARM-specific and relates to the fact that one of the two operands of an arithmetic/logical instruction is fed through a barrel-shifter before it enters the ALU, which means shifts and rotations can be executed "for free" together with other instructions. However, on a 32-bit ARM microcontroller, shifts and rotations are only free for 32-bit operands, but not for 64-bit quantities.

5 Comparison with Other Benchmarking Tools

Besides FELICS, there exist a few other tools for the benchmarking of cryptographic algorithms, of which eBACS and XXBX are the most closely related ones. eBACS (short for ECRYPT Benchmarking of Cryptographic Systems) was developed during the ECRYPT II project to evaluate the performance of cryptographic algorithms on Intel/AMD processors and high-end ARM models capable to run Linux (e.g. the Cortex-A series). It features modules for measuring the performance of public-key cryptosystems (called eBATS), stream ciphers (eBASC), hash functions (eBASH), and authenticated encryption algorithms (eBAEAD). Those modules operate all under a common framework called SUPERCOP (System for Unified Performance Evaluation Related to Cryptographic Operations and Primitives) that allows benchmarking of C, C++ and assembly implementations. It comes with a large collection of implementations of cryptographic algorithms and automatically compiles source code using different compilers and compiler options. The execution time is extracted via a cycle counter (accessed through assembler code) for many different lengths of input data. Since execution time is the only metric measured by this framework, implementations are optimized solely for speed.

The eXternal Benchmarking eXtension [16] is an extension for the SUPERCOP framework developed with the objective of benchmarking hash functions on different microcontrollers in the context of the SHA-3 competition. XBX was the first project to measure, in a unified manner, the performance of cryptographic primitives built for different devices using the same evaluation methodology. In support for the now finished CAESAR competition, XBX was extended for AEAD algorithms and the ability to measure power consumption. However, apart from a 1-page summary of this so-called XXBX extension [6] (published in 2017), we are not of aware any further papers describing concrete details of its inner working, which indicates that XXBX is still under development.

Low-Level API. eBACS (and also XXBX) require AEAD implementations to follow a simple high-level API consisting of just two basic functions, namely `aead_encrypt` and `aead_decrypt`. This simplicity ensures that the API is easy to use (and hard to misuse), even for inexperienced software developers, but yields very coarse-grained results when applied to benchmarking. FELICS-AEAD, on the other hand, defines a low-level API comprising the seven functions specified in Listing 1. This low-level API offers a high degree of flexibility and allows for easy implementation of different kinds of security services, including the high-level functions of eBACS, for which nothing more than simple wrappers are needed. Consequently, adhering to the low-level API does not introduce more development effort than the high-level functions of eBACS. However, the low-level API enables a more fine-grained evaluation of AEAD algorithms since not only their overall execution times can be compared but also the times needed for initialization, encrypting/decrypting the data, processing the associated data, and generating/verifying the authentication tag. All these timings are valuable for algorithm designers when trying to analyze *why* a given AEAD algorithm is faster or slower than others. The fine-grained benchmarking results obtained with the low-level API may also be useful when one has to find the most suitable AEAD algorithm (out of a pool of candidates) for the encryption and/or authentication of a certain amount of data and associated data, respectively.

Evaluation Scenarios. eBACS measures the execution time of AEAD algorithms for combinations of data lengths and associated data lengths ranging from 0 to 2048 bytes in steps of one byte. These more than four million combinations have to be multiplied by the number of compiler options (i.e. optimization levels), which makes the collection of benchmarking results extremely computation-intensive and costly, especially when a large number of AEAD implementations have to be evaluated. The target platforms of eBACS (Intel/AMD and high-end ARM processors) are powerful enough to execute such a workload in an acceptable time, but this is not the case for resource-constrained 8 and 16-bit microcontrollers that can only be accessed via a debug probe and have to be programmed separately for each implementation. Using cycle-accurate instruction-set simulators is also not a solution since most of them lack a stable way of scripting to automate the verification of test vectors and the recording of cycle counts. These issues were the main reason to introduce the two evaluation scenarios (and six sub-scenarios) described in Subsect. 2.1. Namely, by defining very specific use cases that resemble real-world security services in the IoT, FELICS-AEAD becomes capable to evaluate a large number of implementations in a reasonable amount of time. The two scenarios are intended to have very different characteristics and requirements for AEAD algorithms. For example, the amount of data in Scenario 1 is relatively small and the length of the associated data is roughly a quarter of the data length. On the other hand, the amount of data in Scenario 2 is much higher, but the associated data amounts to only a small fraction of the data-length.

Figure-of-Merit. eBACS measures only the execution time of AEAD implementations, which makes it relatively easy to rank candidates by e.g. comparing their average throughput in cycles/byte. In contrast, FELICS-AEAD determines not only the execution time but also the memory footprint and code size of an implementation on each of the three supported platforms. This is reasonable since both RAM and ROM (resp. flash) are usually scarce resources in the IoT. However, taking three different metrics for each AEAD implementation into account makes a comparison of the benchmarking results relatively difficult, which is why FELICS allows the user to define a Figure-of-Merit (FOM) that combines execution time, RAM footprint, and code size into a single number. The FOM metric can use different weight factors for the three metrics, but by default, they have equal weight and, consequently, the execution time is considered to be equally important as RAM footprint and code size.

6 Conclusions and Final Remarks

In this paper, we introduced an extension to FELICS, a free and open-source benchmarking framework for the evaluation of AEAD algorithms. The main motivation behind this development is to give the designers of AEAD algorithms a fair, comprehensive and consistent way of evaluating their algorithms in the context of lightweight embedded devices, as well as a consistent way of comparing performance metrics between different algorithms. More specifically, this paper provided three contributions: (i) an API that allows a fine-grained evaluation of algorithms, while still maintaining design flexibility for the designers; (ii) a series of real-world based evaluations scenarios, allowing a fair comparison of algorithms based on their predicted future use; and (iii) preliminary results with a small set of well-known AEAD algorithms that demonstrate the framework's practical value. Thanks to its modular design, FELICS is very flexible and can be extended to support new metrics, new scenarios, and new devices. Furthermore, new implementations of AEAD algorithms can easily be added to the framework.

With that in mind, we encourage the cryptographic community to contribute optimized C and Assembler implementations of AEAD candidates submitted to the NIST lightweight crypto project and support in this way the fair and transparent evaluation of AEAD algorithms.

Acknowledgements. We would like to thank Daniel Dinu, Yann Le Corre, and Virat Shejwalkar for directly and indirectly helping with the development of this work. Luan Cardoso dos Santos is supported by the Luxembourg National Research Fund through grant PRIDE15/10621687/SPsquared.

References

1. Aumasson, J.-P., Jovanovic, P., Neves, S.: NORX: parallel and scalable AEAD. In: Kutyłowski, M., Vaidya, J. (eds.) ESORICS 2014. LNCS, vol. 8713, pp. 19–36. Springer, Cham (2014). https://doi.org/10.1007/978-3-319-11212-1_2
2. Beer, D.: MSPDebug: Debugging Tool for MSP430 MCUs (2015). http://mspdebug.sourceforge.net
3. Bellare, M., Rogaway, P.: Encode-then-encipher encryption: how to exploit nonces or redundancy in plaintexts for efficient cryptography. In: Okamoto, T. (ed.) ASIACRYPT 2000. LNCS, vol. 1976, pp. 317–330. Springer, Heidelberg (2000). https://doi.org/10.1007/3-540-44448-3_24
4. Bernstein, D.J., Lange, T.: eBACS: ECRYPT Benchmarking of Cryptographic Systems (2009). http://bench.cr.yp.to
5. Bertoni, G., Daemen, J., Peeters, M., Van Assche, G., Van Keer, R.: CAESAR submission: Ketje v2 (2016)
6. Carter, M.R., Velagala, R.R., Pham, J., Kaps, J.P.: eXtended eXternal Benchmarking eXtension (XXBX). In: IEEE International Symposium on Hardware Oriented Security and Trust (HOST 2018) (2018)
7. CryptoLUX Team: FELICS: Fair Evaluation of Lightweight Cryptographic Systems (2016). http://www.cryptolux.org/index.php/FELICS
8. Dinu, D., Biryukov, A., Großschädl, J., Khovratovich, D., Corre, Y., Perrin, L.: FELICS-fair evaluation of lightweight cryptographic systems. In: NIST Workshop on Lightweight Cryptography, vol. 128 (2015)
9. Dinu, D., Le Corre, Y., Khovratovich, D., Perrin, L., Großschädl, J., Biryukov, A.: Triathlon of lightweight block ciphers for the Internet of Things. Cryptology ePrint Archive, Report 2015/209 (2015). https://eprint.iacr.org/2015/209
10. Dobraunig, C., Eichlseder, M., Mendel, F., Schläffer, M.: Ascon v1, submission to the CAESAR competition. CAESAR First Round Submission, March 2014
11. Katz, J., Yung, M.: Unforgeable encryption and chosen ciphertext secure modes of operation. In: Goos, G., Hartmanis, J., van Leeuwen, J., Schneier, B. (eds.) FSE 2000. LNCS, vol. 1978, pp. 284–299. Springer, Heidelberg (2001). https://doi.org/10.1007/3-540-44706-7_20
12. McGrew, D., Viega, J.: The Galois/counter mode of operation (GCM). Submission to NIST Modes of Operation Process, vol. 20 (2004)
13. National Institute of Standards and Technology (NIST): Submission requirements and evaluation criteria for the lightweight cryptography standardization process. Technical report (2018). http://csrc.nist.gov/CSRC/media/Projects/Lightweight-Cryptography/documents/final-lwc-submission-requirements-august2018.pdf

14. Rogaway, P.: Authenticated-encryption with associated-data. In: Atluri, V. (ed.) Proceedings of the 9th ACM Conference on Computer and Communications Security (CCS 2002), pp. 98–107. ACM Press, New York (2002)
15. Titzer, B.L., Lee, D.K., Palsberg, J.: Avrora: scalable sensor network simulation with precise timing. In: 2005 Fourth International Symposium on Information Processing in Sensor Networks (IPSN 2005), pp. 477–482. IEEE (2005)
16. Wenzel-Benner, C., Gräf, J.: XBX: eXternal Benchmarking eXtension for the SUPERCOP crypto benchmarking framework. In: Mangard, S., Standaert, F.-X. (eds.) CHES 2010. LNCS, vol. 6225, pp. 294–305. Springer, Heidelberg (2010). https://doi.org/10.1007/978-3-642-15031-9_20
17. Wu, H.: ACORN: a lightweight authenticated cipher (v3). Candidate for the CAESAR Competition (2016). https://competitions.cr.yp.to/round3/acornv3.pdf

Advances in Side-Channel Analysis

A Comparison of χ^2-Test and Mutual Information as Distinguisher for Side-Channel Analysis

Bastian Richter(✉), David Knichel, and Amir Moradi

Horst Görtz Institute, Ruhr University Bochum,
Bochum, Germany
{bastian.richter,david.knichel,amir.moradi}@rub.de

Abstract. Masking is known as the most widely studied countermeasure against side-channel analysis attacks. Since a masked implementation is based on a certain number of shares (referred to as the order of masking), it still exhibits leakages at higher orders. In order to exploit such leakages, higher-order statistical moments individually at each order need to be estimated reflecting the higher-order attacks. Instead, Mutual Information Analysis (MIA) known for more than 10 years avoids such a moment-based analysis by considering the entire distribution for the key recovery. Recently the χ^2-test has been proposed for leakage detection and as a distinguisher where also the whole distribution of the leakages is analyzed.

In this work, we compare these two schemes to examine their dependency. Indeed, one of the goals of this research is to conclude whether one can outperform the other. In addition to a theoretical comparison, we present two case studies and their corresponding practical evaluations. Both case studies are masked hardware implementations; one is an FPGA-based realization of a threshold implementation of PRESENT, and the other is an AES implementation as a coprocessor on a commercial smart card.

Keywords: Chi squared test · Mutual information analysis · Side-channel attacks

1 Introduction

When developing real-world cryptographic applications, implementation attacks pose a serious threat. The past has shown that cryptographic applications like locking systems [5,17], one-time-password tokens [16], RFID cards [15], and mesh networks [4] not incorporating strong countermeasures are susceptible to Side-Channel Analysis (SCA) attacks. Thus, it is very important to harden these during development and to thoroughly test by performing possible attacks.

Within the area of countermeasures against SCA attacks, masking is widely considered as the most important one since it can give certain guarantees, e.g.

S. Belaïd and T. Güneysu (Eds.): CARDIS 2019, LNCS 11833, pp. 237–251, 2020.
https://doi.org/10.1007/978-3-030-42068-0_14

threshold implementations [14] concerning glitches in the implementation. By splitting the computation into shares, direct leakage of the state can be prevented and not only reduced or covered by noise like with hiding countermeasures. In the univariate case these masking schemes are developed to prevent leakage up to a certain statistical order, i.e. a first-order masking prevents extracting information via the first statistical moment but might still be attackable via the second centered statistical moment. However, higher-order statistics are more susceptible to noise, so the required number of traces to sufficiently approximate the statistics are increasing exponentially with the order [19].

Further, when implementing masking schemes, the designers always have to test whether some physical side-effects of the platform are influencing the effectiveness of the countermeasure. Here, especially coupling [3,10] is a main problem for hardware implementations which can lead to unpredicted leakages in lower orders due to undesired interaction between the shares.

An initial test is usually performed by using a leakage detection method often based on the t-test [8]. In 2018 the χ^2-test [12] was proposed as an addition to the t-test. While the t-test highlights leakage in each order individually, the χ^2-test considers the whole distribution and can thus detect leakage spread over multiple orders. Leakage detected with the χ^2-test but not in the t-tests can indicate that the noise in the measurements is not sufficient to cover the leakage in the higher orders.

However, leakage detected in these tests does not necessarily indicate exploitable leakage. To further examine if detected leakage can be exploited, attacks have to be executed. The original Correlation Power Analysis (CPA) [2] attack correlates the measurements with a hypothetical power model based on a guessed key and thus targets the first order. Fortunately, the attack can be extended to higher orders by preprocessing the measurements [19] (c.f. Sect. 2.5). But still, this only attacks individual orders like the t-test. To attack the whole distribution different attack methods are needed. The first one was Mutual Information Analysis (MIA) presented by Gierlichs et al. in 2008 [7] which computes the mutual information between the measurements and an assumed model to reveal the key. As this is based on histograms or a kernel distribution, it also considers the whole distribution. In addition to leakage detection Moradi et al. also proposed a distinguisher based on the χ^2-test, which tests whether the groups defined by a model are independent and thus can also reveal the keys. In combination with modern measurement methods like on-die EM measurements [6,9] which can monitor the leakage of the cryptographic core independently of the surrounding circuitry, a low noise measurement might defeat a masking implementation when targeting with the combined leakage of all orders.

1.1 Contribution

As both methods follow similar approaches and can actually be calculated on the same precomputed histograms, the question arises whether one of the methods shows an advantage over the other. To evaluate this, we first try to find a theoretical dependency between the two tests and show why these schemes are not directly related in the way the attacks are currently formulated. Further, we present two case studies which successfully exploit leakage in higher orders. The first one is a threshold implementation of PRESENT implemented on an FPGA and the second an SCA-protected AES hardware implementation on a smart card.

2 Background

2.1 χ^2-Test and Distinguisher

Utilizing the χ^2-test to detect leakage independent of statistical moments was initially proposed by Moradi et al. in 2018 [12]. Further, they showed that it can also be used as a distinguisher similar to MIA.

χ^2-Test of Independence. Pearson's χ^2-test of independence checks whether two random variables are independent. For two random variables X and Y, it tests whether

$$H_0 : Pr[X = x|Y = y] = Pr[X = x]$$

which means that they are independent. Let $P \in \mathbb{R}^{r \times c}$ be the matrix with p_{ij} standing for the joint probabilities $Pr[X = x_i \wedge Y = y_j]$ that X takes its i-th category *and* Y takes its j-th. If H_0 holds, the multiplication rule states that $Pr[X = x_i \wedge Y = y_j] = Pr[X = x_i] \cdot Pr[Y = y_j]$. So in a random experiment with N repetitions, the expected frequency that $X = x_i$ and $Y = y_j$ should be $N \cdot Pr[X = x_i] \cdot Pr[Y = y_j]$. Since $Pr[X = x_i]$ and $Pr[Y = y_j]$ are not known, they have to be estimated from the contingency table $F = (f_{i,j}) \in \mathbb{R}^{r \times c}$ where $f_{i,j}$ is the number of times that x_i occurred together with y_j. To estimate $Pr[X = x_i]$ we sum up all frequencies in the corresponding row and divide it by the total number of experiments N. To estimate $Pr[Y = y_j]$ we sum up all frequencies in the corresponding column and divide it by N. This results in the expected frequency being calculated as

$$e_{i,j} = \left(\frac{\sum_{k=0}^{c-1} f_{i,k}}{N}\right)\left(\frac{\sum_{k=0}^{r-1} f_{k,j}}{N}\right) \cdot N = \frac{\left(\sum_{k=0}^{c-1} f_{i,k}\right)\left(\sum_{k=0}^{r-1} f_{k,j}\right)}{N}. \tag{1}$$

Now the Z value is a metric of how much the actual frequencies $f_{i,j}$ differ from the expected ones $e_{i,j}$. It is computed in the same fashion as shown in Eq. (2):

$$Z = \sum_{i=0}^{r-1}\sum_{j=0}^{c-1} \frac{(f_{i,j} - e_{i,j})^2}{e_{i,j}}. \tag{2}$$

With the degree of freedom as $v = (r-1) \cdot (c-1)$. The p-value

$$p = \int_Z^{\infty} \mathsf{f}(Z, v)\, dx, \qquad \mathsf{f}(Z, v) = \begin{cases} \frac{Z^{\frac{v}{2}-1} e^{-\frac{Z}{2}}}{2^{\frac{v}{2}} \Gamma(\frac{v}{2})} & Z > 0 \\ 0 & Z \leq 0 \end{cases}, \tag{3}$$

with the gamma function Γ can be used as a metric in order to test H_0. It expresses the probability whether the null hypothesis is accepted. We use this test for specific leakage assessment and as a distinguisher in a Differential Power Analysis (DPA). More precisely, we test whether the distribution depends of the value of a hypothetical power model. In this case, X corresponds to the value measured by the ADC of the oscilloscope and Y corresponds to the value of the power model. It can also be used in addition to the non-specific t-test [12], where Y is simply 0 or 1, depending of whether a random plaintext or a fixed plaintext is used.

Distinguisher. Very similar to the way the Pearson correlation coefficient is used as a distinguisher in a DPA/CPA, we may use the result of the χ^2-test. In DPA/CPA, it is assumed that for the correct key guess, the values of the power model correlates well with the actual power consumption. In χ^2-test the assumption is that for the correct key guess, the traces depend on the values of the power model, whereas the power consumption is independent of the model for wrong key guesses. For every key guess this can be checked with the χ^2-test of independence. Similar to the t-test, we can state with a certain confidence that the assumption H_0 is wrong, which in our case means that the values of the power consumption depends on the values of the model.

2.2 Mutual Information Analysis

Mutual Information Analysis (MIA) for SCA was initially proposed by Gierlichs et al. in 2008 [7] as a more generic information-theoretic distinguisher.

Mutual Information. The Mutual Information (MI) I is a measure for the information shared between two random variables X and Y.

As the entropy $\mathrm{H}(X)$ is a measure of the information contained in X we can substract the conditional entropy $\mathrm{H}(X|Y)$ as this is exactly the portion of the entropy which is not covered by Y to get the mutual information $\mathrm{I}(X;Y)$.

$$\begin{aligned}\mathrm{I}(X;Y) &= \mathrm{H}(X) - \mathrm{H}(X|Y) \\ &= \mathrm{H}(X) + \mathrm{H}(Y) - \mathrm{H}(X,Y) = \mathrm{I}(Y;X)\end{aligned} \tag{4}$$

Suppose that X and Y are random variables of the discrete spaces $\mathcal{X}$ and $\mathcal{Y}$, we can also formulate the mutual information $\mathrm{I}(X;Y)$ as

$$\begin{aligned}\mathrm{I}(X;Y) = \sum_{x\in\mathcal{X}}\sum_{y\in\mathcal{Y}} Pr[X=x, Y=y]\cdot \\ \log_2\left(\frac{Pr[X=x, Y=y]}{Pr[X=x]Pr[Y=y]}\right),\end{aligned} \tag{5}$$

knowing the joint probability $Pr[X = x, Y = y]$ and the marginal probabilities $Pr[X = x]$ and $Pr[Y = y]$ which can be calculated from the contingency tables.

Distinguisher. Considering this in the side-channel application, we set one variable as our observation of the side-channel and the other a model of the leakage depending on the secret key. Hence, we set X as our observation of the power consumption and Y as the assumed distribution of our leakage model. Hence, if the power consumption behaves similar to our leakage model, the mutual information increases. Only if the key is correct, our observations have the same or a similar distribution as the power model and thus a high mutual information.

2.3 Implementation of χ^2-Test and MIA

The first step needed is the calculation of the histograms for the different models and key candidates. For each key candidate the traces are grouped by the key dependent model. The histograms are then calculated for each group and each point in time. Here, the original oscilloscope quantization (8-bit values as the result of its Analog-to-Digital Converter (ADC)) is kept and the results saved as starting point for the different metric calculations. When using the same model this can be performed as a common precomputation step for χ^2-test and MIA, as both methods can perform their computation on the same histograms.

Based on these basic histograms the next step differs for the two methods. The χ^2-test has a fixed rule for handling empty bins by ignoring them. This can result in different numbers of bins for each point in time. But since we use the p-value for comparison of the candidates, this does not matter as it is accounted for in the degrees-of-freedom v (see Eq. (3)). For MIA the original histograms have to be rebinned. The lowest (highest, respectively) bin contains the lowest(highest, respectively) value measured with the bins in between filled with the corresponding ratio of the original bin counts. Additionally, the number of bins has to be the same for each point in time to be able to compare these. At the same time, also the success of the attack highly depends on the choice of the number of bins as shown by Moradi et al. in [11]. Thus, MIA has to be performed multiple times with different parameters to find the best attack setting which results in a high overhead in comparison to the χ^2-test. These adjustments to the bins, are only performed in memory within the respective calculation.

2.4 Relation Between χ^2-Test and Mutual Information

While at first glance MIA and the χ^2-test seem very similar and can show similar results (see Sects. 3.1 and 4.6), they are based on different approaches. There are different tests which can be performed with a statistical measure like the χ^2-test. Two common ones to perform on data sets are the *test of goodness-of-fit* and the *test of independence* which was already introduced in Sect. 2.1.

The *test of goodness-of-fit* examines whether the contingency table based on an observation f_i of a random variable fits the expected occurrences e_i of a theoretical model. In contrast to the *test of independence* the expected values e_i are given by a theoretical model and not by the observations.

For the same applications as the χ^2-test there is the G-test, which can be used as an alternative for *test of goodness-of-fit* and *test of independence*. It is also based on histograms/contingency tables and also approximates the χ^2 distribution.

$$G = 2\sum_{\forall i} f_i \cdot \ln\left(\frac{f_i}{e_i}\right) \tag{6}$$

As shown in [13] Eq. (6) can also be expressed in terms of probabilities $p_i = \frac{1}{N}\sum_i f_{i,j}$ and $p_{i,j} = \frac{1}{N} f_{i,j}$ with N the total number of observations.

$$G = 2N \sum_{\forall i, \forall j} p_{i,j} \cdot (\ln(p_{i,j}) - \ln(p_i) - \ln(p_j)) \tag{7}$$

By considering the definition of entropy $\mathrm{H}(x) = -\sum_{x\in\mathcal{X}} p(x) \cdot \ln p(x)$ and joint entropy $\mathrm{H}(x,y) = -\sum_{x\in\mathcal{X},y\in\mathcal{Y}} p(x,y) \cdot \ln p(x,y)$ based on the natural logarithm and distributing the sum to the sub-terms we can further express G through entropies and following from these mutual information.

$$G = 2N\,(\mathrm{H}(x) + \mathrm{H}(y) - \mathrm{H}(x,y)) = 2N \cdot \mathrm{I}(x;y) \tag{8}$$

Please note that the entropy and mutual information in computer science are usually calculated with $\log_2$ which introduces an additional factor of $\frac{1}{\ln 2} \approx 1.443$ in Eq. (8).

Based on this, there should only be a constant factor between mutual information and the G value. As G-test and χ^2-test both approximate the χ^2-distribution, these should lead to the same results for reasonable sample sizes. So, there seems to be a connection between χ^2 and mutual information. However, the two tests are currently used in different approaches. For the χ^2-test as presented in [12] we split up the observations into sets based on a model and then perform a test of independence, i.e. whether the distributions of the sets are independent. In contrast, for MIA we calculate the mutual information between our model and the observations which is more like a test of goodness-of-fit, i.e. whether the observed distribution is similar to the theoretical model. Accordingly, the relation via the G-test does not apply. Since we cannot give a direct theoretical connection we further evaluate their behavior by two case studies.

2.5 Higher-Order CPA

CPA as introduced by Bier et al. [2] uses the Pearson correlation coefficient between measurements and hypothetical leakage to extract the secret key. The hypothetical leakage is calculated for each challenge using a key dependent model.

In order to attack masked implementations, it is possible to perform a univariate (i.e., every point in time is considered individually) CPA at higher orders by preprocessing the measurements. To this end, the point-wise mean is subtracted from the measurements t and the results are taken to the power of the order d as $t' = (t - \bar{t})^d$. It is shown by Schneider et al. [20] in 2016 how to efficiently perform these computations.

3 Case Study 1: PRESENT Threshold Implementation

Our first case study is a threshold implementation of the PRESENT cipher as presented in [18]. For better comparison we evaluate the same implementation used by Moradi et al. in [12]. To achieve first-order security the state of the cipher is split into three Boolean shares (x_1, x_2, x_3) where $x = x_1 \oplus x_2 \oplus x_3$. It is saved in three 16-by-4 bit shift registers and from there shifted 4 bits per clock cycle. After key addition, the state is shifted into the S-box which is split up into two functions G and F separated by a register. The S-box lookups are then run as a pipelined serial computation which takes 17 clock cycles with the PLayer run in parallel in one clock cycle after the S-boxes.

The design is implemented on a Xilinx Spartan-6 FPGA on a SAKURA-G board [1]. To collect the measurements, we used the integrated amplifier of the SAKURA-G board and sampled the power consumption at a sampling rate of 1 GS/s. The core was running at a frequency of 160 MHz and the initial sharing performed in the control FPGA to prevent leakage from the inputs, i.e. the target FPGA receives masked plaintext and issues masked ciphertext.

Performing a random-vs-fixed (non-specific) t-test on the traces revealed minimal leakage ($t = 8.2$) in the second and significant leakage ($t = 39.55$) in the third order using 50,000,000 traces. Since we attack the first round of the encryption and the major leakage is right at the beginning of the measurement, we only consider the first 500 ns for the attack.

3.1 Results

As we are analyzing a nibble-serial implementation, we chose the Hamming distance of two consecutive S-box lookups as our power model $\mathrm{HD}(S(p_i \oplus k_i), S(p_{i+1} \oplus k_{i+1}))$. It results in 8-bit key candidates, as it is based on the distance between two consecutive nibbles. To decrease the complexity of the attack, we can assume that we perform the 8 bit attack only for the first distance, continuing from there we always already know one of the two key nibbles and can work with 4 bit candidates. To find the optimal number of bins for the MIA, we first tested which settings lead to the best result for the nibble and then performed the attack with this optimal number of bins.

We performed a key recovery on one of the key nibbles with χ^2-test and MIA using 50,000,000 traces. Figure 1(a) and (c) show the χ^2-p-value and the mutual information after all traces were processed. Both attacks are successful and the correct key can be clearly distinguished. As both methods use the same model they highlight the correct key at the same point in time but the period during which the correct key stands out is longer for MIA. However, correct key and wrong candidates are more clearly separated in the χ^2-test. This is also confirmed by Fig. 1(d) and (b) which plot the maximum MI (p-value, respectively) over the number of traces in the calculation. The χ^2-test needs 30,000,000 traces for the key to stand out while MIA needs 36,000,000 traces for the correct key to be more likely than the ghost peak.

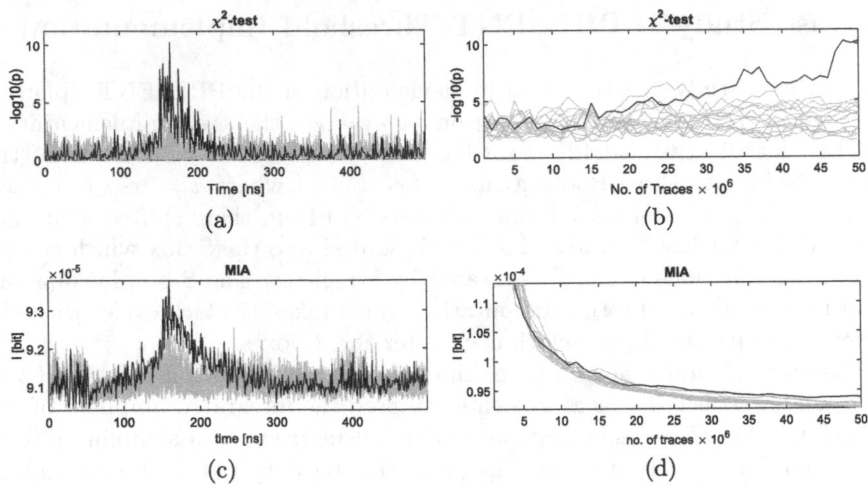

Fig. 1. Results of χ^2-test and MIA on PRESENT threshold implementation.

We also performed CPAs from the first to the third order but were not able to recover the key. We therefore omitted the figures. This indicates that combined leakage in higher order can indeed be better exploited in our case by moment-free methods.

4 Case Study 2: Smart Card

Our second target is a commercially available smart card implementing the Java Card standard with multiple cryptographic hardware cores. In this case study we target the AES encryption which is implemented by a dedicated circuit of the card.

4.1 Measurements

We performed on-die near-field EM measurements on the backside of the die, exposing it by removing the center pad of the smart card contacts and the underlying material.

For the measurements we used a Teledyne-Lecroy Waverunner 8254M with a sampling rate of 5 GSamples/s and the full bandwidth of 2.5 GHz. This high sampling rate and bandwidth is needed since the on-die EM signal includes sharp peaks reflecting the high frequency of the signal. As the EM probe we used a Langer EMV ICR HH150-27 near-field microprobe with a diameter of 150 µm and a bandwidth of 1.5 MHz to 6 GHz.

To find the optimal position on the die we scanned over the die and by visual inspection chose a position which showed a characteristic round pattern of the AES encryption.

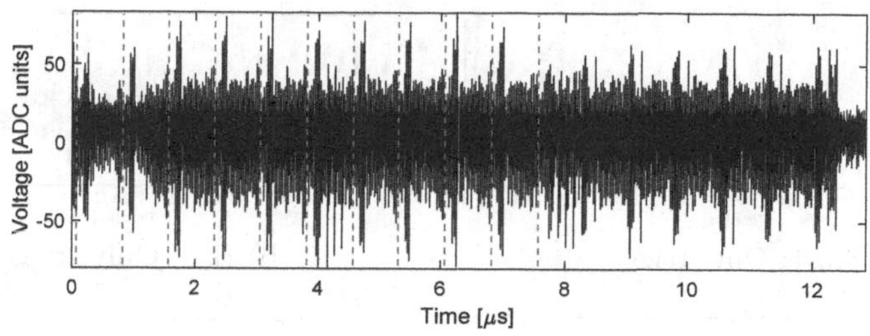

Fig. 2. Mean trace of 2000 aligned traces with clearly visible round structures.

4.2 Architecture

Based on our measurements we were able to identify the rounds of the AES implementation. The rounds are formed by the repeating pattern in Fig. 2 of approx. 0.75 µs length. The rounds are marked by red lines in Fig. 2. We confirmed this using correlation on the key schedule, which is executed at every round. Each round needs 25 clock cycles including the key schedule of 7 clock cylces to complete. The three high peaks within the round pattern are the end of the key schedule. Interestingly, the last round seems to be not shorter than the other ones although the MixColumns operation is missing in the last round of the AES algorithm.

4.3 Countermeasures

While it is based on a smart card IC which is also used in Common Criteria certified software and hardware combinations, the Java card we are attacking is not certified and most likely does not implement all countermeasures which are included in a certified product. Still, we expect that the circuit realizes hardware countermeasures.

A visual inspection of multiple measurements reveals strong random delays of the encryption in relation to the communication and additional high jitter of the clock. Also, we were able to get first order correlations on some plaintext bytes at the beginning of the realigned traces but no first order correlation on intermediates of the first round (see Sect. 4.6). Due to this low first order leakage, we believe that the card also incorporates some kind of masking countermeasures.

From a certified product one would expect additional countermeasures. A typical one would be dummy rounds, which we can exclude here since the traces clearly show 10 rounds, also the leakage of single rounds occurs only within one round pattern and not distributed over multiple ones.

4.4 Alignment

As we already observed random timing and jitter countermeasures we first need to align the traces. In the following, we explain how we did this to achieve the aligned mean trace shown in Fig. 2.

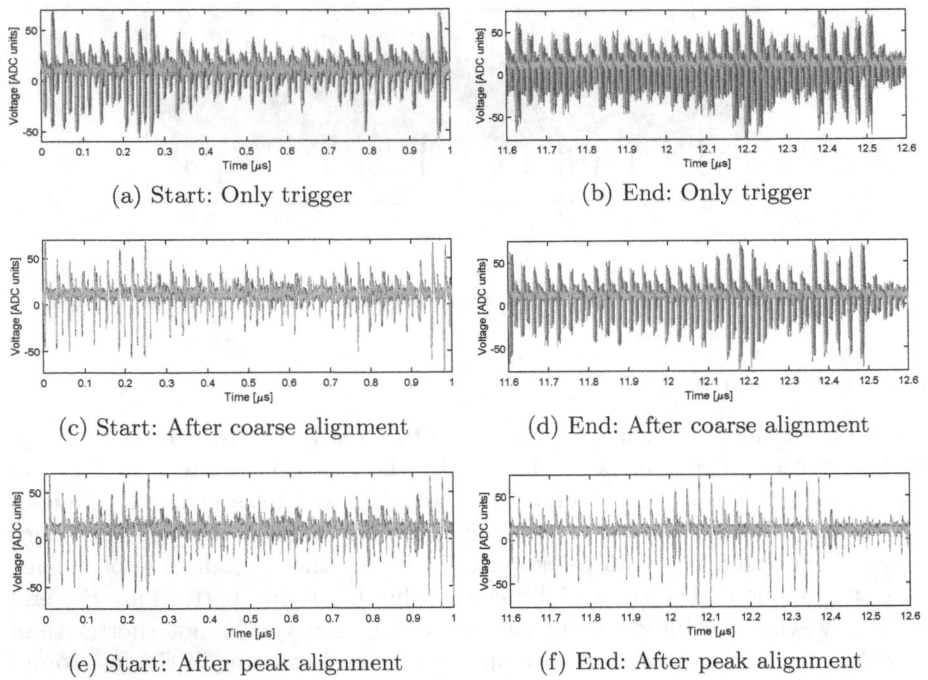

(a) Start: Only trigger

(b) End: Only trigger

(c) Start: After coarse alignment

(d) End: After coarse alignment

(e) Start: After peak alignment

(f) End: After peak alignment

Fig. 3. Beginning and end of ten traces each after the three different stages of alignment.

Trigger on High Peak. To compensate for the long random delays, we used an advanced trigger setting making use of both IO communication signals of the card and the EM signal itself. This approach is possible since we are performing a localized EM measurement which exhibits the highest amplitudes when the encryption is running. Using such a trigger results in traces with only small temporal variation of the beginning of the encryption block as shown in Fig. 3(a) and (b).

Coarse Alignment of AES Block. We selected a reference pattern at the beginning of the first trace. To recover the offset of the other traces, we then correlated the pattern over a window at the beginning. Shifting the traces by the found offset results in Fig. 3(c) and (d). The beginning is now aligned but due to the clock jitter, the difference between the traces increases to the end.

Fine Alignment Against Clock Jitter. To overcome the clock jitter, we followed a windowing approach. For each clock cycle in each trace we searched for the minimum and selected a window around it. By only keeping the part of the trace belonging to the windows of the 150 clock cycles, we created traces whose clock cycles are aligned. As shown in Fig. 3(e) and (f) all peaks are now aligned at the beginning as well as at the end.

4.5 Key Recovery

After performing the alignment, we were able to conduct an attack on a subset of the key bytes. To this end, we used a Hamming distance (HD) model between outputs of the S-box operation $\mathrm{HD}(S(p_i \oplus k_i), S(p_j \oplus k_j))$. We found certain pairs $(i, j) = \{(1, 2), (5, 6), (9, 10), (13, 14), (6, 7), (14, 15)\}$ which lead to successful key recovery. As the model targets the distance between two bytes the size of the key candidates is 16 bits for the first four pairs and 8 bits for the last two ones since one of the bytes is already known from a previous pair. Interestingly, the first four pairs resemble the byte-wise distance between the second and third row of the AES state matrix.

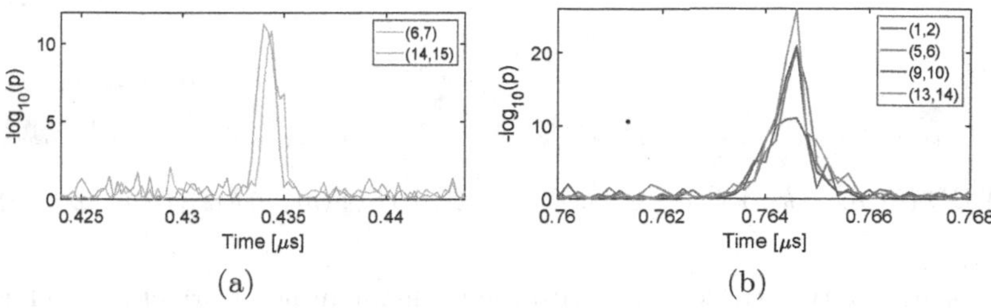

(a) (b)

Fig. 4. Results of χ^2-test over time (a) and zooms of the two peaks we chose for the attack (b) and (c).

The results of the χ^2-test can suffer from outlier categories with only low counts. To prevent this from influencing the analyses, we modified the initial model. Instead of using the normal Hamming distance to categorize the traces, we merged the less frequent HDs which results in the following five categories $[\{0, 1, 2\}, 3, 4, 5, \{6, 7, 8\}]$. In the following we denote this grouping as HD$'$.

Considering the leakage of the different pairs over time we observed that that the pairs $\{(1, 2), (5, 6), (9, 10), (13, 14)\}$ leak at three different times while pairs $\{(6, 7), (14, 15)\}$ only leak at one point. For the attack we chose the peaks with the highest p-value for the respective pairs which are shown in more detail in Fig. 4(a) and (b).

Figure 5 shows the progress of the attack for the different pairs of key bytes. The pair $(13, 14)$ shows the highest probability and can be recovered with less than 200000 traces. With 350000 required traces pair $(6, 7)$ is the most difficult to recover.

Using 350,000 traces only 6 out of 16 key bytes remain unknown with this attack. The remaining 48 bits of entropy are within brute-force range even without specialized hardware.

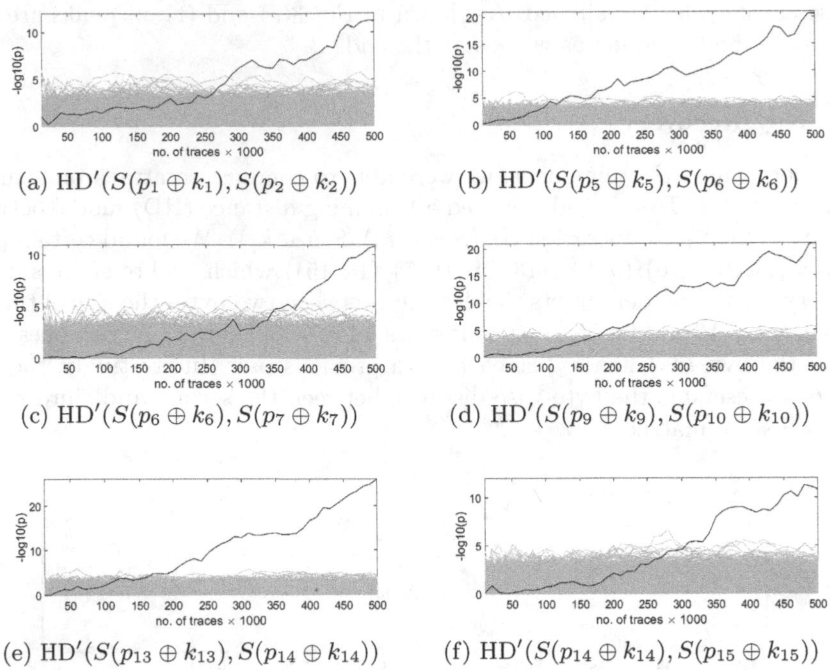

(a) $\mathrm{HD}'(S(p_1 \oplus k_1), S(p_2 \oplus k_2))$ (b) $\mathrm{HD}'(S(p_5 \oplus k_5), S(p_6 \oplus k_6))$

(c) $\mathrm{HD}'(S(p_6 \oplus k_6), S(p_7 \oplus k_7))$ (d) $\mathrm{HD}'(S(p_9 \oplus k_9), S(p_{10} \oplus k_{10}))$

(e) $\mathrm{HD}'(S(p_{13} \oplus k_{13}), S(p_{14} \oplus k_{14}))$ (f) $\mathrm{HD}'(S(p_{14} \oplus k_{14}), S(p_{15} \oplus k_{15}))$

Fig. 5. Progress of the attack results with the χ^2-distinguisher. Correct key highlighted in black.

4.6 χ^2-Test Vs. MIA Vs. HOCPA

In order to compare the different attacks we ran a χ^2-test, a MIA and CPAs from the first to the third order. To speed up the analyses we only used an 8-bit candidate and a small window of the traces. As the target, we picked the pairs (13, 14) and (6, 7) which are the ones requiring the least and most number of traces to succeed.

The CPAs at 1st to 3rd order were not successful in recovering the secret. Further, we used the aforementioned HD′ model for all attacks. Since CPA needs a linear dependency between the power model and the measurements, we also examined the normal HD model but the attacks at all three orders were still not successful.

In contrast, χ^2-test and MIA were both able to recover the keys. For the pair (13, 14) (shown in Fig. 6) both attacks represent a clear peak for the correct key candidate. The χ^2-test needs around 200,000 traces and MIA requires slightly more traces (230,000). The attack targeting the pair (6, 7) show a different behavior shown in Fig. 7. While it was the worst performing pair for the χ^2-test with 350,000 traces, it performs even better than the other pair with MIA. It needs only 180,000 traces to identify the correct candidate. Interestingly, the optimal number of bins for MIA is very different for the two considered key pairs. While the first showed best results with rebinning to 33 bins, the second one was optimal with only 8 bins.

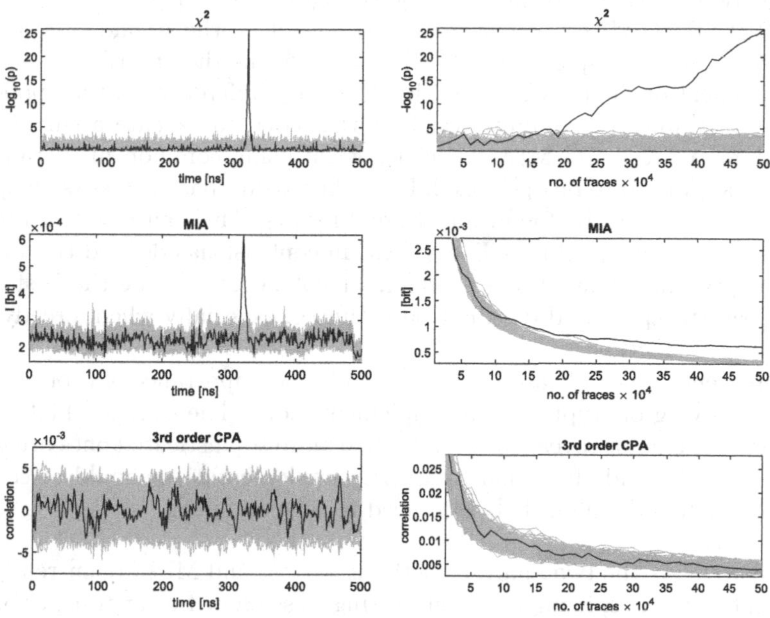

Fig. 6. Results of χ^2-test, MIA and 3rd order CPA attacks on key byte pair (13, 14).

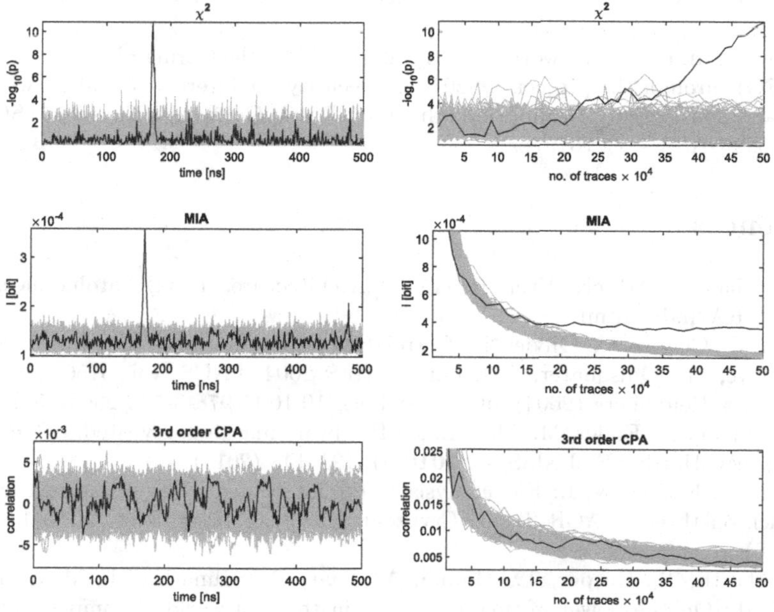

Fig. 7. Results of χ^2-test, MIA and 3rd order CPA attacks on key byte pair (6, 7).

5 Conclusion

As explained in Sect. 2.4, for the current use of χ^2-test and MIA there is no direct relation. This is also shown in the two case studies presented here. While for the PRESENT TI the χ^2-test performed better, in the second case study we also presented an example in which MIA outperforms the other.

Independent of the presented results, there are differences in the application of the tests. While the computational effort needed to execute a single attack is similar for χ^2-test and MIA especially when using common histograms, the settings of MIA need to be optimized. In the histogram-based attacks an optimal number of bins has to be found for optimal results. This can result in the need to run the attack many times. The χ^2-test in contrast has defined rules how to handle empty bins. Thus, the χ^2-test might not necessarily be the best attack but it is easy to apply and does not need tuning, especially when already using it for leakage detection.

The presented second case study highlights the importance of thorough testing and certifying of cryptographic implementations. The common higher-order attacks (CPA) cannot reveal the secret while more sophisticated ones are able to do so. In case the underlying hardware AES implementation should be certified, such moment-free distinguishers also need to be examined.

Future Works. As the two analysis methods χ^2-test and MIA are currently used in different test types, it might be interesting to see how the χ^2-test performs in a *test of goodness-of-fit* scenario. Since the methods might converge differently, they still may lead to different results. It might also be interesting to see whether using the G-test instead of the χ^2-test leads to a faster key recovery.

Acknowledgments. This work is partly supported by the German Research Foundation (DFG) through the project 393207943 "Security for Internet of Things with Low Energy and Low Power Consumption (GreenSec)", and Germany's Excellence Strategy - EXC 2092 CASA - 390781972.

References

1. Side-Channel AttacK User Reference Architecture. http://satoh.cs.uec.ac.jp/SAKURA/index.html
2. Brier, E., Clavier, C., Olivier, F.: Correlation power analysis with a leakage model. In: Joye, M., Quisquater, J.-J. (eds.) CHES 2004. LNCS, vol. 3156, pp. 16–29. Springer, Heidelberg (2004). https://doi.org/10.1007/978-3-540-28632-5_2
3. De Cnudde, T., Ender, M., Moradi, A.: Hardware masking, revisited. IACR Trans. Cryptogr. Hardw. Embed. Syst. **2018**(2), 123–148 (2018)
4. Dinu, D., Kizhvatov, I.: EM analysis in the iot context: lessons learned from an attack on thread. IACR Trans. Cryptogr. Hardw. Embed. Syst. **2018**(1), 73–97 (2018)
5. Eisenbarth, T., Kasper, T., Moradi, A., Paar, C., Salmasizadeh, M., Shalmani, M.T.M.: On the power of power analysis in the real world: a complete break of the KeeLoq code hopping scheme. In: Wagner, D. (ed.) CRYPTO 2008. LNCS,

vol. 5157, pp. 203–220. Springer, Heidelberg (2008). https://doi.org/10.1007/978-3-540-85174-5_12

6. Gandolfi, K., Mourtel, C., Olivier, F.: Electromagnetic analysis: concrete results. In: Koç, Ç.K., Naccache, D., Paar, C. (eds.) CHES 2001. LNCS, vol. 2162, pp. 251–261. Springer, Heidelberg (2001). https://doi.org/10.1007/3-540-44709-1_21
7. Gierlichs, B., Batina, L., Tuyls, P., Preneel, B.: Mutual information analysis. In: Oswald, E., Rohatgi, P. (eds.) CHES 2008. LNCS, vol. 5154, pp. 426–442. Springer, Heidelberg (2008). https://doi.org/10.1007/978-3-540-85053-3_27
8. Goodwill, G., Jun, B., Jaffe, J., Rohatgi, P.: A testing methodology for side channel resistance validation. In: NIST Non-invasive Attack Testing Workshop (2011)
9. Heyszl, J., Mangard, S., Heinz, B., Stumpf, F., Sigl, G.: Localized electromagnetic analysis of cryptographic implementations. In: Dunkelman, O. (ed.) CT-RSA 2012. LNCS, vol. 7178, pp. 231–244. Springer, Heidelberg (2012). https://doi.org/10.1007/978-3-642-27954-6_15
10. Moradi, A., Mischke, O.: On the simplicity of converting leakages from multivariate to univariate (case study of a glitch-resistant masking scheme). In: Bertoni, G., Coron, J.-S. (eds.) CHES 2013. LNCS, vol. 8086, pp. 1–20. Springer, Heidelberg (2013). https://doi.org/10.1007/978-3-642-40349-1_1
11. Moradi, A., Mousavi, N., Paar, C., Salmasizadeh, M.: A comparative study of mutual information analysis under a Gaussian assumption. In: Youm, H.Y., Yung, M. (eds.) WISA 2009. LNCS, vol. 5932, pp. 193–205. Springer, Heidelberg (2009). https://doi.org/10.1007/978-3-642-10838-9_15
12. Moradi, A., Richter, B., Schneider, T., Standaert, F.: Leakage detection with the x2-test. IACR Trans. Cryptogr. Hardw. Embed. Syst. **2018**(1), 209–237 (2018)
13. Morris, A.: An information theoretic measure of sequence recognition performance. Technical report, IDIAP (2002)
14. Nikova, S., Rijmen, V., Schläffer, M.: Secure hardware implementation of nonlinear functions in the presence of glitches. J. Cryptol. **24**(2), 292–321 (2011)
15. Oswald, D., Paar, C.: Breaking Mifare DESFire MF3ICD40: power analysis and templates in the real world. In: Preneel, B., Takagi, T. (eds.) CHES 2011. LNCS, vol. 6917, pp. 207–222. Springer, Heidelberg (2011). https://doi.org/10.1007/978-3-642-23951-9_14
16. Oswald, D., Richter, B., Paar, C.: Side-channel attacks on the Yubikey 2 one-time password generator. In: Stolfo, S.J., Stavrou, A., Wright, C.V. (eds.) RAID 2013. LNCS, vol. 8145, pp. 204–222. Springer, Heidelberg (2013). https://doi.org/10.1007/978-3-642-41284-4_11
17. Oswald, D., Strobel, D., Schellenberg, F., Kasper, T., Paar, C.: When reverse-engineering meets side-channel analysis – digital lockpicking in practice. In: Lange, T., Lauter, K., Lisoněk, P. (eds.) SAC 2013. LNCS, vol. 8282, pp. 571–588. Springer, Heidelberg (2014). https://doi.org/10.1007/978-3-662-43414-7_29
18. Poschmann, A., Moradi, A., Khoo, K., Lim, C., Wang, H., Ling, S.: Side-channel resistant crypto for less than 2, 300 GE. J. Cryptol. **24**(2), 322–345 (2011)
19. Prouff, E., Rivain, M., Bevan, R.: Statistical analysis of second order differential power analysis. IEEE Trans. Comput. **58**(6), 799–811 (2009)
20. Schneider, T., Moradi, A., Güneysu, T.: Robust and one-pass parallel computation of correlation-based attacks at arbitrary order. In: Standaert, F.-X., Oswald, E. (eds.) COSADE 2016. LNCS, vol. 9689, pp. 199–217. Springer, Cham (2016). https://doi.org/10.1007/978-3-319-43283-0_12

Key Enumeration from the Adversarial Viewpoint

When to Stop Measuring and Start Enumerating?

Melissa Azouaoui[1,2(✉)], Romain Poussier[3], François-Xavier Standaert[1], and Vincent Verneuil[2]

[1] Université Catholique de Louvain, Louvain-la-Neuve, Belgium
[2] NXP Semiconductors, Hamburg, Germany
melissa.azouaoui@nxp.com
[3] Temasek Laboratories, Nanyang Technological University, Singapore, Singapore

Abstract. In this work, we formulate and investigate a pragmatic question related to practical side-channel attacks complemented with key enumeration. In a real attack scenario, after an attacker has extracted side-channel information, it is possible that despite the entropy of the key has been significantly reduced, she cannot yet achieve a direct key recovery. If the correct key lies within a sufficiently small set of most probable keys, it can then be recovered with a plaintext and the corresponding ciphertext, by performing enumeration. Our proposal relates to the following question: how does an attacker know when to stop acquiring side-channel observations and when to start enumerating with a given computational effort? Since key enumeration is an expensive (i.e. time-consuming) task, this is an important question from an adversarial viewpoint. To answer this question, we present an efficient (heuristic) way to perform key-less rank estimation, based on simple entropy estimations using histograms.

Keywords: Side-channel attacks · Key rank estimation · Key enumeration

1 Introduction

Key enumeration and key rank estimation are important parts of the security evaluation of cryptographic implementations. These methods allow post-processing the side-channel attack outcomes and determine the computational security of an implementation with respect to a full key recovery. Key enumeration is an adversarial tool that allows testing key candidates without the knowledge of the key by listing the key candidates starting with the most likely one according to the attack results. For example, Veyrat-Charvillon et al. presented a deterministic algorithm for key enumeration [13] that allows the optimal enumeration of full keys by decreasing order of probabilities, by reformulating the key enumeration problem as a geometric problem. Ye et al. proposed a so-called key space finding algorithm [15], that returns the enumeration workload for a

S. Belaïd and T. Güneysu (Eds.): CARDIS 2019, LNCS 11833, pp. 252–267, 2020.
https://doi.org/10.1007/978-3-030-42068-0_15

given success probability, by considering the number of optimal guesses for each subkey. Bogdanov et al. proposed a score-based key enumeration algorithm [2] that reduces the high computational and memory complexity of previous proposals. Martin et al. provided a new method [9] by casting the key enumeration as an integer knapsack problem.

On the other hand, rank estimation is a part of the side-channel evaluator's tool set: given lists of discrete probability distributions for independent parts of the key and the correct key, a key rank estimation algorithm provides tight bounds for the position of the correct key among all possible ones (i.e. the number of guesses required to find the key following an optimal enumeration like above). In 2013, Veyrat-Charvillon et al. showed [14] that in the context of security evaluations (for which the key is usually known), it is possible to estimate the rank of a key beyond the evaluator's practical enumeration capabilities. Bernstein, Lange, and van Vredendaal improved this rank estimation proposals [1] and introduced a new method using polynomial multiplication to calculate lower and upper bounds for the ranks of all keys, by re-writing the problem of counting probabilities larger than the key's probability as finding the number of terms in a generalized polynomial satisfying a specific condition. In parallel, Glowacz et al. proposed a new tool for rank estimation [6] that is conceptually simple and very efficient, based on histogram convolutions, which was later extended to key enumeration by Poussier, Standaert, and Grosso [10]. At CHES 2017, a different and faster approach [5] was finally proposed by Choudary and Popescu. They suggested to bound the guessing entropy with information theoretic measures and inequalities, that do not require the knowledge of the correct key, estimated across multiple side-channel attacks.

In this paper, we tackle a different question than key enumeration or rank estimation, which lies somewhere in between. In a realistic attack scenario, after an adversary has performed a divide-and-conquer side-channel information extraction using a set of N observations, she obtains a vector of probabilities or scores for each subkey. The goal of the adversary is to perform a full key recovery. In this context, if all the subkeys have not been fully recovered immediately from the information extracted, the natural next step is key enumeration, up to a certain limit defined by her computational capabilities. Depending on the attacks, the cryptographic operation(s) targeted, and the size of the key, enumeration can become the most time- and resource-consuming step. Hence, it is very useful (for an adversary) to efficiently estimate the key rank, and therefore to know whether it is worth to start enumerating the key candidates or if the collection of more side-channel observations is needed. We believe that this is an important problem from an adversarial point-of-view, that has not yet been investigated.

We show in this article a simple solution for this purpose and propose a keyless heuristic (i.e. that doesn't require the knowledge of the key) to efficiently approximate the rank of a key given the result of a side-channel attack. Our solution is based on the key rank estimation method from Glowacz et al. [6] using histograms, which we combine with information theoretic metrics to predict the rank of the full key from one single attack. In particular, it differs from the solution of Choudary and Popescu [5] in the sense that it allows estimating the key rank of a single attack (rather than the estimation of the average key rank). Nonetheless, we compare an adaptation of their solution to this single attack setting with our method in Sect. 6.

The rest of the paper is organized as follows. First, Sect. 2 describes more precisely the problem under investigation. Secondly, Sect. 3 introduces the required background. Then, Sect. 4 discusses our proposed method to estimate the rank without the knowledge of the key from an attack perspective. Section 5 suggests an adaptation of the CHES 2017 proposal for rank estimation to the single-attack/attacker scenario. The results of the different methods are further shown in Sect. 6. We additionally discuss the usability and some limitations of our method in Sect. 7. We finally conclude in Sect. 8.

2 Problem Statement

Key enumeration algorithms can offer a trade-off between the required number of side-channel observations and the computational power of the adversary. That is, the use of such algorithms allows recovering the full key with fewer traces, often referred to as the data complexity of a side-channel attack, at the cost of computational/time complexity. However, in practice, it is not trivial for an adversary to know when to start the enumeration. Our goal is to tackle this problem by answering the following question: *Can the attacker infer if more side-channel measurements are required or if she expects a successful key recovery after enumeration, given the current attack outcome?*

To highlight the importance of this question, we picture the strategy that an adversary follows to recover the full key. When performing a side-channel attack it is common to follow a divide-and-conquer strategy, in which parts of the key are targeted and possibly recovered independently. For the rest of this paper, we use the same notations as in [6]. The target of a side-channel attack is an n-bit key $k \in \mathcal{K}$, divided into $N_p = \frac{n}{b}$ parts of b bits, called subkeys and denoted as k_i, for i in $[1 : N_p]$. A side-channel attack makes use of a set of q inputs $\mathcal{X}_q$ and the corresponding set of q leakages $\mathcal{L}_q$ (for example when targeting the AES S-box output, the attacker observes, given an input x_i^j $(1 \leq j \leq q)$, the leakage l_i^j of $\mathrm{S}(x_i^j \oplus k_i)$). After the attack, the adversary obtains N_p lists of probabilities $\Pr[k_i^* | \mathcal{X}_q, \mathcal{L}_q]$ where k_i^* refers to a subkey possibility out of the 2^b candidates. Attacks using Gaussian templates [4] or a linear-regression model [11] output probabilities, but for other distinguishers such as DPA [7] and CPA [3], a Bayesian extension is possible [13].

Let's assume that the adversary is able to perform key enumeration with respect to some computational effort e (e.g. $1 < e < 2^{50}$). A first attack strategy is shown in Algorithm 1. In that case, the attacker first collects a set of measurements, performs the attack, enumerates up to the first e most probable key candidates or until the correct key has been recovered. If the key has not been recovered, she then collects new side-channel observations and repeats the process.

Algorithm 1. Greedy attacker's strategy.

Input. Enumeration effort e.

1: Collect a set of side-channel measurements.
2: Update the attack N_p probability lists P_i for each subkey k_i.
3: Enumerate up to the first e key candidates or until the correct key k is found.
4: **if** k not found **then**
5:     Collect new side-channel measurements and go to step 2.
6: **end if**

The greedy attacker strategy has one main drawback. Indeed, the attacker does not know if the key is reachable via enumeration after step 2. That is, she has no way to know how many times she has to loop over steps 2 to 6. More specifically, if (e.g.) w repetitions of side-channel measurements are required for the attack, the adversary spends an effort of $w \times e$ in enumeration. As the time complexity of such a method is high, it mitigates the original goal of enumeration, which is to trade a lower measurement complexity for a higher computational power.

The aforementioned issue could be avoided if the adversary could assess if the key is reachable with an enumeration effort at most e, using the currently available measurements. Following this idea, we now assume that the attacker is provided with a tool that, from the probability lists P_i and without the knowledge of the actual key, returns an approximate $\hat{\mathrm{R}}$ of the actual rank R. Using this tool, a more efficient attack strategy is shown in Algorithm 2. With this method, enumeration is executed only if the approximated rank $\hat{\mathrm{R}}$ is found to be within the enumeration effort e. If $\hat{\mathrm{R}}$ is close enough to R, this method is obviously more optimal than the previous one and achieves the desired trade-off between side-channel observations and computational power.

Algorithm 2. Efficient attacker's strategy.

Input. Enumeration effort e, and a key-less rank estimation.

1: Collect a set of side-channel measurements.
2: Update the attack N_p probability lists P_i for each subkey k_i.
3: From P_i lists, compute an estimation $\hat{\mathrm{R}}$ of the rank R.
4: **if** $\hat{\mathrm{R}} \leq e$ **then**
5:     Enumerate up to the first e key candidates or until the correct key k is found.
6:     **if** k not found **then**
7:         Collect new side-channel measurements and go to step 2.
8:     **end if**
9: **else**
10:     Collect new side-channel measurements and go to step 2.
11: **end if**

It is worth mentioning that, as a side advantage, the existence of such a tool would also give information to the adversary on whether or not the attack will succeed eventually.

Indeed, observing the trend of $\hat{R}$ either gives some confidence in the efficiency of the attack if it decreases steadily as the number of measurements increases, or shows that the attack has little chance to eventually recover the key (or a significant part of it) otherwise.

3 Background

In this section, we first define the metrics we investigate: the entropy, the rank and the guessing entropy. For the work described in this paper, we make use of the Glowacz et al. key rank estimation method [6], which we describe using the notations introduced in the previous section.

3.1 Entropy, Rank and Guessing Entropy

Entropy. The Shannon entropy H of a discrete random variable $X \in \mathcal{X}$ following a probability distribution Pr is defined as:

$$\mathrm{H}(\mathrm{X}) = -\sum_{x \in \mathcal{X}} \Pr(x) \cdot \log \Pr(x).$$

Rank. The rank R, after a side-channel attack using a set of q inputs $\mathcal{X}_q$ and a corresponding set of q leakages $\mathcal{L}_q$, provides the position of the correct key k in the sorted vector of $|\mathcal{K}| = 2^n$ key candidate probabilities $\mathbf{p} = [p_1, p_2, ..., p_{|\mathcal{K}|}]$, i.e:

$$\mathrm{R}(k) = i \quad \text{if} \quad \Pr[k|\mathcal{X}_q, \mathcal{L}_q] = p_i.$$

Guessing Entropy. The guessing entropy GE [12] measures the average number of key candidates to test after a side-channel attack. It corresponds to the average rank and is defined as:

$$\mathrm{GE} = \underset{k \in \mathcal{K}}{\mathbb{E}}(R(k)).$$

3.2 Key Rank Estimation

Given a set of discrete probability distributions for independent parts of a key and a correct key k, a rank estimation algorithm provides tight bounds for the rank among the set of all possible candidates. Among the different proposals for key rank estimation, we use the histogram-based approach of Glowacz et al. [6]. This algorithm provides efficiently tight bounds for the rank of the key and gives the probability distribution of the full key expressed as a histogram. Given the N_p lists of the log probabilities of the subkeys $LP_i = \log(\Pr[k_i^*|\mathcal{X}_q, \mathcal{L}_q])$, the method of Glowacz et al. starts by constructing the corresponding N_p histograms $H_i = \mathrm{hist}(LP_i, \mathrm{bins})$ where bins is a set of N_{bin} equally-sized bins, used for all the histograms. The convolution of two histograms is denoted as

Algorithm 3. Rank estimation.

Input: The key log probability $\log(\Pr[k|\mathcal{X}_q, \mathcal{L}_q])$ and the histograms H_i.
Output: An approximation of k's rank.

initialization: $H_{\text{curr}} = H_1$;
histograms convolution:
for $i = 2 : N_p$
$H_{\text{curr}} = \mathsf{conv}(H_{\text{curr}}, H_i)$;
end
rank estimation:

$$\text{estimated\_rank} \approx \sum_{i=\mathsf{bin}(\log(\Pr[k|\mathcal{X}_q, \mathcal{L}_q]))}^{N_p \cdot N_{\text{bin}} - (N_p - 1)} H_{\text{curr}}(i).$$

$\mathsf{conv}(H_i, H_j)$. Knowing the key k, its log probability is $\log(\Pr[k|\mathcal{X}_q, \mathcal{L}_q]) = \sum_{i=1}^{N_p} \log(\Pr[k_i|\mathcal{X}_q, \mathcal{L}_q])$. The following steps are described by Algorithm 3. In a nutshell, the rank estimation algorithm provides a very efficient way to estimate and bound the number of key candidates with a probability higher than k.

The estimated rank is then bounded by tracking the quantization error of the histograms as:

$$\text{rank\_lower\_bound} = \sum_{i=\mathsf{bin}(\log(\Pr[k|\mathcal{X}_q, \mathcal{L}_q]))+N_p}^{N_p \cdot N_{\text{bin}} - (N_p - 1)} H_{\text{curr}}(i),$$

and:

$$\text{rank\_upper\_bound} = \sum_{i=\mathsf{bin}(\log(\Pr[k|\mathcal{X}_q, \mathcal{L}_q]))-N_p}^{N_p \cdot N_{\text{bin}} - (N_p - 1)} H_{\text{curr}}(i),$$

By increasing the number of bins, the tightness of the bounds can be arbitrarily reduced. In the rest of this paper, and for the practical experiments, we use a number of bins large enough such that the tightness is below 1 bit. As this precision is enough for our experiments, we consider the estimated rank as the "true" rank and ignore the bounds. We emphasize that the histogram convolutions do not require the knowledge of the key, and only the rank estimation itself does. For the rest of this paper, we use the final histogram constructed, which corresponds to the full key distribution.

4 Using the Entropy to Approximate the Rank

The entropy of the key candidate probabilities produced by an attack intuitively brings some information on the outcome of the attack, since it measures the uncertainty on the key, which amounts to the number of bits of information left to recover on the key. For instance, an attack ran on data that is uncorrelated with the key would tend to attribute average probabilities to most candidates, yielding a high entropy (n bits in the extreme case where all candidates have a probability of 2^{-n}, while the average rank is 2^{n-1}). On the other hand, an attack performing extremely well would give a high probability to the correct key candidate and very low ones to all other candidates. In that case, the entropy tends to 0 (like the rank) as the probability of the wrong candidates also tends to 0. This intuition that in realistic cases entropy and rank are linked – although it's a loose link, as one can show that entropy and rank can diverge in specific cases – leads us to consider the use of the entropy to estimate the remaining enumeration effort of an attack.

In the following, we present how the entropy of the full key can be estimated using the histogram obtained with the convolution-based method from Glowacz et al. Although the histogram is only a compressed representation of the full key candidates' probability distribution, it still is an excellent tool to analyze it. To estimate the entropy, we require a proper probability distribution that sums up to 1. Thus, it is preferred to normalize the full key candidates' probability distribution. This is done by ensuring that the sum of the exponential of log probabilities given by the bins of all keys in all histograms sum to 1. Furthermore, it is recommended to normalize the distribution of the subkeys, prior to the histogram convolution, to avoid that the estimated metrics are weighted by the distributions of the subkeys. The entropy of the full key after a side-channel attack is estimated using the corresponding histogram (H,bin) as:

$$
\begin{aligned}
\mathrm{H} &= -\sum_{k^* \in \mathcal{K}} \Pr(k^*) \cdot \log \Pr(k^*) \approx \sum_{k^* \in \mathcal{K}} \exp(\mathsf{bin}(k^*)) \cdot \mathsf{bin}(k^*) \\
&\approx \sum_{i=1}^{N_p \cdot N_{\text{bin}} - (N_p - 1)} H(i) \cdot \exp(\mathsf{bin}(i)) \cdot \mathsf{bin}(i)
\end{aligned}
$$

We denote by $\tilde{\mathrm{H}}$ the estimation of the entropy using the histogram. Note that bounds on this estimation can be computed. The corresponding formulas are given in Appendix A.

5 Adapting the CHES 2017 Key-Less GE

At CHES 2017, Choudary and Popescu [5] consider a number of information theoretic measures and inequalities that are easy and efficient to estimate in order to bound the guessing entropy of the key. However, in their proposal, they make a distinction between a key-agnostic guessing entropy and one that requires the knowledge of the key[1]. This key-less guessing entropy, that we denote by GE_{kl},

[1] The framework [5] is actually misleading in this respect as it suggests that the GE is the *actual* key rank while it is the *average* key rank. The keyed and key-less versions are equivalent in case the templates used in the key-less estimation are perfect so the difference between both definitions only lies in the knowledge of the key.

is computed given the sorted vector of the $|\mathcal{K}| = 2^n$ key candidate probabilities $\mathbf{p} = [p_1, p_2, ..., p_{|\mathcal{K}|}]$ obtained after a side-channel attack as:

$$\mathrm{GE}_{kl} = \sum_{i=1}^{|\mathcal{K}|} i \cdot p_i$$

The GE_{kl} is impossible to compute since the sum is over all full key candidates. For that purpose Choudary and Popescu use common measures and bounds described in information theory literature. Since this work provides a key-less rank estimation tool, a natural alternative to our previous proposal is to try to adapt it to our single-attack context. This alternative is again only heuristic since the bounds are only valid on average [5]. To describe this alternative solution, we use again the histogram-based PDF estimation provided by the Glowacz et al. Here, GE_{kl} corresponds to the sum of the position of every key weighted by its probability and it can be estimated as:

$$\mathrm{GE}_{kl} = \sum_{i=1}^{|\mathcal{K}|} i \cdot p_i \approx \sum_{k^* \in \mathcal{K}} \left(\sum_{j=\mathsf{bin}(k^*)}^{N_p \cdot N_{\mathrm{bin}} - (N_p - 1)} H(j) \right) \cdot \Pr[k^*]$$

Then, we sum across all histograms and corresponding log probability bins, yielding the estimation of the key-less guessing entropy $\tilde{\mathrm{GE}}_{kl}$:

$$\tilde{\mathrm{GE}}_{kl} \approx \sum_{i=1}^{N_p \cdot N_{\mathrm{bin}} - (N_p - 1)} \left(\sum_{j=i}^{N_p \cdot N_{\mathrm{bin}} - (N_p - 1)} H(j) \right) \cdot \exp(\mathsf{bin}(i))$$

Again, new bounds on the key-less guessing entropy estimation can be computed from the histogram approximation, which are given in Appendix A. However, these bounds are not directly relevant to our work. Precisely, the ones in [6] require the knowledge of the key (i.e. an evaluation setting) while we aim at key-less rank estimation, and the ones in [5] only become tight on average over many experiments (i.e. also in an evaluation setting) while we aim to estimate the rank of single experiments on-the-fly. For the same reason, bounds on the entropy are also irrelevant in our adversarial setting. Subsequently, the rest of this paper ignores the bounds and only focus on the heuristic evaluation of these metrics.

6 Simulated and Real Experiments

In the following sections, we investigate whether the previous metrics can be used to approximate the rank of the correct key after a single side-channel attack. In that purpose, we evaluate two average absolute differences (for multiple side-channel attacks): the first between the logarithm of the rank and the estimated entropy $\tilde{\mathrm{H}}$, and the second between the logarithm of the key rank and the logarithm of $\tilde{\mathrm{GE}}_{kl}$. For that purpose, we use both simulated and real experiments. We start by describing our experimental setups and then show practical results.

6.1 Experimental Setups

Simulated Leakages: We simulated side-channel leakages of the 16 S-box outputs of the first round of an unprotected AES. For each byte x_i out of the 16, we model the leakage of x_i as $\mathsf{HW}(x_i) + b$, where HW denotes the Hamming weight function, and b represents an independent noise distributed according to a normal distribution with mean 0 and standard deviation 10.

Real Leakages: We target a custom constant-time C implementation of an unprotected AES with T-tables. The code runs on an ARM Cortex-M3 microcontroller running at 83 Mhz, mounted on an Arduino Due board. We acquired EM measurements with a Langer near field RF-U 5-2 probe and a Lecroy 610Zi oscilloscope at a sampling rate of 1 GHz. We synchronized the traces at the beginning of the AES computation using a trigger signal. As for the simulated case, we target the output of the S-boxes of the first round. For each of the 16 target bytes, we selected the point of interest that exhibit the highest correlation with the corresponding S-box output value, using a first set of 10,000 traces with a known key.

We performed a template attack [4] for both simulated and real leakage experiments. For the real experiments, we use a set of 100,000 traces with known key and plaintext for the template building phase.

6.2 Results

We show here the practical results using the estimation of the entropy $\tilde{\mathrm{H}}$ and the estimation of the key-less guessing entropy $\tilde{\mathrm{GE}}_{kl}$ to approximate the rank of the key R after a side-channel attack. We additionally compare the performance of both metrics. We recall that we estimate the rank using the histogram method of Glowacz et al. and that we used a large enough number of bins so that the bounds are tight enough for us to use the estimated rank and ignore the bounds. In the following, we refer to the approximation of log(R) using the entropy as the $\tilde{\mathrm{H}}$-based approximation and the one using the logarithm of the key-less guessing entropy as the $\tilde{\mathrm{GE}}_{kl}$-based approximation.

As a preliminary experiment, we ran a single attack against both simulated and real traces. We incremented the number of attack traces until the rank reached one. The results are depicted in Fig. 1. The left (resp. right) part of the figure shows the results for simulated (resp. real) traces. In each case, the X-axis represents the number of attack traces, and the Y-axis is used to represent the different metrics in $\log_2$ scale. We notice that the entropy-based approximation is closer to the logarithm of the rank than the one based on the key-less guessing entropy. More specifically, for the simulated traces the $\tilde{\mathrm{H}}$-based approximation remains within less than 10 bits of log(R), while the gap with the $\tilde{\mathrm{GE}}_{kl}$ goes up to 25 bits. The real experiments show less optimistic results. Indeed, while $\tilde{\mathrm{H}}$ remains mainly within 5 bits of log(R), we can observe a fairly large gap of 30 bits when the rank is around 2^{40}. Results are worse for $\log(\tilde{\mathrm{GE}}_{kl})$ with a maximal gap of 50 bits.

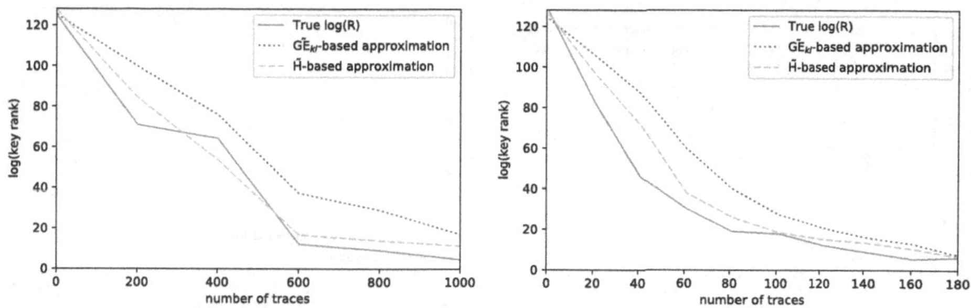

Fig. 1. Comparison of $\log(\tilde{GE}_{kl})$, $\tilde{H}$ and $\log(R)$ for a single random side-channel attack on the AES S-box output. Simulated traces (left) and real EM traces (right).

The previous experiment showed some results for a single attack and that the entropy is neither an upper bound or a lower bound on the logarithm of the rank. While this gives some insight about the interest of the considered metrics, it does not allow deriving any general conclusion. Next, we examine how the $\tilde{H}$-based approximation and the $\tilde{GE}_{kl}$-based one perform on average over many independent experiments. For that purpose, we evaluate the average absolute difference in bits, first between $\tilde{H}$ and $\log(R)$, then between $\log(\tilde{GE}_{kl})$ and $\log(R)$. This is performed over 100 independent attacks for the simulated and the real traces. The results on the simulated traces are shown in Fig. 2. The X-axis corresponds to $\log(R)$. The Y-axis on the left (resp. right) part of the figure gives the mean (resp. standard deviation) of the distance between each measure and the rank. For the left part of the figure, we additionally plot the maximal distance obtained over the 100 attacks in corresponding dashed curves. We notice that the entropy clearly seems to outperform the key-less guessing entropy when estimating the rank for a single attack. First focusing on the average distance on the left part of the figure, the entropy stays within less than 10 bits of R. The maximal difference we obtained among the 100 experiments is slightly above 20 bits. However, the mean distance of $\log(R)$ to $\log(\tilde{GE}_{kl})$ is in most cases above 10 bits and below 25 bits, with a maximum above 45 bits. Also considering the standard deviations of these distances on the right part of the figure, it is reasonable to consider that the entropy provides a more reliable estimation of R than the key-less guessing entropy: since the standard deviation of the distance to $\tilde{H}$ is lower than the one to $\log(\tilde{GE}_{kl})$, the first one is less likely to deviate from its mean value which is below 10 bits.

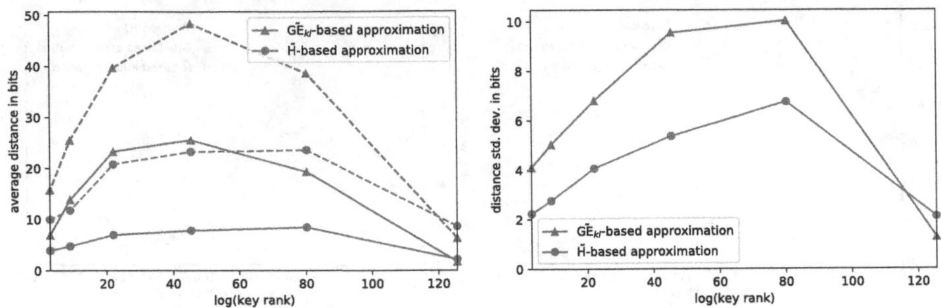

Fig. 2. Simulated HW leakages: (Left) The average distance from the rank to both the $\tilde{\mathrm{H}}$-based approximation and the $\tilde{\mathrm{GE}}_{kl}$-based approximation as function of the logarithm of the rank and the maximal distance observed in corresponding dashed lines. (Right) the distances' standard deviations.

The results for real traces are shown in Fig. 3. Again, the X-axis represents log(R) and the Y-axis on the left (resp. right) part of the figure represents the mean (resp. standard deviation) of the distances, computed over 100 independent attacks. The experiments on real traces coincide with the simulated ones. Accordingly, the entropy-based approximation provides a better estimate of log(R) than the approximation based on the key-less guessing entropy. The average distance between log(R) and $\tilde{\mathrm{H}}$ is below 12 bits while the average distance to $\log(\tilde{\mathrm{GE}}_{kl})$ is always above the average distance to $\tilde{\mathrm{H}}$. The right part of Fig. 3 is similar to the right part of Fig. 2, as the standard deviation of the distance to the entropy is lower than the one to the key-less guessing entropy, confirming that for a real side-channel attack, $\tilde{\mathrm{H}}$ provides a better approximation of log(R) than $\log(\tilde{\mathrm{GE}}_{kl})$.

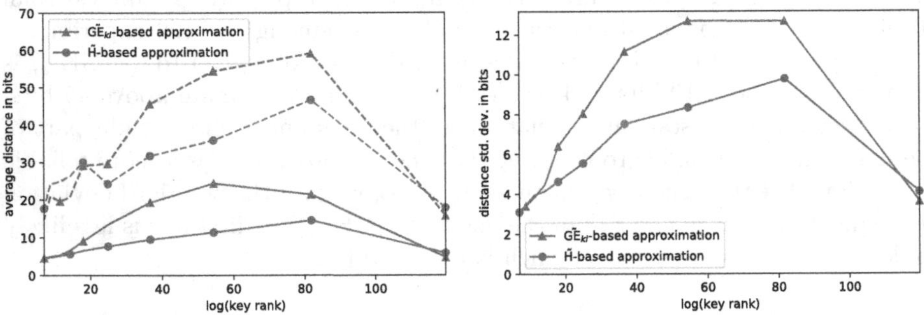

Fig. 3. EM traces: (Left) The average distance from the rank to both the $\tilde{\mathrm{H}}$-based approximation and the $\tilde{\mathrm{GE}}_{kl}$-based approximation as function of the logarithm of the rank and the maximal distance observed in corresponding dashed lines. (Right) the distances' standard deviations.

We highlight the fact that all predictions have a higher variance/standard deviation for middle ranks, which are the most interesting for both evaluators and attackers, as it is typically the range of ranks where enumeration turns from being unfeasible to practically feasible. This has been previously observed by Martin et al. in an evaluation setup [8] with the possibility to perform multiple attacks with the knowledge of the key. Our results and the ones of Martin et al. show that the interesting ranks are the hardest to estimate for an evaluator, and especially in the context of a real attack with the purpose of recovering the key.

Our proposed metric cannot mathematically approximate nor bound the true rank of the key after a single side-channel attack. However, we experimentally show that the entropy tends to stay within reasonable limits from the logarithm of the rank (provided that the attack does not suffer from errors, for e.g. due to a wrong model assumption). As a result, we believe it can be used in a more efficient strategy by trading data complexity for computational effort as illustrated by Algorithm 2 by enumerating key candidates up to (or slightly above) $2^{\tilde{H}}$.

7 Discussion and Limitations

Any attempt to predict the rank from one single attack without the knowledge of the key suffers from a specific caveat. It is possible that the attack is not carried out correctly and is converging towards a wrong key (due for example to wrong intermediates, wrong assumptions about the leakage or unknown countermeasures). The entropy and the key-less guessing entropy would then decrease as the attack tends towards the wrong key candidate, while the rank of the correct key would not. This behavior does not only affect the entropy and the key-less guessing entropy but most probably any metric estimated without the knowledge of the correct key.

Another aspect to consider that affects the considered metrics is the key size. This can be pictured through a simple example: let's consider two attacks that both aim at recovering a bit b whose value is 1, and output two probability distributions $\mathbf{p_1} = [\Pr_1[b = 0] = 0, \Pr_1[b = 1] = 1]$ and $\mathbf{p_2} = [\Pr_2[b = 0] = 0.45, \Pr_2[b = 1] = 0.55]$. Both attacks achieve a rank of one since the correct value of b has the highest probability. On the other hand, the entropy values are quite different. The entropy of the first attack is equal to 0, which is equal to the logarithm of the rank. For the second attack, the entropy of b is higher and equal to 0.99277, albeit the correct value of b is ranked first. These discrepancies can be observed for small keys, but vanish for larger key sizes. This illustrates how independent conclusions on subkeys can be quite misleading when trying to infer conclusions on full key recovery.

To demonstrate this effect, we performed the same experiments as described in the previous section. We estimated the average distance between log(R) and the entropy and then between log(R) and the key-less guessing entropy, but across different key sizes. For each key size, we performed 100 attacks. We normalized the distance with respect to the size of the key in bytes. Indeed, normalizing makes the distances comparable for different key sizes, and allows to infer conclusions based on the distance per byte. As an example, a minor distance for one key byte between R and its key-less prediction is critical, but not so relevant for the full key. The results are given in Fig. 4, for both the simulated traces on the left and real traces on the right. The dashed line indicates the maximum values observed. For the simulated experiments, it was possible to perform experiments on large keys of up to 64 bytes, and up to the AES-128 key size for the real traces we measured. We used 400 attack traces for the simulations, leading to a rank of approximately 2^{55}, and 70 traces for the real attack to achieve a rank around 2^{30} for a 128-bit key (with proportional ranks for smaller key sizes). This was chosen to focus on the interesting ranks and we did not notice any considerable differences for other ranks, when it comes to the effect of the key size on the distance to log(R) of either the $\tilde{\mathrm{H}}$-based approximation or the $\tilde{\mathrm{GE}}_{kl}$-based one. As we can see, the normalized difference indeed decreases when the key size increases, confirming our intuition. Moreover, the trend starts to settle for both simulated and real traces once realistic full key sizes are reached. First, for a 1-byte key size, we can observe on average a two-bit difference between log(R) and $\tilde{\mathrm{H}}$ and a lower difference between log(R) and $\log(\tilde{\mathrm{GE}}_{kl})$. On the other hand, for a 16-byte key size, the distance between the rank and the entropy-based prediction drops to around 0.5 bits of error per byte for both the simulated and the real traces, while the distance between the rank and $\tilde{\mathrm{GE}}_{kl}$ seems to settle at an average distance of 1.5 bits of error per byte even for larger key sizes. For the maximal value, we observe the same trend as previous experiments. The distance to the key-less guessing entropy is higher than the one to the entropy in most cases. Overall, two conclusions can be drawn from this experiment. First, it confirms that the entropy-based estimation seems to be a better tool to approximate the rank than the key-less guessing entropy once real key sizes are reached. Second, it shows that as expected, it is better to estimate the security level in an adversarial scenario on the full key than on a small part of the key, such as a subkey.

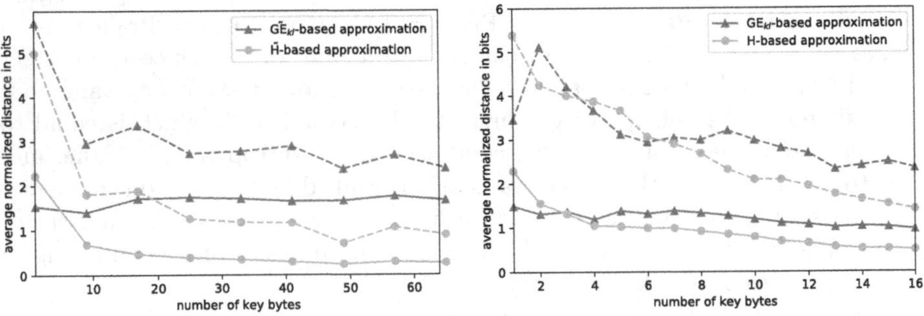

Fig. 4. Average distances between the log of the rank, the entropy and log(GM) as function of the number of key bytes. Maximal distances observed in corresponding dashed lines. Simulated traces on the left and real traces on the right.

8 Conclusion

In this paper, we described a heuristic way to infer an approximation of the key rank for one single attack without the knowledge of the key. This corresponds to a realistic attack scenario, where the adversary aims at figuring out if the correct key can be reached through enumeration. Our proposal helps to devise an optimal attack strategy to trade data complexity for computational effort when possible. For that purpose, we showed that the remaining entropy of the full key can be estimated using the histogram built with the rank estimation method from Glowacz et al. without the knowledge of the key. We showed experimentally that the entropy of the full key distribution after a side-channel attack is close to the logarithm of the rank on both simulated data and real EM side-channel measurements of an AES implementation. We compared this entropy-based approximation of the rank, to a single-attack adaptation of the key-less rank estimation method of Choudary and Popescu [5]. We additionally discussed factors that may affect the accuracy of the entropy (and any measure that lacks knowledge of the key or its probability) as a predictor of the logarithm of the rank. Further research might investigate if the behavior observed in this paper is common to different side-channel datasets. Moreover, it would be interesting to investigate if the tool described in this work can help to identify possible wrong assumptions about the implementation or device that can possibly hinder the success of the attack. Alternatively, an interesting direction is to propose a more precise technique or metric to approximate the rank of the correct key in the single attack scenario.

Acknowledgement. François-Xavier Standaert is a senior research associate of the Belgian Fund for Scientific Research. This work has been funded in part by the European Commission through the H2020 project 731591 (acronym REASSURE) and by the ERC Consolidator Grant 724725 (acronym SWORD). The authors acknowledge the support from the 'National Integrated Centre of Evaluation' (NICE), a facility of Cyber Security Agency, Singapore (CSA).

A Error Bounds on the Histogram Estimations

The bounds on the estimation of the entropy and the key-less guessing entropy using the Glowacz et al. full key distribution histogram and based on its quantization error are given by:

$$\text{H\_upper\_bound} = \sum_{i=1}^{N_p \cdot N_{\text{bin}} - (N_p - 1)} H(i). \exp(\mathsf{bin}(i + N_p)).\mathsf{bin}(i + N_p)$$

$$\text{H\_lower\_bound} = \sum_{i=1}^{N_p \cdot N_{\text{bin}} - (N_p - 1)} H(i). \exp(\mathsf{bin}(i - N_p)).\mathsf{bin}(i - N_p)$$

$$\text{GE}_{kl}\text{\_upper\_bound} = \sum_{i=1}^{N_p \cdot N_{\text{bin}}-(N_p-1)} \left(\sum_{j=i-N_p}^{N_p \cdot N_{\text{bin}}-(N_p-1)} H(j) \right) . \exp(\text{bin}(i+N_p))$$

$$\text{GE}_{kl}\text{\_lower\_bound} = \sum_{i=1}^{N_p \cdot N_{\text{bin}}-(N_p-1)} \left(\sum_{j=i+N_p}^{N_p \cdot N_{\text{bin}}-(N_p-1)} H(j) \right) . \exp(\text{bin}(i-N_p))$$

References

1. Bernstein, D.J., Lange, T., van Vredendaal, C.: Tighter, faster, simpler side-channel security evaluations beyond computing power. IACR Cryptology ePrint Archive, 2015:221 (2015)
2. Bogdanov, A., Kizhvatov, I., Manzoor, K., Tischhauser, E., Witteman, M.: Fast and memory-efficient key recovery in side-channel attacks. In: Dunkelman, O., Keliher, L. (eds.) SAC 2015. LNCS, vol. 9566, pp. 310–327. Springer, Cham (2016). https://doi.org/10.1007/978-3-319-31301-6_19
3. Brier, E., Clavier, C., Olivier, F.: Correlation power analysis with a leakage model. In: Joye, M., Quisquater, J.-J. (eds.) CHES 2004. LNCS, vol. 3156, pp. 16–29. Springer, Heidelberg (2004). https://doi.org/10.1007/978-3-540-28632-5_2
4. Chari, S., Rao, J.R., Rohatgi, P.: Template attacks. In: Kaliski, B.S., Koç, K., Paar, C. (eds.) CHES 2002. LNCS, vol. 2523, pp. 13–28. Springer, Heidelberg (2003). https://doi.org/10.1007/3-540-36400-5_3
5. Choudary, M.O., Popescu, P.G.: Back to Massey: impressively fast, scalable and tight security evaluation tools. In: Fischer, W., Homma, N. (eds.) CHES 2017. LNCS, vol. 10529, pp. 367–386. Springer, Cham (2017). https://doi.org/10.1007/978-3-319-66787-4_18
6. Glowacz, C., Grosso, V., Poussier, R., Schüth, J., Standaert, F.-X.: Simpler and more efficient rank estimation for side-channel security assessment. In: Leander, G. (ed.) FSE 2015. LNCS, vol. 9054, pp. 117–129. Springer, Heidelberg (2015). https://doi.org/10.1007/978-3-662-48116-5_6
7. Kocher, P., Jaffe, J., Jun, B.: Differential power analysis. In: Wiener, M. (ed.) CRYPTO 1999. LNCS, vol. 1666, pp. 388–397. Springer, Heidelberg (1999). https://doi.org/10.1007/3-540-48405-1_25
8. Martin, D.P., Mather, L., Oswald, E., Stam, M.: Characterisation and estimation of the key rank distribution in the context of side channel evaluations. In: Cheon, J.H., Takagi, T. (eds.) ASIACRYPT 2016. LNCS, vol. 10031, pp. 548–572. Springer, Heidelberg (2016). https://doi.org/10.1007/978-3-662-53887-6_20
9. Martin, D.P., O'Connell, J.F., Oswald, E., Stam, M.: Counting keys in parallel after a side channel attack. In: Iwata, T., Cheon, J.H. (eds.) ASIACRYPT 2015. LNCS, vol. 9453, pp. 313–337. Springer, Heidelberg (2015). https://doi.org/10.1007/978-3-662-48800-3_13
10. Poussier, R., Standaert, F.-X., Grosso, V.: Simple key enumeration (and rank estimation) using histograms: an integrated approach. In: Gierlichs, B., Poschmann, A.Y. (eds.) CHES 2016. LNCS, vol. 9813, pp. 61–81. Springer, Heidelberg (2016). https://doi.org/10.1007/978-3-662-53140-2_4

11. Schindler, W., Lemke, K., Paar, C.: A stochastic model for differential side channel cryptanalysis. In: Rao, J.R., Sunar, B. (eds.) CHES 2005. LNCS, vol. 3659, pp. 30–46. Springer, Heidelberg (2005). https://doi.org/10.1007/11545262_3
12. Standaert, F.-X., Malkin, T.G., Yung, M.: A unified framework for the analysis of side-channel key recovery attacks. In: Joux, A. (ed.) EUROCRYPT 2009. LNCS, vol. 5479, pp. 443–461. Springer, Heidelberg (2009). https://doi.org/10.1007/978-3-642-01001-9_26
13. Veyrat-Charvillon, N., Gérard, B., Renauld, M., Standaert, F.-X.: An optimal key enumeration algorithm and its application to side-channel attacks. In: Knudsen, L.R., Wu, H. (eds.) SAC 2012. LNCS, vol. 7707, pp. 390–406. Springer, Heidelberg (2013). https://doi.org/10.1007/978-3-642-35999-6_25
14. Veyrat-Charvillon, N., Gérard, B., Standaert, F.-X.: Security evaluations beyond computing power. In: Johansson, T., Nguyen, P.Q. (eds.) EUROCRYPT 2013. LNCS, vol. 7881, pp. 126–141. Springer, Heidelberg (2013). https://doi.org/10.1007/978-3-642-38348-9_8
15. Ye, X., Eisenbarth, T., Martin, W.: Bounded, yet sufficient? How to determine whether limited side channel information enables key recovery. In: Joye, M., Moradi, A. (eds.) CARDIS 2014. LNCS, vol. 8968, pp. 215–232. Springer, Cham (2015). https://doi.org/10.1007/978-3-319-16763-3_13

Author Index

Alam, Manaar 3
Azouaoui, Melissa 252

Balasch, Josep 176
Becker, Georg T. 40
Beckers, Arthur 176
Bhasin, Shivam 57
Bhattacharya, Sarani 3
Biryukov, Alex 216
Božilov, Dušan 20

Cardoso dos Santos, Luan 216
Chattopadhyay, Anupam 57
Cristiani, Valence 143

Dutertre, Jean-Max 109
Duval, Sébastien 195

Fujimoto, Daisuke 176

Gérard, François 74
Gierlichs, Benedikt 176
Glowacz, Cezary 126
Gravellier, Joseph 109
Grosso, Vincent 126
Großschädl, Johann 216
Gupta, Sourav Sen 57

Hailfinger, Carl-Daniel 159
Hayashi, Yuichi 176
Hiscock, Thomas 143

Imbert, Laurent 95

Kinugawa, Masahiro 176
Knežević, Miroslav 20
Knichel, David 237

Lecomte, Maxime 143
Lemke-Rust, Kerstin 159
Leurent, Gaëtan 195
Lomné, Victor 95

Margraf, Marian 40
Moradi, Amir 237
Moundi, Philippe Loubet 109
Mukhopadhyay, Debdeep 3

Nikov, Ventzislav 20

Olivier, Francis 109

Paar, Christof 159
Poussier, Romain 252
Pratihar, Kuheli 3

Ravi, Prasanna 57
Richter, Bastian 237
Roche, Thomas 95
Rossi, Mélissa 74

Singh, Astikey 3
Soroceanu, Tudor A. A. 40
Standaert, François-Xavier 252

Teglia, Yannick 109
Tobisch, Johannes 40

Verbauwhede, Ingrid 176
Verneuil, Vincent 252

Wisiol, Nils 40

Zengin, Benjamin 40

Printed in the United States
By Bookmasters